Hearing the Victim

Cambridge Criminal Justice Series

Published in association with the Institute of Criminology, University of Cambridge

Published titles

Community Penalties: change and challenges, edited by Anthony Bottoms, Loraine Gelsthorpe and Sue Rex

Ideology, Crime and Criminal Justice: a symposium in honour of Sir Leon Radzinowicz, edited by Anthony Bottoms and Michael Tonry

Reform and Punishment: the future of sentencing, edited by Sue Rex and Michael Tonry

Confronting Crime: crime control policy under New Labour, edited by Michael Tonry

Sex Offenders in the Community: managing and reducing the risks, edited by Amanda Matravers

The Effects of Imprisonment, edited by Alison Liebling and Shadd Maruna

Hearing the Victim: adversarial justice, crime victims and the state, edited by Anthony Bottoms and Julian V. Roberts

Hearing the Victim

Adversarial justice, crime victims and the State

**Edited by
Anthony Bottoms and Julian V. Roberts**

WILLAN
PUBLISHING

Willan Publishing
Culmcott House
Mill Street, Uffculme
Cullompton, Devon
EX15 3AT, UK
Tel: +44(0)1884 840337
Fax: +44(0)1884 840251
e-mail: info@willanpublishing.co.uk
Website: www.willanpublishing.co.uk

Published simultaneously in the USA and Canada by

Willan Publishing
c/o ISBS, 920 NE 58th Ave, Suite 300,
Portland, Oregon 97213-3786, USA
Tel: +001(0)503 287 3093
Fax: +001(0)503 280 8832
e-mail: info@isbs.com
Website: www.isbs.com

First published 2010

ISBN 978-1-84392-272-8 hardback

British Library Cataloguing-in-Publication Data

A catalogue record for this book is available from the British Library

FSC
Mixed Sources
Product group from well-managed
forests and other controlled sources

Cert no. SGS-COC-2482
www.fsc.org
© 1996 Forest Stewardship Council

Project managed by Deer Park Productions, Tavistock, Devon
Typeset by TW Typesetting, Plymouth, Devon
Printed and bound by T J International Ltd, Trecerus Industrial Estate, Padstow, Cornwall

Contents

Abbreviations

ACPO   Association of Chief Police Officers
APR   Accelerated Parole Review (Canada)
ASBO   Antisocial Behaviour Order
BCS   British Crime Survey
BMRB   British Market Research Bureau
CJS   Criminal Justice System
C&JS   Crime and Justice Survey
CPS   Crime Prosecution Service
CSC   Correctional Service of Canada
DPP   Director of Public Prosecutions
ECL   End of Custody Licence
FIS   Family Impact Statement
HDC   Home Detention Curfew
ICVS   International Crime Victims Survey
IDVA   Independent Domestic Violence Advisor
ISVA   Independent Sexual Violence Advocate
LCJB   Local criminal justice board
NCVS   National Crime Victimisation Survey (USA)
NEVA   North of England Victims Association
NPB   National Parole Board (Canada)
NSPCC   National Society for the Prevention of Cruelty to Children
NWNJ   *No Witness, No Justice* Project
OCJR   Office for Criminal Justice Reform
OCJS   Offending, Crime and Justice Survey
OI   Offenders Index
PHSO   Parliamentary and Health Service Ombudsman
PSR   Pre-sentence report

ROTL	Release on Temporary Licence
SAMM	Support After Murder and Manslaughter
SARC	Sexual Assault Referral Centre
SIR	Social inquiry report
VAP	Victims' Advisory Panel
VAS	Victims' Advocate Scheme
VFS	Victims' Focus Scheme
VIP	Victim Impact Panel
VIS	Victim Impact Statement
VNS	Victim Notification Scheme (in Scotland)
VPS	Victim Personal Statement
VSO	Victim Statement of Opinion
WAVES	Witness and Victim Experience Survey
WCU	Witness Care Unit

Tables

Notes on contributors

Anthony Bottoms is Emeritus Wolfson Professor of Criminology at the University of Cambridge, Life Fellow of Fitzwilliam College, Cambridge, and Honorary Professor of Criminology at the University of Sheffield. He is also a Fellow of the British Academy. His most recent empirical research (with Joanna Shapland) is a study of steps towards desistance in a sample of young adult recidivists. Other research interests lie mainly in the fields of theoretical criminology, criminal justice policy and socio-spatial criminology. In 2007, he received the European Criminology Award from the European Society of Criminology for lifetime contributions to criminology.

Andrew Costello is Lecturer in Criminology in the Centre for Criminological Research at the University of Sheffield. His principal research interests lie in the fields of crime analysis and socio-spatial criminology, and he has published on topics such as the localism of crime, repeat victimisation and crime in 'urban villages'. He is the General Editor of the book series 'Environment, Space and Criminology' published by Ashgate Publishing.

Peter Dunn is Director of The Griffins Society. Formerly Victim Support's Head of Research and Development, Peter has written widely about crime victims and victim services, and he has been a frequent conference speaker about these issues. He is also a part-time PhD student at the London School of Economics where the subject of his doctoral research is gay men's experiences of hate crime and its policing.

Edna Erez is Professor and Head of the Department of Criminology, Law and Justice at the University of Illinois at Chicago. She has published widely on victims in the criminal justice system, violence against women including immigrant women, and women in terrorism. Her current National Institute of Justice-funded research, with UIC colleagues, includes the use of GPS tracking technology to protect battered women, and a study of Jihad on the internet.

Matthew Hall is Lecturer in Criminology in the School of Law, University of Sheffield, where he teaches various aspects of criminology and victimology, as well as criminal law and the law of evidence. He is the author of *Victims of Crime: Policy and Practice in Criminal Justice* (2008, Willan Publishing), as well as articles on the use of special measures with crime victims and domestic violence victims in criminal justice. He is currently undertaking a comparative study of the relation of victims with criminal justice across European mainland and Commonwealth countries.

Matt Matravers is Professor of Political Philosophy at the University of York. He has published widely on political and penal theory. He is the author of *Justice and Punishment* (2000, Oxford University Press) and *Responsibility and Justice* (2007, Polity Press). His recent research has focused on dangerousness and the intersection of criminal justice and issues around personality disorders.

Nicola Padfield is a Senior Lecturer at the Law Faculty, University of Cambridge. A barrister by training, she has published widely on criminal law, sentencing and criminal justice. Her books include *The Criminal Justice Process: Text and Materials* (fourth edition 2008, Oxford University Press); *Criminal Law* (sixth edition 2008, Oxford University Press); *Beyond the Tariff: Human rights and the release of life sentence prisoners* (2002, Willan Publishing). She has edited other collections of essays, and is editor of a monthly practitioners' newsletter, *Archbold News*. She sits as a Recorder (part-time judge) in the Crown Court and is a Bencher of the Middle Temple.

Dame Helen Reeves was the first Chief Executive of Victim Support from 1980 to 2005. She has served on many Government policy committees and has recently been a member of the Howard League Commission on English Prisons and an Advisor to the Courts and Sentencing Policy Group for the Centre for Social Justice. She has considerable international experience including founder member and chair of Victim Support Europe, Vice-President of the World Society of Victimology and chair of the Council of Europe expert committee which drafted the 2006 Recommendation on Assistance to Victims of Crime.

Julian V. Roberts is a Professor of Criminology in the Faculty of Law, University of Oxford. He is Editor-in-Chief of the *European Journal of Criminology* and Associate Editor of the *Canadian Journal of Criminology and Criminal Justice*. His recent publications include: *Principled Sentencing* (2009, ed. with A. Ashworth and A. von Hirsch, Hart Publishing); *The Role* *of Previous Convictions at Sentencing: Applied and Theoretical Perspectives* (2010, ed. with A. von Hirsch, Hart Publishing); *Punishing Persistent Offenders* (2008, Oxford University Press).

Paul Rock is Emeritus Professor of Sociology at the London School of Economics and Visiting Professor of Criminology at the University of Pennsylvania. He has been a Visiting Professor at the University of California, San Diego; Simon Fraser University; the University of British Columbia; and Princeton University; a Visiting Scholar at the Ministry of the Solicitor General of Canada; a Fellow of the Center for the Advanced Study of the Behavioral Sciences in Stanford, California; a resident at the Rockefeller Foundation Center at the Villa Serbelloni, Bellagio; and a Visiting Fellow at the Australian National University in Canberra. His interests focus on the development of criminal justice policies, particularly for victims of crime, but he has also published articles on criminological theory and the history of crime. His most recent books include (with David Downes) *Understanding Deviance* (sixth edition 2007, Oxford University Press) and *Constructing Victims' Rights* (September 2004, Clarendon Press). With Professors David Downes and Tim Newburn, his current research focuses on the official history of criminal justice.

Joanna Shapland is Professor of Criminal Justice and Head of the School of Law at the University of Sheffield. She has researched widely in victimology, criminal justice and restorative justice and is the Executive Editor of the *International Review of Victimology*. Most recently, she has published the edited volume, *Justice, Community and Civil Society* (2008, Willan publishing), which looks at how countries have reached out to their publics in terms of restorative justice, court reform, etc., as well as the national evaluation of three restorative justice schemes for adult offenders (Ministry of Justice/Home Office 2003, 2004, 2006, 2007).

John Spencer is a Professor of Law at the University of Cambridge. His interests include criminal law, criminal evidence and comparative criminal procedure. His publications in this area include many articles, and (co-edited with Mireille Delmas-Marty) *European Criminal Procedures* (2002, Cambridge University Press). From 2000–2001 he was a consultant to Lord Justice Auld's Review of the Criminal Courts. He is a QC (*honoris causa*), an Academic Bencher of the Inner Temple, and holds an Honorary Degree from the University of Poitiers.

Michael Tonry is Sonosky Professor of Law and Public Policy and director, Institute on Crime and Public Policy, University of Minnesota, and senior fellow, the Netherlands Institute for the Study of Crime and Law Enforcement, Free University of Amsterdam.

Preface

Anthony Bottoms and Julian V. Roberts

Margery Fry (1874–1958), who was once the Principal of Somerville College, Oxford, was also, as the subtitle of her biography puts it, 'the essential amateur' (Jones 1966) in an age when such people could be hugely influential in British society. In the period after the Second World War, although already in her seventies, as Chairman of the Howard League for Penal Reform she was a major player in English criminal justice policy. Two of her concerns in this field are relevant to this volume. First, in the closing years of her life she campaigned ceaselessly to draw attention to the then much neglected topic of the needs of victims of crime. In particular, she strongly advocated State compensation for victims of violent crime, a policy that was accepted and implemented in the decade after her death. Secondly, in June 1957 the Howard League wrote to the then Home Secretary R.A. Butler, pressing the case for the Government to support the creation of the United Kingdom's first fully-fledged university-based Institute of Criminology; and in the following month Margery Fry followed this up with personal advocacy through a visit to Butler in the Home Office (Radzinowicz 1988: 3). The initiative was successful, and the Institute of Criminology came officially into existence at Cambridge University on 1 January 1960.

It was, however, not until the year 2004 that the Institute of Criminology was finally able to move into its permanent home on the Sidgwick Site in Cambridge (see Walston *et al.* 2009 for the complicated story of this lengthy delay). The new building was officially opened in May 2005 by Lord Woolf, the then Lord Chief Justice of England and Wales, and to celebrate the occasion the Institute arranged two special academic events. The first arose from Lord Woolf's gracious acceptance of the Institute's invitation to be the first holder of a Fellowship endowed by its first Director, Sir Leon Radzinowicz; as a part of his Fellowship duties, Lord Woolf delivered a special formal lecture entitled 'Making Sense of Sentencing' (see Woolf 2008).

The second event was a one-day Cropwood Conference, generously funded by the Barrow Cadbury Trust; and, as is the custom at Cropwood Conferences, this brought together academics and persons active in the criminal justice system for a day of discussion and reflection. Lord Woolf honoured the Institute by attending the whole of this conference, the theme of which was 'Victims and the Criminal Justice System'. Although we did not realise the link until later, the choice of the topic for this conference, at the time of the opening of the Institute's building, therefore constituted a very appropriate recognition, fifty years on, of the work of Margery Fry.

The decision to focus the 2005 Cropwood Conference on the topic of Victims reflects, of course, the much higher profile that this subject now holds, in both policy and academic discussions, than was the case in Margery Fry's lifetime. As David Garland has put it in his important book, *The Culture of Control* (Garland 2001: 121), people used to be able to argue that the crime victim's interest is, in criminal justice policy, appropriately recognised by being subsumed within the interests of the State. However, Garland goes on:

> Since the 1970s this response has come to seem aloof and unresponsive, as well as of doubtful credibility. With the forceful encouragement of elected officials, criminal justice agencies have developed an entirely different relationship to individual victims, and also to the organized victims' movement which became a growing presence on the policy scene in the 1980s and 1990s. In stark contrast to previous policy, victims have become a favoured constituency and the aim of serving victims has become part of the redefined mission of all criminal justice agencies.

The reasons for this major policy shift – which has occurred with varying emphasis in most Western countries – are still a matter of debate, and we shall not pursue that difficult question here. But given this background, it is not surprising that all common law jurisdictions have in recent years struggled to find a more prominent place for crime victims within their adversarial systems of criminal justice. The challenge has been to find a role for victims which allows them some scope for participation in a way that is meaningful to them and to the system, yet which does not fundamentally realign the nature of an adversarial proceeding in which the State, on behalf of the community, conducts a public prosecution. Allowing the victim unfettered freedom to intervene at critical stages of the justice system will undermine the foundational principles of a State-led prosecution system. Yet if a criminal justice system were to prosecute and punish offenders while being blind to the interests of victims – except and insofar as their participation assists the prosecution in (its own view of) its interests – that system would ultimately founder.

Victims and members of the community would see little merit in participation. Indeed, evidence of this can be found in many areas, including rape and other crimes of sexual aggression, where in the recent past victims have often avoided reporting victimisations in part because they were aware that the interests of victims have frequently been marginalised by the justice system – both in police stations and in the courts.

Such issues raise, ultimately, a question of legitimacy, a topic that has attracted growing interest among criminologists (see e.g. Tyler 2007). In our view, the proper treatment of the victim is integral to establishing and maintaining the legitimacy of the criminal justice system. Legitimacy may be defined and achieved in various ways: by criminal justice personnel such as the police service adhering to the law and to internal regulations; by ensuring that criminal justice decision-makers such as judges and juries are representative of the communities from which they are drawn, and appointed after fair competition; by the absence of corruption, and so on. Yet a justice system which fulfilled all these requirements, but completely excluded the victim of the crime would, in contemporary societies, still lack full legitimacy.

It is now widely recognised that a central aspect of achieving legitimacy in the criminal justice system is through procedural justice (Tyler 2003). One of the requirements of procedural justice is that all the key players in a case should have a chance to 'have their say' at some point in the process (Paternoster *et al.* 1997). Does that mean that victims should be allowed to say whatever they wish, whenever they wish, in court? Unfortunately, such unfettered participatory rights could generate conflict with another source of legitimacy, namely the rule of law. For it is inevitable that, for example, some crime victims will demand the imposition of disproportionate punishments on the offender in their case. If the system accedes to such demands, the legitimacy which springs from the application of fairness will drain away; but if it never so accedes, victims could claim that their apparent participatory right is a pointless sham that discredits the legal system. There are intractable dilemmas here.

Pressure to accommodate the victim within the justice system has come from many sources: victims' advocates, victims' rights groups, politicians, and criminal justice professionals charged with responding to the needs of victims. Victims' needs may be conceptualised as falling into three categories: first, Service Needs, including compensation, proper treatment at court, assistance in testifying and so forth; secondly, Expressive Needs, which include having the opportunity to express themselves at key stages of the criminal process, either in a public forum or in private discussions with criminal justice decision-makers; and thirdly, Participatory or Decision-making Needs, that is, to provide a direct input which may influence the key decisions taken, including bail, sentencing and parole (see Hoyle and Zedner 2007).

The threat to the adversarial system is present principally with respect to the third category. This explains why all common-law jurisdictions, other than some in the US, have placed important limits on victim input. For example, under most victim input regimes crime victims are denied the right to express an opinion about whether the offender should be given a custodial sentence, or whether (and when) prisoners should be released on parole; their input is restricted to documenting the effects of the crime upon them (including its emotional effects).

It is important to note that the victims' rights movement cannot be seen as a monolithic enterprise, nor has it exercised a unidimensional influence on criminal justice policy-making. There are indeed several schools of thought regarding victims' rights in the criminal process. One of these may be described as punitive in nature, and is most closely associated with victim policies in the United States (see discussion in Roach 1999); victim advocates who demand the right to intervene at various stages of the criminal process often do so to try to ensure harsher treatment for the offender. A very different victims' rights perspective is one which seeks to ensure that victims are apprised of, and receive, their service rights at all stages of the criminal process. It is not from a desire to enhance the punitiveness of the system that victims claim the right to compensation, or to be informed of significant developments in the case against their offender. A third strand of the victims' movement comes from restorative justice advocates. This perspective, like the second, is also non-punitive in nature. The purpose of a restorative encounter is to reduce conflict and to end the victim's distress – not simply to punish the offender. Indeed, restorative justice advocates recognise that simply making the offender suffer for his crimes may ultimately increase the number of victims, whatever the short-term benefits to the current victim.

The debate over the place for the victim in the criminal justice system has been infused recently with a political element. Public opinion polls in Britain and other Western nations routinely demonstrate that most people subscribe to two 'headline' opinions about the criminal justice system: it is too lenient towards convicted offenders, and it is 'tilted' towards protecting the rights of the offender at the expense of the more legitimate interests of the crime victim. (More detailed analysis of the surveys reveals a more complex picture, but many people do not get beyond the headlines.) Taken together, these opinions provide support for political initiatives such as that launched by New Labour in Britain in recent years, entitled 'Rebalancing the justice system in favour of the victim'. Whether this initiative has benefited crime victims is a question addressed in this volume, but this and other examples of political rhetoric linked to the victims issue show clearly that one cannot now escape the macropolitical dimension in contemporary discussions of policies for victims.

It should be clear from these brief remarks that the issues addressed in the Cropwood Conference, and in the papers in this volume, are complex, multifaceted and controversial. Our authors do not all speak with one voice, so no 'party line' will be found within these covers; and we believe that the volume has benefited from this approach to the subject. But all the authors have grappled seriously with issues which demand sustained reflection and debate. We hope that readers will find that the volume as a whole makes a valuable contribution to these debates.

Purpose and overview of this volume

This volume is deliberately restricted in its scope, being not about the general topic of victims and their needs, but specifically about the role of victims in contemporary criminal justice systems in the common law (adversarial) tradition. It also deliberately omits any direct discussion of the restorative justice alternative to criminal justice. This is not because we wish in any way to downplay the importance of that topic, but simply because there has been much recent writing on restorative justice, and we wanted to focus attention on the rather different topic of the victim within more conventional criminal justice processes.

The essays that follow fall broadly into two groups, each comprising five chapters. The first half of the book contains a series of chapters which could reasonably be described as 'contextual' in character. These begin with a paper by Matt Matravers in which, as a political philosopher, he explores the relationship that should exist between the State and the individual victim; in the process, he produces a robust defence of the State's leading role in criminal justice systems, on behalf of the whole community. Themes raised by Matravers are further explored by Anthony Bottoms in Chapter 2, where the argument is advanced that the State carries a 'duty to understand' in various criminal law contexts, and that this duty has consequences for victim participation. Helen Reeves and Peter Dunn provide an authoritative summary of recent policy developments with respect to the role of the victim in England and Wales, from the perspective of the respected charity Victim Support. They draw attention to several salutary developments, while arguing that much remains to be accomplished. Michael Tonry sounds a note of caution in his chapter, in which he highlights the politics of victims' issues. Tonry argues, in particular, that being tougher on offenders does not necessarily help victims, and that New Labour's 'Rebalancing' policy (see above) is 'nonsensical and dangerous'. Politicians often portray offenders and victims as two entirely distinct groups; they are not, however, and criminologists have long known about the so-called 'victim–offender overlap', especially for violent offences. In Chapter 5, Anthony Bottoms and Andrew Costello report findings from an empirical research project which show that this overlap is strongly present even for household offences (burglary and cognate offences), and they discuss the implications of these findings for crime policies.

The remaining chapters of the volume explore the role of the victim in the practice of adversarial criminal justice, beginning with the relationship between the victim and the prosecutor, which is discussed by John Spencer. Spencer also briefly explores the differences between the adversarial model and the *partie civile* system used in various Continental jurisdictions. Joanna Shapland and Matthew Hall analyse how victims are treated in court, and they argue a robust case for a return to something like the 'centre stage' which victims once held. In Chapter 8 Paul Rock reports some fascinating findings from his detailed study of the use of victim impact statements in homicide trials in London. The volume concludes with two contributions focusing on victim input into the punishment of convicted offenders. First, Julian Roberts and Edna Erez argue for an expressive rather than an instrumental role for victim personal statements at the sentencing stage. Then, in the concluding chapter, Nicola Padfield and Julian Roberts highlight the differences between sentencing and parole, and argue that victim input into the decision to release prisoners should be carefully conceptualised and circumscribed.

Acknowledgements

The principal organiser of the 2005 Cropwood Conference was Dr Amanda Matravers, then on the staff of the Institute of Criminology, now of American University, Washington, DC. This whole enterprise owes a great deal to her, and we are sorry that the duties of her new post have made it impossible for her to help to edit this volume. The Institute is also most grateful to the Barrow Cadbury Trust for funding the conference, one of many significant Cropwood Conferences that the Trust has funded over the years.

As sometimes happens on these occasions, for fully understandable reasons some of those who contributed preliminary papers to the conference have not been able to develop these papers into chapters for this volume. We therefore recruited other contributors, to whom we are most grateful for their willingness, and indeed enthusiasm, to participate. We are also very grateful for the patience and forbearance of those who produced chapters after the Conference, and then – in view of the delay in publication – have had to update their work to take account of more recent developments.

Brian Willan of Willan Publishing has been a great source of encouragement by making it clear how much he believes in the volume. We hope we have justified his confidence. In the closing stages of the work, we have benefited greatly from the copy-editing skills of Catherine Byfield of the Institute of Criminology, to whom we are most grateful.

References

Garland, D. (2001) *The Culture of Control: Crime and social order in contemporary society*. Oxford: Oxford University Press.

Hoyle, C. and Zedner, L. (2007) 'Victims, victimization, and criminal justice', in M. Maguire, R. Morgan and R. Reiner (eds), *The Oxford Handbook of Criminology* (4th edn). Oxford: Oxford University Press, pp. 461–95.

Jones, E.H. (1966). *Margery Fry: The essential amateur*. London: Oxford University Press.

Paternoster, R., Brame, R., Bachanan, R. and Sherman L.W. (1997) 'Do fair procedures matter? The effect of procedural justice on spouse assault', *Law and Society Review*, 31(1): 163–204.

Radzinowicz, L. (1988) *The Cambridge Institute of Criminology: Its background and scope*. London: HMSO.

Roach, K. (1999) *Due Process and Victims' Rights: The new law and politics of criminal justice*. Toronto: University of Toronto Press.

Tyler, T.H. (2003) 'Procedural justice, legitimacy and the effective rule of law', in M. Tonry (ed.). *Crime and Justice: A review of research*, 30: 283–357.

Tyler, T.H. (ed.) (2007) *Legitimacy and Criminal Justice: A comparative perspective*. New York: Russell Sage Foundation.

Walston, C., Bottoms, A.E., Eisner, M. and Lösel, F. (eds) (2009) *Challenging Crime: A portrait of the Cambridge Institute of Criminology*. London: Third Millennium.

Woolf, Lord (2008) 'Making sense of sentencing', in Lord Woolf (ed. C. Campbell-Holt), *The Pursuit of Justice*. Oxford: Oxford University Press, pp. 293–307.

Chapter 1

The victim, the State, and civil society[1]

Matt Matravers

Crime victims are increasingly of interest to politicians, criminologists and criminal justice practitioners. However, their place in criminal justice is disputed. In this chapter I consider the proper roles of the State and the victim in relation to criminal justice. The discussion is largely framed by the issue of who properly 'owns' crimes: the State or the parties involved? However, before getting to that rather abstract question, it is worth briefly considering the growing importance of victims in contemporary criminal justice, and the reasons some scholars respond to this growth with suspicion.

The rise of the victim

The web page of the British Government ministry responsible for policy on crime claims that it puts 'the concerns of victims of crime at the heart of the work we do' (Home Office 2009). In the USA, there is an Office for Victims of Crime that has, since 1981, helped communities to celebrate an annual National Crime Victims' Rights Week. A similar event takes place every year in Canada, where there is also a federal Office for Crime Victims. More generally, there is a great deal of public discussion of victims' rights; politicians regularly surround themselves with victims whenever they announce new criminal justice policy; and statutes are often proposed and enacted while attached to the names of particular victims: Megan, Sarah, and Jessica Lunsford.[2]

It is important to distinguish two rather different, although interconnected, elements in 'the rise of the victim'.[3] First, a great deal has been done to improve the experience of victims during the criminal process. Much of this is at worst benign and at best to be welcomed. There is nothing heinous or dangerous in improving the conditions of the waiting rooms in court buildings; in protecting vulnerable victim witnesses; or in trying to keep informed those victims who wish to be informed about the progress, or lack of it, in the investigation and prosecution (if any) of the case. That said, there is no reason to think that these kinds of welfare reforms are exclusive to crime victims. We surely have an interest in improving the experience of everyone involved in criminal proceedings so that there is, for example, no more reason to be concerned with vulnerable victim witnesses than vulnerable witnesses who are not victims. The fact that many of these reforms have been implemented by association with victims' rights is sociologically and politically interesting, but does not tell us anything in particular about the relative position of the victim, the State, and any other party in criminal justice.

The kinds of welfare reforms mentioned above need to be kept separate from the second, more fundamental, component in the rise of the victim. Recent debates have included the question of whether victims should have the right to make personal or impact statements and, if so, what role such statements should have; whether victims should play a role in decisions over whether to prosecute, over how much to punish, and over parole and other decisions regarding release from prison. Still more fundamentally, there is the proposal that the existing criminal justice paradigm should be rethought in terms of dispute resolution and restorative justice.

These proposals elicit varied and often hotly contested reactions. My purpose is not to take each proposal separately, but rather to approach them by asking about the relative position of the parties involved in criminal justice, where those parties include the victim, the offender, the State, and civil society. Before that, however, it is worth considering why some people and groups have reacted with such suspicion to the emergence of the victims' rights movement.

The grounds of suspicion

There is little doubt that while victims' rights movements have attracted a certain level of popular and academic support, many legal and social theorists have sounded a notably cautious tone both in general and in relation to specific measures. The arguments are many and complex; nevertheless it is possible to discern rather different sets of concerns that have motivated those who oppose, or are cautious about, recent developments in relation to victims.

First, there are those who see the rise of the victim as part of the process of increased punitiveness that characterises the UK and the USA. This is what Andrew Ashworth has neatly called 'victims in the service of severity' (2000: 186). Those worried by this development point to the fact that some victims' movements actively lobby for harsher sentences; juxtapose the interests of offenders and victims in a zero-sum game; campaign for victim impact/personal statements that are little more than mechanisms to generate harsher penalties; and contribute to the de-monisation of offenders.

Second, there are those who worry that the rise of the victim is part of the individualisation of late modernity. These worries can take a number of forms, and the relations between them are not at all clear. For some, the focus on the victim and the offender (rather than on the society and the State) is associated with a methodological invasion of rational choice theory from economics into sociology and the other social sciences; of *homo economicus* replacing *homo sociologicus*. For others, the individualisa-tion of crime is evidence of a politics in which the focus is on individual offenders as rational actors rather than on the social causes of crime. It is not that 'there is no such thing as society', as Mrs Thatcher famously put it, but that society has abdicated its responsibilities under the pretence of restoring the individual to the centre of politics. For still others, the victim now takes centre stage as a point of reference in an individualised postmodern world in which the traditional sources of morality have receded. The victim's suffering offers something shared – in a world of diminishing shared moral values – on which to ground a 'victimalized morality' (Boutellier 2000).

It is noticeable from the above that the various explanations of the rise of the victim, and of the suspicions with which that rise has been met, do not fit neatly together. Critics of 'victims in the service of severity' worry that victims are, more or less willingly, being appropriated by politicians with substantive moralising, communitarian agendas. The victims' movement is to be feared because it is a tool of non-liberals who wish to use it to press home their critiques of modern value-less societies and to restore 'Victorian', 'Christian', or just 'old-fashioned' values to the public domain.[4]

This is in sharp contrast to those who fear victims' rights as represen-ting the thin edge of an individualist, rational-choice wedge. These fears relate the rise of the victim to the triumph of free market individualism, the focus on citizens as individual rational actors, and the loss of community. On the one hand, the victim's claim is made on behalf of the restoration of community and old values (and resisted for the same reason). On the other, the victim's special significance is understood within the triumph (or disaster) that is the modern, pluralistic, disen-chanted West where the old values have withered away.

The State and its citizens

Perhaps the confusion identified above suggests that one should approach the issue of the relative place of victims, the State, and civil society in criminal justice by first giving an account of the State and its relation to morality and community – or at least by giving a series of such accounts – and then extrapolating from each to find the proper place of the victim given a certain understanding of politics.[5] This would be neat, but I do not think it can be done. Of course, it is true that political philosophers have long debated the merits of liberal versus communitarian understandings of politics. Moreover, it is also true that it is only possible to make sense of some policies or political phenomena given a certain understanding – liberal or communitarian – of the State. However, while one can work backwards in this way from a suggested policy to the presuppositions on which it rests, it is much more difficult to work from a general account of the State, such as is found in communitarianism, to specific concrete policy proposals. Nothing much can be said to follow from a communitarian theory of the State until it is established what kind of values inhere in the State, and what traditions and communities are properly embodied within it.

Similarly, there are contractarian theories of the State; that is, accounts of the legitimacy of the State that are grounded in asking what individuals would agree to in a hypothetical choosing situation (in a 'state of nature'). These are often associated with the individualistic neo-liberalism identified as problematic in the second account of the rise of the victim mentioned above. However, again it is very hard to see how anything as specific as the role of the victim in the criminal justice system can be derived from a contractarian theory of the State.

In short, theories of the State and/or of justice – whether communitarian or contractarian – generate rather abstract principles of justice or political authority that merely set parameters on public policy. No amount of abstract theorising, or of analysis of the debate between those who espouse communitarianism and those who favour contractarianism, will resolve fine-grained issues surrounding victims and their proper place in criminal justice.

One might conclude from the above that political philosophy cannot contribute much to the debate over the proper place of victims in the criminal justice system because its concern is with abstract and general principles and these seldom dictate specific policies. However, in what follows, I propose that there are at least two arguments that can be given to frame the debate between advocates of victims' rights and their opponents. First, all such debates need to be understood within parameters set by demands of justice and equality. Second, and more importantly, they need to be understood in a context in which the State – or a state-like entity – must take responsibility for the regulation of crime not simply because it is the entity most likely to be effective, but because its doing so is in part constitutive of what makes co-operative social life possible.

The narrow contribution of political philosophy

The narrow contribution that political philosophy can make to debates over policy, including policy relating to victims of crime, lies in the fact that parameters, while they cannot tell us precisely what to do, can tell us what not to do. For example, the most general statement about justice – that it requires that each gets his or her due – tied to the most general statement about equality – that it requires that relevantly like cases be treated alike – can shed light on, for example, the proper use of victims' personal/impact statements at sentencing and parole.

The argument turns on what counts as 'relevantly like'. For example, two otherwise similar crimes, committed by similar offenders, may result in very different financial costs to the victims. In assessing any court-ordered compensation to be awarded to the victim and paid by the offender, the court might legitimately consider this difference and do so by listening to a victim's statement. Here, the different financial impact of the crimes is relevant in distinguishing the cases.

Contrast this with two similar offenders convicted of similar offences with similar results for the victims, whose punishment – say, the length of their prison sentences – is different because the court was moved in one case by the eloquence of the victim's statement in favour of a harsh penalty prior to sentencing. Here, the difference between the cases – the fact that one victim is eloquent and the other not – is irrelevant and the demands of equality and justice are not met. Thus, if it can be shown that victims' statements, delivered at a certain point in the procedure, result in relevantly like offenders receiving different penalties, then that is unjust and the use of such statements in that way is improper.

Of course, these are easy examples, but they demonstrate how even thin, general principles of justice (as well as formal principles of consistency, and so on) can show what ought not to be done. Moreover, clarifying the nature of the debate also helps in locating the proper battleground for the different parties. What often matters is what people count as 'relevant' in the demand that equality requires relevantly like cases to be treated in relevantly like ways. Putting it this way can help at least to make the issues clear. For example, consider a proposal that speeding fines should be in some way proportionate to income rather than be in simple fixed amounts. In discussing this, we can ask whether the millionaire and the poor pensioner who commit identical offences are subject to 'relevantly like' treatment if each receives a fixed penalty of, say, £60 rather than a penalty of 1 per cent of net monthly income. Similarly – albeit even more controversially – the debate over when and in what ways a history of previous offending ought to make a difference to current cases is clarified (although not, of course, resolved) if one asks whether there is anything about having a history of previous offending that renders one offender relevantly different from another who, without such a history, is convicted of an identical offence.

The broad contribution of political philosophy

So far, I have made only modest claims for abstract theorising about the nature of justice or of the State. In part, this is because the kinds of issues addressed so far – victim personal/impact statements, humdrum welfare reforms, and so on – have been quite specific and, for reasons given above, political philosophy is not well equipped to deal with such detail. However, it is also in part because in order to make progress we need to step back from asking about the nature of the State and its relations to its citizens and ask the more basic question, 'why have a State at all?'

The question of why we should have a State at all arises because answering it sheds light on the issue of who owns a crime and its consequences. This is the heart of the matter. On the one hand, it is natural to think of crime as being 'between' the offender and his victim. On the other, crime is public. The debate, of course, is at its crudest between those for whom crime is 'owned' by the parties involved and 'stolen' by the State (Christie 1977), and those who think crime is the proper business of the State and the victim is little more than a contingent fact about this or that particular crime.

Ordinary language suggests that there is nothing wrong with thinking of crimes, offenders, and criminal proceedings as the victim's. Victims will often initiate the case by reporting it to the police; the wrong, if there was one, was done to them; they may well be the most important witnesses; and they may well have to sacrifice time and energy in the pursuit of the case. Given all that, it is natural to think of the case as 'theirs'. However, the case is theirs only in the sense that they are closely associated (perhaps, together with the offender, most closely associated) with it, not in the (possessive) sense that it belongs to them.[6] In all but exceptional circumstances, the case belongs to, and is prosecuted (in both the broad and narrow senses of that word) by the State. Moreover, the State does not prosecute the case on behalf of the victim, but on behalf of the public.

As noted above, this question of who owns the case lies at the heart of the most fundamental issues dividing those who think differently about the respective roles of the State and of victims in criminal justice. Moreover, on the face of it the State does seem to be the intruder: if D assaults V in the car park of a pub after a heavy drinking session, this would seem to be between D and V. The State, of course, might assist D in pursuing his dispute with V, or in establishing the facts about the incident, but in doing so it would be no more than a tool in a conflict between those directly involved. In what follows, I argue that this position cannot be defended and that crime does belong to the State. The arguments are of two kinds. First, even if it is granted that a particular crime belongs to the parties involved, it is hard to stop the set 'parties involved' from expanding outwards to include the citizen body. Moreover, on at least one understanding of the wrong done (in part or whole) in a given crime, this is not a contingent matter. Second, and more fundamentally, the argument is that State ownership of crime is a constitutive element of one precondition of co-operative social life.

'The parties involved'

Grant for the moment that a particular crime does belong to the parties involved: the victim and the offender. What reason is there for the State, or any other body, to 'steal' the crime? One answer that does not depend upon any particular philosophical commitments arises if one asks who are 'the parties involved'. The example given above in which D assaults V might be thought to be a paradigmatic case of a crime – a conflict – that belongs to the assailant and his victim. However, the parties affected by D's actions extend far beyond V; even the most private of acts tend to have some public dimensions and this is no exception. D's actions, together with those of others, result in insurance premiums being higher than they would otherwise be; they may cause people to invest in expensive security; and they may cause people to forego opportunities for welfare (such as going to the pub) for fear of being assaulted (and this may be true of people geographically distant from the scene of the crime who have read about the assault in the newspaper).

A second argument appeals to the duty we have to one another as citizens to obey the law (at least, in most circumstances). On this account, the wrong done by the assailant is not just the violence inflicted on the victim, but also the wrong of failing to restrain the pursuit of his interests in accordance with the law. Since that is an obligation on us all, and since we accept it only as a reciprocal obligation, the assailant fails to honour an obligation he has to us all. He is a free rider and that part of his wrong is one that is done to all those who participate in society.

In short, both these arguments appeal to the thought that, even if we admit that the crime belongs to the parties involved, the actions of the parties involved have public dimensions and so the State has a legitimate claim on the case as the only institution with the resources to represent everyone. However, in granting in the first instance that offences are owned by the parties directly involved and then showing that it is difficult to stop the category of 'party involved' extending outwards, these arguments do not go to the heart of the matter. The traditional view is not that criminal offences are owned by the parties and, lo and behold, it turns out that we are all involved parties. Rather, it is that criminal offences are owned by the State and the wrongs done by criminal offenders are public wrongs, and not simply wrongs done to all of the public.

I think this view can be defended. To do so requires, as mentioned above, that we ask why we should have a State at all. Of course, the answers to this question are themselves hotly contested. In particular, those in the anarchist tradition deny that there is any need for, or legitimacy in, a State. Putting them to one side, though, one can identify an agreed purpose of the State that runs through a number of different writers and traditions, although it should be noted that the purpose of the State need not be the same as what makes it legitimate. This purpose is to protect those who reside within its borders and, to a (much disagreed-about) extent to secure their welfare.

The State and the condition of sufficient security

In order to achieve its ends, the State takes to itself what, according to Max Weber, defines it: a monopoly on the legitimate use of physical force (Weber 1948: 78). This need not be understood simply as an instrumental claim; that is, that it so happens that in order to secure the protection and welfare of its citizens, the State needs this monopoly. Rather, we can understand the State claiming this monopoly as essentially tied to the relevant idea of security. Consider Hobbes, who argued that the only way in which to secure peace was for each person 'to conferre all their power and strength upon one Man, or upon one Assembly of men, that may reduce all their Wills, by plurality of voices, unto one Will' (Tuck 1991: 120). This was necessary, according to Hobbes, not because he believed men to be innately savage or bad, but because he believed that unless an individual had 'sufficient security' that others, too, would submit their judgement to that of the Sovereign, that individual would have no reason to do so himself (Tuck 1991: 215).

In the modern jargon, what Hobbes identified is an assurance problem (Sen 1967). Each person has reason to co-operate (in a joint venture) only if she is assured that others will co-operate. In the absence of such assurance, the danger is not only that each person will defect from the agreement (or that no agreement will be possible), but that each will anticipate future non-cooperation and attempt to 'get her retaliation in first'. It is this that threatens to land people without a Sovereign to guarantee security to a life that is famously 'solitary, poore, nasty, brutish, and short' (Tuck 1991: 89). On this account, then, what is clear is that the State's monopoly on the legitimate use of physical force is not simply a means to security, but is in part constitutive of such security.

Although Hobbes is unusual in granting as much power as he does to the Sovereign, the idea that the State ensures peace (and all that goes with it) by taking to itself a monopoly on the legitimate use of physical force is by no means unique to Hobbes. Even those natural law theorists like Pufendorf and Locke, who believe that there is an obligatory law of nature such that individuals have a right to punish violations of it, argue that the problems that would result from any such free-for-all are so severe as to require the concentration of the individual's natural right to punish at the level of the community and by delegation to the magistrate. For Locke, political power is thus defined as *'a Right* of making Laws with Penalties of Death, and consequently all less Penalties, for the Regulating and Preserving of Property' (Laslet 1988: ii, paragraph 3; see also Tully 1991: 2.5).[7]

That the State plays the role of guarantor of assurance can be found in other thinkers as diverse as the utilitarian Jeremy Bentham and the contemporary neo-Kantian John Rawls. What grounds their accounts is very different. For Bentham, the State is justified only if it promotes happiness. In order to do that, it must ensure stability such that people's reasonable expectations of the future will not prove to be false by removing, as far as possible, the chances of arbitrary interference in their plans (Burns and Hart 1970). Rawls, whose account is very different, also recognises the need to respond to the assurance problem. The problem, he writes, is that 'each person's willingness to contribute is contingent upon the contribution of the others'. So, what is needed is 'to assure the cooperating parties that the common agreement is being carried out'. Thus, he argues, 'to maintain public confidence in the scheme that is superior from everyone's point of view, or better anyway than the situation that would obtain in its absence, some device for administering fines and penalties must be established' (Rawls 1971: 270; cf. Kant 1991: 307–8).

The point of citing these different arguments and thinkers is not to say that there is universal agreement on the nature, purpose and justification of the State and nor is it to appeal to the argument from authority (if all these great men think this, then it must be true). Rather, it is to illustrate the positive argument, which is that the State – understood in a Weberian form – claims a monopoly on the use of legitimate force not merely as a means to securing security, but because the State's doing so is partly constitutive of one kind of security – the security that comes with assurance – which is itself a necessary condition for peaceful coexistence.[8]

It follows from adopting this vision of the State that cases that properly fall within the laws of the State belong to it. In return, the State must try to ensure that such cases are prosecuted (again in both senses) properly and impartially so as to contribute to mutual assurance. To allow a free-for-all in which disputes remain solely the property of the parties involved would introduce an arbitrariness that would undermine the condition of sufficient security that makes social life in the State possible.

However, to say that offences and their resolution are rightly the property of the State acting for the public is not yet to resolve the issue of the proper roles of the State and the victim in relation to *criminal* justice. First, clearly not all disputes are properly the property of the State. Second, to say that the State must try to ensure a proper and non-arbitrary prosecution of relevant offences is not to say that it must do so directly or by itself. After all, in a sense the State acts merely as a guarantor in tort and family law and, on occasions, it delegates its powers to other bodies (such as the General Medical Council). Why then should the State not stand back and allow, as advocates of restorative justice would like, those directly involved to resolve their dispute under State guidance and regulation?

What these two issues point towards is the need for an account of criminalisation and the criminal law. That is, granting that some disputes are the property of the State, why should the State claim them as crimes and deal with them itself rather than allowing their status as disputes to be dealt with by those involved, albeit under the supervision of the State?[9]

Regulation and criminalisation

The argument so far is as follows: peaceful and successful social co-operation (in complex societies) requires the condition of 'sufficient security'; it requires that each participant is reasonably assured that others will co-operate in accordance with the rules. This condition is not contingently secured by the State – or by whatever State-like entity exists – but is rather constituted by the existence of the State as the monopoly guarantor of assurance. Thus, the State must 'own' those rules, and disputes over them, that together ensure the condition of sufficient security is met. Again, this is not a contingent claim – it is not that the State just happens to be best at securing assurance – it is constitutive: the State's ownership of these rules and disputes is part of the condition of sufficient security itself.[10]

Even if this is right, though, it does not explain the State's (and the victim's) role in criminal justice in particular. Why should the State move beyond regulation to criminalisation? And, more pertinently, is there anything about that move that changes the relative position of the State and those involved (including the victim)? In what follows, I shall only gesture at an answer to the first question. However, it seems unlikely that the answer to the second is affirmative. No matter how the State enforces the rules – whether through devolved regulation or direct criminalisation – it must retain ownership if it is to fulfil its function.

In addressing the move from regulation to criminalisation, it is worth considering what is peculiar about the criminal law. The answer cannot be simply that breaking the criminal law brings down on the offender, if caught, criminal prosecution and punishment. Moreover, the wrong done in core criminal cases is not only that the offender has failed to restrain himself in accordance with the law. Rather, with Antony Duff, we can say that the mark of the criminal law is that it calls the offender to account and, if no excuse or justification is forthcoming, it condemns him in the name of the public for his wrong (Duff 1986; Duff 2001).

For Duff, there is a distinct sense in which core criminal wrongs are public: they are wrongs in which the public share. Serious criminal wrongs, he writes, are 'wrongs in which the community shares ... [and] as members of the community, we should see them not merely as the victim's wrongs but as "our" wrongs' (2001: 63). It is because of this that such wrongs are 'matters on which the community as a whole can and should take a stand, through ... authoritative, communal condemnation' and that 'those who commit [such wrongs] should be called to account and censured by the community' (Duff 2001: 61).

If Duff is right then there is another sense of 'public wrong' (particular to criminal justice) that was not considered in the earlier part of this chapter and that might, by itself, account for the proper roles of the State and the victim in criminal justice. Serious wrongs are wrongs in which the community shares; they are wrongs done to the public as well as to the particular victim. However, although richly suggestive, I do not think Duff is right or that there is any such sense of a shared public wrong.

Duff's argument is (as always) subtle and nuanced. However, it is also hard to pin down. In what sense are the victim's wrongs also 'ours'? One answer appears in an earlier paper in which Duff and his co-author Sandra Marshall offer the examples of sexually, and racially, motivated attacks. In these cases, they argue, 'an attack on a member of the group is ... an attack on the group – on their shared values and their common good' (Marshall and Duff 1998: 19).

Marshall and Duff's examples are well chosen, but even so it requires some imagination to get the argument to work. A small close-knit community of women in a society in which women are generally discriminated against may come to think of themselves as sufficiently interconnected for a wrong done to one of them to be a wrong done to all (and much the same could be said in the racial case). However, in run-of-the-mill criminal cases – even core, serious cases – it is implausible to think of wrongs as shared in this way. When someone is the victim of a gang-related murder in Nottingham, I do not feel that I share the wrong as a *wrong done to me*. Moreover, that is not because I do not share in an (admittedly fairly minimal) moral community that is united around liberal values including the value of life. The point is that I may – indeed, do – feel that a serious wrong has been committed, but it is not a wrong in which I share as a victim.[11]

Perhaps the answer lies in separating Duff's (and Marshall's) claim that the wrong is done to the public from the other claims cited above: that serious criminal wrongs are 'matters on which the community as a whole can and should take a stand, through ... authoritative, communal condemnation' and that 'those who commit [such wrongs] should be called to account and censured by the community'. For Marshall and Duff it seems that the community must take a stand because the wrong is done to the community (as well as to the victim), but it seems more plausible to say that the community must take a stand because of the seriousness of the wrong done to the victim, because only communal condemnation can convey the appropriate degree of censure for that degree of wrong-doing, and because it is a violation of a rule the affirmation of which by the State in part constitutes a necessary condition of co-operative social life.[12]

Conclusion

The argument above depends on two claims about the nature and purpose of the State. First, by effectively taking to itself the monopoly on the legitimate use of physical force it removes a degree of uncertainty that would undermine trust and the conditions of social co-operation. Second, it is a carrier of values – values, as Duff puts it, 'by which the political community defines itself as a law-governed polity' (2003: 47) – and core criminal wrongs violate these values. As a constitutive element of sufficient security, the State must own the rules, and disputes over the rules, which constitute the 'game' of social co-operation. As the bearer of values, the State has reason not merely to regulate some disputes, but to consider them as 'offences' and to condemn those who commit them for their serious wrongdoing.

To say this, though, is to leave unanswered many aspects of the question: what are the proper roles of the State and the victim in relation to criminal justice? I want to end with three comments on what is not resolved.

First, nothing follows from the above arguments in relation to the humdrum welfare reforms mentioned at the start of the chapter. Second, a great deal is left open about the exact roles victims should play in processes of criminal justice. For example, if restorative conferences are effective – as they seem to be for some crimes, some offenders, and some victims – then the State may use them. However, this is not to say that the arguments above have nothing to contribute to the debate between advocates of restorative justice and advocates of more traditional ap-proaches. The argument requires that all procedures within the criminal justice system must guarantee (as far as possible) just and equal treatment for those involved. If some restorative justice practices fail to do so then they are unacceptable. Moreover, restorative justice practices are, accord-ing to this argument, manifestations of the State's power and authority. They exist, and have legitimacy, only insofar as they are invoked by the State. They are not, then, an alternative to the State's ownership of criminal cases – or, to use the dominant contemporary jargon, an alternative paradigm for criminal justice (see Ashworth 1993) – but rather are simply different ways of realising the State's role in criminal punishment. Whether, as a matter of fact, restorative justice practices are good or bad in achieving their goals is, of course, hotly debated (the literature is vast and good arguments, on both sides, can be found in Crawford and Goodey 2000; and von Hirsch *et al.* 2003).

Third, and finally, I think that it follows from this picture of the State and its legitimate authority that, in conditions in which sufficient security does not obtain, all political (and, in my view, moral) bets are off. That opens up a whole new way of thinking about the issue of victims. That is, I have concentrated in this chapter entirely on claims made by, and on behalf of, those victims of crime who are, or wish to be, involved in the processes that follow a crime. However, this is a tiny percentage of the overall number of victims. For most victims of crime – even when they report the crime – questions of possible involvement in decisions over prosecution, penalties, and release are entirely irrelevant. The case stops with the police officer, or community support officer, leaving the house after having recorded what has happened. The challenge those victims pose for a political theory of the kind I have just defended is a substantial one. It may make it both reasonable and legitimate for groups to suspend their commitment to the political association whether by retreating to a gated community or by organising local private protection groups. However, that is an issue for another time.[13]

Notes

1 Earlier versions of this paper were given at the Cropwood Conference hosted by the Institute of Criminology at Cambridge in 2005; the Morrell Theory Workshop in the Politics Department at York; and the Issues in Criminal Law Theory seminar series in the Law School at Birmingham. I am grateful to Tony Bottoms, Amanda Matravers, Sue Mendus, Julian Roberts, Stephen Shute, and to the participants at the above gatherings for their comments.

2 Megan's Law is named after Megan Kanka, a seven-year-old who was raped and killed by a known child molester in New Jersey; a campaign for a similar law in the UK is named after Sarah Payne, another child murder victim. The Florida Jessica Lunsford Act followed the rape and murder of a nine-year-old of that name. I should note that my concerns in this chapter will be limited to developments in UK and US politics and law, and the philosophical analysis will similarly be in the Anglo-American analytic tradition. I am sure that there would be a great deal to learn from a comparison of Anglo-American and Continental European developments, but (sadly) I am not in a position to offer such an account.

3 I am conscious that the phrase 'the rise of the victim' is rather too crude. Moreover, there is always the professional hazard in writing papers of this kind that posterity might judge that one had mistaken a short-term fashion for an important development. For what it is worth, I think the rise of the victim a genuine, if complex, phenomenon that has the potential to alter significantly the shape of (parts of) the criminal justice system. That said, even if it is a

short-term fashion, the proposals that have emerged from the victims' rights movements still need to be critically assessed.

4   This is perhaps more apparent in the USA, where there seem to be implicit and explicit connections between some victim advocacy groups (particularly those concerned with homicides and the death penalty) and some of those advocating the return to the public domain of Christian values and the reassessment of the constitutional separation of church and State.

5   The best summary of the arguments is Mulhall and Swift (1996).

6   It is interesting to note that when authors refer, for example, to victims being informed about the progress of their case, the 'their' is very often put in scare quotes. A quick trawl through the literature revealed (among others) the following: 'how much ... victims should be told about the sentencing of "their" offender' (Williams 2005: 495); 'the importance attached by victims to being kept informed of the progress of "their" case' (Zedner 2002b: 432); 'victims are encouraged to demand better information about the progress of "their" case' (Zedner 2004: 145); 'several American states now permit individual victims to make recommendations to the judge prior to sentencing, and to put their views to the parole board prior to the release of "their" offender' (Garland 2001: 179); 'The "rights" of victims in relation to "their" cases' (Sanders 2002: 211).

7   I am very grateful to my colleague, Jon Parkin, for his comments. He should not, however, be held responsible for the interpretations of Hobbes, Locke and Pufendorf offered here.

8   A contemporary variation on this argument can be found in Loader and Walker's rich and interesting book, *Civilizing Security*. They, too, argue that security is a good, and for the 'necessary virtue of the State in delivering the public good of security' (Loader and Walker 2007: 195).

9   I want to put to one side the issue of what offences ought to be criminal (assuming that some should be). This issue is of the first importance, but it is not one I can deal with here. I will, therefore, take examples from core *mala in se* offences, which I assume are rightly criminal (if anything is).

10 Modern States, of course, came into existence for all sorts of different contingent reasons. The claim here is not historical, but conceptual. In reconstructing why we should have a State at all, ensuring the condition of sufficient security is part of the answer, and thus part of the justification of the State. It is not part of any story of the State having come into existence. I am grateful to Gordon Woodman for encouraging me to clarify this point.

11 Duff might retort that this is because I have too thin a notion of 'belonging' to a community (see, for example, his contribution to the debate with Andrew von Hirsch in Matravers 1999 and Duff 2001).

12 This conclusion shares something with the conclusion of Grant Lamond's paper, 'What is a Crime?' Lamond (2007) argues that core criminal wrongs are public 'because the public is responsible for punishing them', rather than because they are wrongs done to the public. However, his argument for why the public should be responsible for punishing core criminal wrongs is rather different from the above.

13 I should note that I am not saying that the modern State has broken down, or that we live in Hobbes' State of nature. Nor do I mean to contribute to a 'dangerous penal pessimism' (Zedner 2002a). Rather, I raise the issue as a

conceptual possibility. That said, I do think such analysis is useful when thinking about issues such as gated communities and how to do penal justice in a distributively unjust society (see Matravers 2000: ch. 9).

References

Ashworth, A. (1993) 'Some doubts about restorative justice', *Criminal Law Forum*, 4(2): 277–99.

Ashworth, A. (2000) 'Victims' rights, defendants' rights and criminal procedure', in A. Crawford and J. Goodey (eds), *Integrating a Victim Perspective within Criminal Justice: International Debates*. Aldershot: Ashgate/Dartmouth.

Boutellier, H. (2000) *Crime and Morality: The Significance of Criminal Justice in Post-modern Culture*. Dordrecht: Kluwer Academic.

Burns, J.H. and Hart, H.L.A. (eds) (1970) *The Collected Works of Jeremy Bentham: An Introduction to the Principles of Morals and Legislation*. London: Athlone Press.

Christie, N. (1977) 'Conflicts as property', *The British Journal of Criminology*, 17(1): 1–15.

Crawford, A. and Goodey, J. (eds) (2000) *Integrating a Victim Perspective within Criminal Justice: International debates*. Dartmouth: Ashgate.

Duff, R.A. (1986) *Trials and Punishments*. Cambridge: Cambridge University Press.

Duff, R.A. (2001) *Punishment, Communication, and Community*. Oxford/New York: Oxford University Press.

Duff, R.A. (2003) 'Restoration and retribution', in A. von Hirsch, J. Roberts, A. Bottoms, K. Roach and M. Schiff (eds), *Restorative Justice and Criminal Justice: Competing or reconcilable paradigms?* Oxford: Hart Publishing.

Garland, D. (2001) *The Culture of Control: Crime and social order in contemporary society*. Oxford: Oxford University Press.

von Hirsch, A., Roberts, J., Bottoms, A., Roach, K. and Schiff, M. (2003) *Restorative Justice and Criminal Justice: Competing or reconcilable paradigms?* Oxford: Hart Publishing.

Home Office (2009) 'Keeping crime down: crime and victims'. http://www.homeoffice.gov.uk/crime-victims/.

Kant, I. (1991) (trans. M. Gregor) *The Metaphysics of Morals*. Cambridge: Cambridge University Press.

Lamond, G. (2007) 'What is a crime?', *Oxford Journal of Legal Studies*, 27(4): 609–32.

Laslet, P. (ed.) (1988) *Locke: Two Treatises of Government*. Cambridge: Cambridge University Press.

Loader, I. and Walker, N. (2007) *Civilizing Security*. Cambridge: Cambridge University Press.

Marshall, S. and Duff, R.A. (1998) 'Criminalization and sharing wrongs', *The Canadian Journal of Law & Jurisprudence*, 11(1): 7–22.

Matravers, M. (ed.) (1999) *Punishment and Political Theory*. Oxford: Hart Publishing.

Matravers, M. (2000) *Justice and Punishment: The rationale of coercion*. Oxford: Oxford University Press.

Mulhall, S. and Swift, A. (1996) *Liberals and Communitarians* (2nd edn). Oxford: Blackwell.

Rawls, J. (1971) *A Theory of Justice*. Cambridge, MA: Harvard University Press.

Sanders, A. (2002) 'Victim participation in an exclusionary criminal justice system', in C. Hoyle and R. Young (eds), *New Visions of Crime Victims*. Oxford: Hart Publishing.

Sen, A. (1967) 'Isolation, assurance, and the social rate of discount', *Quarterly Journal of Economics*, 81(1): 112–24.

Tuck, R. (ed.) (1991) *Hobbes: Leviathan*. Cambridge: Cambridge University Press.

Tully, J. (ed.) (trans. M. Silverthorne) (1991) *Samuel Pufendorf: On the duty of man and citizen according to natural law*. Cambridge: Cambridge University Press.

Weber, M. (1948) 'Politics as a vocation', in H.H. Gerth and C. Wright Mills (eds, trans.), *From Max Weber: Essays in Sociology*. London: Routledge.

Williams, B. (2005) 'Victims', in C. Hale, K. Hayward, A. Wahidin and E. Wincup (eds), *Criminology*. Oxford: Oxford University Press.

Zedner, L. (2002a) 'Dangers of dystopias in penal theory', *Oxford Journal of Legal Studies*, 22(2): 341–66.

Zedner, L. (2002b) 'Victims', in R. Morgan, R. Reiner and M. Maguire (eds), *The Oxford Handbook of Criminology* (3rd edn). Oxford: Oxford University Press.

Zedner, L. (2004) *Criminal Justice*. Oxford: Oxford University Press.

Chapter 2

The 'duty to understand': what consequences for victim participation?

Anthony Bottoms

Dispute settlement has, historically, taken many different forms, but in the legal systems of modern nation states there is normally a well-established division between (i) adjudicative processes in which the State makes available facilities within which disputes between private citizens and/or corporate bodies may be pursued ('civil law'), and (ii) adjudicative processes in which the State takes the lead, on behalf of the community, in pursuing or 'prosecuting' the dispute ('criminal law').

As is well known, theorists such as Nils Christie (1977) and Louk Hulsman (1981, 1982) have argued that, in modern States, too many adjudicative processes are State-led, and we should therefore deliberately attempt to pursue an agenda for the 'civilisation' of disputes. (The use of the term 'civilisation' in this context has of course, in the eyes of its advocates, a helpful *double entendre*.) However, as Matt Matravers has argued in the first chapter of this book, a strong normative case can still be made for the use of the criminal law (or 'State-led adjudicative processes') as an appropriate mechanism for dispute resolution in many contexts.

In this chapter, it is not my concern to debate the issues raised in the preceding paragraph. Rather, I shall simply assume for the sake of argument that there is, at least in the case of many disputes, an ethically justifiable case for the use of State-led adjudicative processes. Within that framework, I shall try to explore in detail one of the duties that appropriately rests upon adjudicative tribunals in such cases, namely the 'duty to understand'. To simplify the discussion, I shall restrict the general analysis to adversarial legal systems in the common law tradition, and all the specific legal examples will be derived from England and Wales.

Given the focus of this volume, a particular concern will be the consequences of the analysis for issues of victim participation in the criminal justice system. I am naturally aware that, conceptually, a duty-led approach of this kind is unusual when considering such questions; the more customary manner of considering the issues is through a discussion of the rights of victim(s) to a say in the processes relating to 'their' dispute. There is, however, a reason for adopting the different conceptual approach utilised here. This reason can perhaps best be appreciated by considering an imaginary dialogue between a victim of a street robbery and a strong advocate of the State's predominant role in dealing with alleged incidents of robbery:

> *Victim*: It was me that was injured and frightened when they took my wallet off me by force. Because of this, I can't help being interested and involved. So I surely have the right to be heard when it comes to the sentencing of these offenders.
>
> *State Advocate*: No, there are good theoretical reasons why the State takes the lead in cases of this sort. So, talk of your 'right' to participate is misplaced. Rather, to quote Professor Andrew Ashworth (1993b: 499), 'the touchstone for deciding [issues of victim participation] should not be the wishes of victims so much as the nature and goals of the criminal process as a social and legal institution'.

This is, of course, not a very productive dialogue: the speakers are largely talking past each other. But let us immediately concede to the State Advocate that she has a serious point. If (as this chapter assumes: see above) there is an ethically justifiable case for the adjudicative process to be State-led, then it certainly does not straightforwardly follow that the victim has a 'right' to participate.

The State Advocate cannot, however, so easily brush aside questions relating to the duties that appropriately rest upon an adjudicative tribunal when considering a State-led case. Accordingly, the *modus operandi* for this chapter is a deliberate omission of any discussion of victims' rights, and instead a serious focus on the duties of the tribunal, with particular reference to the 'duty to understand'. The principal purpose of this analytical strategy (which might be regarded as a kind of thought-experiment) is to enable readers of this volume to compare this approach with those represented in some other chapters, which employ more conventional approaches based on victims' rights. As will become clear, one of the contentions of this chapter is that careful attention to the question of the tribunal's duties yields rather more by way of victim participation than might initially have been thought likely.

A flawed example of sentencing

To give some practical context to these issues, I propose to consider in depth a specific case of sentencing in which, by common consent, the legal process was flawed, and in which – under the rules in force at the time of the case – the victims had no role in the court proceedings except as potential witnesses at the trial stage. Careful examination of the weaknesses revealed by the case might lead us to a better understanding of the duties of the court at the sentencing stage of the criminal process. It should be said at the outset that the case to be discussed was decided some years before the introduction of so-called 'Victim Personal Statements' in England and Wales, and later in the chapter I shall consider briefly how far the introduction of such statements has altered the system as described here.

The case is usually referred to as the 'Ealing Vicarage Rape Case', although as we shall see it was not only about rape. Between noon and 1 p.m. on 6 March 1986, the doorbell rang at Ealing vicarage in West London, and the vicar (Michael Saward, a prominent clergyman in the Church of England) answered it. He was confronted by three men he had never seen before, one of whom was holding a large, sharpened kitchen knife, its blade pointing at the vicar's stomach.

Michael Saward's account of the incident, restricted to facts which he personally witnessed, is given in his autobiography (Saward 1999: 380–1). There were two other people in the house that morning; Saward's daughter Jill, aged 21, and her boyfriend David Kerr, who had come to visit her. Michael Saward writes:

> Robert Horscroft, leader of the trio, was the man with the knife. He pushed me backwards into my study, followed by Martin McCall and Christopher Byrne ... Horscroft began by screaming, 'Where's the f—ing safe?' which he repeated again and again. I explained quietly that there was no safe, but only some loose money in a desk drawer which I indicated ...
>
> One of the others left the room and returned with Jill and David ... from the sitting-room next door. The three of us were made to sit down in a corner of the room with the knife against Jill's face. David stiffened, as if to fight, and I held his wrist firm. 'Sit still,' I said. We had no chance against three thugs with knives and my brain was racing as I wrestled with a way to keep us alive. Passivity was absolutely vital. More threats and effing. We had no money. 'Vicarages aren't places where church money is kept,' I said.
>
> Jill was taken off, by one man, to 'find the jewellery'. 'My wife has nothing of value,' I said but, obviously, seeing a large modern house, Horscroft and co. assumed that we were well-heeled. A few minutes

passed. 'You two come upstairs!' shouted Horscroft and forced David and me to drop our trousers to our ankles and shuffle along. Upstairs we entered the second bedroom, at the south front, to see Jill's naked back. She was quickly hustled out, after we had been ordered to lie face downwards on the floor. Only at that moment did the idea of a sexual attack enter my head but we saw nothing, beyond her back, before she was lost to view.

Face down, unable to see anything but the carpet, the blow was quite unexpected. There was a crash, I saw stars, and thought I had been shot. [In fact, he had been hit on the head with a cricket bat.] Just conscious, I was still alert enough to think 'sham dead' and I did just that. In any case, I passed out almost at once. Not till days later did I learn that David, also struck, had rolled around and the villains beat him up badly, damaging, probably permanently, his hearing.

The offenders' original motive for coming to the house – to obtain cash and valuables – had yielded little. They had, however, seriously assaulted two men, and indeed it was later found that both the victims' skulls had been fractured. It was, however, what two of the offenders did to Jill Saward, out of sight of her father and boyfriend, that subsequently attracted the greatest publicity. Jill was forced to undress at knifepoint by Martin McCall, who then raped her both vaginally and anally, and also 'used a knife handle to penetrate her' (Saward 1999: 382). McCall then suggested to Christopher Byrne that he looked 'hungry for sex'. Byrne agreed, drew the curtains and also raped Jill Saward; the two men then tied her hands and feet with a skipping rope (Saward with Green 1990: ch. 4). Robert Horscroft, though the leader of the three offenders, had said to McCall at the beginning of the rape, 'we didn't come here for this'; and to Jill, as they left, he said, 'remember, I didn't do it' (Saward 1999: 382).

Jill Saward was and is a practising Christian, and, true to her principles, as an unmarried woman she was a virgin at the time of the attack. Not surprisingly, she found the events of March 1986 and their aftermath extremely traumatic. With a friend, Wendy Green, she eventually wrote a book about her experiences (Saward with Green 1990), detailing what her father later called her 'four-year agony' (Saward 1999: 393); and, many years later, in a frank interview she disclosed further details (Grice 2006). Her difficulties included initial worries about pregnancy and AIDS (fortunately, she was spared both), followed by multiple fears and anxieties and 'total exhaustion' (Saward with Green 1990: 141). It was three and a half years before the 'flashbacks' and nightmares stopped; and, in that time, 'she came close to suicide on three occasions' (Grice 2006). Some extracts from the final two chapters of her book convey some of her feelings (Saward with Green 1990: 143, 150–1, 153):

The rape has changed my whole outlook on life. Suddenly something happened that affected everything I did, what I talked about, the way I lived, the questions I had to face ... The trauma associated with rape is very great. Anyone who does not believe that should try living through it. There are definite stages, though nobody really explained that to me at first. That's one of the reasons I want to share my experience. So nobody need feel she is cracking up, or going mad, when she is sitting there feeling the greyness, the nothingness. If someone else has gone through similar feelings there can be some form of reassurance that it is all part of a normal pattern, however abnormal it feels.

I still don't know how some women get over it if they don't have the kind of support I have received. God provided me with some very special friends who kept very close to me. Even so, it was touch and go at times. Women need to be able to talk about their experience to get it out of their system. Trying to ignore the fact that it's happened can create far more problems ...

Rape is totally and utterly destructive, striking right at the roots of a person's sense of self and worth. I would not have believed that the events of one hour on 6 March 1986 could have such devastating effects.

The Ealing vicarage case came up for trial at the Old Bailey in February 1987, 11 months after the crime. All three defendants pleaded guilty to the offence of aggravated burglary (that is, burglary while armed with a weapon); McCall and Byrne also pleaded guilty to rape.

Horscroft, as the ringleader, and as an older man with many previous convictions, was sentenced to 14 years' imprisonment for aggravated burglary. McCall was sentenced to five years' imprisonment for aggravated burglary and five years for rape, to run consecutively – 10 years in all. Byrne received five years for aggravated burglary and three years for rape, to run consecutively – eight years in all. The judge, following normal sentencing practice, took into account the guilty pleas of all three men, the relative youth of McCall and Byrne, and the fact that these two had shorter criminal records than Horscroft.

As regards the rape, the police officer in charge of the case gave evidence to the effect that, in Jill Saward's subsequent words, 'I come from a supportive family, am recovering fairly well, and ... it is hoped I will be able to lead a normal life', which Jill commented was 'true – as far as it goes' (Saward with Green 1990: 132). Following this, the judge, Mr Justice Leonard, made an apparently 'off the cuff' (Saward 1999: 392) remark, the exact wording of which is variously reported. Jill Saward's account is that 'according to the judge the trauma I have suffered is "not so great"' (Saward with Green 1990: 133), while according to Michael Saward (1999: 392) the judge stated that Jill had 'suffered "no great trauma'''. According to a 2002 obituary of Mr Justice Leonard (Sir John Leonard), he went further, explicitly linking the 'trauma' assessment with the proposed sentence: 'Because I have been told the trauma suffered by the victim was not so great . . . I shall take a lenient course with you' (*Daily Telegraph*, 14 August 2002). Whatever the exact words, it seems clear that the judge had interpreted the police officer's evidence, together with Jill Saward's controlled and dignified demeanour in court (Saward 1999: 392), as meaning that her suffering was limited, because of the good social support she was receiving. It was, unfortunately, a completely false inference.

There was a deluge of public criticism of the sentences, some of it ill-informed. But two points in particular were made by better-informed critics. The first was the inappropriateness of the judge's 'no great trauma' comment. The second was the proportionality, or lack of it, between the sentences for aggravated burglary and those for rape. The aggravated burglary, of course, was not simply a property offence – it had involved serious assaults on Michael Saward and David Kerr.[1] But it is clear from all the evidence (see especially Saward with Green 1990; Grice 2006) that the rape, and the attendant humiliations, perpetrated upon Jill Saward were significantly more traumatic for her, and more disturbing to her long-term sense of what kind of a person she was (that is, to her self-identity), than were the assaults on the two male victims. Hence, the sentence of 14 years' imprisonment on Horscroft (who had not participated in the rape) by comparison with the shorter sentences awarded to the other offenders (who were both convicted of rape as well as aggravated burglary), seemed to many to be very hard to defend. That was also Horscroft's view; after being sentenced, 'he left the court screaming "what about the effing rape?"' (Saward 1999: 392).

One might, of course, dismiss all this as simply the fault of an incompetent judge. But the evidence does not support such an interpretation. In the week that the sentences were pronounced, when public criticism was at its height, *The Times* published a profile of Mr Justice Leonard (James 1987). In this profile, a number of comments were quoted from the judge's fellow lawyers. Among them were: 'a most careful craftsman'; 'not a man for the ill-judged impulse'; a 'brilliant mind'; 'one of the great criminal specialists of his generation'; an 'engaging and approachable man'. To which one might add that, as revealed a decade later in Michael Saward's autobiography, after the sentence Mr Justice Leonard had the courtesy, the courage and the humility to take the unusual step of writing in confidence to Michael Saward, in reply to a letter of measured criticism from Saward. 'It would be improper for me to betray his confidence . . . suffice to say that he admitted (and later did so publicly)[2] that he had made a serious error, and deeply regretted the "no great trauma" remark' (Saward 1999: 393).

So this case is one of admitted 'serious error', but it was an error committed by a very competent and highly respected judge. Perhaps he just had an 'off' day. But perhaps, on the contrary, the Ealing case is a particularly striking example of some fault lines deeply embedded within the institutional structures of the English sentencing process, as it was in the mid-1980s. I shall consider that possibility later, but first I shall discuss a very different type of issue, that of sociological methodology.

Evaluation and three senses of understanding

A quarter of a century ago, the Cambridge sociologist W.G. Runciman (1983) proposed a fresh way of conceptualising the basic elements of social theory, though one that remained broadly faithful to Max Weber's view that 'a satisfactory theory of social explanation must take account of both the meanings and the causes of social phenomena' (Skinner 1985: 6).[3] Runciman argued, first, that social theory consists of both 'understanding' and 'evaluation'; and second, that there are, in the social sciences, three separate strands within the generic concept of 'understanding', namely 'reportage', 'explanation' and 'description'. The originality of this proposal lies particularly in the threefold differentiation of 'understanding', and in later sections of this chapter I shall try to show how that conceptualisation can help us to think about the adjudicating tribunal's 'duty to understand' at different stages of the criminal process. But first, it is necessary to explicate Runciman's approach more fully.

Runciman's distinction between 'understanding' and 'evaluation' is set within a particular tradition of social scientific methodology, namely that of theorists who accept the so-called 'fact–value distinction'. Within that framework, his concept of 'evaluation' self-evidently involves value-choices, and thus in intellectual terms it takes us into the territory of ethics and political theory. By contrast, his concept of 'understanding' is located on the 'factual' side of the fact–value distinction, as is clear from the language used by Runciman for what he describes as the three 'senses' of understanding, namely reportage, explanation and description. Thus, 'understanding' involves empirical discourse, and 'evaluation' involves normative discourse.

This chapter is focused ultimately on the question: 'What duties does an adjudicative tribunal properly have in relation to victims at different stages of an adversarial criminal process?' The end-point of a tribunal's work in a specific case is a *decision*; in Runciman's language, in making a decision a tribunal necessarily engages in 'evaluation'. A key subsequent question then becomes: how can 'understanding', in its various senses, help the tribunal towards a good solution to its evaluative task?

The first strand of 'understanding' is *reportage*, that is, the provision of an accurate factual account of what has happened on a given occasion or over a given period of time. While this is often straightforward (for example, 'the apple fell from the tree onto Isaac's head'), it is by no means always so. For example, where necessary, 'reportage' must include a report of the agent's intention, but such a report might well – to make adequate sense – require an understanding of the social context within which the intention was formulated. Hence, the observer who wishes to make a fully accurate report 'has to be sure that he knows all that he needs to know about the context *and* the intention' (Runciman 1983: 62, emphasis in original); and clearly, this can be quite a complex matter.

The second strand of 'understanding' is *explanation*. Where reportage asks the 'what' question, explanation asks the 'why' question (Runciman 1983: 19). Like reportage, the concept of explanation is reasonably familiar in everyday discourse, but it can contain within it some formidable philosophical complexities (see for example Ruben 1993). Fortunately, it is not necessary to venture into these complexities in the present context.

Runciman's inclusion of a third strand within the concept of 'understanding' is where his conceptual approach to empirical issues becomes most innovative. He suggests that while reportage asks the 'what' question, and explanation asks the 'why' question, the third strand of 'understanding' asks the question 'what like?' (Runciman 1983: 19). Moreover, as George Homans (1984) pointed out in a review of Runciman's book, this third strand of 'understanding' itself seems to have two sub-categories. The first of these is *individual*, and is well exemplified by a quotation that Runciman (1983: 17) cites from the work of the distinguished historian Marc Bloch. At the age of 53, Bloch, as a reservist officer in the French Army, reported for duty at the beginning of the Second World War (although in view of his age he could have declined the call-up). Sadly, his army was soon comprehensively defeated. Writing later, Bloch asked rhetorically: 'Did I truly know, in the full sense of that word, did I know from within, before I myself had suffered the terrible, sickening reality, what it meant for an army to be encircled, what it meant for a people to meet defeat?' (Bloch 1954: 44). Clearly, he did not.[4]

The second dimension of the 'what like' question is more *general*. It, too, can be encapsulated in a single quotation from Runciman (1983: 19), though this example is lengthier:

When, therefore, a twentieth-century writer on the social structure of ancient Rome speaks of his need to understand the institution of, say, chattel slavery, he should be taken to mean this in all three senses. He must in the first place be sure that he has not misread his evidence in such a way as would lead him to misreport what has actually taken place: he must have established that the Romans did buy and sell people as things. In the second place, he is likely to have some idea about the causes of the origin and continuation of their practice of doing so. But if he goes on, in the third place, to discuss the nature of Roman slavery in such a way as to reveal that he is unaware that not only miners and factory hands but bankers, doctors and naval captains could all be of servile status, then he will be guilty of misunderstanding in the tertiary, descriptive, sense. He may not be reporting anything which is inaccurate or offering any explanation of an event, process or state of affairs which is not validated by his evidence, yet at the same time be failing to convey to the reader what the institution of slavery was like in terms of the possibilities known to be inherent in it by the members of the society in which it operated and was recognized as legitimate.

As previously noted, Runciman's term for the third strand of understanding is 'description', though he acknowledges he is using this term in a special sense. It is a small matter, but I would personally prefer to use the phrase 'appreciative description'. This alternative suggestion picks up Matza's (1969: ch. 2) use of the term 'appreciation' to refer to 'the internal view of the subject', an approach that Matza saw as having been 'begun by the Chicago School' of Sociology in the interwar period, and continued by others thereafter (p. 37).

Terminological issues aside, the important point is that, for Runciman, *description* (or 'appreciative description') is an identifiably different task for the social scientist than either *reportage* or *explanation*. Moreover, Runciman goes on to contend that whereas reportage and explanation operate in a similar fashion in the natural sciences and the social sciences, *appreciative description* is a task unique to the social sciences.

Yet, as the Roman slavery example suggests, appreciative description is not simply a trivial addendum to the social scientist's task; for if the social scientist gets an appreciative description wrong, he or she can be said to be, in a real sense, failing. A little later in his text, Runciman (1983: 34) makes this point explicit. Writing about a hypothetical example of a 'wave of strikes', he asks:

What did [the strikers] think they were ('really') doing? That they thought they were deciding to withdraw their labour is enough to furnish the explanandum from which the researcher has begun. But it is not enough to convey to the reader an adequate sense of *their* sense of the context within which their actions took place and of the nature of the institutions and practices of the society, region, industry, community and plant as experienced by them. What were their ideas of their relations with their workmates, their supervisors and their union officials? What was, to them, the nature of the sense of grievance or discontent to which they were giving expression? These questions are not answered by even the most rigorous degree of secondary understanding [i.e., 'explanation'] except to the extent that the topics which they raise feature among the counterfactual conditionals and presumptive generalizations on which the validated explanation depends; and even then, they will not so feature in a way which answers them completely. Yet the sociologist who is unable to answer may fairly be told that he writes of things which he knows little or nothing about – 'knows', that is, in the sense that Evans-Pritchard knows about the Azande but you and I do not, or that Bloch knows about the 'sickening reality' of defeat in war but you (or at any rate I) do not . . . [Emphasis in original]

Notice the harsh judgement here: 'the sociologist who is unable to answer may fairly be told that he writes of things which he *knows little or nothing about*' (emphasis added). Good appreciative description, it is being suggested, is therefore of central importance for the credibility of a social scientist's work; moreover, it is a task that is identifiably different from either reportage or explanation.

The two specific examples given by Runciman at the end of the preceding quotation also illustrate a further point. One example is Bloch's individual and subjective appreciative description of the 'sickening reality' of defeat in war; the other is that of a highly respected anthropologist who wrote a detailed, and now classic, ethnographic account of witchcraft and related phenomena among the Azande (Evans-Pritchard 1937). Runciman's clear suggestion, though he does not make this point explicit, is therefore that, using Homans' (1984) distinction, both 'individual' and 'general' appreciative descriptions are vital to the social scientist's task.

It is necessary to add a couple of comments about the individual element of appreciative description. First, in an important sense, for Runciman 'the agent is privileged' in his or her accounts of certain matters; not only does (s)he normally understand 'what [in the primary sense of reportage] he thinks, feels, says and does; he also understands in the tertiary sense *what it is like* to think, feel, say and do it' (Runciman 1983: 17, emphasis in original). Thus, when seeking information about the individual element of appreciative description, it is always appropriate to go first to the agent him/herself. But secondly, we should not assume that the agent will necessarily be able to articulate, immediately, the best available individual appreciative description. Rather, it could be the case that an agent fails 'initially to see that the way in which she [is] describing her feelings . . . could be bettered' (Runciman 1983: 238). In such circumstances, a sympathetic third party could bring her 'to the point of coming to share his view that she had previously misapprehended and/or mystified her own experience', in which case 'his redescription does qualify as authentic' (Runciman 1983: 238). Hence, it would seem, it is worthwhile for social scientists who are seriously interested in truth to spend time helping agents to clarify exactly what certain social events and circumstances were like – in a subtle, nuanced sense – for them.

This section should perhaps be concluded with what might be described as a 'health warning'. It must be said that Runciman's conceptualisation of the basic elements of social theory has not been as strongly influential within sociology as its quality might lead one to expect, although of course some have taken serious note of it. Nor has his approach been free from criticism (see e.g. Callinicos 2004: 111–19). Why, then, have I chosen to give it prominence? I have done so because, whatever its precise merits in the strict field of social theory (where many complex issues arise that are of little relevance in the present context), I believe it has a great deal to offer to the discussion in this chapter. That is particularly the case, I would argue, because the most innovative element in Runciman's conceptual scheme is his emphasis on the separateness of three different questions within the *empirical understanding* of social situations: namely, 'what?', 'why?' and 'what like?' Those three questions, I shall suggest, offer a very useful framework as we begin to consider the 'duty to understand' of tribunals within the criminal justice system.

The adjudicative tribunal's duty to understand

What duties does an adjudicative tribunal owe to various people (and especially, in the present context, to the victim) within a State-led dispute resolution process? Various duties are of course important, such as the *duty of respect* for all participants in the case. But I propose to focus here especially on what I shall describe as the *duty to understand*.

The essence of the 'duty to understand' in the present context is, I would suggest, that it requires the adjudicative body to consider fully all the factual matters relevant to a particular evaluative decision before proceeding to make that decision. But a key word in the preceding sentence is 'relevant'. It was noted earlier that, when considering normative questions relating to aspects of the criminal justice system as a whole, Andrew Ashworth (1993b: 499) placed emphasis on the 'touchstone' constituted by 'the nature and goals of the criminal process as a social and legal institution'. In like manner, when considering the tribunal's 'duty to understand' at specific stages of the criminal justice system, it would seem vital to bear in mind the nature and goals of the particular type of adjudication being made. Thus, adjudications relating to guilt or innocence have a different character from adjudications relating to possible early release from a prison sentence, and the 'duty to understand' consequently plays out in a different way in these different contexts. In what follows, I shall suggest that Runciman's analysis of 'understanding' is particularly helpful in facilitating a clear appreciation as to how the varied purposes of different stages of the criminal justice system require tribunals to emphasise different elements of 'understanding' when exercising their 'duty to understand'.

I turn now, therefore, to three separate stages of the criminal justice system: the trial, sentencing, and decisions as to early release.[5] In respect of each, I shall consider the application of the tribunal's 'duty to understand'. As we shall see, the second of the three stages, that of sentencing, raises the most complex issues.

The trial stage

At the trial stage, the adjudicative requirement is to assess whether the defendant(s) is/are guilty of the offence as charged. This of course requires the presentation of significant amounts of evidence; or, in Runciman's language, *reportage*. It may also require a degree of *explanation*. For example, in a trial in which a defendant is charged with dangerous driving, he might claim that the admitted loss of control of the vehicle was due to mechanical failure, rather than any fault of the driver; and the court will then necessarily have to assess whether this causal claim is plausible. In this example, however, a focus on explanation is central to the adjudicative requirement. Where that is not the case, it has often been pointed out that, in accusatorial systems, explanation is very secondary to reportage, and hence major explanatory puzzles can exist even after a lengthy trial.[6] As to *appreciative description*, since the central players in the courtroom drama (judge, jury, counsel, witnesses, defendant) usually belong to social groups that broadly understand one another, there is normally little need for this at the trial stage, where the focus is on reportage (and explanation) that might establish guilt or innocence. However, occasionally aspects of a differing culture, such as that prevailing among a group of habitual drug users, might need to be explicated in order to provide an appropriate contextual background for the reportage.

So, the primary focus of the tribunal's 'duty to understand' at the trial stage in accusatorial legal systems is on reportage, as an aid to the assessment of guilt or innocence. Within the trial, no special duty is owed to the victim, over and above that owed to other witnesses, because the victim's role is simply as a potential witness.

Sentencing decisions: the Ealing case reconsidered

As an initial step in teasing out the character of the tribunal's 'duty to understand' in sentencing decisions, let us return to the Ealing case. The central weakness in that case was, it would seem, the failure of the court to comprehend how serious the rape was, and how traumatised Jill Saward was by her victimisation. In other words, there was an admitted failure in the duty to understand, which adversely affected the quality of the subsequent adjudication. Two things in particular appear to have contributed to this failure: the first was Jill Saward's calm demeanour in court, and the second was the police officer's evidence about how she had coped with life in the months after the rape. Each of these matters deserves some careful attention.

As regards demeanour, there is recent evidence from a study of mock jurors that ordinary people, not surprisingly, have a limited appreciation of how varied women's psychological responses to rape victimisation can be. One response is to try 'to stay in command of their feelings, ... emotionally detaching from the rape experience' (Ellison and Munro 2009a: 211). Unfortunately, this emotional detachment is not always understood for what it is, and negative inferences may be drawn by jurors if the complainant fails to appear distressed while testifying (though marked distress can also be regarded as suspect). Hence, 'concerns regarding juror (mis)evaluation of complainant post-assault demeanour are merited' (Ellison and Munro 2009a: 211). This is an *inferential error*, whereby a false conclusion about what the experience of rape was really like for the victim is based on the factually incorrect assumption that only women who appear distressed in court could have been truly traumatised by their experience. To refer back to one of Runciman's examples, this is somewhat akin to drawing inferences about what the institution of chattel slavery in ancient Rome was like for those who experienced it (whether as slaves or citizens), based on treating evidence about the institution of slavery in nineteenth-century America as a reliable guide to its more ancient counterpart. In the Ealing case, it would appear that the judge made exactly this kind of inferential error, based on Jill Saward's dignified demeanour in court.[7]

To adopt Homans's (1984) useful commentary on Runciman, the preceding paragraph refers to a mistake of a *general* kind relating to 'appreciative descriptions' (i.e. what, if any, inferences may be drawn from dignified demeanour), rather than focusing upon any specific individual. But, as we have seen, appreciative description of individual experiences is frequently also of great importance in the social sciences; and, in respect of this, the agent's own account is privileged, though not necessarily definitive. How does this translate to legal contexts, and in particular to the Ealing case?

Jill Saward's account of what happened in court is very telling. The police officer gave evidence that she came from a supportive family, that she was recovering fairly well from the attack, and that it was hoped she would be able to lead a normal life. Jill's terse comment was that this was '*true – as far as it goes*' But, she immediately added, '*they only know half the story*' (Saward with Green 1990: 132, emphasis added). Translating her comment into Runciman's categories, what she seems to be saying is that (i) the officer's evidence constituted accurate *reportage*, but (ii) it did not begin to convey what the experience of victimisation, and its aftermath, really felt like: there was no adequate *appreciative description* of her trauma.[8]

If the interpretation offered in the preceding paragraphs is correct, then in the Ealing case there appears to have been: (i) an inferential error relating to appreciative description in the general sense, based on the victim's demeanour in court; and (ii) an absence of evidence relating to appreciative description in the specific case of Jill Saward. A social scientist seeking to 'understand' the court proceedings through Runciman's conceptualisation would therefore probably conclude that while the *reportage* was apparently accurate ('so far as it went') nevertheless the victim-focused *appreciative description* available to the court when sentencing was inadequate.

But that conclusion simply raises another question, this time a normative one; namely, *should* sentencing decisions take account of victim-oriented appreciative descriptions? To assess this question, it is necessary to consider some of the complexities of the act of sentencing as a judicial activity.

Sentencing decisions: 'standard harms' and appreciative description

Sentencing decisions normally take into account both 'backward-looking' or offence-centred factors (focusing on the harm inflicted or intended, and the offender's degree of culpability) and 'forward-looking' or consequentialist factors (such as the rehabilitation of the offender or the deterrence of future potential offenders). Hence, the court needs to develop an evidence-based *understanding* (in Runciman's language), both of the offence itself and of various future risks and possibilities, as a precursor to the act of sentencing.

For these purposes, the court clearly requires relevant factual *reportage*. Interestingly, however, for half a century now, it has also been recognised, as regards the offender, that one needs to go beyond simple reportage. What used to be called the *social inquiry report* (SIR) and is now called the *pre-sentence report* (PSR) was introduced precisely so that courts could obtain a better understanding, first, of the 'social and domestic background of the offender which is relevant to the ... assessment of his culpability' (to be achieved both through *reportage* and through *appreciative description*, or 'information which helps to give a better picture of the offender'); and secondly, of the causal factors leading to his/her offending (*explanation*), in order to inform a 'consideration of how his criminal career might be checked' (Home Office and Lord Chancellor's Office 1961: 94–5).[9] The defendant's legal representative might also raise issues in some of these areas.

As the use of the SIR/PSR increased in the 1960s and 1970s, what was often not recognised was that the court had no standard mechanism, akin to such reports, by which to receive any appreciative description from the perspective of the victim(s). Yet one must also recognise that to introduce an element of victim-oriented appreciative description at the sentencing stage can have its complications. Foremost among these are two linked issues that arise when assessing the seriousness of the offence(s), namely the issues of 'unforeseen consequences' and 'standard harms'. To take a well-known hypothetical example, suppose that a burglar breaks into a house, wrongly believing it to be unoccupied. In an ensuing physical struggle with the householder, he seriously injures the latter's hand and arm. Unfortunately, and unbeknown to the offender, the householder is a professional concert pianist. Clearly, in any victim-oriented appreciative description arising from such a case, the householder is likely to emphasise not only his loss of earnings, but also his severe distress at having his pleasurable career severely disrupted. Yet, given that the primary purpose of the criminal law is to punish wrongdoing against the public good, rather than to compensate individuals for their loss or distress, it would be inappropriate for the sentencing judge to take account of such matters when passing sentence; only the reasonably foreseeable risks of injuries to a 'standard' householder should be considered.[10] Similarly in the Ealing case, it is certainly arguable that the psychological harm to Jill Saward was greater because she had made a principled commitment to chastity until marriage. However, this was not known to or reasonably foreseeable by her attackers, so it would be wrong to take this into account when sentencing.[11]

A powerful further argument can be offered in favour of a 'standardised' approach to assessing the seriousness of offences within the process of sentencing. In what has been described as a 'seminal' paper on gauging crime seriousness (see Simester and Sullivan 2007: 585), Andrew von Hirsch, Nils Jareborg and Andrew Ashworth (2005) argue that 'particular criminal acts are too diverse' for sentencing systems to rate the harm that they cause 'on an individualized basis'.[12] Rather, what these authors recommend is a two-stage approach: namely, one which '(1) rates the standard case of an offence, and then (2) addresses unusual cases through supplemental principles (e.g. of aggravation and mitigation)' (p. 188).

These considerations raise some important conceptual issues for the present analysis. In particular, if sentencing is to be approached on the basis of the (necessarily largely objective) concepts of the 'standard case' and 'reasonable foreseeablility', does this render the suggestion of introducing an element of (necessarily subjective) individualised victim-oriented 'appreciative description' into the sentencing process actually *inappropriate*? This is a difficult question, but I shall contend that ultimately it has to be answered in the negative. Two separate strands of argument both point to this conclusion, of which the first is the more important.

Incontestably, it makes good practical sense for sentencers to begin with certain 'standard' features of cases (though, as von Hirsch *et al.* (2005)

rightly emphasise, the selection of such features always involves normative choices about penal values). In the first stage of their two-stage
approach, von Hirsch and his colleagues (2005) propose a 'living
standard' approach to the assessment of harm, and they offer various
illustrations as to how this would work out in practice. Thus, for example,
they classify rape at knifepoint as a very serious crime, because it violates
both of what they consider to be the two most fundamental categories of
'living standard': first, there is a threat to kill or seriously injure the victim
(through the threat with the knife), which contingently threatens the
'survival' lifestyle level; and secondly, there is a major intrusion into the
victim's self-respect, which violates the 'minimal wellbeing' lifestyle level,
since in our culture 'forced sex is about the most demeaning imposition
that can be imagined – far more humiliating than a beating' (p. 210).[13] In
terms of the general argument being pursued in this section, the key point
to notice in this discussion is that one does not need victim-oriented
'appreciative description' to identify these characteristics of 'standard
harm'; *the basic reportage is sufficient.*

But the above constitutes only the first stage in von Hirsch *et al.*'s (2005)
recommended two-stage procedure for the assessment of harm, and it will
be recalled that the second stage consists of 'supplemental principles ...
of aggravation and mitigation' (see above). In order to keep their paper
within manageable bounds, the authors say little about these aggravation/
mitigation principles, but one can capture something of what they
presumably intended from an important Court of Appeal 'guideline
judgment' on sentencing in rape cases that was enunciated not long before
the Ealing trial.[14] This judgment usefully identified a number of 'standard'
aggravating factors, many of which were later found to be present in the
Ealing case, and each of which could be said to further violate the
'minimal wellbeing' living standard; these heightened intrusions into the
victim's self-respect included (i) the victim was raped by intruders in her
own home; (ii) the rape was repeated; (iii) the victim was subjected to
'further sexual indignities' in addition to rape; and (iv) the crime was
committed by two men acting together.[15]

So far, the analysis is clearly fully compatible with a straightforward
'standard harms' approach. But at one point von Hirsch *et al.* (2005: 189)
describe their recommended two-stage procedure in the following way:
'one can rate the harm category – and also take certain features of the
harmfulness *of the particular event* into account through ... aggravation/
mitigation principles' (emphasis added). Given that, in this description,
the focus of the second stage is on the 'particular event', might it follow
that that 'event' would be usefully illuminated not only by a PSR, but also
by a victim-oriented appreciative description; and therefore the court has
a duty to seek such information?

As noted above, von Hirsch *et al.* do not fully discuss the aggravation/
mitigation stage, but they do make one comment which might seem, on

first reading, to suggest that even at this further stage there is little room for information of a more personal kind:

> [O]ne cannot reasonably expect to approximate, in legal judgements of seriousness, the particularity of everyday judgements ... The rehabilitative penal ethic lost its credibility in part because of unrealistic claims it made about the individualization of sentence ... The criminal law reflects a system of public standards, not an arena for personalized judgements. What the law realistically can accomplish is to assess crime seriousness in standard cases, and then permit deviations from that assessment for specified types of special circumstances. (von Hirsch *et al.* 2005: 189, emphasis added)

Careful scrutiny of this passage reveals, however, that what is being discouraged is a personalised or individualised *sentencing decision*, and not the presentation of personalised or individualised *information* to the court. This might seem to constitute a fine distinction, but in Runciman's terms (see earlier discussion) the former is an *evaluative* activity, while the latter is potentially an aid to the court's *understanding*. The distinction is therefore important, since it allows one in principle to argue that (i) von Hirsch *et al.*'s case against individualised sentencing is correct, yet (ii) in certain cases, to maximise its understanding prior to sentencing, the court needs (and hence has a duty) to receive personalised appreciative-descriptive information. Is such an argument sustainable?

In order to assess this issue, let us return to the Ealing case and first consider – using information from Jill Saward's autobiographical book – what evidence might have been presented to the court had the court had a duty to consider a victim-oriented appreciative description. There were, first of all, the medical consequences:

> The pains in my ribs and chest persisted for at least four months after the attack ... My gums are bleeding again, and I feel sick tasting the blood in my mouth ... [I have made] twenty-two trips to ten different doctors, seven blood tests, two X-rays and one short admission to hospital. All in one year ... Coming to terms with bleeding, of whatever kind is not ... straightforward. Anal bleeding particularly. My new GP reckons that cauterising the vein could do more harm than good ... (Saward with Green 1990: 105, 121, 139)

None of this comes into the category of unforeseeable harm (like the burglary victim being a concert pianist); if a woman is repeatedly raped, the offenders ought reasonably to foresee that she could suffer serious internal injuries and significant personal inconvenience. Moreover, the evidence being presented is clearly evidence of *harm*, and it therefore seems *prima facie* reasonable that the sentencing court should consider it.

Similarly with the psychological consequences, which, given the severe humiliations inflicted by the offenders in the Ealing case (anal as well as vaginal rape; forced insertion of a knife handle into the victim's vagina) must also be regarded as having been reasonably foreseeable:

> If I'd known beforehand about the terrible sense of aloneness, it could have blown my mind. It's tough acknowledging that people can only help me so far. The rest is up to me. There is no way around the feelings . . . It wouldn't be so bad if I could get a decent night's sleep, but I can't. Once I am in bed I feel even more alone. Every morning the pillow is soaked with my tears . . . [In December, nine months after the attack] I pull on my dressing gown and go to find [Mum] . . . It's probably the first admission of hurt on my part she has seen. Now she knows something is seriously wrong. (Saward with Green 1990: 120–1)

It is worth recalling that most of the above evidence (medical and psychological) was not presented to the court. Given that the judge then made a serious factual error in stating that the victim had experienced 'no great trauma', it seems reasonable to conclude that the absence of this personalised information allowed the court to draw inappropriate conclusions from the other evidence presented. Therefore, it would seem, a victim-oriented appreciative description potentially adds a valuable further dimension to the total evidence before the court, *and in the absence of such information, the court might misread other (more 'standardised') evidence before it*. Note also that this justification for the presentation of victim-oriented appreciative evidence does not fall foul of the danger suggested by von Hirsch *et al.* (2005: 189), namely that of turning the sentencing procedure into 'an arena for personalised judgements'. Rather, it allows the court to assess the placement of the crime into the standard categories and sub-categories of harm, having taken account of appreciative-descriptive evidence as well as reportage and (where relevant) explanation. Further reflection on this important point enables one to see how right the Cambridge moral philosopher Simon Blackburn (1998) was when he argued that the relationship between the empirical facts in a case ('understanding', in Runciman's terms) and any subsequent normative decision ('evaluation') is, in the real world, very variable. Sometimes, the linkage can be 'mechanical' or 'automatic', as when a case seems to fit easily into a well-established ethical category; but in other instances, understanding the full character of the empirical situation may require 'the most delicate exercise of observation and imagination' before one can be sure what are its 'ethically salient' features (Blackburn 1998: 5), after which it can be placed in an appropriate ethical category.

It will be apparent that the analysis in the preceding paragraph has, to a significant extent, been influenced by various aspects of Runciman's discussion of the concept of 'understanding'. Recall that, for Runciman, the absence of appreciative description can significantly distort one's overall understanding; that is, even accurate reportage and explanation of a social situation can be misleading if one has no adequate appreciative-descriptive understanding (see his Roman slavery example). I have argued that the same can be true of the understanding required before a sentence is passed. Indeed, we might draw further parallels from other parts of Runciman's analysis. In particular, consider Runciman's comments on the hypothetical example of the strikers (see earlier section). The author's suggestion was that a sociological analyst who was unable to answer appreciative-descriptive questions about what it felt like to be one of the strikers 'may fairly be told that he writes of things that he knows little or nothing about'. Would it be reasonable to adapt that comment, and to say that a sentencing court that sentences a rapist while not fully appreciating, in the appreciative-descriptive sense, what it is like to be the victim of such a crime, 'may fairly be told that it is acting on behalf of society while knowing little or nothing about what it is called upon to judge'? The answer, I think, has to be in the affirmative. Indeed, this comment captures exactly the central flaw in the Ealing case and, as shown in an earlier section, the failure in that case involved, in Homans's terms, both the general and the specific types of appreciative description. Moreover, it should by now be fairly clear that the flaws were by no means simply attributable to the judge (though certainly he was not faultless). Rather, the system's patterned exclusion of relevant evidence must bear a large part of the blame.

A further argument also favours acceptance of the principle that the sentencing court may have a duty to receive a victim-oriented appreciative description. However, this further argument is unquestionably secondary, because it is only about process, and (unlike the first argument) not about the substance of the 'duty to understand'. We noted in the introduction to this chapter that some scholars advocate the so-called 'civilisation thesis', according to which (in its strong form) disputes 'belong' to the disputing parties themselves. Therefore, in the view of such advocates, fewer incidents than at present should be 'removed' from the parties and treated as 'State-led' cases, processed through the criminal courts. The premise of this chapter (see the introduction) is that the strong form of the 'civilisation thesis' is not normatively convincing. It is important to note, however, that advocates of this thesis place considerable emphasis on the importance of the parties being allowed (indeed, encouraged) to offer any evidence they wish (including appreciative-descriptive evidence, or 'what like' statements) within the informal procedures that are advocated (see especially Christie 1977). Moreover, there is empirical evidence from various sources that the freedom to present this kind of evidence is valued by the parties, not least by victims.[16] The State, in *justifiably* asserting its right to take the lead in a case on behalf of the whole community, needs – as a normative matter – to ensure that it does not *unjustifiably* exclude appreciative-descriptive evidential opportunities that the parties would value; though, clearly, there is no point in allowing evidence if it adds nothing substantively to the tribunal's proceedings (which is why this process argument is necessarily secondary). As an empirical matter, unjustifiable exclusions of this sort could potentially weaken the legitimacy of the court process (on legitimacy and criminal justice, see for example Tyler 2007).

I conclude, therefore, that in appropriate cases the sentencing court has a duty to consider evidence relating to a victim-oriented appreciative description, principally as part of its overall 'duty to understand'. Where such evidence refers to matters that should not properly be considered by the sentencer – such as harm that is not reasonably foreseeable by a 'standard' offender – it should be discounted.[17]

But this conclusion raises a further question, namely: is it necessary in every case for the sentencing court to seek out an appreciative description? At this point, it is appropriate to return once more to Runciman's methodological discussion. Runciman (1983: 20) explicitly states that 'appreciative description' is not 'relevant or necessary' to social scientific understanding in all contexts. He gives an example of a discussion with a cyclist:

> If I am puzzled by your putting out your hand, I may need to ask you both why you are putting out your hand (or better, what you are doing in putting out your hand), and on receiving the reply that you are, say, performing the action of signalling, to ask you to explain why you are signalling. But once you have told me that you are signalling because there is a vehicle behind you whose driver would not otherwise know that you are about to turn right (and have gone on, if required, to tell me that you are about to turn to your right because that is the way to where you want to go), I am unlikely to want to ask you 'what is it *like* to signal that you are about to turn right?'. All this means however, is that signalling of this kind is so far conventional that the state of the mind of the agent performing it is, in the absence of special circumstances, unproblematic. (Runciman 1983: 20–1, emphasis in original)

In a similar manner, in sentencing standard cases of shoplifting from supermarkets or high street clothes shops, it would certainly seem to be redundant for the court to enquire carefully of the store owners, shop assistant or store detectives: 'What was it *like* to be the victim of this crime?' (That is not to say that such a question will always be redundant where the victim is a corporate body, as is quickly shown by the example of an armed bank robbery during which bank staff have been very frightened by the raid.) Rather, the distinction that we are seeking would seem to be provided by an adaptation of the final sentence of the quotation from Runciman (above): the 'what like' question will be irrelevant where 'victimisation of this kind is so far straightforward that the state of mind of the victim is, in the absence of special circumstances, unproblematic'. Thus, in practice the need to seek an appreciative description as part of the duty to understand will be focused especially on more complex and serious cases.[18]

Decisions as to early release

I turn finally to a further stage of the criminal process, that of decisions about *early release* from prison sentences. Here, we can assume, the primary concern of the State-led adjudicative process will be *risk*: 'safe' cases should be released, 'risky' ones detained. Assessing risk of course requires adjudicators to think about prediction, and that in turn means that early release decisions place a particular emphasis on the *explanatory* element within Runciman's threefold concept of understanding, since causal explanation of past events is an important (although not the only) dimension in considering the prediction of future events. Indeed, *explanation* plays a larger proportionate role in relation to early release than it does in either of the two types of decision (guilt/innocence; sentence) that have been previously discussed.

But what about the potential role of victim-oriented 'appreciative description' in early release decisions? Some care is needed at this point. Because, in this kind of decision-making, the focus of the adjudicative body is on prediction, except in rare cases (where, for example, he/she has received a specific threat) the victim will have no special factual evidence to offer to the tribunal. Moreover, if the adjudicative body is performing its task effectively, by definition it will release only those prisoners who are considered to present little future risk to any former victim. Nevertheless, many victims and their families may be understandably nervous, particularly in serious cases, about impending releases. The tribunal, it can reasonably be contended, has a duty to understand such anxieties fully, and to take appropriate steps to alleviate them. This might take the form, for example, of placing restrictions on the offender entering the area around the victim's home during the period of early release. Thus, in appropriate cases, it will be the tribunal's duty to consider evidence based on victim-oriented appreciative description. Given the remit of the tribunal, however, such evidence will necessarily focus upon the future, and not – as was the case at the sentencing stage – on the past experience of the offence and its aftermath. Some of these issues are more fully discussed in Chapter 10 by Nicola Padfield and Julian Roberts.

Victim statements and appreciative description

It has been argued in this chapter that, both at the sentencing stage and at the early release stage, the tribunal's 'duty to understand' will, at least on a significant number of occasions, and especially in more serious cases, require it to seek out an appreciative description from the victim.

But, of course, in England and Wales victim-oriented appreciative descriptions are now quite often provided to tribunals, for example through Victim Personal Statements (introduced in 2001) at the sentencing stage, or through representations that victims might offer to the Parole Board through the probation service. It is, therefore, important to consider how far such statements already adequately meet the requirements discussed in earlier sections. To keep the discussion short, in considering this topic I will restrict the focus to the sentencing stage, and I will comment on only three points.

The first and most important issue is the conceptual basis of the Victim Personal Statement (VPS) scheme. The official governmental leaflet about VPS, *Making a Victim Personal Statement* (Home Office 2009), does not suggest that the criminal justice system positively values, needs or requires any information from the victim; rather, the making of a VPS is presented as entirely a matter of choice for the victim:

> A victim personal statement adds to the information you have already given to the police in your statement about the crime. The victim personal statement *gives you the chance to tell us* about any support you might need, and how the crime has affected you. (Home Office 2009: 2, emphasis added)

The reasons for this emphasis on voluntariness, the 'support you might need', and so on, are spelt out in the next chapter by Helen Reeves and Peter Dunn. As they summarise the matter, the original intention in introducing the VPS was 'simply to provide a service to victims of crime'. This constitutes, conceptually, a significantly different emphasis from that argued in this chapter, namely that, as part of its 'duty to understand', the tribunal sometimes actively *requires* a victim-oriented appreciative-descriptive perspective.[19]

Secondly, in England and Wales (which differs in this respect from some other jurisdictions), the normal practice is for the police to ask victims 'if [they] want to fill in a victim personal statement when they have finished filling in the witness statement' [or 'evidential statement'] (Home Office 2009: 5). Perhaps not surprisingly, it seems that victims sometimes become confused about the difference between these two types of statement, normally completed on the same occasion (Office for Criminal Justice Reform 2005: 5). Runciman's conceptualisation, which is readily comprehensible, would almost certainly help here. Thus, the police could emphasise that the evidential statement is firmly about the 'what' of the crime itself (*reportage*); whereas the VPS focuses on 'what it was like' to experience the crime, and its aftermath (*appreciative description*).

Thirdly, there is the question of how information for the VPS is best collected. In an interesting small-scale qualitative study on the VPS in England, Graham *et al.* (2004) found that, in research interviews, some victims reported that they had left out some significant 'impacts' when completing their VPS. The reasons for these omissions were said to be that, at the time of the statement (just after the evidential statement), respondents felt 'too shocked or numb to yet know how the crime had affected them, or were too emotionally exhausted . . . . to do justice to the impacts they felt'; or that 'the impacts were too numerous to document in the VPS'; or that the impacts only really emerged later, after the initial VPS was made[20] (Graham *et al.* 2004: iii). From the point of view of this chapter, with its emphasis on tribunals sometimes needing victim-oriented appreciative descriptions as part of their 'duty to understand', these findings – although based only on a small study – are potentially worrying. Recall that, for Runciman, while the agent is ultimately the best judge of 'what an experience has been like', it can easily be the case that an agent's first attempt at 'describing her feelings . . . could be bettered' (Runciman 1983: 238). That must be especially the case if the circumstances in which the person is being asked to describe her feelings are not ideal – as is surely likely when a VPS is sought immediately after a (frequently lengthy) session devoted to the making of an evidential statement. Hence, if the system is interested in maximising the quality of victim-oriented appreciative descriptions, as part of the tribunal's 'duty to understand', it needs to think carefully about how such information is best collected.

Two reasonable conclusions from this brief discussion would therefore seem to be: first, that the VPS, as it currently operates in England and Wales, will sometimes very valuably aid the tribunal's overall understanding; but, secondly, that if we are serious about victim-oriented appreciative descriptions being sometimes necessary to fulfil the tribunal's 'duty to understand', then some conceptual and other changes to current practice are necessary.

Conclusion

In summary, then, the three different stages of the criminal process that have been considered – trial, sentence, and early release – produce different duties of (or requirements for) *understanding* for their respective adjudicative bodies. At the trial stage, the emphasis (in accusatorial systems) is on *reportage*, with some *explanation*. At the sentencing stage, reportage remains important but *explanation* and *appreciative description* (from both the offender's and the victim's point of view) are of generally enhanced significance; and careful analysis shows that the inclusion of victim-oriented appreciative-descriptive evidence does not have to (and should not) lead to individualised sentencing. Finally, at the early release stage *explanation* (being closely linked to risk assessment) becomes dominant, but *reportage* and a degree of victim-oriented *appreciative description* remain significant. Within the conceptual framework adopted in this chapter (i.e. prioritising the analysis of the tribunal's 'duty to understand' within State-led adjudicative processes), the role of the victim in the adjudicative process therefore varies as the primary purpose of the adjudication changes, and as the character of the tribunal's 'duty to understand' alters with these variations in primary purpose.

As noted in the introduction, this chapter has deliberately adopted a particular conceptual approach, focused on the tribunal's duties within State-led adjudicative procedures. (The approach might therefore reasonably be described as, at least in one sense, deontological.) This path has been chosen in an endeavour to show that the issue of victim participation in State-led adjudicative processes cannot be ignored even if one takes no account of victims' rights. However, no attempt has been made to contrast the merits and demerits of this deontological approach with a more traditional 'victims' rights' framework; there has been enough to do in attempting to establish the *prima facie* plausibility of a duty-based framework. It is hoped that readers might find this sketch to be of interest as a contrast to other conceptual approaches to the same issues, as represented in other chapters in this volume.[21]

Notes

1 Most sources describe the sentences in this case in the manner given in a previous paragraph, i.e. mentioning only the convictions for aggravated burglary and rape. However, *The Times* for 3 February 1987 (the day after McCall and Byrne were sentenced) reported also that: 'Horscroft and Byrne admitted inflicting grievous bodily harm on Mr Saward, [and] Byrne ... admitted inflicting grievous bodily harm on the second man'. Presumably therefore the sentences for these GBH offences were passed concurrently with the sentences for aggravated burglary.
2 This refers to Sir John Leonard's valedictory speech at the Old Bailey in 1993, when he retired as a judge. According to an obituary in the *Daily Telegraph* (14 August 2002), Sir John on that occasion referred to the Ealing sentences as 'a blemish – I make no bones about it'.
3 Runciman had previously written an appreciative critique of Max Weber's philosophy of social science: see Runciman (1972).
4 On the same page, Bloch, in his role as historian, went on: 'In the last analysis, whether consciously or no, it is always by borrowing from our daily

experiences and by shading them, where necessary, with new tints that we derive the elements which help us to restore the past.' On the French defeat, see also and more fully Bloch (1949), described in the Foreword by Georges Altman as 'a great book', containing 'a vivid and precise description of the disaster of 1940' (p. x). Marc Bloch was later a leader in the French Resistance movement, and in June 1944 he was put to death for his part in it.

5   Obviously, other decisions within the criminal process could also have been selected; for example, bail hearings. The three selected decision points, however, provide an adequate range of topics, and also some important contrasts.

6   See for example Louis Blom-Cooper's (1963) short book on what was then the longest murder trial in English legal history, that relating to the so-called 'A6 murder'. This trial concerned offences committed by a gunman who, at dusk, approached two lovers sitting in a car parked in an empty Buckinghamshire cornfield; he then required them to drive at gunpoint for many miles before, eventually, he shot the man dead and raped and shot at the woman. A man named James Hanratty was charged with this murder, and convicted. But his defence was that he was elsewhere that night, and that the police had therefore got the wrong man. Hence, the trial 'never came near to revealing ... [a key issue, namely] ... what was Hanratty, an urban thief, ... doing wandering round a cornfield ... carrying a loaded revolver, a weapon he had never been known to use in his quite extensive criminal career?' (Blom-Cooper 1963: 40). According to Blom-Cooper (1963: 49) a principal reason for this explanatory failure was that 'the [English] trial system is concerned only with hearing evidence directly relevant to the criminal act and the accused man's connexion with it ... There is therefore no incentive – indeed almost a compelling disincentive – for a policeman to dig deeply and find out all he can about the circumstances of the crime'.

7   In 2006, in England and Wales, the government published proposals to allow prosecutors to adduce 'general' expert witness testimony in rape cases. It has been said that 'this initiative was based on two assumptions – first, that jurors currently lack an adequate understanding of rape complainants' post-assault behaviour ... and, second, that expert testimony offers a useful vehicle for addressing such juror ignorance' (Ellison and Munro 2009b). See this source for a fuller discussion of the initiative.

8   This interpretation is supported by Jill Saward's next sentence, which explicitly contrasts an unrelated piece of reportage with a 'what like' comment: 'It feels as though more emphasis is being placed on how a hairdresser in Isleworth provided valuable information about a group of three scruffy men who went to her for haircuts, than on the far-reaching effects all this has had on the three people in the Vicarage, and on their friends and family' (Saward with Green 1990: 132).

9   These quotations are taken from the report of an Interdepartmental Committee (known as the 'Streatfeild Committee' after its Chairman, Mr Justice Streatfeild) which had a particular influence in promoting the increased use of SIRs in England and Wales in the 1960s. It should be noted that SIRs/PSRs have never been simply 'appreciative-descriptive' in character, but they undoubtedly often contain an 'appreciative-descriptive' element. For further discussion of SIRs as they were in the 1980s, see Bottoms and Stelman (1988).

10 Of course, in the civil courts, applying the law of torts, matters can be very different, precisely because the primary purpose of tort law is to compensate individuals for losses incurred by the wrongs of others. On issues of foreseeability in the criminal law, see more fully Ashworth (1993a).

11 This conclusion is reinforced by a separate normative principle, namely that as a matter of public policy it would be wrong to take into account the previous sexual experience of the victim when assessing the seriousness of an offence of rape. If such a principle were not upheld, then for example the rape of a prostitute might be rated as not very serious, but this would very significantly disregard the victim's human rights.

12 The cited 2005 paper is a revised version of a paper originally published in 1991; in that earlier version the authors were Andrew von Hirsch and Nils Jareborg.

13 This insightful comment provides a convincing explanation for an observation made earlier in this chapter, namely that in the Ealing case Jill Saward found her victimisation significantly more disturbing to her long-term self-identity than did either of the two male victims, notwithstanding that both of them suffered serious physical injuries.

14 *R v. Billam* (1986) 8 Cr App R (S) 48. A 'guideline judgment' on sentencing has been authoritatively defined as one in which the Court of Appeal, in deciding the case, has expressed the view that 'the guidance given in the judgment was intended to apply more widely than the case before it': see Sentencing Guidelines Council (2005: iii). There is now a more recent guideline judgement on rape, which retains the basic structure of the *Billam* judgement, but amends and updates it: *R v. Milberry* (2003) 2 Cr App R (S) 31.

15 These factors are all aggravating factors, but standard mitigating factors relating to offences also exist, such as an individual committing a crime under threat from others. These mitigating factors relating to the offence should be distinguished from so-called 'personal mitigation' factors, such as age and remorse. See generally Ashworth (2005: ch. 5).

16 See for example Heather Strang's (2002: 193) summary: 'victim research shows clearly that victims want ... a less formal process [than that offered by the adversarial court system], where their views count'. See also the evaluation of the pilot victim statement schemes in Scotland, in which 'the most common reason given' for making a statement (by one-third of respondents making a statement) was 'simply to express their feelings about the crime' (Leverick *et al.* 2007: 40)

17 Although space forbids detailed discussion, the question of reasonable foreseeability arguably also requires some reconsideration in the light of the analysis in this chapter. For example, von Hirsch, Jareborg and Ashworth (2005: 189) state that 'the burglar may be expected to understand the typical consequences of a burglary, but not, ordinarily, [the victim's] particular situation – for example, the extraordinary personal value the gift taken from her apartment had for her as a gift from a deceased friend.' Arguments of this kind clearly have some force, especially when the focus is on the specific features of the 'personal value' of a particular object. Nevertheless, from a victim-oriented appreciative-descriptive perspective, the 'standard' burglar ought to understand that, in the average household, many of the non-utilitarian objects (vases and jewellery rather than DVD players) will have

sentimental value to the household members; hence, in a more general sense 'personal value' can indeed be among what von Hirsch *et al.* describe as the 'typical consequences of a burglary'.

18 This raises a difficult issue as to how one would operationalise this criterion in daily court practice, a topic which is beyond the scope of the present discussion.

19 Of course, even within the 'duty to understand' approach discussed in this chapter, it would be open to the victim to decline a court's request to make an appreciative-descriptive statement.

20 Official guidance is that if 'impacts' emerge later, after the initial VPS has been completed, then it is appropriate to complete a supplementary VPS containing this additional information. An official document recognises that victims 'will not always realise the full impact that a crime has had upon them at point of statement', but admits that 'they are not always given the opportunity to update or add to their statement at a later date' (Office for Criminal Justice Reform 2005: 5).

21 I am most grateful to Andrew von Hirsch and to Julian Roberts for their constructively critical comments on an earlier draft of this chapter.

References

Ashworth, A.J. (1993a) 'Taking the consequences', in S. Shute, J. Gardner and J. Horder (eds), *Action and Value in Criminal Law*. Oxford: Clarendon Press, pp. 107–24.

Ashworth, A.J. (1993b) 'Victim impact statements and sentencing', *Criminal Law Review*: 498–509.

Ashworth, A.J. (2005) *Sentencing and Criminal Justice* (4th edn). Cambridge: Cambridge University Press.

Blackburn, S. (1998) *Ruling Passions: A theory of practical reasoning*. Oxford: Clarendon Press.

Bloch, M. (1949) *Strange Defeat: A statement of evidence written in 1940* (translated from the French by Gerard Hopkins, with a Foreword by Georges Altman). London: Oxford University Press.

Bloch, M. (1954) *The Historian's Craft* (translated from the French by P. Putnam, with an introduction by J.R. Strayer). Manchester: Manchester University Press.

Blom-Cooper, L. (1963) *The A6 Murder, Regina v. James Hanratty: The semblance of truth*. Harmondsworth: Penguin Books.

Bottoms, A.E. and Stelman, A. (1988) *Social Inquiry Reports: A framework for practice development*. Aldershot: Wildwood House.

Callinicos, A. (2004) *Making History: Agency, structure and change in social theory* (2nd edn). Leiden: Brill.

Christie, N. (1977) 'Conflicts as property', *British Journal of Criminology*, 17(1): 1–15.

Daily Telegraph (2002) 'Sir John Leonard' (14 August). http://www.telegraph.co.uk/news/obituaries/1404335/Sir-John-Leonard.html

Ellison, L. and Munro, V.E. (2009a) 'Reacting to rape: exploring mock jurors' assessments of complainant credibility', *British Journal of Criminology*, 49(2): 202–19.

Ellison, L. and Munro, V.E. (2009b) 'Turning mirrors into windows?: assessing the impact of (mock) juror education in rape trials', *British Journal of Criminology*, 49(3): 363–83.

Evans-Pritchard, E.E. (1937) *Witchcraft, Oracles and Magic among the Azande*. Oxford: Clarendon Press.

Graham, J., Woodfield, K., Tibble, M. and Kitchen, S. (2004) *Testaments of Harm: A qualitative evaluation of the Victim Personal Statements Scheme*. London: National Centre for Social Research.

Grice, E. (2006) 'It's not whether you can or can't forgive; it's whether you will or won't', *Daily Telegraph*, 8 March.

von Hirsch, A, Jareborg, N. and Ashworth, A.J. (2005) 'Gauging crime seriousness: a "living standard" conception of criminal harm', in A. von Hirsch and A.J. Ashworth, *Proportionate Sentencing: Exploring the principles*. Oxford: Oxford University Press, pp. 186–219.

Homans, G.C. (1984) 'Review of *A Treatise on Social Theory: Vol. 1, The Methodology of Social Theory* by W.G. Runciman', *Theory and Society*, 13: 137–40.

Home Office (2009) *Making a Victim Personal Statement*. London: Home Office. http://www.homeoffice.gov.uk/documents/victimstate.pdf

Home Office and Lord Chancellor's Office (1961) *Report of the Interdepartmental Committee on the Business of the Criminal Courts* (Cmnd. 1289). London: HMSO.

Hulsman, L.H.C. (1981) 'Penal reform in the Netherlands: Part 1 – Bringing the criminal justice system under control', *Howard Journal of Penology and Crime Prevention*, 20(3): 150–9.

Hulsman, L.H.C. (1982) 'Penal reform in the Netherlands: Part 2 – Criteria for deciding on alternatives to imprisonment', *Howard Journal of Penology and Crime Prevention*, 21(1): 35–47.

James, B. (1987) 'A thinker, not a soft touch: Times profile of Mr Justice Leonard', *The Times*, 5 February.

Leverick, F., Chalmers, J. and Duff, P. (2007) *An Evaluation of the Pilot Victim Statement Schemes in Scotland*. Edinburgh: Scottish Executive Social Research.

Matza, D. (1969) *Becoming Deviant*. Englewood Cliffs, NJ: Prentice-Hall.

Office for Criminal Justice Reform (2005) *Local Criminal Justice Board Toolkit 4: Taking victims' views into account (Victim Personal Statements)*. London: Office for Criminal Justice Reform. http://frontline.cjsonline.gov.uk/search/index.php?searchterm=Toolkit+4&page=1

Ruben, D.-H. (ed.) (1993) *Explanation*. Readings in Philosophy Series. Oxford: Oxford University Press.

Runciman, W.G. (1972) *A Critique of Max Weber's Philosophy of Social Science*. Cambridge: Cambridge University Press.

Runciman, W.G. (1983) *A Treatise on Social Theory: Vol. 1, The Methodology of Social Theory*. Cambridge: Cambridge University Press.

Saward, J. with Green, W. (1990) *Rape: My Story*. London: Bloomsbury.

Saward, M. (1999) *A Faint Streak of Humility: An autobiography*. Carlisle: Paternoster Publishing.

Sentencing Guidelines Council (2005) *Guideline Judgments Case Compendium*. London: Sentencing Guidelines Council. http://www.sentencing-guidelines.gov.uk/guidelines/other/courtappeal/default.asp

Simester, A.P. and Sullivan, G.R. (2007) *Criminal Law: Theory and doctrine* (3rd edn). Oxford: Hart Publishing.

Skinner, Q. (1985) 'Introduction', in Q. Skinner (ed.), *The Return of Grand Theory in the Human Sciences*. Cambridge: Cambridge University Press, pp. 1–20.

Strang, H. (2002) *Repair or Revenge: Victims and restorative justice*. Oxford: Clarendon Press.

Tyler, T.R. (ed.) (2007) *Legitimacy and Criminal Justice: International perspectives*. New York: Russell Sage Foundation.

Chapter 3

The status of crime victims and witnesses in the twenty-first century

Dame Helen Reeves and Peter Dunn

Introduction

The first decade of the twenty-first century is turning out to be a significant time for victims of crime in the United Kingdom. The 2004 Domestic Violence, Crime and Victims Act introduced a new *Code of Practice for Victims of Crime*. This was implemented on 6 April 2006, providing victims for the first time with statutory rights and a means of redress if those rights are not upheld. Throughout England and Wales, local criminal justice boards (LCJBs) have been given responsibility for ensuring that victims and witnesses are properly considered by all the criminal justice agencies. One hundred and sixty-five Witness Care Units have been set up jointly by the police and the Crown Prosecution Service to ensure that witnesses are kept informed of the progress of their cases and that any special needs are identified in good time. There are now independent domestic violence advocates, independent sexual assault advocates, and 22 Sexual Assault Referral Centres (SARCs) in England and Wales. Victims can make victim personal statements to the police that become part of the CPS case file if an offender is caught, and people who have been bereaved by homicide can make a family impact statement setting out how they have been affected by the crime (see Chapter 8 by Paul Rock in this volume).

The main question this chapter seeks to address is the extent to which these developments are motivated by a desire to meet the needs of victims and witnesses, in which case their success will be judged on that basis, or whether they are designed to achieve other, more traditional, criminal justice objectives. We set out some of the difficulties inherent in trying to address these issues and reflect on the questions that policy-makers may need to tackle in determining the direction in which victims' policies and services will develop in the future.

Some conceptual frameworks for understanding victim policy developments

Before getting into the substance of this chapter, it might be helpful first to summarise some key conceptual perspectives that could help explain the flurry of policy development concerning victims and witnesses that has taken place in the UK in the first few years of this century.

David Garland proposes that there is now 'a new collective meaning of victimhood' which is seen in a reworked relationship between individual victims, symbolic victims, and the criminal justice system (Garland 2001: 12). This, he argues, has its roots in the decline of 'penal welfarism' during the 1970s and 1980s in Britain, the USA and elsewhere. This decline was fuelled by rising crime rates attributable to social changes that loosened traditional structures of informal social control; at the same time ever-increasing numbers of highly desirable and easy-to-steal consumer goods were becoming available. Penal welfarism and its focus on rehabilitating offenders and ameliorating the most destructive aspects of punishment became associated with a failure to control crime. This, when combined with the political realignments that were expressed in the politics of Thatcher and Reagan, led to a new 'zero-tolerance' approach to crime control. The limitations of the criminal justice system in controlling crime were all too apparent, with the police in particular driven by ineffectiveness and corruption into a period that Reiner calls 'post legitimacy' (Reiner 2000). So the policy shift moved away from treating offenders to developing new policies concerned with dealing with the effects of crime. This, according to Garland, accounts for the emergence of much current victim policy. It may be that the most significant aspect of this change is that victims' interests are no longer subsumed within the public interest: hence the creation of 'symbolic' victims that mark out publicly the ending of that subsumption. Meanwhile, the third sector has emerged as a further way of dealing with crime and its effects: part of a wider State-sponsored package of voluntary organisation provision, networks, and inter-agency partnerships. Together, these ensure that the crime control field 'now extends beyond the state' (Garland 2001: 170).

The development of that State-sponsored package and the policy activity of the Government in both supporting and sustaining it gathered pace following the election of the Labour Government in Britain in 1997. Rather than completely eschewing the doctrine of penal punitivism expressed by the former Conservative Home Secretary's mantra that 'prison works', New Labour looked for a new way to reform the criminal justice system that could help them avoid being described by tabloid newspapers as soft on crime. This new approach was expressed as being 'tough on crime, tough on the causes of crime'. Concern with reducing the impact of crime on victims and witnesses was, as Garland shows, an important component of this new approach to criminal justice policy. Improvements in provisions for victims and witnesses, initiated by the previous Conservative Government in the shape of (among other things) greatly increased funding for Victim Support and the establishment of the *Victims' Charter* in 1990, were part of a package of reform that included at least two components of significance to victims. These included a new multi-agency approach to dealing with antisocial behaviour, which for the first time recognised the destructive impact of so-called 'low level' crime on victims and communities; and reform of the police in light of the recommendations of the 1999 report of the Macpherson Inquiry into the bungled police investigation of Stephen Lawrence's racist murder. At the same time, the Human Rights agenda and pro-victim policy developments in the European Union, which included the *European Framework Agreement on the Standing of Victims in Criminal Proceedings*, gave added impetus to the imperative to improve the experiences of victims and witnesses in the criminal justice system.

Paul Rock (2004) describes in detail the political and social dynamics that lay behind the new victim policy of the post-1997 Labour Government. These dynamics had included the identity politics of race and gender, which had been successful in drawing public attention to the continued pervasiveness of racism and the victimisation of women. The politics of victimisation was much less exciting and less likely to gain public attention than those of race and gender, but campaigns for better treatment of victims became swept up in those identity politics, both benefiting from them and informing them further. The scale of some of the conceptual changes that took place in just 10 years and some loss of power by the more established interest groups is described in Rock's publications. These changes are indicated by on the one hand a 1995 Law Society response to the Justice Report on *The Role of the Victim in the Criminal Justice Process* that argued victims' standing as victims could not be confirmed until an admission or finding of guilt (at which point they could be treated with special favour); to the establishment of the Victims' Advocate Scheme less than 10 years later that gave victims or their surviving relatives a limited but nevertheless formal role in trials (see Chapter 8 by Rock, and Chapter 10 by Padfield and Roberts, in this volume). Behind such significant reforms was a process that Rock argues was driven by a 'common pool of stakeholders' active in social movements. The Macpherson Report was spurred by the politics of race 'set within the framework of the criminal justice system', while the *Speaking up for Justice* report (Home Office 1998), which stimulated new provisions for vulnerable and intimidated witnesses, had been triggered by the politics of gender. Meanwhile, restorative justice was also being experimented with by some police and youth justice services: this was about bringing victims and offenders together to reduce crime. Rock writes that 'what contributed in time to their becoming merged together in a loosely connected bundle of policies for victims was the continual traffic in ideas between the committees served by that common pool of stakeholders' (Rock 2004: 100).

So the criminal justice policy shift in the last decade of the twentieth century had ostensibly been from a position in which victims 'had little role in the criminal justice system other than as a source of evidence' (Zedner 1997: 600) to one in which the Government had announced it wanted victims to be 'at the centre of the criminal justice process' (Alun Michael MP quoted in Rock 2004: 7). The rest of this chapter explores the extent to which the Government's ambition for victims that Alun Michael articulated has been achieved. By looking at the unfolding experience of victims in their engagement with the criminal justice system, we consider the question of whether policy reform has brought real improvements for victims or whether it has created a type of enhanced state of 'symbolic victimhood' that has served other, less honourable purposes. Before doing that, it may be helpful to include some information about Victim Support and its work during the period under consideration in this chapter.

Victim Support

The views expressed in this chapter are based on the authors' experience of having worked for Victim Support, an independent national charity which aims to provide access to comprehensive services for all victims of crime. Victim Support provides both a community-based service for victims and the Witness Service in every criminal court in the country. It also runs a confidential national Victim Supportline to provide better access for victims, even if they do not choose to report their victimisation to the police. It works closely with other agencies, both statutory and voluntary so that, where necessary, victims can be referred to other sources of help. Currently, over 1.75 million people are referred to Victim Support each year, mainly by the police. Despite a recent reduction in recorded crime, there has been a steady increase in referrals: in 2006/7 there was an increase of almost two per cent in the number of referrals received over the previous year's figure (Victim Support 2007). Victim Support's services are delivered by 1,700 paid employees and about 9,000 trained volunteers (Victim Support 2007). As well as providing services, the charity has been actively involved in the development of policy for victims and witnesses, public education, and training for staff in other agencies.

In 1995, Victim Support published a policy paper, *The Rights of Victims of Crime*. The rights it identified in relation to criminal justice were based on the charity's first-hand experience of working with victims and witnesses and were designed only with their interests at heart. These rights were:

- To be free from the burden of decisions relating to the offender;
- To receive, and have an opportunity to provide, information;
- To be protected;
- To receive compensation;
- To receive respect, recognition and support.

In the next few pages we will explore the extent to which these rights have become reflected in recent criminal justice policy.

Victims' and witnesses' experiences with the criminal justice system

For more than 20 years it has been known that a significant proportion of victims are dissatisfied with the way they are treated by the criminal justice system. In 1982, Mike Maguire demonstrated that 16 per cent of victims of burglary were somewhat or very dissatisfied with the treatment they received from the police (Maguire 1982: 137). In 1985, Joanna Shapland and colleagues demonstrated that satisfaction actually decreases as the victim passes through the criminal justice process (Shapland *et al.* 1985: 84). It appeared that the more contact victims had with the various aspects of criminal justice, the more dissatisfied they became. In this study 78 per cent were satisfied or very satisfied with police performance during their first contact, falling to 58 per cent at the end of the process. One of the key elements of victims' dissatisfaction was the lack of information they received about the case.

British Crime Survey (BCS) data show that in 2007/8, victims were satisfied with the way the police handled the matter in 59 per cent of incidents that the police came to know about. The figure for the 2006/7 BCS had been almost the same at 58 per cent. Similarly, 60 per cent of those who had witnessed a crime in the previous 12 months were satisfied with the way the police handled it. The BCS report points out that over the longer term, victim satisfaction with the police fell in the 1990s but since 2000 it has remained broadly stable between 58 per cent and 60 per cent (Kershaw, Nicholas and Walker 2008). However, other research raises questions about the suitability of relying on victim satisfaction as the principal measure of the quality of the criminal justice system's engagement with victims.

The Office for Criminal Justice Reform's WAVES project (Witness and Victim Experience Survey) is a telephone survey undertaken in regular sweeps with people who have attended court as a victim or a prosecution witness. The 2008 WAVES report draws on data collected from 22,000 victims and witnesses whose cases were concluded between February 2005 and January 2006. The report reminds us that improving victims' and witnesses' experiences of the criminal justice system is 'a key Government priority. . . central to the Government's ambition to rebalance the criminal justice system in favour of victims and the law-abiding majority' (Moore and Blakeborough 2008: ii). While the survey records generally high levels of satisfaction, with up to 86 per cent being fairly to very satisfied with the overall experience, other findings are disturbing. For example, while more than three-quarters of respondents reported that they had been informed that someone had been charged with their offence, only 51 per cent reported being re-contacted about their case within one month of their initial contact with the police. The Victim Personal Statement scheme is intended to apply to all victims, but only just over one-third of those interviewed (36 per cent) remembered being given the opportunity to make such a Victim Personal Statement. More than half (53 per cent) stated that they had not been given the opportunity. Of those who attended court to give evidence, only 60 per cent were offered a court familiarisation visit (professional witnesses are excluded from the survey). Only half of the 4,000 victims who reported having been injured as part of the crime recalled being told about the Criminal Injuries Compensation Scheme.

It is important to note here that these findings are from interviews with victims and witnesses whose cases were heard before the victims' *Code of Practice* was implemented. The WAVES sample was relatively small and may not have been representative. Some of those interviewed might have simply forgotten they were told about criminal injuries compensation or the opportunity to make a Victim Personal Statement. Nevertheless, bearing in mind Shapland and others' findings that access to accurate information is a key factor in victim satisfaction with the criminal justice system, one cannot help questioning the following conclusion that the WAVES report draws:

A large proportion of victims and witnesses interviewed recalled having been kept informed at key stages in the criminal justice process including when someone had been charged. While the initial survey may not be representative of the experiences of all victims and witnesses across England and Wales, these findings indicate that for those interviewed, progress has been made against the requirements set out in service standards such as the Code of Practice for Victims of Crime (Moore and Blakeborough 2008: 15).

Perhaps more significantly, those substantial numbers of victims and witnesses who are not being told about their entitlement to compensation or the chance to make a Victim Personal Statement might in ignorance still be satisfied with the rather second-rate service they have received.

The Witness Service

Victim Support was developing rapidly during the 1980s, and victims frequently asked the charity's staff and volunteers to accompany them to court. It became evident that attending court was frequently a very unpleasant experience. There was no separate place to wait; victims and witnesses might be subjected to intimidation in or around the courthouse by the defendant, or his or her family and friends. They were not told when the case was likely to begin or how it was progressing. Inside the courtroom they were frequently subjected to the type of cross-examination which could be described as intimidating or humiliating.

In 1991 Victim Support published research, commissioned from Professor John Raine, which confirmed that most witnesses found the experience of attending court distressing and many would not wish to give evidence again (Raine and Smith 1991). A frequent complaint was that witnesses felt undervalued and that they were needed only for the role they could play in convicting the offender. The two key concerns highlighted in this research were the lack of information received by the witness both before and on arriving at court and the risk of meeting the defendant and their family or friends. The report contained many examples of what became known as 'secondary victimisation' – that is the aggravation of the primary offence by the insensitive behaviour of others, including those in authority.

The findings led to the establishment of Victim Support's Witness Service which by 2002 had developed to cover all Crown Court centres and all magistrates' courts. The Witness Service offers witnesses separate waiting rooms, personal support and information as well as practical help, including a pre-trial court familiarisation visit.

Recent significant developments for victims and witnesses

A new deal for victims and witnesses

Despite the low levels of victim satisfaction with the criminal justice system, it was not until 2003 that the Government published its first national strategy, *A New Deal for Victims and Witnesses* (CJS 2003). This paper was welcomed by Victim Support as a major milestone. It contained many improvements the charity had been calling for.

The strategy set out an ambitious agenda to provide both rights and services, not only in criminal justice but also in the community. It drew together and extended the existing duties of the various criminal justice agencies to provide victims with information about their cases and also to refer them to victim services for help. An important development was the recognition, for the first time in a government publication, that victims' needs go beyond the criminal justice system and extend, for example, to health, housing and social security provisions.

However, it is important to note that the stated aims of this strategy were not only to improve services to victims but also to improve public confidence in the criminal justice system and to increase the number of offenders brought to justice. It appears therefore that the Government's proposals for improving the experience of victims were at least in part aimed at making the criminal justice process more effective in dealing with offenders. Although this is a valid aim, there were and are concerns that the new provisions could be at risk if the desired criminal justice targets were not achieved.

Domestic Violence, Crime and Victims Act 2004

The Domestic Violence, Crime and Victims Act 2004 enacts some of the developments proposed in the strategy. It introduced a statutory *Code of Practice*, placing obligations on criminal justice agencies to deliver specified services to victims of crime. It contained provisions to appoint a Commissioner for Victims to oversee the implementation of provisions, both in the criminal justice system and in the wider community. Recruitment of the Commissioner started in January 2006 but no suitable candidate was found (Hansard 8 February 2007). It appears that at the time of writing (January 2009) a new recruitment campaign to appoint a Commissioner is planned by the Ministry of Justice.

The Government Code of Practice

The criminal justice system's *Code of Practice for Victims of Crime* provides victims, for the first time, with statutory rights to information and consideration of their own interests in the process of criminal justice. Previous provisions, such as the Victims' Charter in 1990, had been described as a statement of the rights of victims of crime, although these rights could not be enforced and the Charter was never fully implemented. By the time of the second Victims' Charter in 1996, the word 'rights' had been dropped.

Some of the statutory provisions had already been put in place before the *Code of Practice* was implemented in 2006. One of these is the duty of the probation service to contact victims of sexual and violent crime whose offenders are sentenced to more than 12 months' imprisonment and to provide them with information about the release of the offender. Added to this is the new provision that the victims of mentally disordered offenders now also have the right to information about their offender's discharge from detention under the Mental Health Act, an improvement long called for by Victim Support.

Also included in the Code is the duty of the Crown Prosecution Service (CPS) to inform victims of any decisions, in serious violent or sexual crimes, to reduce or to discontinue charges and to provide information as to the reasons. This development had already been implemented and a major training programme has been conducted throughout the CPS to prepare lawyers for this task.

Some provisions of the draft Code go considerably further than previous procedures. There is a requirement for the police to maintain monthly contact with victims whose offenders have remained undetected to provide them with information about the progress of investigations. They must inform victims of certain key events in an investigation, such as an arrest or the offender being bailed, within five working days or within one day if the victim is vulnerable or intimidated. The police must inform them when the case has been closed. Where suspects have been identified, the police will be required to keep victims informed of progress, including all court dates and outcomes such as bail decisions or adjournments. Despite the requirements involving additional work for the police, no new resources were allocated for its implementation.

The effectiveness of the Code will depend to some extent on the degree to which it can be enforced. Victims will not be able to sue for a failure to deliver these rights, although they can make a complaint through their MP to the Parliamentary Ombudsman. Failure to deliver a *Code of Practice* right can be used to support a civil action, but cannot be the basis of that action itself. The 2007 Parliamentary and Health Service Ombudsman's *Annual Report* records that the Ombudsman received three complaints about the police and two about the CPS under the *Code of Practice*. The report states that 'we lack any firm evidence to suggest why the volume of complaints has not been as high as we expected' (PHSO 2007: 13). The following year's *Annual Report* records just two complaints under the Code, both about the National Probation Service (PHSO 2008).

The existence of the Code, together with the right of complaint to the Parliamentary Ombudsman and the creation of a new Commissioner for Victims, are certainly steps in the right direction. But there is considerable concern about the absence of additional resources for implementing the Code, and it seems inconceivable that the small number of complaints is due to almost total victim satisfaction with the criminal justice system.

The enhanced status of witnesses

A number of high-profile cases in the 1990s highlighted the problem of the physical and sexual abuse of children and vulnerable adults, both in care homes and in the community. It was apparent that too few prosecutions were being brought because of doubts as to the ability of vulnerable witnesses to cope with the trial process. The 1999 Youth Justice and Criminal Evidence Act put in place special measures to help vulnerable and intimidated witnesses give their best evidence. These are applicable to children, people with learning difficulties and other disabilities, victims of certain offences such as rape and those who are at risk of intimidation by the defendant. Plans were also announced to improve the layout of courts to allow witnesses and defendants to be kept apart although, again, the issue of resources caused concern.

Ministers had begun to take notice of research revealing the number of trials, in all categories of crime, which fail to go ahead due to the non-attendance of witnesses. The 2003 Government strategy, *A new deal for victims and witnesses*, quotes research commissioned by the Justice Gap Task Force in 2002 and noted that:

> Even when crimes are reported and a suspect is arrested and charged, a high proportion of cases fail because the victim or witness is not prepared to give evidence in court. A recent study suggested that witness problems were responsible for 60% of Crown Court cases that did not result in conviction. (CJS 2003: 9)

This led, in March 2003, to the establishment of the *No Witness, No Justice* Project (NWNJ) when the Prime Minister and the Attorney General commissioned a partnership of the Prime Minister's Office of Public Services Reform, the Home Office, the CPS and the Association of Chief Police Officers (ACPO) with the dual aim of improving public confidence and narrowing the justice gap. The *No Witness, No Justice* document states that:

> The guiding principle [of NWNJ] is that providing better information, reassurance and support will not only produce more confident and willing victims and witnesses, it should also reduce ineffective trials, help to bring more offenders to justice and improve public confidence in the criminal justice system. [Working with other criminal justice agencies and Local Criminal Justice Boards the] programme is designed to ensure that the service provided to victims and witnesses is properly tailored to the needs of each individual, so that they are able to attend court. (CJS 2004)

Witness Care Units

Under the NWNJ project, trial witnesses are allocated a Witness Care Officer to give information and assistance. They are based in Witness Care

Units, run jointly by the police and the CPS, and 165 units have been established.

Certainly, these units go some way towards enabling the police and the CPS to achieve their new duties towards victims under the *Code of Practice for Victims of Crime*. They give each witness a single point of contact if they need information and they keep them routinely informed of all developments in the case.

The Witness Care Units also identify, at an early stage, any particular needs witnesses may have. Practical concerns, such as the need for childcare while attending court, or arranging with employers to have time off work, can be dealt with in good time before the hearing. Similarly, vulnerable or intimidated witnesses can be identified early enough for any special measures to be arranged to assist them in giving their evidence. This task is particularly important as it has become clear to Witness Service staff that not everyone who could benefit from special measures had been getting access to the help they needed. In 2004/5, the Witness Service dealt with 47,000 witnesses who could easily be classified as vulnerable or intimidated under the terms of the Act, but only approximately 26,000 of these were identified by the statutory agencies prior to the court appearance (Victim Support 2005). A very high proportion of the people not identified in advance were under the age of 17 – a group automatically entitled to the statutory provisions. It should be expected that all these witnesses are identified early in the preparation of the case so that special measures and witness preparation can be arranged.

The Government's view is that Witness Care Units have been successful in their purpose. The then Home Office Minister, Tony McNulty MP, noted in the House of Commons in June 2006 that the number of trials that did not go ahead as planned because a witness did not attend had declined from a national average of 908 in September 2004 to 727 in August 2005, a decrease of almost 20 per cent. In those cases handled by Witness Care Units, the witness attendance rate has increased from 78.5 per cent in the three months before WCUs went live to 84 per cent in August 2005 (Hansard 7 June 2006).

Having welcomed the establishment of Witness Care Units, two key concerns must be highlighted: the first is the number of additional witnesses who will be referred to the Witness Service for enhanced preparation. The early referral of witnesses, particularly those who are vulnerable or intimidated, is welcome but the preparation they will require involves considerable resources and so far no extra funding has been provided. Findings from the WAVES survey indicate that the early referral of witnesses has not been happening in a large number of instances. The second concern is that the units have been set up to deal with victims and witnesses after the offender has been charged, but it is important to remember that only approximately three per cent of all crimes reach the courts (Victim Support 2002; Kershaw *et al.* 2008). No provisions have been made for the much larger numbers of victims whose offenders have not yet been detected or for any victim or witness during the early stages of the investigation, although they too could benefit from better information and a single point of contact.

Rob Mawby draws attention to the lack of evaluation of the effectiveness of many of the Government's recent policy initiatives concerning victims and witnesses. This, he observes, reflects an established tendency to introduce victim policy without first evaluating it. This is especially notable 'when compared with New Labour's evidence-based approach to probation and crime reduction initiatives' (Mawby 2007: 234). Failure to put in place robust evaluation of initiatives might be accounted for by a lack of research findings about 'what works' with victims of crime with which new projects could be benchmarked; but it could also suggest that while resources are committed to evaluating the treatment of offenders, provisions that help victims are, with some exceptions, based not so much on 'what works' as on 'what looks good'.

Provisions for young witnesses

Reference has already been made to the various provisions for supporting all vulnerable witnesses, including children and young people. Video technology enables them to give evidence away from the courtroom and special training has been provided for officials, including prosecutors and judges. However, in 2004, Victim Support and the NSPCC conducted research into the experiences of children attending criminal courts. The resulting report, *In Their Own Words: The experiences of 50 young witnesses in criminal proceedings*, cited examples of long delays before the trial actually took place, children waiting for long periods in the court building, use of inappropriate language by lawyers, and cross-examination which was clearly found by children to be distressing and humiliating (Plotnikoff and Wolfson 2004).

The research found that young witnesses waited on average over five hours to give evidence while a fifth of those interviewed attended court but were sent home without testifying on that day, sometimes more than once. It was also apparent that more could be done by lawyers to ask the court to intervene when inappropriate or aggressive cross-examination took place. Nearly a third of the young witnesses in the survey reported feeling very upset, distressed or angry.

Home Office Ministers welcomed the research, announcing at its launch the establishment of the Child Evidence Review. The Government's response included commissioning an evaluation of services for young witnesses, comparing those run by Victim Support, by Local Safeguarding Children Boards and by the National Society for the Prevention of Cruelty to Children (NSPCC); but the purpose of this was mainly to evaluate the cost-effectiveness of support schemes. Staff from the Office for Criminal Justice Reform (OCJR)[1] explained that Ministers would be persuaded to increase resources for young witnesses only if it could be demonstrated that support contributed to reducing attrition in trials, while the evaluation's advisory group were concerned that the imperative of safeguarding children's well-being was not apparently of primary importance. As predicted, reduction in attrition turned out to be impossible to demonstrate. The research could only conclude that 'rates of young witness non-attendance reported by the six schemes were lower than national estimates' (Plotnikoff and Wolfson 2007: 5). Other findings from the governmental evaluation were similar to those of the authors of *In Their Own Words*. The evaluation recommended that there should be a more co-ordinated national approach to young witness support, an update of National Standards for Witness Care, and better inter-agency work.

OCJR used the evaluation findings to produce a toolkit for local use in developing support for young witnesses, though the Witness Service seems to have had little involvement in its production. The NSPCC in particular are frustrated by the long time taken to address the recommendations of the Child Evidence Review, whose consultation closed in October 2007 and about which decisions were expected in autumn 2008 (Hansard 29 September 2008).

Victim Personal Statements

The development and implementation of the Victim Personal Statement (VPS), probably more than any other example, highlights the difficulty of introducing a truly victim-centred provision in the context of criminal justice. We shall therefore chart its troubled 10-year history in some detail.

The concept of the VPS was first introduced by Victim Support in 1995 as part of its policy that victims should receive, and have an opportunity to provide, information. We were aware of the use of victim impact statements in North America and we were concerned about this initiative reaching the UK. The victim impact statement, which began in California, is a statement made by the victim which is to be taken into account only during the sentencing of the offender. It is prepared with the assistance of the prosecuting authority and in some states it is used as a central part of the adversarial sentencing process.

Victim Support had never supported the introduction of the victim impact statement in that form. We recognised, however, that research demonstrated consistently that victims valued being asked about the effects of the crime on themselves and their families. Consequently, we worked on a way in which the positive effects could be achieved, without the pitfalls. Our proposal was the introduction of a personal statement, to be made early on in the case, which would inform both the police and the

CPS of any special needs or sensitivities about which they should be aware and other important issues such as whether or not the victim wished to be kept informed or wished to apply for compensation if the case went to court. The statement could also be used at the time of sentence to identify any legitimate interests of victims such as the need for protection or compensation.

Victim Support's proposal was introduced at a seminar in 10 Downing Street, hosted by the then Prime Minister, John Major. Following the seminar, a working party was set up to explore the possibility of a system being introduced in the UK. After four years' deliberations, the VPS scheme was ready to be tested. The pilot projects were monitored and the first analysis made it clear that problems already existed (Morgan and Sanders 1999).

There was widespread confusion about the purpose of the VPS, with some victims clearly either believing or having been told that they were for the purpose of sentencing. Briefings to the police made it quite clear that the statements were to be used throughout the management of the case and that victims would not be able to express an opinion as to sentence. However, neither the police nor the CPS had recognised any other use for the statements prior to sentence and many had not even read them. As a result, the statements were largely ineffective in ensuring better treatment for victims or in identifying any services they might need.

However, the Youth Justice and Criminal Evidence Act had been passed in 1999, and the police and the CPS now needed additional information in order to identify vulnerable witnesses and to ensure that special measures were applied for when necessary. There was also growing pressure on the police to be more consistent in their referrals to Victim Support, and the VPS would be an additional source of information about the level and type of support that was needed. The additional responsibilities of the CPS in relation to the victim also meant that they needed greater awareness of the individuals and families they might have to contact, sometimes with disappointing news. At a policy level, the VPS became more of a priority.

The press, a major player in most criminal justice initiatives, was keen to present the VPS as a development in the adversarial system. When the programme was rolled out nationally in 2000, the Government press release was clear about the use of the statement throughout the case. However, when the story appeared, headlines announced that victims would now have a say in the punishment of their offender and that victims would have a right to be heard in court.

The roll-out was introduced to practitioners in a Government circular,[2] which stressed that victims would take part on an entirely voluntary basis, that no pressure should be put on them, and that the absence of a VPS should not influence the court in any way. The intention was simply to provide a service to victims of crime. However, less than a year later, a

Government newsletter contained an item on the need for courts to recognise the severity of crimes committed by animal rights demonstrators. The newsletter advised that 'Prosecutors and the police should ensure that in each case a victim personal statement is obtained which sets the offence in the correct context'.[3] Clearly, once a provision had been made, the temptation to use it for the purposes of criminal justice had proved hard to resist.

By 2004, research by Graham *et al.* was demonstrating that not all victims were being offered the opportunity to make a VPS, and there remained a wide lack of understanding about the purpose of the scheme by both victims and the police. The report notes that 'There is a clear need for further training of those front line staff administering the scheme, improved communication and understanding for police officers and victims of crime' (Graham *et al.* 2004).

Put another way, a culture change is needed to ensure that the new provision, intended for the benefit of victims, is understood, valued and implemented consistently with its original purpose. Otherwise, there is the constant danger that it will be treated simply as a tool to be used in the service of the criminal justice system.

Legal representation for victims in court

Shortly before the May 2005 General Election the Government announced it was planning to introduce legal aid to enable victims to be independently represented in criminal courts for cases such as homicide, rape and domestic violence. In addition to representation during the trial, victims would be allowed, either personally or through an advocate, to make a statement in the courtroom after a guilty verdict and before sentencing. It was proposed that the new provisions would be funded from a reduction in expenditure on legal aid for defendants.

The Government announcement made no reference to the review of the criminal justice system it had commissioned from Lord Justice Auld in 2001. In his review, Lord Justice Auld considered the position of victims in the criminal courts and ruled out the idea of victims having a more active role in the system. He concluded: 'I recommend against giving victims, as some have suggested, a formal role in the trial process similar to that of the continental *partie civile* or auxiliary prosecutor, or any outwardly special position in relation to the prosecutor' (Auld 2001).

The Review gave detailed consideration to models of representation in Continental Europe and, after analysis of the relative merits of the various systems, it appeared that victims were no better served by procedures in other countries. For example, victims in France were parties to the case only insomuch as they could claim compensation, but it was clear from the evidence that victims are far more likely to receive compensation in the UK where a claim is made on their behalf by the prosecutor and the debt is enforced by the court.

Although the proposed Victims' Advocate Scheme was welcomed by many bereaved relatives and by some victim campaigning groups, it was also felt that there could be a serious danger that victims might have their expectations raised as to the extent of their perceived new role and on the effect their statements could have on sentencing. For those victims who do wish to influence the sentence, there could be disappointment if the outcome is not as they had wished. For those who do not wish to speak, there could be the added burden of thinking they are failing in their duty. There were also concerns that with the introduction of this possibly expensive initiative, currently directed at only a minority of cases, attention could be diverted from ensuring that the VPS is used more effectively. Considering that the VPS can provide access to a wider range of rights and services and that it is available to all victims whose cases reach the courts, perhaps it would be more beneficial to direct resources and effort to its proper implementation.

The Victims' Advocate Scheme was piloted from April 2006 in five Crown Court Centres and has been evaluated. It contains three elements: enhanced pre-trial support, a Family Impact Statement, and up to 15 hours of free personal and social legal advice (though legal advice about the trial is excluded). Because one of the evaluators has contributed a chapter on the Scheme for this book (see Rock, Chapter 8, this volume), we will not attempt an inevitably much less satisfactory summary of it here, but in the context of this chapter's overall argument, it may be helpful to note that separate legal representation for victims in court appears to be in conflict with some aspects of the CPS role. The prosecutor can already ask the bench to intervene in unnecessarily aggressive cross-examination, draw the court's attention to elements of a VPS, apply for compensation on a victim's behalf and challenge derogatory comments about a victim or other third party in a plea of mitigation. The CPS *Prosecutor's Pledge* specifies that:

Where mitigation casts unwarranted or unsubstantiated attacks on the character of another who may or may not be a victim, the prosecutor will challenge the account and may ask the court to hear evidence to correct the defendant's account. Where this takes place the prosecutor may also make an application to the court to prevent the defendant's account being reported by the media. (CPS 2009)

It seems important to ask why potentially problematic but superficially attractive initiatives are introduced when improvements such as those specified in *The Prosecutor's Pledge* could be made to work for the benefit of victims and witnesses.

Specialist victim services, narrowing the justice gap

There has been growing concern about the failure of the criminal justice process to secure convictions in serious crimes such as rape and domestic violence (see for example Kelly *et al.* 2005). The Government strategy known as 'Narrowing the Justice Gap' has been developed specifically to tackle this problem. For each of these crimes, the reluctance of victims to contact the police or to remain involved with the prosecution is now recognised as a major obstacle to be overcome. As a result, new specialist services aimed at providing more support to victims of these sensitive and distressing crimes are currently being promoted.

Domestic violence

In March 2005, the Government published a plan proposing an improved response to domestic violence. Part of the plan was the expansion of Specialist Domestic Violence Courts. It was hoped that more sensitive treatment of domestic violence victims would increase confidence in the criminal justice system and encourage more victims to come forward.

> The core principles of the [Domestic Violence Courts] include: access to lay advocates (who act as a liaison between the victim and the court); coordination of partner agencies; providing a victim and child friendly court and providing specialist personnel trained in domestic violence awareness and procedures.[4]

The 'lay advocates', known as Independent Domestic Violence Advisors (IDVAs), support victims in the community and guide them through both the criminal prosecution and any civil procedures relating, for example, to the care and custody of children, housing and financial maintenance. IDVAs are independent, paid staff who provide professional advice, information and support aimed at improving the safety of victims of domestic violence. According to the Home Office statement, 'the focus of an advisor's work is with high-risk victims where their safety can only be assured through this approach' (Home Office 2005).

Extra support is welcome for victims of domestic violence who are at higher risk of death or serious injury. It is important, however, that resources are also made available to help the many thousands of other victims of domestic violence to ensure that they too receive the support they need and to prevent the violence from escalating.

Rape and sexual assault

Many victims of sexual violence, probably a significant majority, find it difficult to report their experience to the police. Sexual Assault Referral

Centres (SARCs), pioneered by the St Mary's Centre in Manchester since 1986, provide an opportunity for victims to receive medical and social support whether or not they choose to report the offence. Forensic evidence is gathered and preserved so that it can be used in the event of a later prosecution. The value of these centres has only recently been more widely recognised and they are being actively promoted and supported by both the police and the Government, with funding from the Victim's Fund.

SARCs normally involve local partnerships between the police, health services and voluntary organisations, including Victim Support. They are therefore able to provide a comprehensive service focused on both the immediate and longer-term needs of the victim.

According to guidance issued by ACPO,[5] there are two imperatives to service provision given by a SARC following sexual assault:

- forensic examination so that evidence can be collected for use in the investigation of crime;

- care of the victim to minimise the risk of subsequent physical and mental difficulties and promote recovery.

ACPO point out that the unique aspect of a SARC is that victims can make use of all the facilities before deciding whether or not to report the crime to the police, and their anonymity is preserved. The partnership between the police, the health services, and good liaison with other statutory and voluntary agencies is therefore essential in meeting victims' needs. Services required following sexual assault will depend on the needs and wishes of victims and the time that has elapsed since the assault. SARCs aim to provide an efficient and sensitive service to all victims of serious sexual assault.

The priority therefore is for victim care, though ACPO clearly hopes that better treatment and support will result in improved confidence in the criminal justice system and an increase in both reporting and convictions.

Independent Sexual Violence Advocates (ISVAs) have been introduced in 38 areas of England and Wales and the Government plans to evaluate their role with a view to wider roll-out. They are funded primarily through the Victim's Fund and the Victim's Surcharge (a levy of £15 on fines, which has been controversial and has been resisted by some magistrates). Working with SARCs, the police and other agencies, the role of ISVAs is to support and accompany victims of sexual violence through the criminal justice process to enable them to give evidence and to free up police time for better investigation.

All these new provisions clearly have the potential to provide valuable support to victims of two of the most distressing types of crime. They may also be successful in achieving a higher level of reporting and subsequent convictions. It is too early to know if their future is secure or if their continuation as specialist services to victims will depend on their success in narrowing the justice gap. Encouragingly, Home Office Minister Alan Campbell, in a November 2008 speech to a police conference about the investigation of rape cases, said that 'the victim experience of the process is just as important as the conviction rate'.[6] This seems to signal a degree of official acceptance of the imperative to focus on the needs of victims not just as witnesses but as people who have a right to fair treatment irrespective of their status in the criminal justice system. However, he is referring here to victims' experience of the criminal justice system, not to the overall aftermath of the offence, which will precipitate needs around health, housing, benefits etc. that go well beyond the remit of criminal justice agencies.

The use of the 'victim' label

In this chapter we have described various initiatives which have been presented as services for victims but which have clearly been prioritised because they also fulfil criminal justice objectives. Recently, a far more worrying phenomenon has appeared. This is the tendency to introduce new provisions that are likely to be controversial by describing them as efforts to 're-balance the system in favour of victims'.[7] This was used in relation to the 2003 Criminal Justice Act, which introduced the provision for retrials, referred to as 'double jeopardy', and to reduce the number of cases which would be eligible for a jury trial. Although there were some provisions to assist witnesses, such as the right to read their statement prior to giving evidence, most of the publicity focused on the more controversial issues. This resulted in comments both in Parliament and in the press about the danger of the pendulum swinging too far in favour of victims.

Michael Tonry, former Director of the University of Cambridge Institute of Criminology, expressed his concerns about this trend while discussing the 2002 Criminal Justice White Paper, which resulted in the 2003 Criminal Justice Act:

> So what can the White Paper mean when it says the system needs rebalancing in favour of victims? If it means only that some procedures and processes can be made more effective or efficient, that may be true, but it has nothing to do with rebalancing. If it means that procedures should be changed to produce more convictions, that may or may not be true, but again it's nothing to do with rebalancing. It may mean, and probably does mean, that victims and the rest of us resent and dislike offenders and that the Government wishes to

manipulate those emotions so that we will think it tough on crime. That has nothing to do with rebalancing and it is ignoble. (Tonry 2004: 29)

Returning for a moment to the decline of the 'penal welfarism' approach that we discussed earlier in this chapter, Zedner's assessment of the dangers in the (ab)use of the victim label seem particularly relevant here. She wrote: 'at a time when the impulse to punish dominates, it remains doubtful whether reorientation towards the victim will in fact foster reintegrative or reparative ends. The danger is that concern for the victim may be used to justify the pursuit of punitivism in their name . . .' (Zedner 1997: 607).

The growth of restorative justice

Zedner's reference above to 'reintegrative ends' brings us to another important development, the increased use of restorative justice in all aspects of dealing with young offenders and the proposed extension of this approach to adult offenders. Victim Support always welcomed the concept of restorative justice and it acknowledged that the process is very beneficial for those victims who wish to take part and under the right circumstances. However, the idea that restorative justice has been designed primarily as a service for victims is highly questionable. Restorative justice was introduced with the aim of preventing reoffending and the systems are therefore in place to meet this objective. For example, the timing of the offer of restorative justice clearly depends on the point the case has reached in the criminal justice process and not on the point of recovery reached by the victim. Victim Support proposed a number of safeguards to ensure that victims' interests are always protected, for example, a minimum of three weeks for the victim to decide whether or not they wish to take part, with the possibility of independent advice and support being provided. There should also be an assurance that offenders will not be penalised if the victim chooses not to take part (Victim Support 2003). These important conditions would help to ensure that victims do not feel responsible for decisions relating to the punishment of the offender.

Many of Victim Support's proposals were adopted by the Government and appear in recent guidelines to mediation practitioners. The charity welcomed the development of occupational standards to help ensure the competence of mediators. However, it is vital to recognise that if victim/offender mediation is not properly conducted the end result could be detrimental for the victim, rather than a positive experience.

Beyond criminal justice

It is important to note here that almost all the developments described so far in this chapter are entirely dependent on an offender having been identified. The new provisions available to victims are mostly intended to ease their progress through the criminal justice system and also to encourage them to participate. The Government judges the success of these developments by their ability to improve the operation of the criminal justice system (see Tony McNulty's statement about Witness Care Units, above). But as noted, only a small percentage of all crimes ever reach the courts (Victim Support 2002; Kershaw *et al.* 2008), which means that the new services are available to only a tiny minority of victims of crime. If asked to prioritise the problems they have faced following a crime, most victims would list health, financial and housing issues as well as the need for general emotional support in coping with the consequences of an unexpected and unwanted experience. These problems will occur whether or not an offender has been detected. Services designed to meet these needs would include personal support to help victims understand their own reactions and those of other family members, practical help with home security, the replacement or repair of stolen or damaged items and the need for a victim-aware health service responsive to providing appropriate support and treatment.

The Government strategy in 2003 included statements about the social needs of victims of crime, and a new department has been created within the Office for Criminal Justice Reform aimed at liaising with other Government departments and agencies, such as health and housing, to promote the wider interests of victims. However, at this point the absence of references to the social needs of victims in Government strategy documents suggests that there may not be any tangible developments and that it remains the case that the criminal justice aspects have been given much higher priority. Orthodox criminal justice interventions are not always the most effective responses to criminal victimisation, especially when criminal justice agencies are themselves a source of secondary victimisation or where victimisation is committed corporately; nor do criminal justice agencies always provide the help that victims most want, particularly in the short term (see Dunn 2007; Mawby and Walklate 1994; Spalek 2006; Victim Support 2006). While many victims may want satisfactory sanctions to be applied to the person who offended against them, some may want or need other interventions such as rehousing, reinstatement of their loss, or the engagement of the offender in a programme aimed at stopping their offending. Many of these desirable outcomes, most of which do not feature in the current flurry of Government-initiated criminal justice policy reforms, may have very little to do with established and increasingly populist methods of punishment.

The Government's strategy for the criminal justice system, *Working Together to Cut Crime and Deliver Justice: A Strategic Plan for 2008–2011*, sets out a range of measures to make the criminal justice system more effective in bringing offenders to justice. Key principles in the Plan include the importance of ensuring 'the needs of the victim (are) at the heart of the system' (CJS 2007: 7). The Plan reports on considerable progress in improving the treatment of victims and witnesses who are involved in the criminal justice system. There is no recognition that promoting justice and fairness in society (particularly in relation to victims of crime, many of whom do not report their victimisation to the police) calls for the input of other State agencies that are not part of the criminal justice system, but whom victims will approach for help, such as the National Health Service. Indeed, the only context in which health provision is mentioned is in a reference to mentally disordered offenders. This exclusive focus on the criminal justice system offers nothing to victims who do not report their victimisation and very little to the majority of victims who do not have the satisfaction of seeing the person who victimised them becoming subject to criminal justice sanctions.

Conclusion

There is no doubt that very significant advances have been made in improving the position of victims and witnesses and that further important developments are still taking place. The introduction of Witness Care Units, the implementation of the *Code of Practice*, the introduction of a range of standards and performance indicators that require the police and other criminal justice agencies to monitor and improve the quality of their engagement with victims and witnesses, and the extended role of the CPS will undoubtedly help victims and witnesses to cope more effectively with the criminal justice process.

However, we suggest that there are two difficult and important issues that policy-makers have not yet resolved. The first is the priority still being given to rights and services which also contribute to the achievement of criminal justice objectives including meeting targets on conviction rates, narrowing the justice gap and increasing confidence in the criminal justice system. As a result, there is continuing concern that victims and witnesses are being recognised less for their own needs than for the role they can play in helping to deal with offenders. The second problem is the preoccupation with measuring victim and witness satisfaction, rather than being clear about what are desirable outcomes for victims, then setting out to measure how well those outcomes have been achieved. While victim and witness satisfaction is important and must be monitored, it should not be the main measure of progress. This is because preoccupation with satisfaction rather than with other equally important outcomes (such as every eligible victim being invited to make a VPS) will tend to inhibit the type of real cultural change that would ensure substantive improvements in the treatment victims and witnesses receive.

In addition, there is a danger that the 'victims' cause is being hijacked for political use. In Garland's terms we have seen the creation of 'symbolic victims' to justify controversial policies such as the reduction in expenditure on criminal legal aid and limiting access to jury trials. If this continues, it will risk provoking unjustified opposition to the otherwise uncontroversial development of victims' rights. It also obscures the fact that penal measures that are expensive (thereby drawing resources away from services to victims) and not very effective at reducing offending, are of little benefit to victims and should not be promoted as something that victims want or need. There is the further problem of the 'tainting' of victims' interests in the media, such as with the Victim's Surcharge scheme where an association is created between public resentment of, for example, speeding fines with funding for victims' organisations. We could ask if it might be better for the Government to fund prisons from the Victim's Surcharge and fund victim services from general taxation?

Meanwhile, the notion – so often expressed in Government statements about the criminal justice system – that the system needs to be 're-balanced' in favour of the victim is, as Newburn points out, misleading. This is because it suggests that offenders already have too many rights 'and that somehow the position of defendants needs to be worsened in order to improve the situation of victims' (Newburn 2007: 366). There is much that can be done to improve the situation of victims without having to make things worse for defendants.

It is not yet clear how some of the new services within the criminal justice system will be evaluated. If they are successful in improving the experience of victims and witnesses, will this be sufficient to safeguard their future or will their survival depend on the extent to which they contribute to the achievement of criminal justice objectives? A truly victim-centred strategy would prioritise services aimed at reducing the impact of crime on those most directly affected and would not be driven by ulterior motives.

The greatest concern, however, and the issue which affects the majority of victims, is the comparatively low priority given to the many needs of victims that can be dealt with only outside the criminal justice system. This is demonstrated by the relative absence of initiatives within community-based public services and the inadequate funding of victim services in the voluntary sector. The Government has previously said that it is aware of this discrepancy, but there is little evidence of awareness of the need for social provisions within its strategy for victims. It remains to be seen whether funds will be provided to enable these proposals to become a reality.

Important choices will made during the next two to three years. But at the moment it looks as if, despite tremendous efforts to reform the criminal justice system for the benefit of victims and witnesses, priorities are still determined by relatively narrow criminal justice objectives. These unfortunately bring significant benefits only to witnesses in criminal proceedings and to a minority of victims of crime, while most victims are still not entitled to receive services on the basis of their own needs rather than the needs of the criminal justice system.

Notes

1   The Office for Criminal Justice Reform is a governmental unit that reports to the Attorney General, Home Secretary, and Minister of Justice.
2   Justice and Victims Unit, 14/08/2001, Home Office Circular 35/2001.
3   Criminal Justice Performance Directorate newsletter for Local Criminal Justice Boards. Update 23, Ref: LCJB/07/2004, 7 June 2004.
4   CPS Press Release 112/04, *Specialist Domestic Violence Courts point the way ahead*, 22/03/04, accessed at www.cps.gov.uk/news/pressreleases/archive/112_04.html
5   Association of Chief Police Officers, Rape Working Group (2002) 'Sexual assault referral centres: getting started', accessed at: www.crimereduction.homeoffice.gov.uk/sexual/sexual15a.pdf
6   Speech by Alan Campbell MP to Lancashire and Cumbria constabularies' joint conference 7 November 2008. Available at: http://press.homeoffice.gov.uk/Speeches/alan-campbell-speech-responding
7   Press Release by David Blunkett, Home Secretary, Lord Irvine, Lord Chancellor, and Lord Goldsmith, Attorney General, 21 May 2003. CJS online: www.cjsonline.org.uk/publications/archive.html

References

Auld, Lord Justice (2001) *Review of the Criminal Courts of England and Wales*. http://www.criminal-courts-review.org.uk.
Criminal Justice System (2003) *A New Deal for Victims and Witnesses: National strategy to deliver improved services, July 2003*. London: Home Office Communication Directorate. http://www.crimereduction.homeoffice.gov.uk/victims/victims24.htm
Criminal Justice System (2004) *No Witness, No Justice: The National Victim and Witness Care Programme*. London: The Cabinet Office. http://archive.cabinetoffice.gov.uk/opsr/documents/pdf/cjs_final.pdf
Criminal Justice System (2007) *Working Together to Cut Crime and Deliver Justice: A Strategic Plan for 2008–2011. An overview* Cm 7247. London: Office for Criminal Justice Reform. http://www.cjsonline.gov.uk/downloads/.../pdf/1_CJS_Public_ALL.pdf
Crown Prosecution Service (2009) *The Prosecutor's Pledge*. http://www.cps.gov.uk/publications/prosecution/prosecutor_pledge.html
Dunn, P. (2007) 'Matching service delivery to need', in S. Walklate (ed.), *Handbook of Victims and Victimology*. Cullompton: Willan Publishing, pp. 255–81.

Garland, D. (2001) *The Culture of Control: Crime and social order in contemporary society*. Oxford: Oxford University Press.

Graham, J., Woodfield, K., Tibble, M. and Kitchen, S. (2004) *Testaments of Harm: A qualitative evaluation of the Victim Personal Statements Scheme*. London: National Centre for Social Research. http://www.natcen.ac.uk/natcen/pages/publications/AcrC2101.pdf

Home Office (1998) *Speaking Up for Justice: Report of the Interdepartmental Working Group on the treatment of vulnerable and intimidated witnesses in the criminal justice system*. London: Home Office. http://www.homeoffice.gov.uk/documents/sufj.pdf

Home Office (2005) *Domestic Violence*: A National Report. London: Home Office.

Kelly, L., Lovett, J. and Regan, L. (2005) *A Gap or a Chasm? Attrition in reported rape cases*. Home Office Research Study 293. London: Home Office. www.crimereduction.homeoffice.gov.uk/sexual/sexual13.htm

Kershaw, C., Nicholas, S. and Walker, A. (2008) *Crime in England and Wales 2007/08: Findings from the British Crime Survey and police recorded crime*. Home Office Statistical Bulletin 07/08. London: Home Office. www.homeoffice.gov.uk/rds/pdfs08/hosb0708.pdf

Maguire, M. with Bennett, T. (1982) *Burglary in a Dwelling: The offence, the offender and the victim*. Cambridge Studies in Criminology 49. London: Heinemann.

Mawby, R. (2007) 'Public sector services and the victim of crime', in S. Walklate (ed.), *Handbook of Victims and Victimology*. Cullompton: Willan Publishing, pp. 209–39.

Mawby, R. and Walklate, S. (1994) *Critical Victimology: International Perspectives*. London: Sage.

Morgan, R. and Sanders, A. (1999) *The Uses of Victim Statements*. London: Home Office. http://www.homeoffice.gov.uk/rds/pdfs/occ-vicstats.pdf

Moore, L. and Blakeborough, L. (2008) *Early findings from WAVES: Information and service provision*. Ministry of Justice Research Series 11/08. London: Office for Criminal Justice Reform. http://www.cjsonline.gov.uk/downloads/application/pdf/WAVES.pdf

Newburn, T. (2007) *Criminology*. Cullompton: Willan Publishing.

Parliamentary and Health Service Ombudsman (2007) *Annual Report 2006–07: Putting principles into practice*. London: The Stationery Office. www.ombudsman.org.uk/improving_services/annual_reports/ar07/

Parliamentary and Health Service Ombudsman (2008) *Annual Report 2007–08: Bringing wider public benefit from individual complaints*. London: The Stationery Office. http://www.ombudsman.org.uk/pdfs/ar_08.pdf

Plotnikoff, J. and Wolfson, R. (2004) *In Their Own Words: The experiences of 50 young witnesses in criminal proceedings*. London: National Society for the Prevention of Cruelty to Children/Victim Support. http://www.nspcc.org.uk/Inform/research/Findings/intheirownwords_wda48258.html

Plotnikoff, J. and Wolfson, R. (2007) *Evaluation of Young Witness Support: Examining the impact on witnesses and the criminal justice system*. London: Ministry of Justice. http://www.justice.gov.uk/docs/MoJresearchSummary2Mk2.pdf

Raine, J.W. and Smith, R.E. (1991) *The Victim/Witness in Court Project. Report of the Research Programme*. London: Victim Support.

Reiner, R. (2000) *The Politics of the Police* (3rd edn). Oxford: Oxford University Press.

Rock, P. (2004) *Constructing Victims' Rights: The Home Office, New Labour, and victims*. Oxford, Oxford University Press.

Shapland, J., Willmore, J. and Duff, P. (1985) *Victims in the Criminal Justice System*. Cambridge Studies in Criminology 53. Aldershot: Gower.

Spalek, B. (2006) *Crime Victims: Theory, policy and practice*. Basingstoke: Palgrave Macmillan.

Tonry, M. (2004) *Punishment and Politics: Evidence and emulation in the making of English crime control policy*. Cullompton: Willan Publishing.

Victim Support (1995) *The Rights of Victims of Crime: A policy paper by Victim Support*. London: Victim Support.

Victim Support (2002) *Criminal Neglect: No Justice Beyond Criminal Justice*. London: Victim Support. http://www.victimsupport.org/About%20us/Publications%20section/ResearchReports

Victim Support (2003) *Policy on Restorative Justice in Criminal Justice*. London: Victim Support. http://www.restorativejustice.org.uk/.../Vic_Supp_on%20RJ_in_CJOct03.pdf

Victim Support (2005) *Victim Support Annual Report and Accounts 2005*. London: Victim Support.

Victim Support (2006) *Crime and prejudice: The support needs of victims of hate crime. A research report*. London: Victim Support. http://www.victimsupport.org/About%20us/Publications%20section/ResearchReports

Victim Support (2007) *Victim and Witness Review: Annual Report and Accounts 2007*. London: Victim Support. http://www.victimsupport.org/About%20us/Publications%20section/ResearchReports

Zedner, L. (1997) 'Victims', in M. Maguire, R. Morgan and R. Reiner (eds), *The Oxford Handbook of Criminology* (2nd edn). Oxford: Oxford University Press.

Chapter 4

'Rebalancing the Criminal Justice System in favour of the victim': the costly consequences of populist rhetoric

Michael Tonry

No informed person doubts that the Labour Government's crime control policies were in part cynical efforts to win electoral support by demonstrating that Labour was tougher on crime than the Conservatives (e.g., Windlesham 1996). Rod Morgan, formerly head of the Youth Justice Board of England and Wales and Her Majesty's Inspector of Probation, attributed Labour's illiberal policies to a tendency to seek 'short-term electoral gain rather than effectiveness in changing behaviour or creating a safer world' (Morgan 2006: 111; to like effect: Downes and Morgan 2007: 214–16, 221–22). At least in part, Labour's policies were 'expressive', meant at least as much to acknowledge public anxieties and resentments as to accomplish anything substantive (Garland 2001).

Two phrases – 'rebalancing the Criminal Justice System in favour of the victim' and 'restoring public confidence' – recur in policy documents and politicians' speeches. A 2001 Home Office report to Parliament, *Criminal Justice: the Way Ahead*, combining them, set the goal of 'putting the needs of victims more at the centre of the CJS to raise public confidence' (Home Office 2001: 10). In subsequent usage, 'centred' victims were usually invoked in relation to policies meant to treat offenders more severely or less fairly and public confidence in relation to antisocial behaviour orders.

The White Paper announcing the Criminal Justice Act 2003 averred in its first paragraph, 'This White Paper aims to rebalance the system in favour of victims, witnesses, and communities' (Home Office 2002: 1). Comparable language appears again and again. In a more prosaic setting, the Home Office Departmental Report for 2007 specified 'Rebalancing the criminal justice system in favour of the law-abiding majority and the victim' as 'Strategic Objective IV' (Home Office 2007b: 38).

Both phrases were invoked to justify policies and practices that violate or undermine fundamental, long-standing, and widely shared ideas about personal liberty and procedural fairness. Conspicuous examples include the 2003 Act's abrogation of the eight-centuries-old double jeopardy rule,[1] incursions into jury trial rights, and weakening of evidentiary and procedural rules designed to protect against wrongful convictions (Tonry 2004a: 21–2). The best-known example is the antisocial behaviour order (ASBO), which sidesteps defendants' traditional criminal law protections by authorising civil proceedings for allegations of broadly defined 'antisocial behaviour' and making breaches of the resulting civil orders criminal offences punishable by prison sentences up to five years (Tonry and Bildsten 2009).

My aim here is to identify a range of undesirable unintended consequences that flowed from recent Labour Government policies. This essay has four sections. The first examines the rebalancing rhetoric and what it might mean. It is a non sequitur. Treating defendants badly has nothing to do with treating victims well, and vice versa. The defendants/victims distinction in any case is empirically untenable; most people have been or will be offenders; victims and offenders are often the same people at different times (or their parents, children, or neighbours).

The second section discusses programmes for victims in England and Wales and the United States. The 'centring' rhetoric, by shifting attention away from aiding victims and towards disadvantaging offenders, is making English policies more similar to American ones. This is a pity. Any informed and fair-minded person would agree that England runs rings around the United States in its constructive policies towards victims.

The third section discusses ASBOs, because of their association with political rhetoric and their controversial nature. Often, as in the 2003 Home Office document, *A New Deal for Victims and Witnesses*, ASBOs were expressly linked to restoration of public confidence and 'new ways of protecting and providing resolution to victims' (2003: 5–6). There is no credible evidence that their use decreased the prevalence of antisocial behaviour or public anxiety. Although Government documents regularly claim substantive success, those claims are neither well-founded nor credible. The best example of disingenuous argument is a repeated practice of claiming declining public discontent about antisocial behaviour by comparing later years' British Crime Survey (BCS) findings with those from 2002–03, when discontent was the highest ever measured. If other plausible comparison years are used, BCS data show that public dissatisfaction has increased since enactment of the ASBO legislation.

The fourth section discusses the unhappy consequences of England's shift from substantive to expressive crime and antisocial behaviour policies. There are seven. The first four – the rebalancing rhetoric's displacement of attention from victims to offenders, and the ASBO's fostering of a culture of complaint, exacerbating public discontent, and worsening intergenerational conflict – are discussed in the second and third sections. There are three others. First, public anxieties and fears about crime victimisation have increased. Second, Labour's preoccupation with repressive crime policies increased public dissatisfaction and intolerance and risked exacerbating social cleavages between the haves and the have-nots. Third, by insisting that traditional ideas about civil liberties, procedural protections, and human rights are expendable in the name of public order, the Labour Government risked undermining normative beliefs and human rights policies long seen as fundamental in Western societies.

Under the Labour Government, England slipped well down the slope of obliviousness to important issues of civil liberty and procedural fairness. This is a pity in its own right, and it may be why there was less resistance in contemporary England than would have occurred in earlier times, or than occurs now in other countries, to policies that sacrifice fundamental liberties and interests of citizens in the name of public order. Examples besides ASBOs include proposals for national identity cards, ubiquitous CCTV and speed cameras, creation of the world's most extensive criminal justice system DNA database, and regular police surveillance of non-violent protestors.

Rebalancing rhetoric

The Criminal Justice Act 2003 enacted new policies and programmes for victims and reduced procedural and human rights protections for alleged offenders. Shortly after the Act's enactment, the National Victims Conference was told that government 'must ensure that the criminal justice system is rebalanced in favour of victims' (National Victims Conference 2004: 10).

The notion of rebalancing is fundamentally misconceived, as John Humphrys of Radio Four's *Today* programme explained in *Lost for Words: the mangling and manipulation of the English language*:

> Politicians from all parties tell us endlessly that the criminal justice system needs 'rebalancing' in favour of the victim. That's a pretty safe proposition to defend. Surely we must all be on the side of victims. So if the system needs rebalancing in their favour let's get on with it.
>
> But this is a manipulation of the word's meaning. Those famous scales in the hands of Blind Justice are not meant to symbolize balancing the interests of the victim against the interests of the accused. They are there to weigh the evidence of the prosecution

against that of the defence. That's it. The interests of the victim are no different from the interests of society as a whole: to see justice done, nothing more, nothing less. Victims might well want revenge – it is the most human of instincts – but the judicial system should not. One of its purposes is to prevent it.

What is generally meant by 'rebalancing' the system is making it easier to get a conviction by lowering the burden of proof – by tipping the scales a bit. It means that fewer of the guilty will be acquitted. It also means that more of the innocent will be convicted. That may or may not be a good reason for doing this but it has nothing to do with redressing the system in favour of the victim. How would sending an innocent man to jail do that? (Humphrys 2004: 307)

Senior police officers including Sir John Stephens, long-time Commissioner of the Metropolitan Police, regularly used similar rhetoric. It came straight from the tabloids. Lord Windlesham examined the crime coverage of *The Sun*, the *Daily Mail* and *The Times* in the early 1990s and interviewed their editors. Here is how he summarised the newspapers' messages:

The balance in the criminal justice system had been tilted towards the protection of the innocent at the expense of failing to convict the guilty; and too often the interests of the offender (the description 'the criminal' being invariably preferred) were put above those of the victim. (Windlesham 1996: 48)

What can the undertaking to balance the system more in favour of the victim mean? Such language can be understood in three principal but irreconcilable ways. The first is phatic. The words do not mean anything literal, but are meant to give comfort, much as hospital visitors mumble reassurances to dying patients when no genuine reassurance is possible. Empathy is the message, and both the speaker and the listener understand that. That's the most generous – but least plausible – way to characterise the Labour Government's symbolic communications. The second is that the rebalancing language is merely expressive, cynical political spin meant to demonstrate to the public that the Government takes crime and victimisation seriously, can be trusted to be tough on crime, and thus when the time comes should be re-elected. The third is substantive. Most likely, some combination of expressive and substantive meanings was in Labour leaders' minds.

If something substantive was meant, what might that be? One possibility is that the criminal justice system really is a zero-sum game in which everything that benefits offenders hurts victims. Justice on this account is a pie of fixed size; a larger piece for victims means a smaller piece for offenders and vice versa. A second is that victims suffer psychic harm or personal frustration when alleged offenders are not convicted, or are punished less severely than victims want. A third is, as the Government's language asserts, that the system is somehow, in some real way, 'balanced against' the victims.

On these arguments, reducing procedural protections for offenders, and increasing the prevalence of wrongful convictions, hurts offenders, helps victims, and rebalances the system. None of these arguments, however, withstands scrutiny.

The parties to a criminal prosecution are the State and the defendant. The victim is an interested party, and as a witness may be a desirable or necessary participant, but the litigation is not between the victim and the defendant. The ultimate questions are whether the defendant has committed a crime and, if so, in what ways the awesome power of the State will appropriate the offender's property and liberty.

The idea that the criminal justice system is a zero-sum game in which every gain for one player is a loss for the other is wrong. This can be shown in a number of ways. Consider, for example, a case where a mentally disordered suspect is deemed incompetent to stand trial and therefore by definition, whether he committed the harmful acts or not, cannot be convicted. Few would suggest that a victim in such case would have any lesser claim for sympathy, assistance and compensation than if the offender were tried and convicted. Neither is it easy to imagine such a suggestion being made if the defendant were acquitted because some crucial piece of incriminating evidence was deemed inadmissible, or if the assailant was never identified. The victim's ethical claim is the same, no matter what happens to the defendant.

Turning the subject around, I've never heard anyone make a zero-sum game argument from the offender's perspective. Nothing that is done to provide assistance or support to victims adversely affects offenders. Treating victims well, better, or sympathetically does no damage to offenders. To the contrary, because many offenders at other times in their lives are victims, as a class they have a substantial self-interest in having victims be treated well.

There are good reasons why the State should be sympathetic to victims' suffering and needs, and should develop programmes to address them. Chapter 2 of the White Paper (Home Office 2002) offered a raft of proposals, many worthy, for improvements in addressing victims' needs, and the corresponding provisions of the Criminal Justice Act enacted most of them. Reasonable people can disagree about details, but few will disagree that victims should be dealt with sympathetically and supportively. That implies nothing, however, about treating defendants and offenders badly.

The reverse implication also is true: treating offenders well, better, or sympathetically does no damage to victims. Victims have the same interests as other citizens in having a criminal justice system that is fair, efficient, and humane, and it is hard to see how they benefit from its degradation.

There are self-interested reasons why victims should oppose changes that treat defendants and offenders worse. Many of today's victims have been offenders or in future will be, or their children or other loved ones have been or will be, and will therefore themselves suffer from weakened procedural protections. The evidence for this is overwhelming and comes from many sources. I focus on the Crime and Justice Survey (C&JS), a large-scale representative household survey on self-reported offending conducted by the Home Office. To substantiate its conclusions, more briefly I refer to the Government's 'Offenders Index' of people who have been convicted of crimes, and to a plethora of more narrowly focused surveys and data sources.

In the first six months of 2003, the C&JS interviewed around 12,000 people aged 10 to 65 living in private households in England and Wales (Budd, Sharp and Mayhew 2005). People were asked whether they had ever committed any of 20 core offences falling into seven broad categories: burglary, thefts of or from vehicles, other thefts, vandalism, robbery, assault, and drug sales. Absent from the list were lower-seriousness offences including drunk driving and other driving offences and higher-seriousness offences such as child abuse, sexual assaults, and homicides.

Fifty-two per cent of male respondents and 30 per cent of female respondents admitted to committing one of the target offences. The offences were not primarily trivial. Thirty-two per cent of men and 17 per cent of women admitted committing assaults and, in majorities of incidents, causing physical injuries.

Those numbers substantially understate the real prevalence of offending. The C&JS researchers point out that the survey seriously under-counted several categories of people who are disproportionately likely to be offenders (Budd, Sharp and Mayhew 2005: ch. 1). The research design omitted people living in institutions; many of those in prisons and jails are active offenders, and those in mental institutions and student accommodation typically have higher offending rates than does the general population. Moreover, a household survey does not reach homeless and highly mobile people, other social categories likely to be characterised by higher than average offending probabilities.

In addition, the C&JS managed to interview only 74 per cent of its sample. The researchers point out that 'those with particularly chaotic lifestyles might be difficult to contact and more likely to refuse' to participate, and that 'non-respondents tend to be more antisocial than respondents' (Budd, Sharp and Mayhew 2005: 3). Farrington et al. (2006), reporting on interviews at age 48 in the Cambridge Study in Delinquent Development, observe:

Surveys in which only about 75 per cent of the target sample (or even less) are interviewed are likely to produce results which seriously underestimate the true prevalence and frequency of antisocial and criminal behaviour. An increase in the percentage interviewed from 75 per cent to nearly 95 per cent leads to a disproportionate increase in the validity of the results. (2006: 14–15)

Lesser reasons to regard the lifetime prevalence figures as significant underestimates are such familiar methodological problems as individuals' reluctance to talk about embarrassing subjects and, probably more serious, recall problems. We tend to forget lots of details about our lives including, as we get older, less serious misconduct when we were young.

When these things are added together, the 52 per cent male and 30 per cent female offending prevalence figures probably underestimate true prevalence by a third or more. If so, 78 per cent of men and 45 per cent of women at some time will be offenders *concerning the sets of offences the C&JS asked about.* When omitted offences such as drunk driving, other serious driving offences, child abuse, and sexual crimes are added in, the rates will be higher still.

This conclusion about the wide prevalence of offending is confirmed by other sources. The Government's Offenders Index (OI) showed that 33 per cent of men and 9 per cent of women born in 1953 had been convicted of a standard list offence by age 46 (Budd, Sharp and Mayhew 2005: 7). These numbers are lower than the C&JS numbers but there is a ready explanation: most offenders are not caught. In the C&JS, '[Only] a quarter of those who had offended at some time in their lives had been arrested at least once, a fifth had been to court charged with an offence, and 16 per cent sentenced to a fine, community penalty or custody' (Budd, Sharp and Mayhew 2005: viii).

Home Office research on self-reported delinquency shows that 57 per cent of males and 37 per cent of females aged 12–30 admitted committing at least one serious offence (Flood-Page *et al.* 2000). Those figures are probably low. The Cambridge Study in Delinquent Development found that 92 per cent of a sample of London working-class males born in 1953 admitted committing a serious offence by age 32 and 93 per cent by age 48 (Farrington *et al.* 2005: 3). Other Home Office research shows that offenders have especially high rates of victimisation and that victims and offenders are often the same people, repeatedly changing roles over time (Stratford and Roth 1999).

Many victims will benefit from changes designed to treat offenders better. Likewise, many of them and others they love will suffer from changes that treat today's and tomorrow's offenders worse. There is thus little positive to be said about a shift away from a substantive focus on addressing victims' needs towards a rhetorical focus on treating offenders more harshly. Whatever case can be made for the Labour Government's adoption of severer crime policies, it cannot reasonably be claimed that benefiting victims is a credible part of it.

Programmes for victims in England and America

Policies and politics in England and Wales concerning victims are schizophrenic. In many ways, programmes for victim assistance, compensation, and support are admirable, especially compared with those in the United States. They are well established, respected, and financially supported by the central government, and extensive efforts have long been underway to improve them (e.g. Home Office 2002: ch. 2; Home Office 2003).

In other ways, they are being undermined. Governmental financial support in recent years in constant pounds has been declining. The claim that policies that hurt offenders benefit victims has shifted emphasis away from meeting victims' social welfare and service needs towards more expressive policies along American lines such as making offenders pay for victims' programmes and allowing victims a voice in parole release decisions.[2]

In this section I discuss victims' programmes in England and America. This is not entirely easy to do. Evaluations of the effectiveness of these programmes are rare. Basic data on national-level funding and on programme outputs are scant and in both countries are usually several years out of date when they are published.[3]

Programmes for support of victims and assistance to them are considerably more advanced in England and Wales than in the United States.[4] Victim Support has existed since 1974. Largely funded by the national government, its mission is one-on-one provision of information, advice and assistance to crime victims. No national organisation remotely like Victim Support exists in the United States, and equivalent State programmes are fragmented and highly dependent on erratic income flows from fees and fines paid by offenders.

A victim compensation programme, funded by the central government, has existed in England since 1964. Such programmes operate in all American States and receive three-eighths of their funding from the federal government; the federal money, however, comes not from general government revenues but from fines and restitution paid by offenders. Victims' needs for medical and hospital care in England are met by the National Health Service. In the United States, such expenses must generally be met from private funds or insurance, the latter being a resource nearly 60 million Americans lack.[5] Recent national-level initiatives in England have included extensive attention to victims' needs and services and a host of programmes are in place or under development. Fewer new initiatives were underway in the United States and in 2008 victim programme advocates were struggling to find political support to prevent a Bush Administration plan to transfer $2 billion from the federal Crime Victims Fund to general revenues; if the transfer had occurred, it would have brought grant programmes 'to a close at the end of that fiscal year, dropping from $590 million in compensation and victims assistance support to zero on October 1, 2009' (National Association of VOCA Assistance Administrators 2008).

Thirty years ago, the victims' movements of England and Wales and the United States had more in common than in contrast, with one crucial difference. What they had in common was a sense that victims' welfare needs were generally overlooked, that victims often needed assistance such as information, sympathy, counselling, and money, and that judges and prosecutors were not very good at keeping victims informed. Programmes were started or expanded in both countries under the rubrics of victim assistance, victim compensation, and victim/witness notification. Victim support and compensation received comparatively greater emphasis in England and witness notification programmes and victim impact statements received more emphasis in the United States. In recent years, England has more than caught up in relation to notifications and victim impact statements. The United States continues to lag far behind England with respect to victim support and compensation.

The crucial difference was that the victims' movement in the US was primarily negative, angry at offenders and vindictive towards them. When the victims' movement began in England, it was positive, sympathetic towards victims, and constructive in its efforts to help them. This greater determination to punish offenders probably explains greater US emphasis on witness notification programmes and victim impact statements at sentencing. The US movement was an odd-bedfellows alliance of right-wing law-and-order politicians, and usually-left-wing-but-on-these-issues-right-wing radical feminists who were primarily concerned with domestic violence (Zimring 1989; Gottschalk 2006).[6] The English alliance was between liberal reformers and social work-influenced probation officers (Rock 1991).

The US movement quickly took on the vindictive tint it retains. President Ronald Reagan appointed the President's Task Force on Victims of Crime (1982), headed by a right-wing ideologue named Lois Haight Herrington. It promoted four key ideas. First, criminal justice is a zero-sum game; you're for victims or for offenders; you can't be both; claiming to be for both is being for offenders.[7] Second, it's unfair that constitutional provisions give procedural rights to offenders but not to victims; victims need a victims' bill of rights enshrined in the US constitution. Third, victims' impact statements should be prepared in every case and victims should be entitled to offer their views on prosecution, sentencing and paroling decisions. Fourth, victim compensation and assistance programmes, funded by offenders and not by public funds, should be established.

These beginnings had pernicious effects. First, the idea of a zero-sum game endures. The 2004 Office for Victims of Crime *Report to the Nation*

2003 described the 'underlying philosophy of everything OVC does' (p. vii): 'putting victims first'. The report went on, 'That is why, for example, Attorney General John Ashcroft gave victims and survivors of the Oklahoma City bombing the option [in person, on site, by closed-circuit television, at federal government expense] to view the execution of Timothy McVeigh' (p. 3).

Second, the proposed federal constitutional amendment by 2004 had been supported in 33 states; only 34 are needed to amend the US Constitution. It provides, 'The victim, in every criminal prosecution, shall have the right to be present and to be heard at all critical stages of critical proceedings' (p. v). That primarily symbolic effort failed. No other State legislature endorsed it.

Third, the US Supreme Court decision in *Payne v. Tennessee*, 501 US 808 (1991), took the idea of victim impact statements to its extreme. It allowed evidence of the worthiness of two homicide victims and the grief suffered by their survivors to be introduced into a death penalty hearing as aggravating circumstances as part of a 'victim impact statement'. *Payne* overturned an earlier decision, *Booth v. Maryland*, 482 US 496 (1987), in which the Supreme Court had held that victim impact statements could not be introduced in death penalty hearings because of the risk that they would distract juries from offenders' blameworthiness to the value of the particular life their act extinguished. The court observed there is no 'justification for permitting such a decision [death] to turn on the perception that the victim was a sterling member of the community rather than a person of questionable character' (p. 506).

Fourth, federal victim compensation funding is entirely derived from fines and confiscations from offenders, not, as the December 2004 *Report to the Nation* proudly declaims: 'appropriated taxpayer dollars' (Office for Victims of Crime 2004: 1). A 2008 congressional briefing document prepared by the National Association of VOCA Assistance Administrators indicates that federal victims' programme funds come from offenders – 'not taxpayer revenues' – and warned that closing the Victims Compensation Fund into which offender fees and fines were deposited would mean that 'taxpayer money may be needed to replace offender-based revenue to support victim services' (2008: 2, 4). The symbolic message is that the State itself has no responsibilities towards citizens suffering the pains of criminal victimisation.

In England, by contrast, until the Labour Government adopted its rebalancing rhetoric, the emphasis remained on meeting victims' real needs. Over the years, support for victims increased steadily, including during the early years of the Labour Government. Governmental funding grew from £11.7 million in 1997 to £28 million in 2002 (Home Office 2002: 40). More recently, Victim Support's 2005 annual report documented £29 million expenditure on services to victims and witnesses. This supported community-based Victim Support services to 1.3 million people and

Witness Services support to 400,000 witnesses and victims and their families and friends.

Both demagoguery and earnest efforts to help people characterise both countries' policies towards victims. The more vindictive and punitive origins of US programmes have importantly shaped what has been done. Except for the shelter movement, rape crisis centres and related ancillary services, which are attributable to the determination and political influence of feminists and others concerned about violence against women, a large fraction of American federal resources has been used to improve law enforcement operations rather than to meet victims' welfare needs.

Table 4.1 shows the distribution by States of federal victim assistance money in fiscal years 2001 and 2002 (Office for Victims of Crime 2004: 19). Grants are made to States which then make sub-grants. One third of sub-grants went to domestic violence and rape crisis centres. More than half of those served were categorised as domestic violence victims (Office for Victims of Crime 2004: fig. 3).

Table 4.1 Distribution of US victim assistance funds, fiscal years 2001 and 2002 combined

Domestic violence shelters	22%
Rape crisis centres	12%
Mental health agencies	5%
Other private non-profit agencies	26%
Prosecutors offices	17%
Other law enforcement	9%
Other criminal justice agencies	4%
Government social service agencies	4%
American Indian tribes or support organisations	1%

Source: Office for Victims of Crime (2004)

A third of sub-grants went to law enforcement agencies. Substantial amounts are also expended on federal criminal justice agency operations. Federal victim funds (it bears repeating, derived from fines paid by offenders) are set aside to support personnel in all 93 US Attorneys' offices and in 56 FBI field offices and to operate a federal victim notification scheme. As the 'funding source of last resort' for a number of federal agencies, the Office for Victims of Crime funds a variety of purely law enforcement efforts, presumably on the rationale that victimisation will be prevented, and supports the US Department of Justice for 'victim travel to executions of federal prisoners when travel costs would be a financial hardship' (Office for Victims of Crime 2004: 35).[8]

I am unable to compare the relative levels of funding on victim assistance, compensation and support in the two countries. Because US federal government support for victims programmes comes primarily from the offender-derived federal Crime Victims Fund, because other State-funded programmes such as the National Health Service address English victims' needs, and because Victim Support mobilises millions of annual hours of volunteer effort, it is almost certain that comparatively more is invested in victims' programmes in England than in America.

US approaches towards victims are afflicting England and Wales. The most conspicuous is the adoption of the zero-sum game mentality, which shifts the focus from assistance and compensation to victims to anger and vindictiveness towards offenders. Particularly telling is the recent an-nouncement in *Cutting Crime – A New Partnership 2008–11* (Home Office 2007a: 37) that the 'Victims Fund (which invested £5.25 million over the past three years) will now be resourced by a Victims Surcharge, diverting money from offenders back into new support services for victims'.

Antisocial behaviour in England and Wales

ASBOs are the signature rebalancing, public confidence programme. Former British Prime Minister Tony Blair made it clear that they were designed to circumvent the criminal law. To the Labour Party Conference in September 2005, he made his displeasure with the criminal justice system clear: '[W]e are trying to fight twenty-first century crime – antisocial behaviour, drug dealing, binge-drinking, organised crime – with nineteenth century methods, as if we lived in the time of Dickens' (quoted in Morgan 2006: 110). There is a small irony here. Blair's 'twenty-first century crime' includes antisocial behaviour and binge-drinking. The latter, though unwise, is not criminal and the former need not be. After describing various measures taken to strengthen ASBOs, Blair explained, 'All of these measures ... have one thing in common: they bypass the traditional way the criminal justice system used to work ... the rules of the game have changed' (quoted in Morgan 2006: 97).

ASBOs mostly encompass behaviours that are not criminal, or are only minor crimes or ordinance violations, not because of the behaviours themselves but because of their possible effects. English Government documents invoke this concern as a primary theoretical rationale for ASBOs. Following the heading 'The Spiral of Antisocial Behaviour', the first major Government report to Parliament on the 'Respect Agenda' observed:

> If a window is broken or a wall is covered in graffiti it can contribute to a climate in which crime takes hold, particularly if intervention is not prompt and effective. An abandoned car, left for days on end, soon becomes a burnt-out car; it is not long before more damage and vandalism takes place. Environmental decline, antisocial behaviour, and crime go hand in hand and create a sense of helplessness that nothing can be done. (Home Office 2003: 14)

This closely resembles the highly suspect 'broken windows' logic in James Q. Wilson and George Kelling's celebrated *Atlantic Monthly* article (Wilson and Kelling 1982).[9] The hypothesis is that antisocial behaviour can start or contribute to a spiral of neighbourhood decline that leads people to become demoralised and alienated and in turn leads to more serious forms of crime and antisocial behaviour. The evidence supporting the hypothesis is at best mixed; the current near-consensus is that it has not been validated (Taylor 2001; Harcourt 2002; Sampson and Raudenbush 2004; Harcourt and Ludwig 2006; Hinkle and Weisburd 2008; Tonry and Bildsten 2009).[10] Even James Q. Wilson is agnostic. In an interview in 2004, Wilson observed, 'I still to this day do not know if improving order will or will not reduce crime. People have not understood that this was a speculation' (Hurley 2004: 1).

ASBOs were authorised by the Crime and Disorder Act 1998. The term antisocial behaviour was broadly defined to include any action that 'caused or was likely to cause harassment, alarm, or distress' to someone outside the actor's household. ASBOs enable police, local authorities and others to initiate *civil* legal proceedings against individuals alleged to have engaged in acts someone considers antisocial. The prohibited behaviour need not be criminal; it can be as innocuous as 'entering the city of Manchester'. Because ASBO cases involve civil actions, they are subject to 'more probable than not' standards of proof rather than the criminal law's 'proof beyond a reasonable doubt' and are not subject to procedural and evidentiary rules that restrict admission of evidence in criminal courts. Sometimes they are issued *ex parte*, without a trial being held or the defendant being notified. Violations of ASBOs constitute criminal offences that can be punished with prison sentences up to five years, with the issue being not whether, for example, entering Manchester is itself criminal, but whether by entering Manchester the defendant violated the terms of the ASBO.

The Government aggressively promoted their use, broadened their scope in the Police Reform Act 2002, established an Antisocial Behaviour Unit in the Home Office in 2003 and announced that the Audit Commission would assess local governments' performance in attacking antisocial behaviour. The Government promulgated the 'Respect Agenda', and developed a large number of other policies – citations for minor misbehaviour, 'antisocial behaviour contracts', ASBOs targeting young children, systems of fines and court orders for underperforming parents – aimed at regulating private behaviour considered unsuitable (Prime Minister's Strategy Unit 2006).

Many police forces, local governments and social service agencies were initially reluctant to seek ASBOs. In their first 30 months of operation, only 466 were issued and those mostly in a small number of places (Campbell 2002). Thereafter, under Government prodding, ASBOs proliferated through 2005, before declining in 2006 (the latest date through which data

Table 4.2 Antisocial behaviour orders issued, 1 April 1999 to 31 December 2006

Period	No. issued	No. breached (cumulative total)	% breached
2001	350		
2002	427		
2003	1,349	565	
2004	3,479	1,410	
2005	4,123	2,163	
2006	2,706	1,801	
Total through 2006	12,675	6,526	52

Source: Home Office Crime Reduction Website (4/1/99–2006);
http://www.crimereduction.homeoffice.gov.uk/asbos/asbos2.htm

were publicly available at the time of writing). Table 4.2 tells the tale. Burney (2005) notes that over the period April 1999 to September 2004, magistrates rejected only one per cent of applications for their issuance (Burney 2005: Appendix 1). Nearly half result in court determinations that they had been breached; through the end of 2003, 55 per cent of breaches resulted in prison sentences (Burney 2005: table 5.1). By 2006, approximately half the orders issued had been breached. The overall breach rate that year was 49 per cent, including 61 per cent among juveniles and 43 per cent among adults (Home Office data summarised in Ford 2008).

Many thousands have been issued, some of astonishing breadth. They have been used bizarrely (for example, forbidding a 13-year-old to ride his new dirt bike, an autistic child to stare over the fence from his family's yard, a child with Tourette's Syndrome to shout at passers-by, a prostitute to possess condoms in the environs of a public health clinic that distributed them free) and sometimes forbade surprising activities (for example, feeding seagulls, honking by taxi drivers for passengers, pigs escaping from sties). They have also been used illiberally (for example, forbidding entry into any retail store in Devon or Cornwall or a family to enter a town where its home is located). Finally, they have been used unjustly: sentencing shoplifters to longer terms for violating ASBOs than they would have received had they been convicted of shoplifting; prostitutes to prison for engaging in non-criminal acts of prostitution; beggars to prison at a time when prison sentences were not authorised following criminal convictions for begging.[11]

Whether the ASBO campaign has reduced the prevalence of antisocial behaviour is unknown. The Home Office neither funded nor undertook evaluation research to assess the effects of ASBOs on antisocial behaviour (Morgan 2006: 106). The National Audit Office observed, 'The absence of formal evaluation by the Home Office of the success of different interventions ... prevents local areas targeting interventions in the most efficient way to achieve the best outcome . . .' (2006: 5).[12] There are no data sources that allow measurement of temporal variation in the amorphous set of behaviours that have fallen within the scope of ASBOs. The British Crime Survey measures people's concern about antisocial behaviour, not its incidence.

Government reports often claim, on the basis of two sources of evidence, that ASBOs reduced the prevalence of antisocial behaviour (sometimes ignoring the conflation between people's views about antisocial behaviour and its occurrence). The Youth Crime Action Plan 2008, for example, claimed ASBOs 'can be very effective in reducing crime and antisocial behaviour' (Her Majesty's Government 2008: 20). The Home Office report *Cutting Crime – A New Partnership 2008–11* claimed that there is 'strong evidence' of effectiveness (Home Office 2007a: 22).

The first claim is that the percentage of BCS respondents describing various forms of antisocial behaviours as 'very' or 'fairly' big problems has declined since 2002/03 (e.g. Home Office 2007a: 9; Prime Minister's Strategy Unit 2007: 38). This is disingenuous. The percentages of respondents characterising behaviours as very or fairly big problems were at the highest levels ever recorded in 2002/03. As Table 4.3 shows, if 1998, the year of ASBO adoption, were used for comparison, or even the period 2003–04, levels in 2006–07 and 2007–08 were higher and the Government would have had to explain why levels of concern about antisocial behaviour increased.

Table 4.3 Percentage saying antisocial behaviours very or fairly big problem in their area, British Crime Survey, 1992–2007

Category	92	94	96	98	00	01–02	02–03	03–04	04–05	05–06	06–07	07–08
Noisy neighbours	8	8	8	8	9	10	10	9	9	10	11	10
Drunks, rowdies	n/a	n/a	n/a	n/a	n/a	22	23	19	22	24	26	25
Drug use/dealing	14	22	21	25	33	31	32	25	26	27	28	26
Teens hanging out	20	26	24	27	32	32	33	27	31	32	33	31
Rubbish, litter	30	26	26	28	30	32	33	29	30	30	31	30
Vandalism	26	29	24	26	32	34	35	28	28	29	28	27

Sources: Simmons and Colleagues 2002: table 9.13; Nicholas, Kershaw and Walker 2007; Home Office 2008; Kershaw, Nicholas and Walker 2008: table 5.03

The second claim is the observation that a National Audit Office study based on a study of 893 case files in six local areas showed that 'a majority of people [in their sample of cases] who received an antisocial behaviour intervention did not re-engage in antisocial behaviour' (Home Office 2007a: 22; parenthetical in original). 'In their sample' and 'antisocial behaviour intervention' are important qualifications. The sample cases were mostly not ASBO cases and young people were underrepresented. 'Just under a quarter' of the sample received ASBOs (actually, 21 per cent: 211) and of these 38 per cent were 17 and under (this compares with well over 50 per cent under 18 during the ASBO's early years) (National Audit Office 2006). Home Office data through December 2006 show that 61 per cent of people under 18 who received ASBOs breached them, compared with 43 per cent of those 18 and older (Ford 2008). The National Audit Office study thus undercounted young people, who fail at higher rates than their elders. As a result, the study's findings cannot fairly be generalised to the population of people who receive ASBOs. Thus neither claim that ASBOs have been effective withstands scrutiny.

Defining deviance up

There appear to be three related adverse negative effects of ASBOs. They have made English people more querulous, they have heightened levels of discontent, and they have exacerbated intergenerational conflict.

Elizabeth Burney (2005: 80) observed that ASBOs contributed to the growth of a 'culture of complaint': 'Service providers are increasingly expected to deal with problems that, before, might either have been ignored or dealt with between those involved.' Home Office data bear that observation out. Table 4.4 presents data from the 2003/04 British Crime Survey on respondents' designations of antisocial behaviour problems as 'big' or 'fairly big'. Three patterns leap out. First, most of the behaviours listed are not crimes. They are everyday irritants of life everywhere – speeding and illegally parked cars, litter, irresponsible dog owners, graffiti; only drug dealing and vandalism typically involve criminal

Table 4.4 'Biggest' antisocial behaviour problems reported by respondents, British Crime Survey, 2003–04

Category	Very big problem (%)	Fairly big problem (%)	Both combined (%)
Speeding	12	31	43
Illegally parked cars	9	22	31
Rubbish, litter	9	20	29
Fireworks	10	19	29
Vandalism, graffiti	8	20	28
Loitering teens	9	19	28
Drug use, dealing	9	16	25
Loose dogs and mess	6	18	24
Drunk, rowdy people	5	14	19
Abandoned cars	4	11	15

Source: Wood 2004: figure 3.2

behaviour. Second, levels of discontent are astonishingly high. Speeding was seen as a very or fairly big problem by 43 per cent of respondents and illegal parking by nearly a third. Just under a third were troubled by litter, graffiti and young people hanging about.[13] Third, two of the items – loitering teenagers and rowdy people – are in effect complaints about other people's use of public space.

What sociologists sometimes call the amplification of deviance has taken place. Behaviours such as speeding, parking illegally and depositing rubbish are routine frictions of everyday life. Perceptions of their veniality depend on perspective. Speeding is a nuisance, even a menace, to a resident of a crowded neighbourhood but a venial lapse to a driver late for an appointment. Most drivers sometimes cluck disapprovingly at other people speeding and at other times rationalise their own speeding as justified under the circumstances. Ditto illegal parking. Not quite ditto rubbish. Most people probably feel at least a twinge of guilt tossing crisp bags on the street, but as sins go it is a minor and commonplace one.

There are other signs that ASBOs increased public discontent and fostered intolerance. Findings from a survey in England's North-East by Halifax Pet Insurance showed that four in five adults believe that owners of troublesome pets should be issued a PASBO (a Pet Antisocial Behaviour Order), including 26 per cent who favoured issuance of PASBOs to owners of dogs that bark in the night (Womack 2005).

Exacerbating citizens' discontent

It is more likely that ASBOs increased than decreased citizens' concern about antisocial behaviour. English citizens are unhappier about antisocial behaviour in recent years than they were in the early 1990s, when the BCS began asking questions about it or in 1998 when the ASBO legislation was enacted. Table 4.3, on page 86, presents data from 12 waves of BCS data beginning in 1992. It shows percentages of respondents who said particular types of disorder were 'very' or 'fairly' big problems at two-year intervals between 1992 and 1998 and annually since 2000. For most behaviours, the percentages have risen substantially since 1998, in most cases by 20 per cent or more. British citizens were more troubled by antisocial behaviour in 2007–08 than they were in 1992 or 1996, before the ASBO had been conceived of, or than they were in 1998.

A 2006–2007 household survey of residents from 387 English local authorities (all but the Scilly Isles), the Best Value User Satisfaction Survey, showed extraordinarily high levels of dissatisfaction with various forms of antisocial behaviour (Department for Communities and Local Government 2007). The triennial survey attempts to measure citizens' satisfaction concerning a range of public services and subjects. Table 4.5 shows percentages of respondents saying various behaviours were a 'very' or 'fairly' serious problem in their areas in the Best Value User

Table 4.5 Percentages saying antisocial behaviours very or fairly big problem in their area, British Crime Survey (BCS), 1998, 2002–03, 2006–07, and Best Value User Satisfaction Survey, 2006–07

Category	BCS 1998 (%)	BCS 2002–03 (%)	BCS 2006–07 (%)	User survey 2006–07 (%)
Noisy neighbours	8	10	11	16
Drunks, rowdies	n/a	23	26	31
Drug use/dealing	25	32	28	43
Teens hanging out	27	33	33	57
Rubbish, litter	28	33	31	42
Vandalism	26	35	28	38

Sources: Department of Communities and Local Government 2007: table 15; Kershaw, Nicholas and Walker 2008: table 5.03

Survey for 2006–07 and, for comparison, in the British Crime Survey for 1998, 2002–2003 and 2006–2007. The 1998 data are shown because that is the year the ASBO legislation was enacted and 2002–03 because that year is usually used by the Government as a comparison year to claim subsequent falls in public dissatisfaction. The 2006–2007 BCS data show about the same levels of dissatisfaction as in 2002–2003 (the highest rates recorded to date) and significantly higher rates than in 1998.

The Best Value User Survey levels of dissatisfaction are substantially higher than those shown in BCS data for each behaviour. 'Teenagers hanging around' is a big or fairly big problem for 57 per cent of respondents and four out of 10 respondents gave those ratings to rubbish, vandalism and people using or dealing drugs.

Fostering intergenerational tensions

ASBOs, and the intense publicity campaigns associated with them (Burney 2005; Morgan 2006; Morgan and Newburn 2007), appear to have stoked the fires of adult resentment of common, developmentally predictable teenage behaviour. In June 2008, the Government's four children's commissioners were quoted in *The Times* as saying that 'attitudes have hardened towards older children since Labour came to power, mainly because of its antisocial behaviour agenda' (Bennett 2008). Table 4.6 shows data from the 2003–04 British Crime Survey on respondents' emotional responses to 'young people hanging around'. Fifty-four per cent expressed annoyance and 26 per cent expressed anger (Wood 2004; Bottoms 2006).

The teenage years are a period of experimentation and include the peak years for criminality (let alone lesser acting out) (Farrington 1986). A Home Office Survey on Young People and Crime showed that 25 per cent

Table 4.6 Emotional responses to 'young people hanging around' reported by respondents, British Crime Survey, 2003–04

Emotional response	Percentage of respondents*
Annoyance	54
Anger	26
Frustration	23
Worry	22

*Responses exceed 100 per cent; multiple responses allowed
Source: Wood 2004: table A 8.2

of 10 to 25-year-olds admitted to committing a crime in the preceding 12 months (30 per cent of males) and that just under a quarter admitted to committing at least one of four forms of antisocial behaviour in public (being rude or noisy so that people complained, behaving in a way that a neighbour complained, graffiti, or racial abuse). Among boys aged 14–19, well over a third admitted to antisocial behaviour so defined. Those rates would have been much higher if all the forms of antisocial behaviour covered in the BCS were asked about (Wilson, Sharp and Patterson 2006).

A subsequent survey carried out in 2006 reported similar findings for that year and also observed that 'the proportion of young people who reported committing an offence showed no change across all four waves of the survey [2003–2006] ... This pattern held for all offence categories. Similarly, there was no statistically significant change in the proportion of 10 to 17-year-olds and 18 to 25-year-olds who reported committing an offence' (Roe and Ashe 2008: 13). Among people 10 to 17 years-old, 27 per cent admitted to committing one of the four forms of antisocial behaviour and more than a third of 14 to 15 year-olds (Roe and Ashe 2008: table 3.1).[14]

One of the two 'biggest' BCS problems reported in 2004, and the biggest in the Best Value User Survey in 2006–07, was 'teenagers hanging around' (Wood 2004: 12). Teenagers hanging around is a fact not of modern but of human life. Kids do things in groups, home is a less appealing venue than almost anywhere else, and kids have to go somewhere. That sometimes they are numerous, noisy and untidy is not peculiarly characteristic of or endemic to England. Keith Towler, the children's commissioner who then led on juvenile justice issues, observed in June 2008 'that he and the other commissioners detected little understanding of the pressures on teenagers and a growing intolerance of the perfectly normal things most get up to' (Bennett 2008).

The House of Commons Home Affairs Committee, responding to criticisms about the trivial nature of many ASBOs, indignantly insisted that 'activities such as playing football in the street are not necessarily harmless' (Home Office 2005: 6). That improbable statement exemplifies a core ASBO problem. It is hard to imagine children playing in the streets being portrayed as harmful, much less seriously harmful and warranting criminal court action, anywhere but in England during the ASBO regime. The redefinition of speeding, illegal parking, football-playing children and loitering teenagers as serious antisocial behaviour in many British citizens' minds is not an accomplishment to celebrate.

The ASBO's glory days are past. Their use declined after 2005 and newspaper reports predict their slow death (Branigan 2007; Ford 2008; Travis 2008). Ed Balls, the Secretary of State for Children, in 2008 expressed the hope of living in 'the kind of society that puts Asbos behind us'. Jacqui Smith, the Home Secretary, however, referred to them as 'a ground-breaking innovation' (Travis 2008) and early in 2009 proposed their use to forbid young people 'wearing certain clothes' (Prince 2009).

Sir Simon Jenkins, long one of Britain's most distinguished journalists and sometime editor of *The Times*, shall have the last word on ASBOs here (because he writes more eloquently than I do):

> While some antisocial restraint short of court action may be needed in collapsed communities, such is the chaos of the Asbos that it is impossible to pick out the worthwhile from the counterproductive. The cynicism of these measures is beyond satire. Orwell would hang up his pen and retire. (Jenkins 2006)

Rhetorical excesses and expressive policy-making matter

Historian Clive Emsley (2005) at the end of *Hard Men*, his account of violent crime in England since 1750, observes that in our time of declining crime rates but demagogic tabloid treatment of crime, 'politicians themselves seem fully prepared to employ populist rhetoric and to undermine still further a legal system in which many have lost faith' (2005: 184).

Undermining public confidence in the legal system is *prima facie* not a good thing to do, and a perverse thing for a government to do. It is especially unfortunate at a time when other aspects of the contemporary world, variously referred to as conditions of late modernity or post-modernist angst, are commonly believed to have fostered insecurity generally and undermined faith in public institutions.

Over and above the ASBO's negative effects, the costs of populist posturing have been heavy. First, public anxieties and fears about real crime have increased. Second, populist posturing risks exacerbating social cleavages between the comfortable haves and the unruly and awkward have-nots. Third, by insisting that traditional ideas about civil liberties, procedural protections and human rights are expendable in the name of public order, Labour's criminal justice policies risk undermining norma-tive beliefs and human rights policies long seen as fundamental in Western societies.

Anxiety and risk aversion

Many newcomers to England are surprised by how much attention is paid to crime and crime prevention. Surveillance of people's lives by CCTV and speed-trap cameras is much more pervasive in England than in any other country. CCTV is everywhere: on city streets, in shops, in staircases, in parks, in parking garages, in the forecourts of petrol stations, even around private homes. Speed-trap cameras are ubiquitous in metropolitan areas. Nearly every car park has signs warning, 'Thieves operate here. Lock your car'. Many are as brightly lighted at night as football stadiums. Neighbourhood Watch signs festoon trees everywhere, including in tiny rural villages from which crime is nearly absent.

Not surprisingly, all of this emphasis on crime, vulnerability to crime, and prevention of crime makes people more aware of crime and makes them fearful. All of the blame should not fall on New Labour. Since the early 1980s, a succession of English governments has persistently focused on crime prevention, both visibly in the form of innumerable situational and urban design crime prevention programmes and rhetorically in the form of countless public warnings about risks of crime for citizens and consequences of crime for offenders. People who are repeatedly told that they are in jeopardy come to believe it, and to reify minor everyday crimes into existential threats (e.g. Tonry 2004a). The Labour Government continued those programmes but added to them its own rhetoric of institutional failure and unfairness to victims.

Evidence from the International Crime Victims Survey (the ICVS) shows that people in England and Wales (and the UK generally) worry more about crime than do people in most other Western countries. Since the second wave of the ICVS in 1992, respondents have been asked whether they feel unsafe or very unsafe on the street after dark. In most years, the percentages of English respondents saying yes is highest among Western European countries and among the major English-speaking countries (Australia, Canada, New Zealand, Scotland and the US). Since the first wave in 1989, the survey has also asked whether respondents have installed burglar alarms in their homes or high-security locks on their doors. More English homes have burglar alarms than in other Western European or English-speaking countries, and English rates are among the highest for special locks.

Victimisation rates for England fall in the middle range among the dozen or so countries that participate regularly in the ICVS. Nonetheless, fear of crime, as measured by feeling unsafe on the street at night, is highest among English respondents. Table 4.7 shows results from the second through fifth waves of data collection for Western European (the original EU 15 plus Switzerland) and English-speaking countries that participated in at least three waves. In three of the four waves the English percentage of respondents saying they feel unsafe is highest and in the other one (2000) it is second to Australia.

Table 4.7 Percentages of population feeling unsafe or very unsafe on the street after dark, ICVS second through fifth waves, Western European and English-speaking countries (participating in at least three waves)

Country	1992	1996	2000	2004–5
England	33	32	26	32
Scotland	***	26	19	30
Australia	31	***	34	27
N. Ireland	***	22	22	26
Belgium	20	***	21	26
Switzerland	***	17	22	***
France	***	20	22	21
Austria	***	20	***	19
Netherlands	22	20	18	18
Canada	20	26	16	17
USA	***	25	14	19
Sweden	14	11	15	19
Finland	17	17	18	14

***means data unavailable
Source: van Dijk, van Kesteren and Smit 2007: table 27

Three things stand out about the English results. Nearly a third of English respondents say they feel unsafe in all years, compared with 11 to 20 per cent of respondents in other European countries. English rates in most years are at least a third higher than those in Canada and the US and in some years are nearly double. Unlike in Canada and the US, where feelings of unsafeness have fallen in line with declining crime rates since 1996, in England they have held steady, despite similar declines in crime rates.

The last pattern is the most interesting. Canadian and US fear-of-crime patterns mirror the empirical reality of reduced chances of victimisation in both countries since the early 1990s. The same objective reduction in victimisation risk also existed in England, but levels of fear remained unchanged. Nothing can be proven from that pattern but an inference can reasonably be drawn that the high levels of fear are at least in part a consequence of the Labour Government's unceasing (to the date of writing) and highly visible preoccupation with crime and antisocial behaviour. The barrage of Government reports on crime and antisocial policies and proposals cited in this essay have no equivalents in Canada and the US. By contrast, crime has not for many years been a major partisan political issue in Canada (Webster and Doob 2007), and it has been absent from American political wars since the mid-1990s (Tonry 2004b: ch. 1).

Much the same pattern characterises ICVS data on respondents' efforts to protect themselves from crime. Questions in all five waves asked

Table 4.8 Percentages of households with burglar alarms, ICVS, all waves, Western European and English-speaking countries (participating in at least two waves)

Country	1989	1992	1996	2000	2004–5
England	24	22	27	34	42
Scotland	20	***	25	26	33
Australia	16	14	***	26	27
N. Ireland	8	***	11	16	38
Belgium	15	12	***	21	22
Switzerland	6	***	5	***	***
Italy	***	13	***	***	24
France	14	***	15	13	15
Austria	***	***	6	***	14
Germany	10	***	***	***	14
Netherlands	9	8	10	11	15
Denmark	***	***	***	7	9
Portugal	***	***	***	8	14
Canada	15	13	20	23	28
USA	16	***	21	24	28
Sweden	***	5	7	10	16
Spain	4	***	***	***	8
Finland	2	1	2	4	9

***means data unavailable
Source: van Dijk, van Kesteren and Smit 2007: table 28

whether respondents have installed burglar alarms or high-security door locks in their homes. Table 4.8 summarises results concerning burglar alarms. It reports data from Western European (EU 15 plus Switzerland) and English-speaking countries that participated in at least two waves of data collection on the burglar alarm question.

Three patterns stand out. First, the percentages of English respondents saying they had burglar alarms are the highest of the 18 countries shown in all five waves. Second, the English percentage in 1989 (24 per cent), the first ICVS year, is higher than that of any other non-UK European country except Italy in the fifth wave in 2004–05 (9 to 22 per cent). Third, the English percentages are generally about 50 per cent higher than those for the other English-speaking countries.

Focusing so assiduously on risks of crime and the perfidiousness of antisocial people, and putting the victim at the centre of the criminal justice system, has not demonstrably made English residents less fearful. Fear of crime and the felt need to take self-protective measures have not decreased since the ASBO was created in 1998 or since the victim-centring rhetoric came into wide use in 2001. These initiatives most likely worsened public anxieties in the same way they fostered discontent more generally.

Social cohesion

Poverty, disadvantage and diminished life chances are in no country randomly distributed. People who live lives of comparative disadvantage are much likelier than their more fortunate brethren to be poor, ill-educated, unemployed, mentally ill, drug dependent and involved in 'antisocial behaviour' and crime. In the United States, young blacks and Hispanics, especially males, are disproportionately poor and disadvantaged (Western 2006). In England, young Afro-Caribbeans and young whites of working-class backgrounds, again mostly males, occupy those social positions. Policies against crime and disorder that increase intolerance of the disadvantaged, and that diminish respect for their rights and liberties, further marginalise the marginalised, and lengthen the odds against their ever achieving normal, productive, satisfying patterns of life.

David Garland's magisterial *The Culture of Control* (2001) made 'expressive policies' a widely recognised term of art. He observed that rising crime rates, coupled with widespread belief among officials in the 1970s and 1980s that they could do little that would significantly affect crime rates and patterns, led policy-makers to search for ways to acknowledge citizens' fears and anxieties and at least appear to be doing something about crime. Expressive policies were the answer. Whether or not they were likely to work, their adoption expressed solidarity with law-abiding citizens and, if politicians were lucky, established tough-on-crime credentials for use in re-election campaigns. Zero-tolerance policing, mandatory minimum sentences, three-strikes laws and the 'War on Drugs' are the best-known American examples and ASBOs and 'rebalancing the system in favour of the victim' in myriad ways are the best-known English examples (Tonry 2004a).

One characteristic of this strategy, Garland noted, is that it is often accompanied by a 'criminology of the other', a tendency to target expressive policies on behaviours that are disproportionately committed not by members of the political majority but by more marginalised members of society. This is surely a reason why American drug policies focus on drug dealing in the streets rather than in the suites, and on cocaine, methamphetamine and marijuana rather than on the much more objectively dangerous drugs alcohol and nicotine. It is also why English ASBOs focused on 'yobs' and louts and targeted behaviours, whether or not criminal, that disturbed the law-abiding, and promised severer punishment and lessened procedural protections for the feckless and underclass people who commit most of the high-volume but low seriousness crimes that fill magistrates' and criminal court dockets.

The associations between social and economic disadvantage, chemical dependence, mental disorder and crime exist everywhere. England is not exceptional in those regards. Nor is England exceptional in having criminal courts or in punishing criminal behaviour. England's Labour

Government, however, has been exceptional in choosing to aggravate social discontent and to exacerbate tensions and weaken sympathies between the privileged and their less fortunate brethren. In most countries, small right-wing parties adopt such positions.

Fundamental norms

Prime Minister Blair in 2005 expressed impatience with traditional criminal justice values: 'The whole of our system starts from the proposition that its duty is to protect the innocent from being wrongly convicted . . . But surely our *primary* duty should be to allow law-abiding people to live in safety' (emphasis added; quoted in Morgan 2006: 110–11).

The element of New Labour's victims policy that is primarily rhetorical, in the putative name of reassuring the public and restoring public confidence, is unlikely to do either but is likely to undermine support for traditional human rights and procedural protections. By posing victims' and offenders' interests as being in fundamental conflict, Government policies threaten to undermine the foundation of liberal democracy itself.

Experiences with preventive detention in the United States and ASBOs in England demonstrate the risk. Under nearly two centuries of constitutional law doctrine, people accused of crimes in the United States could be held in detention before their trials only to prevent their absconding. They could not be held because of concern they might commit additional crimes. The law was clear, even if in practice judges sometimes disingenuously got round it by setting bail amounts so high (presumably often because particular offenders seemed especially dangerous) that the money could not be raised and the suspect remained in custody.

A fierce battle took place in the 1970s between due process liberals and law-and-order conservatives over proposals for an explicit preventive detention law for the District of Columbia. After several years' congressional conflict, a narrowly crafted law was enacted and its constitutionality was upheld. Another fierce battle ensued in the Congress over extension of the concept to the federal courts generally. Preventive detention provisions were enacted in the Bail Reform Act of 1984. The conservative post-1960s Supreme Court upheld them in *US v. Salerno*, 481 US 739 (1987). Preventive detention laws have since proliferated and are no longer especially controversial, culminating in the Court's decision in *Kansas v. Hendricks*, 521 US 346 (1997), upholding a Nebraska law permitting the continued confinement of dangerous offenders after expiration of their prison sentences (the 'dangerous offenders' provisions of the Criminal Justice Act 2003 are comparable).

Many in England's Government seem likewise to have forgotten why ASBOs were so controversial and resisted so vigorously in their early years. The House of Commons Home Affairs Committee in 2005, though nominally a body constituted to review policy and policy problems, expressed disappointment that 'social service departments and other key players such as local education authorities, the Children and Adolescent Mental Health Service, Youth Services, and some children's NGOs are often not fully committed to local ASB strategies' (Home Office 2005: 7). This is the same committee I quoted above that observed that children playing football is 'not necessarily harmless'.

The important point about the US preventive detention and the English ASBO stories is that policies that were initially widely seen as radical intrusions into individual liberty and as profoundly illiberal in time became accepted as normal and then led to adoption of broader policies that at the outset would have been unimaginable (e.g. broad-based and routine preventive detention in the United States in the 1970s; criminalisation of children playing football in the streets in 1970s–1990s England). The public, policy-makers and policy critics became accustomed to policies that were once unthinkable and in a sense forgot about issues of principle that only a few years earlier had seemed terribly important. Sensibilities, prevailing ways of looking at and thinking about things, changed, and profoundly anti-liberal policies became not only imaginable but difficult even to imagine as objectionable (Tonry 2004b).

Conclusion

The idea that government 'must ensure that the criminal justice system is rebalanced in favour of victims' (National Victims Conference 2004: 10) is nonsensical and dangerous. It is also fundamentally misconceived.

The Labour Government has been playing a dangerous game. By repeatedly talking and acting as if crime has reached crisis proportions and requires radical responses, at a time when crime rates have long been falling, the Government increased public anxieties and fears.[15] By repeatedly insisting that the criminal justice system was not working satisfactorily, the Government undermined faith in the legal system. By insisting that traditional procedural rights and protections are unimportant and can be cut back without sacrifice of anything important, public understanding and support for fundamental ideas about liberty, fairness and justice were undermined. Further diminutions may happily be accepted on receipt of similar assurances. It is a pity and does not augur well for the future of civil liberties and rights in England and Wales.

Notes

1 'The controversy between Henry II and Archbishop Thomas à Becket – and Henry's concession in 1176 following Becket's murder – that clerks convicted in the ecclesiastical courts were exempt from further punishment in the King's courts probably was primarily responsible for bringing about the

adoption of the concept of double jeopardy in the common law' (Friedland 1969: 5).

2   As Julian Roberts (2009) has recently, cogently, pointed out, arguments that might apply to provision of victim impact statements at sentencing, or allowing victim statements about the sentence to impose, have no substantive relevance to parole release decisions.

3   In the US, for example, *Office for Victims of Crime Report to the Nation 2007*, covering fiscal years 2005 and 2006 (ending 30 September 2005), was released late in 2008.

4   Developments through 1990 in both countries described in this and the following paragraph are based on the comprehensive and scholarly account in Maguire (1991). The American story through 1990 is told more passionately, and with much more who-what-where-when-and-why detail, by Marlene Young (1997), long-time director of the (US) National Organization for Victim Assistance. Two weighty books by Paul Rock (1991, 2004) tell the English story pretty much to their dates.

5   In fiscal years 2005 and 2006 combined, 53 per cent of victim compensation benefits were for medical and dental expenses, 11 per cent for mental health care and 4 per cent for forensic examinations in sexual assault cases (Office for Victims of Crime 2008: fig. 10).

6   This may explain why federally supported victim assistance programmes are heavily weighted towards domestic violence; 52 per cent of all victims served during fiscal years 2005 and 2006 were categorized as domestic violence victims (Office for Victims of Crime 2008: 15).

7   The late Norval Morris and I in 1985 had the pleasure of being told by Mrs Herrington that in her view we were for criminals. She at that time had some power over us. She was Assistant Attorney General for Justice Programs and had ultimate authority over funding for *Crime and Justice*, a book series Morris and I edited. Our offence was in publishing an essay on sex offences and offenders by Professor Donald West (1983) in which he asserted that some victims of child sexual offences suffer long-term adverse effects, but for others the experience has no lasting consequence. In Herrington's view no one who was for victims could possibly accept that conclusion or publish an essay expressing it. Funding was held up for 22 months. The then annual series barely survived.

8   Figures for fiscal years 2006, 2007 and 2008 can be found in National Association of VOCA Assistance Administrators (2009). The real net amounts available for direct assistance and compensation to victims have steadily been falling. They are not adjusted for inflation increases. The total amount appropriated (from offender-source funds) increasingly includes charges for other federal activities. Of a nominal $590 million in 2008 (down from $625 million in 2006 and 2007) a new $34 million charge was made for Department of Justice administrative costs and long-established charges were made for training ($18.4 million), US Attorney and FBI staff ($23.6 million), and federal victim notification programmes ($6.4 million).

9   As restated a few years later, 'If the first broken window in a building is not repaired, then people who like breaking windows will assume that no one cares, and more windows will be broken ... Likewise, when disorderly behavior – say, rude remarks by loitering youths – is left unchallenged, the

signal given is that no one cares. The disorder escalates, possibly to serious crime' (Wilson and Kelling 1989: 3).

10 A small number of early evaluations of the 'broken windows' hypothesis reported some confirmatory evidence (e.g. Skogan 1992); recent claims of validation are polemical (e.g. Kelling and Sousa 2001) or self-justificatory (e.g. Bratton and Knobler 1998; Bratton and Kelling 2006). William Bratton was the New York City Police Department chief when the 'Zero Tolerance' strategy, based on the Broken Windows logic, was introduced.

11 I have not cited the newspaper sources on which I draw. Web search engines can find the relevant stories and many others describing similar cases in London newspapers.

12 In like vein, two California governors who supported that State's three-strikes law killed initiatives to evaluate the law's effects. Governor Pete Wilson, in vetoing legislation creating a commission to study the law's effects, said its aim was to 'disprove the obvious positive impact of the Three Strikes law ... There are many mysteries in life, but the efficiency of "Three Strikes" ... is not one of them' (quoted in California District Attorneys Association 2004: 32). Wilson's successor, Democrat Grey Davis, vetoing a similar bill, observed that 'the savings associated with the law, in terms of lives not destroyed, injuries not sustained, and property not stolen ... is ultimately incalculable, but very serious' (quoted in California District Attorneys Association 2004: 32). Labour Government leaders presumably feel likewise; they *know* the ASBO has achieved good things but are unwilling to chance research that might show otherwise.

13 A subsequent national survey found even higher levels (several around 40 per cent, one – for teenagers hanging around – at 57 per cent) of characterisation of forms of antisocial behaviour as very or fairly big problems (Department for Communities and Local Government 2007).

14 Published results were not disaggregated by gender as in the earlier study.

15 I first offered this observation in a 2004 book (Tonry 2004a). Supporting evidence has continued to accumulate (e.g. ICVS data) and it appears now to be conventional wisdom: 'Some ministers also believe that the tone of previous law and order pronouncements stoked up public fears of crime and anti-social behaviours unnecessarily, creating a vicious cycle which made it easier for the Tories to attack the Government and warn that society is breaking down' (Branigan 2007).

References

Bennett, R. (2008) 'Ministers promise to rehabilitate young offenders as well as punishing them', *The Times*, 9 June: 13. http://www.timesonline.co.uk/tol/news/uk/crime/article4093084.ece

Bottoms, A.E. (2006) 'Incivilities, offence, and social order in residential communities', in A. von Hirsch and A.P. Simester (eds), *Incivilities: Regulating offensive behaviour*. Oxford: Hart, pp. 239–80.

Branigan, T. (2007) 'Every ASBO a failure, says Balls, in break with Blair era on crime' *Guardian*, 28 July: 13. http://www.guardian.co.uk/politics/2007/jul/28/ukcrime.immigrationpolicy

Bratton, W. and Kelling, G. (2006) 'There are no cracks in the broken windows', *National Review* (Feb 28): 2.

Bratton, W.J. and Knobler, P. (1998) *Turnaround: How America's top cop reversed the crime epidemic*. New York: Random House.

Budd, T., Sharp, C. and Mayhew, P. (2005) *Offending in England and Wales: First results from the 2003 Crime and Justice Survey*. Home Office Research Study 275. London: Home Office. http://www.homeoffice.gov.uk/rds/pdfs05/hors275.pdf

Burney, E. (2005) *Making People Behave: Anti-social behaviour, politics, and policy*. Cullompton: Willan.

California District Attorneys Association (2004) *Prosecutors' Perspectives on California's Three Strikes Law: a 10-Year retrospective*. Sacramento, CA: California District Attorneys Association. http://www.toodoc.com/search.php?q=Prosecutors%27+Perspectives

Campbell, S. (2002) *A Review of Antisocial Behaviour Orders*. Home Office Research Study 236. London: Home Office. http://www.homeoffice.gov.uk/rds/pdfs2/hors236.pdf

Department for Communities and Local Government (2007) *Best Value User Satisfaction Surveys 2006–07*. London: Department for Communities and Local Government. http://www.communities.gov.uk/localgovernment/localregional/servicedelivery/usersatisfaction/

Downes, D. and Morgan, R. (2007) 'No turning back: the politics of law and order into the millennium', in M. Maguire, R. Morgan and R. Reiner (eds), *The Oxford Handbook of Criminology* (4th edn). Oxford: Oxford University Press, pp. 201–40.

Emsley, C. (2005) *Hard Men: the English and violence since 1750*. London: Hambledon and London.

Farrington, D.P. (1986) 'Age and Crime', in M. Tonry and N. Morris (eds), *Crime and Justice: A Review of Research*, Vol. 7. Chicago: University of Chicago Press, pp. 189–250.

Farrington, D., Coid, J.W., Harnett, L.M., Jolliffe, D., Soteriou, N., Turner, R.E. and West, D.J. (2005) *Criminal Careers up to Age 50 and Life Success up to Age 48: New findings from the Cambridge Study in Delinquent Development*. Report to the Home Office. Institute of Criminology, University of Cambridge.

Farrington, D., Coid, J.W., Harnett, L.M., Jolliffe, D., Soteriou, N., Turner, R.E. and West, D.J. (2006) *Criminal Careers up to Age 50 and Life Success up to Age 48: New findings from the Cambridge Study in Delinquent Development* (2nd edn). Home Office Research Study 299. London: Home Office. http://www.homeoffice.gov.uk/rds/pdfs06/hors299.pdf

Flood-Page, C., Campbell, S., Harrington, V. and Miller, J. (2000) *Youth Crime: Findings from the 1998/99 Youth Lifestyles Survey*. Home Office Research Study 209. London: Home Office. http://www.homeoffice.gov.uk/rds/pdfs/hors209.pdf

Ford, R. (2008) 'ASBOs quietly dropped as most young offenders ignore them', *The Times*, 9 May: 4.

Friedland, M. (1969) *Double Jeopardy*. Oxford: Clarendon Press.

Garland, D. (2001) *The Culture of Control: Crime and social order in contemporary society*. Oxford: Oxford University Press.

Gottschalk, M. (2006) *The Prison and the Gallows: The politics of mass incarceration in America*. Cambridge: Cambridge University Press.

Harcourt, B.E. (2002) *Illusion of Order: The false promise of broken windows policing.* Cambridge, MA: Harvard University Press.

Harcourt, B.E. and Ludwig, J. (2006) 'Broken windows: new evidence from New York City and a five-city social experiment', *University of Chicago Law Review,* 73(1): 271–320.

Hinkle, J.C. and Weisburd, D. (2008) 'The irony of broken windows policing: a micro-place study of the relationship between disorder, focused police crack-downs and fear of crime', *Journal of Criminal Justice,* 36(6): 503–12.

Her Majesty's Government (2008) *Youth Crime Action Plan 2008.* London: Home Office. http://www.homeoffice.gov.uk/documents/youth-crime-action-plan/

Home Office (2001) *Criminal Justice: The Way Ahead,* Cm 5074. London: The Stationery Office. http://www.archive.official-documents.co.uk/document/cm50/5074/5074.htm

Home Office (2002) *Justice for All – A White Paper on the criminal justice system,* Cm 5563. London: The Stationery Office.

Home Office (2003) *A New Deal for Victims and Witnesses: National strategy to deliver improved services,* July 2003. London: Home Office. http://www.homeoffice.gov.uk/documents/vicwitstrat.pdf?version=1

Home Office (2005) *The Government reply to the Fifth Report from the Home Affairs Committee, Session 2004–05, HC 80: Antisocial behaviour,* Cm 6588. London: The Stationery Office.

Home Office (2007a) *Cutting Crime – A New Partnership 2008–11.* London: The Stationery Office. http://www.homeoffice.gov.uk/documents/crime-strategy-07/

Home Office (2007b) *Home Office Departmental Report 2007,* Cm 7096. London: The Stationery Office. http://www.homeoffice.gov.uk/documents/ho-annual-re-port-07

Home Office (2008) *Crime in England and Wales – Quarterly Update to December 2007,* Home Office Statistical Bulletin 04/08. London: Home Office.

Humphrys, J. (2004) *Lost for Words: The mangling and manipulation of the English language.* London: Hodder and Stoughton.

Hurley, D. (2004) *On Crime as Science (A Neighbor at a Time).* http://crab.rutgers.edu/~goertzel/CollectiveEfficacyEarls.html

Jenkins, S. (2006) 'All this drivel does is bring Basra to our doorsteps', *Guardian,* 11 January. http://www.guardian.co.uk/politics/2006/jan/11/prisonsandprobation.labour

Kelling, G.L. and Sousa, Jr., W.H. (2001) *Do Police Matter? An analysis of the impact of New York City's police reforms.* New York: Manhattan Institute.

Kershaw, C., Nicholas, S. and Walker, A. (2008) *Crime in England and Wales 2007/08,* Home Office Statistical Bulletin 07/08. London: Home Office. http://www.crimereduction.homeoffice.gov.uk/statistics/statistics074.htm

Maguire, M. (1991) 'The needs and rights of victims of crime', in M. Tonry (ed.), *Crime and Justice: a Review of Research,* Vol. 14. Chicago: University of Chicago Press, pp. 363–433.

Morgan, R. (2006) 'With respect to order, the rules of the game have changed: New Labour's dominance of the "law and order" agenda', in T. Newburn and P. Rock (eds), *The Politics of Crime Control: Essays in honour of David Downes.* Oxford: Oxford University Press, pp. 91–116. http://fds.oup.com/www.oup.com/pdf/13/9780199208401.pdf

Morgan, R. and Newburn, T. (2007) 'Youth justice', in M. Maguire, R. Morgan and R. Reiner (eds), *The Oxford Handbook of Criminology* (4th edn). Oxford: Oxford University Press, pp. 1024–60.

National Association of VOCA Assistance Administrators (2008) 'Victims of Crime Act (VOCA) Crime Victims Fund – Briefing Background 2009 Budget'. Washington, DC: National Association of VOCA Assistance Administrators.

National Association of VOCA Assistance Administrators (2009) 'Victims of Crime Act (VOCA) – 2009 Fact Sheet'. Washington, DC: National Association of VOCA Assistance Administrators.

National Audit Office (2006) *The Home Office: Tackling anti-social behaviour*, Report by the Comptroller and the Auditor General. London: The Stationery Office. http://www.nao.org.uk/whats_new/0607/060799.aspx?alreadysearchfor = yes

National Victims Conference (2004) *Conference Report: Supporting and protecting victims – making it happen*. London: Home Office.

Nicholas, S., Kershaw, C. and Walker, A. (eds) (2007) *Crime in England and Wales 2006/07*, Home Office Statistical Bulletin 11/07. London: Home Office.

Office for Victims of Crime (2004) *Report to the Nation 2003: Fiscal Years 2001 and 2002*. Washington, DC: US Office for Victims of Crime, US Department of Justice. http://www.ojp.usdoj.gov/ovc/welcovc/reporttonation2003/welcome.html

Office for Victims of Crime (2008) *Office for Victims of Crime Report to the Nation 2007: Fiscal Years 2005–2006: Rebuilding lives, restoring hope*. Washington, DC: Office for Victims of Crime, US Department of Justice. http://www.ojp.usdoj.gov/ovc/welcovc/reporttonation2007/welcome.html

President's Task Force on Victims of Crime (1982) *Final Report*. Washington, DC: US Government Printing Office.

Prime Minister's Strategy Unit (2006) *Respect Action Plan*. London: Cabinet Office.

Prime Minister's Strategy Unit (2007) *Building on Progress: Security, crime and justice*. London: Cabinet Office.

Prince, R. (2009) 'Home Secretary launches new gang Asbo', *Daily Telegraph*, 5 February: 6.

Roberts, J. (2009) 'Listening to the crime victim: evaluating victim input at sentencing and parole', in M. Tonry and N. Morris (eds), *Crime and Justice: a Review of Research*, Vol. 38. Chicago: University of Chicago Press.

Rock, P.E. (1991) *Helping Victims of Crime: The Home Office and the rise of victim support in England and Wales*. Oxford: Clarendon Press.

Rock, P.E. (2004) *Constructing Victims' Rights: The Home Office, New Labour, and victims*. Oxford: Oxford University Press.

Roe, S. and Ashe, J. (2008) *Young People and Crime: Findings from the 2006 Offending, Crime and Justice Survey*, Home Office Statistical Bulletin 09/08. London: Home Office. www.crimereduction.homeoffice.gov.uk/youth/youth081.htm

Sampson, R.J. and Raudenbush, S.W. (2004) 'Seeing disorder: neighborhood stigma and the social construction of "broken windows"', *Social Psychology Quarterly*, 67(4): 319–42.

Simmons, J. and Colleagues (eds) (2002) *Crime in England and Wales 2001/2002*, Home Office Statistical Bulletin 702. London: Home Office. http://www.homeoffice.gov.uk/rds/crimeew1.html

Skogan, W. (1992) *Disorder and Decline: Crime and the spiral of decay in American neighborhoods*. Berkeley, CA: University of California Press.

Stratford, N. and Roth, W. (1999) *The 1998 Youth Lifestyle Survey*. London: Home Office.

Taylor, R.B. (2001) *Breaking Away from Broken Windows: Baltimore neighborhoods and the nationwide fight against crime, grime, fear, and decline*. Boulder, CO: Westview Press.

Tonry, M. (2004a) *Punishment and Politics: Evidence and emulation in the making of English crime control policy*. Cullompton: Willan.

Tonry, M. (2004b) *Thinking about Crime: Sense and sensibility in American penal culture*. New York: Oxford University Press.

Tonry, M. and Bildsten, H. (2009) 'Antisocial behavior', in M. Tonry (ed.), *The Oxford Handbook of Crime and Public Policy*. New York: Oxford University Press, pp. 578–98.

Travis, A. (2008) 'ASBOs in their death throes as number issued drops by a third', *Guardian*, 9 May: 6.

van Dijk, J., van Kesteren, J. and Smit, P. (2007) *Criminal Victimisation in International Perspective: Key findings from the 2004–2005 ICVS and EU ICS*. The Hague: Ministry of Justice, Directorate for Crime Prevention.

Victim Support (2005) *Victim Support Annual Report and Accounts 2005*. London: Victim Support.

Webster, C.M. and Doob, A.N. (2007) 'Punitive trends and stable imprisonment rates in Canada', in M. Tonry (ed.), *Crime and Justice: a Review of Research*, Vol. 36. Chicago: University of Chicago Press, pp. 297–369.

West, D.J. (1983) 'Sex offences and offending', in M. Tonry and N. Morris (eds), *Crime and Justice: a Review of Research*, Vol. 5. Chicago: University of Chicago Press, pp. 183–233.

Western, B. (2006) *Punishment and Inequality in America*. New York: Russell Sage Foundation.

Wilson, J.Q. and Kelling, G.L. (1982) 'Broken windows', *Atlantic Monthly*, March: 29–38.

Wilson, J.Q. and Kelling, G.L. (1989) 'Making neighborhoods safe: sometimes "fixing broken windows" does more to reduce crime than conventional "incident-oriented" policing', *Atlantic Monthly*, February: 46–52.

Wilson, D., Sharp, C. and Patterson, A. (2006) *Young People and Crime: Findings from the 2005 Offending, Crime and Justice Survey* (Home Office Statistical Bulletin 1709. London: Home Office. http://www.homeoffice.gov.uk/rds/pdfs06/hosb 1706.pdf

Windlesham, Lord D. (1996) *Legislating Within the Tide*, Vol. 3 of *Responses to Crime*. Oxford: Clarendon Press.

Womack, S. (2005) 'Four out of five want Asbos for unruly pets', *Daily Telegraph*, 23 September: 17. http://www.telegraph.co.uk/news/uknews/1498989/Four-out-of-five-want-Asbos-for-unruly-pets.html

Wood, M. (2004) *Perceptions and Experience of Antisocial Behaviour: Findings from the 2003/2004 British Crime Survey*, Home Office Online Report 49/04. London: Home Office. http://www.homeoffice.gov.uk/rds/pdfs04/rdsolr4904.pdf

Young, M. (1997) 'The Victims Rights Movement: A confluence of forces', text of an address delivered to the first National Symposium on Victims of Federal Crime, in Washington, DC, on 10 February 1997. Washington, DC: National Organization for Victim Assistance.

Zimring, F.E. (1989) 'Toward a jurisprudence of family violence', in L. Ohlin and M. Tonry (eds), *Family Violence*, M. Tonry and N. Morris (eds), *Crime and Justice: A Review of Research*, Vol. 11. Chicago: University of Chicago Press, pp. 547–70.

Chapter 5

The phenomenon of victim–offender overlap: a study of offences against households

Anthony Bottoms and Andrew Costello

To most members of the public, and to many politicians, victims and offenders represent identifiably distinct elements of the population: one group preys upon the other. Yet a growing volume of criminological research has, since the early 1980s, demonstrated that, in a non-trivial number of cases, offenders may become victims, and victims may become offenders. This research clearly has potentially important consequences for the study of crime, as well as for criminal justice policies.

The phrase 'victim–offender overlap' has increasingly come to be used as a shorthand description of this phenomenon. But some care is needed in the definition of this term. For example, the minutes of a discussion in the National Crime Reduction Board for England and Wales include the following comment: 'Important to note that the victim/offender overlap is very large and often children coming into the CJS [Criminal Justice System] have themselves been victims' (National Crime Reduction Board 2008: 3). The victimisation mentioned here appears to refer primarily to child abuse at a significantly earlier age. That is obviously a very important matter, and unfortunately there is indeed empirical evidence that such abuse can heighten the risk of later offending by the abused child (for a review see Widom 1997). However, the term 'victim–offender overlap' is more usually restricted to situations in which a person is identified *both* as a victim *and* as an offender within a reasonably short time period, such as a year; and that is how we shall use the phrase in this chapter.

In principle, a victim–offender overlap, defined as above, can be identified in one of two ways. First, one might take a population or sample of victimisations, and check to see whether a disproportionate number of offenders appears within this victimised group. Or secondly, one might take a population or sample of offenders, and check to see whether they receive a disproportionate number of victimisations, as compared with the general population. Both of these approaches are adopted in the present chapter, the first in the initial sections of the chapter and the second in a small-scale interview study on which we report later.

In an important recent article, Janet Lauritsen and John Laub (2007) have reviewed evidence and theorisation on the victim–offender overlap. Among their conclusions are the following:

- The victim–offender overlap has been very widely reported: it 'has been found to exist in numerous countries, across various time periods, among adults as well as youths, and for many types of crime ranging from homicide to bicycle theft' (p. 55).

- Despite this extensive empirical confirmation of the overlap, too often 'the field of criminology has failed to take seriously' the evidence and its implications (p. 65). Among the reasons for this failure is academic specialisation: 'in general, there has been little exchange between victimisation research and more traditional criminological approaches' (p. 65).

- There is a particular need for the field of criminology to make fuller attempts 'to sort out the causal mechanisms underlying these [statistical] associations' (p. 55).

- There is in many countries a significant 'political reticence' that inhibits adequate attention being given, in discussions on criminal policy, to the victim–offender overlap (p. 66). In this respect, Lauritsen and Laub (2007: 66) quote the observation by David Garland (2001: 11) that, in political debates on crime, frequently 'a zero-sum policy game is assumed wherein the offender's gain is the victim's loss, and being "for" victims automatically means being tough on offenders'. (On this topic, see further chapter 4 by Michael Tonry in this volume.) Clearly, the victim–offender overlap does not sit comfortably with such assumptions.

In the final paragraph of their article, Lauritsen and Laub (2007: 70), echoing an earlier challenge by Farrall and Maltby (2003), urge criminologists to renew and sustain their focus of attention upon the victim–offender overlap. Only in this way, they suggest, can we begin to overcome 'the limitations of our knowledge' on this important topic, and also to tackle the 'political and ideological challenges' likely to be encountered by those engaging in 'this important line of inquiry' (p. 70). We will return to the political/ideological issues at the end of this chapter, but first we will concentrate on strictly criminological questions.

The present chapter can be regarded as a tentative and exploratory response to these challenges. Focusing on property offences against households, it presents some fresh empirical data, including a small-scale interview study of offender-victims. After these data have been considered, we seek to locate the findings within the wider literature on explanations of the victim–offender overlap. Finally, we consider the implications of the findings for criminal justice policy.

It is hoped that this discussion will contribute to the literature on the victim–offender overlap in three principal ways. First, the focus on *property offences against households* is unusual within this literature. Secondly, *police crime records* are used as a major data source and it is shown that, even for incidents in which the police have been brought into the picture, there is often a significant degree of victim–offender overlap. Hence, contrary to the beliefs of some, it is not the case that known offenders never report their victimisations to the police. Thirdly, in a limited response to Lauritsen and Laub's (2007) justifiable challenge to criminologists to focus more fully on causal mechanisms (see above), this chapter emphasises, for property offences against households, the apparent importance of *acquaintanceship* in helping to account for the victimisation of offenders – and in so doing, it adds to the growing literature on the role of peers in relation to the victim–offender overlap. For the time being, we will postpone further comment on this third matter; but the first two topics (the focus on offences against households, and the use of police crime records) require brief preliminary discussion before we turn to our empirical data.

Preliminary issues: household crimes and police crime data

The British Crime Survey (BCS) has, since its inception in the early 1980s, distinguished between 'offences against households' and 'personal offences'. The BCS is a regularly conducted victimisation survey of the general population; hence its focus is on crimes against individuals. (Offences against organisations are measured in more occasional and separate surveys.) But an individual might be victimised either *personally* (as in an assault, or by having his/her pocket picked or handbag snatched), or *as a member of a household* (as when a house is burgled, toys are stolen from the garden, or the shed is deliberately vandalised). To obtain a complete count of crimes against individuals, those commissioning surveys clearly need both these types of offence to be included. But the distinction is nevertheless important, when it comes to which crimes will actually be reported in the survey. For example, at least in a perfect world, any member of a given household who is randomly selected as a survey respondent should report the same set of household offences occurring over the survey period. By contrast, different household members (Mum, Dad, their 17-year-old son) will very possibly have different experiences of personal victimisation to report, and if one of them is selected as a BCS respondent, she/he will not be asked about the personal victimisations of other household members. The BCS therefore rightly reports results from the two kinds of offence separately, and it uses different denominators for them: offences against households are counted 'per 10,000 households', and personal offences 'per 10,000 respondents'. 'Crimes against households' include burglaries of the dwelling, or of a shed or garage; thefts in or around the home; criminal damage to the home or to a shed or garage or the garden; and offences against private vehicles. This last type of offence is the only 'household offence' that can be committed away from the family dwelling (or extensions of it such as a nearby garage); but – despite the doubts of some – it remains classified as a household offence on the basis that a car is normally seen as belonging to the whole family, and not just to an individual.

The research literature on the victim–offender overlap does include some studies with data on victimisations for household offences, sometimes set within a broader group of offences.[1] However, in general this literature has focused much more fully on personal crimes rather than on offences against households;[2] and, among personal crimes, offences of violence have received special attention.[3] Good examples of the primary focus on personal crimes may be found in two large-scale British self-reported offending studies (the Edinburgh Youth Transitions Study and the Home Office-sponsored Offending, Crime and Justice Survey (OCJS)), both of which have significantly enhanced our knowledge of the victim–offender overlap, but each of which has limited its published victimisation analyses entirely to personal offences, omitting household offences altogether.[4] Given this background, the present study constitutes one of the very few systematic studies of the victim–offender overlap in relation to offences against households.[5]

In the first part of our study, the main data source utilised is police-recorded crime data. This is an unusual source in the study of the victim–offender overlap,[6] and there are probably two main reasons for this. The first is that criminal justice data sources in most countries typically keep separate their computerised records of *crimes* and of *identified offenders*; hence, bringing them together requires a special effort. However, at least in England and Wales, although it is undoubtedly a laborious task to link the appropriate records, there are no difficulties in principle in doing so. The second obstacle to the study of the victim–offender overlap through the use of police data is probably the assumption that, in addressing this particular topic, police crime data are even more hopelessly flawed than is normally the case (for a general review of the deficiencies of police crime data, see Maguire 2007). For example, it is well known that a major deficiency of police-recorded crime data is that many offences are not reported to the police by their victims; and *a priori* it would seem highly likely that this is especially the case for crimes committed against known offenders. Indeed, there is empirical support for such an assumption in the impressive series of studies of active offenders conducted by criminologists in St Louis, Missouri (see Jacobs and Wright 2006, and further references therein). In these studies, offenders report a hidden world of self-reliance and retaliation in which victimisations, while not uncommon, are dealt with as private matters, and there is a deep cultural resistance to involving the police. Obviously, in situations where such conditions apply, the study of the victim–offender overlap using police data will be a deeply flawed, and possibly even pointless, exercise. However, it is not impossible that the study of offences against households is less susceptible to problems of this kind than is the study of personal crime, because the police might be seen, by offender-victims of household crime, as a useful ally in trying to recover stolen property. Additionally, David Matza's (1964) warning – issued long ago and in another context – seems relevant here: namely, that we should not necessarily assume that offenders, even some persistent offenders, inhabit a totally different social and moral world than the rest of us. If, as Matza suggests, many offenders share many mainstream social values, then reporting crimes to the police may not necessarily be a totally alien activity for them.

The Sheffield Recorded Crime Study

The first element of the empirical study reported here involved an analysis of police-recorded offences against households for the year 1995 in Sheffield, UK, a city with a population of approximately half a million, and, in the relevant year, 207,000 households. For the crimes selected, all offences recorded in the city in 1995 were included in the analysis.

The offences studied were the following (all offences include attempts as well as the full crime):

1. Burglary in a dwelling;

2. Shed and garage burglary (but only including sheds and garages owned or rented by private individuals, and where the shed or garage is directly associated with a residential household);

3. Criminal damage to a dwelling or to property directly associated with it (e.g. in a garden or shed/garage; damage to vehicles is also included where the listed complainant is a private individual);

4. Unlawful taking of a motor vehicle ('TWOC')[7] (restricted to cases in which the listed complainant is a private individual; hence for example taking a commercial vehicle, even one parked outside residential premises for the night, would be excluded);

5. Theft from a motor vehicle (restricted to cases in which the listed complainant is a private individual).

This list of offences does not include either thefts in the home,[8] or thefts outside the home (for example, from the garden or a doorstep). Clearly, these are 'household offences' within the normal meaning of that term (see above); however, in the police dataset being used, they were included within a broad grouping of 'other thefts', and within this they could not be reliably distinguished from more personal thefts. Although this omission is regrettable it does not, we think, seriously compromise the main purposes or results of this part of the study. Hereafter, in this section of the chapter, when we refer to 'household offences' we mean the five offences listed above.

The primary data source used is offence data recorded by the police. These data were very kindly made available to the authors by the South Yorkshire Police.[9] The police also made available relevant offender data, and by a process of detailed individual comparison, it was possible to identify all those households in the city that were *both* recorded as having been victimised for a household offence in 1995 *and*, in the same year, contained at least one recorded offender.[10] We describe these households, in shorthand, as 'offender households', but it is important to note from the outset that this shorthand potentially embraces some very diverse sets of circumstances – from, for example, an active and persistent offender living alone, to a family of five in which a 13-year-old boy was formally cautioned for one minor theft at some point in 1995.

The available data did not enable us to establish reliably whether the victimisation preceded or was followed by the event leading to a given household being identified as an 'offender household' in 1995. Therefore, the analysis that follows is essentially cross-sectional; it seeks to establish the existence or otherwise of a victim–offender overlap, but says nothing about temporal order (an issue that is discussed later in the chapter).

A recurring problem in the literature on the victim–offender overlap concerns whether an apparent over-representation of offenders among a given victimised population might be explicable by the general demographic risks of victimisation. For example, on an overall comparison offenders might seem to have a high victimisation rate for offences of violence, but the validity of such a simple comparison might rightly be questioned, given that recorded offenders live disproportionately in high-crime areas (Craglia and Costello 2005) and they are also disproportionately young men, an age/gender group which the BCS has repeatedly shown to have a higher risk of violent victimisation. In the present study, it was possible to control for risk factors of this kind only as regards area of residence, but the control used for this variable was rigorous. In brief, we calculated the area-based household victimisation rate (for the five offences listed above, taken together in aggregate) for one thousand small areas of the city, and then banded these areas together into quintiles based on the area victimisation rate.[11] Thus, Quintile 1 contains about 200 small areas (widely scattered through the city) with a very low household victimisation rate, while Quintile 5 contains all the small areas in the city with the highest victimisation rates. Within each quintile, we could then compare the victimisation rate for 'offender households' (see above) and other households, having controlled for the area victimisation rate.

Using this analytic strategy, Table 5.1 provides data on the overall crime incidence rates for all household offences taken together. As will be seen, within each quintile there is a highly statistically significant difference in the household crime rate between 'offender households' and 'other households'; that is, a victim–offender overlap in the incidence of household crime is to be found not only in high crime areas but also in low crime rate areas.

Table 5.1 Incidence rates (per 1,000 households) for recorded offences against households in Sheffield in 1995, distinguishing between 'offender households' (OHH) and 'other households' (NOHH)

Household crime quintile	Incidence rates		Sig.
	OHH	NOHH	
1	192.0	108.7	$P < 0.001$
	(536)	(42,223)	
2	267.2	146.0	$P < 0.001$
	(857)	(42,073)	
3	295.6	175.8	$P < 0.001$
	(954)	(40,340)	
4	274.4	204.9	$P < 0.001$
	(1,261)	(39,862)	
5	359.3	261.2	$P < 0.001$
	(1,965)	(36,999)	
ALL	299.1	177.0	$P < 0.001$
	(5,573)	(201,497)	

Note: Figures in parentheses are the Ns for each cell

This overall picture can be considered in more detail by disaggregating the data in two respects: first, by analysing different types of offence; and secondly, by breaking down the concept of 'crime incidence' by consider-ing separately data on the *prevalence* of each offence, and subsequently data on *repeat victimisation*.[12]

We consider first a series of tables measuring prevalence rates. Table 5.2 summarises data on burglaries, and we can immediately note that there is a marked difference between the results for residential burglary and for

Table 5.2 Prevalence rates (per 1,000 households) for recorded household-related burglaries in Sheffield in 1995, distinguishing between 'offender households' (OHH) and 'other households' (NOHH)

Household crime quintile	Residential burglaries			Shed/garage burglaries		
	OHH	NOHH	Sig.	OHH	NOHH	Sig.
1	42.9	18.3	P<0.001	14.9	10.4	NS
2	58.3	26.8	P<0.001	18.7	17.3	NS
3	83.9	40.6	P<0.001	25.2	18.4	NS
4	88.0	53.3	P<0.001	17.4	21.7	NS
5	120.6	82.1	P<0.001	14.8	25.3	P<0.01
ALL	89.9	43.2	P<0.001	17.8	18.4	NS

Note: Ns for each cell are as shown in Table 5.1

shed and garage burglary. In the former, offender households are at significantly greater risk of having been victimised once or more in each of the five quintiles; but for shed and garage burglaries, there are no statistically significant differences except for the areas in the highest crime quintile, where offender households have a *lower* prevalence rate than other households.

This is clearly an interesting difference, but it is also not a straightforward one, because not all households have a shed or garage linked to them, and we have no data on which do and which do not. It is therefore possible that, at least in some quintiles, the proportion of households with a shed or garage might be significantly different as between offender households and others – we do not know. For example, it seems *prima facie* possible that such a difference might be present in the most socially disadvantaged/high-victimisation areas, with offender households having fewer sheds/garages because of a high proportion of offenders living in bedsits. If this is so, then it could of course explain the significantly lower level of shed/garage burglaries in offender households in the highest crime quintile.

Turning to Table 5.3, we note that for the offence of household criminal damage, offender households have significantly higher prevalence rates for every quintile except the least victimised. This result is congruent with that obtained by Farrall and Maltby (2003: 40–1) where a small sample of probationers aged 17–25 had significantly higher victimisation rates for household criminal damage than did a general population sample of the same age group previously asked the same question (by Graham and Bowling 1995).

Table 5.4 presents data on two different types of vehicle crime, and as for burglaries (Table 5.2) there is an interesting difference in the pattern of

Table 5.3 Prevalence rates (per 1,000 households) for recorded household-related criminal damage in Sheffield in 1995, distinguishing between 'offender households' (OHH) and 'other households' (NOHH)

Household crime quintile	OHH	NOHH	Sig.
1	20.5	19.3	NS
2	65.3	26.2	P<0.001
3	50.3	32.0	P<0.01
4	48.4	36.6	P<0.05
5	78.4	46.2	P<0.001
ALL	59.7	31.6	P<0.001

Note: Ns for each cell are as shown in Table 5.1

results for the two offences. For unlawful takings or 'TWOCs', offender households have a significantly higher prevalence rate than other households in all quintiles; while for thefts from motor vehicles, there are no significant differences except in the highest crime quintile, where (as for shed and garage burglaries) the prevalence rate for offender households is *lower* than for other households. Analogously with shed/garage burglaries, however, one should note that the interpretation of the data in Table 5.4 is more uncertain than for residential burglary and criminal damage, because we have no data on which households had regular use of a vehicle, and it is of course possible that this is something that might vary as between offender households and others. But a further complication in the present instance is the very different statistical patterns (shown in Table 5.4) for TWOC and for theft from vehicles, notwithstanding the

Table 5.4 Prevalence rates (per 1,000 households) for household-related offences against vehicles in Sheffield in 1995, distinguishing between 'offender households' (OHH) and 'other households' (NOHH)

Household crime quintile	Unlawful takings			Thefts from motor vehicles		
	OHH	NOHH	Sig	OHH	NOHH	Sig.
1	61.6	26.7	P<0.001	26.1	28.8	NS
2	60.6	31.4	P<0.001	43.2	35.2	NS
3	61.8	34.5	P<0.001	38.8	37.5	NS
4	53.9	38.6	P<0.01	33.3	39.6	NS
5	56.0	41.5	P<0.01	23.9	39.6	P<0.001
ALL	57.6	34.3	P<0.001	31.8	36.0	NS

Note: Ns for each cell are as shown in Table 5.1.

fact that both these offences have vehicles as their target. Accordingly, there is every reason to believe that the divergent statistical patterns displayed for the two offences in Table 5.4 are not artefactual, but represent a real difference, with the data for TWOCs clearly suggesting a victim–offender overlap.

We now turn from data on offence prevalence to consider instead the results for *repeat victimisation*, that is, whether (within the calendar year 1995) each victimised household was subject to a further victimisation for the offence(s) specified.[13] In relation to this issue, by definition the analysis is restricted to those already victimised once in 1995; hence the Ns are substantially smaller than those for Tables 5.1–5.4, and it is accordingly necessary to restrict the area-based control to two broad groups, respectively Quintiles 1–3 and Quintiles 4 and 5. Relevant data on this basis are shown in Table 5.5.[14] Generally speaking, the results are similar to those for prevalence. Thus, for example, there is no significant difference between the revictimisation rates for offender households and others for either shed/garage burglaries or thefts from motor vehicles, either in higher-crime or in lower-crime areas. By contrast, the three offences showing strong statistical differences in the prevalence tables (residential burglary, criminal damage and TWOC) all again show at least one statistically significant result. There is however a contrast between, on the one hand, residential burglary and criminal damage, where in both higher and lower crime areas offender households are very significantly more likely to be revictimised (P<0.001); and, on the other hand, TWOC, where the revictimisation rate is only weakly greater for offender households in high-crime areas, and not at all in lower crime areas. This difference could

Table 5.5 Revictimisation rates (per 1,000 victims) for offences against households in Sheffield in 1995, distinguishing between 'offender households' (OHH) and 'other households' (NOHH)

	Household crime quintiles 1–3			Household crime quintiles 4 and 5		
	OHH	*NOHH*	*Sig.*	*OHH*	*NOHH*	*Sig.*
Residential burglary	18.3	5.9	P<0.001	23.6	12.2	P<0.001
Shed and garage burglary	11.8	7.7	NS	7.5	12.4	NS
Criminal damage	15.7	7.2	P<0.001	23.7	10.4	P<0.001
TWOC	8.4	7.9	NS	16.3	10.5	P<0.05
Theft from motor vehicle	11.4	5.1	NS	9.0	8.4	NS
All household crimes	18.4	13.8	P<0.001	26.6	18.0	P<0.001

be related to the lower absolute rates for repeat-TWOC than for repeats of the other two offences.[15]

A final piece of empirical evidence in this part of the research concerns the so-called 'clear-up rates' for the various offences being studied. The 'clear-up rate' is an official measure used in the national *Criminal Statistics* for England and Wales; it measures the proportion of offences in a given category which are 'detected' or 'cleared up', i.e. for which an offender has been identified. Data on this matter are shown in Table 5.6, again distinguishing between offender households and others. Some readers might be surprised that, when the five offences are taken together, offences against offender households have a statistically significantly higher clear-up rate than do other offences. When each offence is considered separately, once again there is no difference between offender households and others for either shed/garage burglaries or thefts from motor vehicles. On this occasion, that is also the case for residential burglary; but for both criminal damage and TWOC, the clear-up rates are significantly higher for offences against offender households.

Table 5.6 Clear-up rates (%) for recorded offences against households in Sheffield in 1995, distinguishing between 'offender households' (OHH) and 'other households' (NOHH)

	Clear-up rate		Significance
	OHH	*NOHH*	
Residential burglary	17.8	16.5	NS
Shed and garage burglary	5.9	8.4	NS
Criminal damage	20.4	7.9	P<0.001
TWOC	19.5	12.3	P<0.001
Theft from motor vehicle	8.7	7.6	NS
All household crimes	15.8	11.8	P<0.001

How should we interpret the information in these various tables? This is a complex question, with several layers to it. The first thing to say is that there are admitted limitations to the data. For example, the absence of information concerning which households possessed vehicles or sheds/garages has already been noted. Additionally, the simple 'offender household *versus* other households' comparison is in some respects a crude analytic tool. Not only do the circumstances of 'offender households' vary widely (see above), but it is of course to a degree a matter of chance whether a given household counts as an 'offender household' – for example, a young offender officially cautioned in December 1994 would not qualify his household for categorisation as an 'offender household', but if he were cautioned a month later, the household would be so counted.

Yet despite these imperfections in the data source, there is an interesting degree of consistency across offence types in the three different aspects of the overall study – that is, the prevalence analyses, the revictimisation analyses, and the analysis of clear-up rates – each of which is, statistically speaking, independent. As regards all three of these types of analysis, neither shed/garage burglaries nor thefts from vehicles show any hint either of data supporting the victim–offender overlap, or of a differential clear-up rate between offender households and others. However, in several respects there were substantially different results for the other three offences in the analysis (namely, residential burglary, criminal damage and TWOC), where the data typically seemed to provide positive evidence – and sometimes very strong evidence – supporting the existence of a victim–offender overlap. For two of these offences (criminal damage and TWOC) there was also evidence of a higher clear-up rate for victimisations in offender households. Moreover, it is as well to reiterate that these results have been obtained with *police-recorded data*. At a minimum, therefore, we can confirm that the use of police data does not necessarily mean that one will fail to find evidence in support of the victim–offender overlap. It is true, of course, that the rates for offender households will sometimes reflect someone other than the offender having reported the crime (as for example where the parent of a delinquent boy reports that the house has been burgled or the family car taken), but it seems probable that the data also include many instances of offenders themselves reporting victimisations. We shall return to this issue in the second part of this chapter.

The pattern of results described above naturally raises the question why the five offences should vary in their statistical patterns. To begin to tackle this issue, let us focus on clear-up rates. It is well known that, in the national criminal statistics, the clear-up rates for offences of violence are in general substantially higher than those for most offences against households, such as residential burglary or criminal damage. For example, in the year 1995 (to which the Sheffield data relate), the clear-up rate for all violent offences in England and Wales was 77 per cent, while the rate for residential burglary was 24 per cent (Home Office 1996: Tables 2.15 and 2.17). It is equally well known that a main reason for this difference is that, in offences of violence, the perpetrator of the offence is frequently known (at least by name or sight) to the victim, who is therefore able to provide powerful evidence to the police seeking to detect the offence; by contrast, victims of burglary rarely know who has attacked their premises. By analogy, might it be the case that, in the offences in this study where there is a higher clear-up rate for offender households than other households (namely, criminal damage and TWOC), this is because a higher proportion of those committing these offences can be identified by the victim? Recorded crime data, of course, cannot answer this question, but it is an issue that we shall consider, using exploratory interview data, in the second part of this chapter.

A possible objection to this line of argument is that it seems to make little sense (i.e. it is, formally speaking, *irrational*) for someone to commit an acquisitive offence against an acquaintance, precisely because doing so will enhance the risk of detection – *unless* the offender is certain either that the victim will not know who is the perpetrator, or that the victim will not report the offence to the police. Pursuing this logic, since we are dealing here with a dataset of offences recorded by the police, surely there will be relatively few acquisitive offences in this dataset where the offender and the victim are acquainted?

Issues related to these questions were tackled in an interesting paper by Felson, Baumer and Messner (2000) with regard to a different kind of acquisitive crime, namely robbery. These authors noticed that, in the US National Crime Victimization Survey (NCVS, the American counterpart to the BCS), no fewer than a quarter of respondent-reported robberies were said to have been committed either by family members or by 'nonfamily acquaintances'. This seemed surprising, especially since robbery – unlike, say, burglary – requires the co-presence of offender and victim in the same location, thus making the identification of the offender by a victim-acquaintance more probable. What then were the reasons for the high proportion of acquaintance robberies – or, putting it another way, 'why [might] offenders . . . commit acquaintance robbery in spite of the potential cost?' (Felson *et al.* 2000: 300). The authors naturally considered the possibility that offenders might have committed such crimes in the belief that the victims would not report the robbery to the authorities; but, in the NCVS data, the rate of reporting of crimes to the police was actually *higher* for victims who were family members and nonfamily acquaintances than for other victims (p. 298), so it is very unlikely that this was a major element in the explanation of the high proportion of acquaintance-based robberies.[16] Felson *et al.* therefore went on to suggest (on an *a priori* basis) three principal situational contexts in which people might be tempted to commit acquisitive crimes against acquaintances:

(a) *'Inside information'*. These are robberies which are financially motivated, and which rely upon information that would not be widely known, e.g. that on a particular day a particular person will be carrying a large amount of cash down a given street. It is postulated that 'offenders are more likely to have inside information about acquaintances' than about strangers (Felson *et al.* 2000: 287).

(b) *'Proximity and impulsiveness'*. This category also refers to financially motivated offences. It draws on the well-attested research finding that property offenders frequently commit crimes when they feel in urgent need of cash – perhaps because of the perceived need to maintain a hedonistic lifestyle, or to feed a drug habit. Hence, although they typically give some thought to the consequences of their actions, offenders rarely display cool rationality when selecting targets. Instead, they tend to act impulsively and to settle 'for the first, rather than the best target available to them' (Wright and Decker 1997: 94).[17] In such circumstances, argue Felson and his colleagues, offenders 'may target anyone in proximity, and people they know may be convenient targets. They are likely to be acquainted with many of the people who live near them' (Felson *et al*. 2000: 288).

(c) *'Dispute-related offences'*. In these offences, unlike the first two categories, the primary motivation is not financial; instead, 'retribution and revenge rather than remuneration' are sought by the offender (Felson *et al*. 2000: 287). In most financially motivated robberies, targets are substitutable, and if a particular target seems unattainable the potential offender moves on to another. In dispute-related offences, however, this is not the case, and 'offenders are mainly interested in one target – the person with whom they have a grievance ... [the person who has] provoked their anger in some way' (p. 287).

What is particularly helpful about these suggestions is that they are based on specific *explanatory mechanisms* regarding how acquaintance-based acquisitive crimes might come to be committed – and a mechanism-based approach to social-scientific explanation has a very great deal to commend it (see Hedström 2005). Unfortunately, however, the NCVS dataset that Felson *et al*. (2000) used for their research allowed only limited scope for further exploration of these suggested mechanisms. Moreover, their paper does not specifically consider the victim–offender overlap. Nevertheless, the mechanisms that they postulate are, in our view, worthy of very careful exploration, since there is significant empirical evidence that offenders are often socially acquainted with other offenders. For example, studies in geographical criminology have shown that offenders frequently live near one another (see Craglia and Costello 2005). As regards friendships, unpublished data from the ongoing Sheffield Desistance Study (see Bottoms *et al*. 2004) show that, at approximately 20 years of age, 90 per cent of a sample of mostly persistent male offenders said that more than half of their mates 'had been in trouble', while two-thirds said that this applied to 75 per cent or more of their mates.[18] Given this amount of residential propinquity and actual friendship with other offenders, it seems plausible to hypothesise that acquaintance-based acquisitive crime might well sometimes feature in offenders' criminal records, and that the mechanisms suggested by Felson *et al*. might be relevant in the explanation of such offences.

Briefly recapitulating some of the arguments of this section, we have noted significant evidence for the existence of a victim–offender overlap for some offences (residential burglary, criminal damage, TWOC), but not for others (theft from vehicles, shed/garage burglaries). Also, higher clear-up rates for offender households tended to be associated with the offences with a victim–offender overlap (though residential burglary was an exception in this regard). That led to a speculation that the higher clear-up rates in offender households might be explained by a higher proportion of victimisations by acquaintances, and an exploration – through the work of Felson *et al.* (2000) – of possible motivations in property crimes against acquaintances. The implication might be – though the data considered so far certainly do not demonstrate this – that a high rate of household victimisations in offender households might be explicable, at least in part, by a high rate of acquaintance victimisation, and that such offences might be committed for the kinds of reasons suggested by Felson *et al.* (2000). But at this stage, and before we pursue speculation too far, we need more data.

An exploratory interview study

In order to explore more fully some of the issues raised in the study of recorded crime, it was decided to conduct an exploratory interview study with a limited number of offenders. At its main office in central Sheffield, the South Yorkshire Probation Service has dedicated the whole of the ground floor to interview rooms, grouped around a central waiting space. With the kind co-operation of the Probation Service, it was arranged that, on certain days, we would place notices in the central waiting space saying that anyone who wished to earn a small sum of money by being interviewed for a Sheffield University research project should speak to the receptionist.[19] There was no attempt to select respondents, except by checking that they were currently required to visit the probation service (i.e. people such as girlfriends, who were merely accompanying probation clients, were excluded). Since the minimum age for probation – as opposed to youth justice – supervision is 18, there were no respondents below that age. Hence, in technical language this was *an unselected opportunity sample of adult offenders* and, of course, it follows from this that the sample is not necessarily representative of all probation clients. (Indeed, as we shall see, it seems likely that the sample contains an over-representation of probationers who were living alone and short of money.) The main purpose of the interviews was *to explore the victimisation experiences of known offenders.*

It was originally intended that we would interview 100 offenders, but our research assistant miscounted on the last day and so the sample actually contains 101.[20] Of these, 82 are male and 19 female. The age range was fairly broad, from 18 to 46, with a mean age of 27. As regards ethnic group, white offenders are over-represented in the sample at 92 per cent, perhaps because of a reluctance of members of ethnic minority popula- tions to volunteer for an opportunity sample. All of the eight ethnic minority respondents were male, and all were black, so Sheffield's Asian-origin population is unrepresented in this sample. We have no exact knowledge of the extent of the criminal record of sample members, though it was clear that many of them had been before the courts on several occasions.

As regards housing (an important matter when studying household offences), as many as 43 of the sample lived alone, either in self-contained accommodation (e.g. a bedsit) (28) or in a hostel room (15). As expected, the great majority of non-hostel residents lived in rented accommodation (77 out of 86), mostly in the social housing sector (i.e. their landlord was either the local authority or a housing association). Nearly 60 per cent of the sample had lived at more than one address in the last nine months.

Victimisation questions similar to those asked in the BCS formed a central part of the interview schedule. However, on this occasion the list of offences was restricted, with only household offences being covered. Where a respondent's household had been victimised, as is standard in crime surveys a 'victimisation sheet' seeking further details of the offence (and the victim's response to the offence) was completed for each such incident. In this survey, however, as it was a small and exploratory study and as we were not primarily interested in multiple victimisations, we decided to work to a maximum of three victimisation sheets per respondent. Where a respondent reported more than three victimisations, we asked him/her to provide details of the three most recent events.

Interviews were conducted in September 2000, and respondents were asked to recall victimisations occurring 'since last Christmas'. It was thought that 'last Christmas' would constitute a readily understood time-marker, especially given the widespread celebrations for the new Millennium that occurred on New Year's Eve 1999. We have treated the results as referring to victimisations during a nine-month period, and where appropriate we have converted them into an annual rate using a simple 4/3 formula.

Table 5.7 gives basic details of victimisation in the sample. Column one of the table shows that, overall, as many as 70 (69 per cent) of the sample reported a victimisation during the nine months of the study, a figure that contrasts strikingly with the British Crime Survey covering the same year (2000), where only 27.6 per cent of respondents reported one or more victimisations for *any crime* (i.e. including personal as well as household crimes) during the full calendar year (col. 2 of Table 5.7). On this simple overall comparison, then, there seems to be obvious evidence of a high victimisation prevalence rate in this offender sample. However, at this point the need to compare like with like, discussed previously, must be

Table 5.7 Victimisations for household offences in an opportunity sample of offenders, with comparisons with the British Crime Survey 2000

Offence type	Offender sample: % victimised in 9 mths	BCS prevalence rate for full year (%)**	Offender sample: total no. of incidents	Offender sample: incidents expressed as annual rate per 1,000 households	BCS incidence rate for full year, per 1,000 households**
	(1)	(2)	(3)	(4)	(5)
Residential burglary with entry	25.7	2.1	46	613	27
Attempted residential burglary	16.8	1.5	24	320	21
Theft in dwelling	31.7	5.2*	72	960	71*
Theft outside dwelling	24.8	}	54	720	}
Criminal damage to household	11.9	2.8	30	400	51
TWOC (incl. attempts)	5.9	1.9†	11	146	21†
Theft from vehicle	4.0	7.5†	6	80	104†
Damage to vehicle	5.9	4.9	6	80	71
All	69.3	27.6††	249	3,319	n/a

Notes:
*Using the BCS category 'other household theft' which excludes bicycle theft.
†BCS data for acquisitive vehicle crimes are given in three sub-categories: TWOC, theft from vehicles, and attempts (relating to both offences). The figures given here have apportioned the 'attempt' sub-category on the basis of the proportions for the full crimes.
**BCS data are derived from Simmons et al. (2002: Tables 3.02 and 3.03).
††Includes personal offences as well as household offences.

borne in mind. For example, BCS data for the year 2000 show, for residential burglary with entry, that the overall prevalence rate was 2.1 per cent for all households (Table 5.7, col. 2), but this rate rose to 6.0 per cent in 'council areas' and to 7.6 per cent among households where the head of household is aged 16–24 (Kershaw *et al.* 2001: Tables A4.3 and A4.4).[21] Presumably, for households in council areas with a young head of household, the rate was even higher. Given the relative youth of the offender sample, and their geographical clustering in poorer housing areas, it is therefore clear that some upward adjustment needs to be made to the 'national average' rates in the BCS if one is to make a credible comparison. Even on this basis, however, the offender sample prevalence rate for some offences seems high: for example, the prevalence rate for burglary with entry in the offender sample is 25 per cent in nine months (Table 5.7, col. 1).

As well as prevalence data, we also need to consider repeat victimisations. There was a high rate of revictimisation in this sample – 49 out of 101 reported being the subject of more than one offence. Putting this another way, only 21 of the 70 victimised respondents (or 30 per cent) reported just a single victimisation, whereas in the BCS results for 2000, the proportion of single victims among all victims of household crimes was much higher than this (Kershaw *et al.* 2001: Table A2.9).[22] Additionally, the mean number of victimisations per victim was very high at 3.5 in the nine-month period (median = 3).[23] When, therefore, victimisation incidence rates (i.e prevalence × repeat victimisations) for the offender sample are calculated as an annual rate and compared to the average national BCS figures (see the final two columns of Table 5.7), the offenders' victimisation level is very much higher for all offences except thefts from and damage to vehicles. For example, the rate for burglary with entry is over 20 times the BCS rate, that for attempted burglary 15 times, that for criminal damage eight times. As we have seen, given the 'like versus like' problem, such comparisons have to be treated with great caution, but taken as a whole the data do nevertheless suggest a picture of disproportionately high victimisation levels in this sample.

The main reason for the relatively low rate of vehicle victimisation per household in the offender sample is because only 28 of the sample reported that anyone in their household had regular use of a car or other vehicle. Given such a low opportunity base, however, the reported victimisation rate for TWOC and attempted TWOC (six out of 28 available vehicles victimised, and a total of 11 victimisations in nine months) must be considered high.[24]

In the offender sample, the two offences with the highest rates of victimisation are residential burglary (taking full crimes and attempts together) and theft in a dwelling (see Table 5.7, col. 4). The prominence of offences of theft in a dwelling in this sample makes for an important difference from the empirical data in the first part of this chapter, where for technical reasons theft in a dwelling was not included in the analysis. This offence has some special features, which we shall consider in more detail below.

The relative rates of victimisation for different types of respondent were also considered. There were no significant differences by age or gender, and the most striking finding was the high victimisation levels for persons living alone in a non-hostel setting.[25] There were 28 sample members in this category, of whom as many as 20, or 71 per cent, reported two or more victimisations during nine months, as compared with 29 out of 73 (39 per cent) for the remainder of the sample.

How often were these victimisations reported to the police? To answer this question – and further detailed questions about specific victimisations – it is necessary to turn to the data obtained from the victimisation sheets. As previously indicated, in this survey we worked to a maximum of three such sheets per respondent, and in consequence there is a total of only 116 completed sheets, although (see Table 5.7, col. 3) our respondents reported, in all, 249 victimisations.

Table 5.8 shows (in col. 2) the rates of reporting to the police for the different offences covered in the survey, with (in col. 3) a comparison of the national BCS figure for the same offence(s) in the same year. Because of the small numbers in the survey data for many offences (especially the vehicle offences), any comparisons need to be made with care. Neverthe-

Table 5.8 Frequency of reporting of offences to the police in an opportunity sample of offenders, with comparisons with British Crime Survey data for 2000

Offence type	No. of victimisation sheets (N)	% of N reported to police	Reporting rate in BCS 2000*
Residential burglary with entry	32	66	74
Attempted residential burglary	17	41	55
Theft in dwelling	34	18	30
Theft outside dwelling	15	27	
Criminal damage to household	9	(56)	39
TWOC (incl. attempts)	3	(67)	90†
Theft from vehicle	4	(25)	47†
Damage to vehicle	2	(0)	24
All	116	40	42**

Note: percentages in brackets are based on Ns of less than 10.
*Derived from Simmons *et al.* (2002: Table 3.06).
†These data refer to the full crimes of TWOC and theft from vehicles. The combined reporting rate for attempts to commit these two crimes was 32%; the published data give no breakdown of this figure.
**This overall BCS figure includes personal crime as well as crimes against households.

less, a few points of general interest arise from the data. First, and not surprisingly, for most offences the reporting rates in the offender sample are lower than the corresponding rates in the BCS. Secondly, and more surprisingly, the reporting rates in the offender sample are in fact only slightly lower than the national rates – suggesting that (as one could also infer from the recorded crime study) it is not uncommon for offenders to report victimisations to the police. Thirdly, it is noteworthy that, for the more numerous offences, the rank ordering of reporting rates is very similar in both the BCS and the offender sample – so, burglary with entry has the highest rate, followed by attempted burglary, followed by thefts in and around the home, which have a low rate. This similarity of data patterns is reassuring (although not conclusive) as regards the validity of the data from the offender sample.

A potentially important variable in relation to the reporting of property offences is whether the property is insured (most insurance companies will meet a claim for theft or damage to property only if the offence has been reported to the police). Perhaps surprisingly, in over half the crimes for which a victimisation sheet was completed (65 out of 116, or 56 per cent), insurance had been taken out. However, in only five of these cases was the property insured by the offender-victim him/herself; in other instances it was normally the landlord or, in the smaller number of family contexts, a family member who had bought the insurance. We did not ask detailed questions about insurance cover, but we can reasonably assume that in the case of landlords (as opposed to family members) the insurance covered only damage to the structure of the dwelling, and not theft of the tenant's personal possessions. This helps to explain the two main findings of the study as regards insurance. These were first, that in the case of residential burglaries (including attempts), the offence was significantly more likely to be reported to the police where insurance was in place; and of course structural damage to, for example, doors or windows will often have occurred in these crimes. Secondly and by contrast, for thefts in a dwelling, where there would normally be no structural damage to the property, there was no 'insurance effect' on whether crimes were reported, and reporting rates were uniformly low.

While the rate at which victimisations were reported varied significantly by offence, and to an extent according to insurance, there was no significant association of the reporting rate with the age or gender of the respondent, or whether he/she was currently on drugs.

The rates of reporting to the police found in this survey are clearly higher than those in the series of ethnographic studies carried out by criminologists in St Louis among active street criminals (see e.g. Wright and Decker 1994, 1997; Jacobs and Wright 2006). In part, this could reflect what is obviously a very different cultural setting (including, perhaps, differences in insurance practices), but it is also almost certainly linked to the fact that the Sheffield and St Louis samples contain different kinds of offenders. From the published interview extracts, it would appear that most of the St Louis offenders were very active, semi-professional offenders. That was not the case for the Sheffield sample, many of whom were living 'on the social margins', short of money (hence they were glad to volunteer for our research interview), and fairly frequently living alone. Some of them were quite persistent offenders, but they were not semi-professional offenders. A good description of them would be, in the parlance of the English police, 'volume offenders'; that is, those who primarily commit those (non-motoring) offences that are most frequently dealt with by the police, such as theft, burglary, TWOC and criminal damage. The fact that, in such a sample, the reporting of victimisations to the police is clearly not a rare event is, in our view, a matter of some significance for criminal policy. We shall return to this point in our concluding section.

We asked those respondents who had reported crimes to the police for a comment on how they viewed the police response. The responses were coded into broad categories of 'positive', 'neutral' and 'negative', and on this basis negative comments outweighed positive ones by about two to one. However, many of the negative comments were mild, of the sort that one might easily obtain in a survey of the general population (e.g. 'they just took details'; 'there was nothing they could do'; 'they weren't really interested'; and so on). Only a few were very negative, with for example two respondents being disgusted because, they claimed, the police responded to the report of the victimisation by saying that the known offender making the report had in reality either done the crime himself, or had colluded in it. To set against these negatives, there were a number of positive comments, from the specific (such as 'they were good – they're still looking through the [CCTV] videos', or 'they took statements, they were sympathetic') to the more general ('they were quite good, actually'). Again, we shall return to the significance of these comments in our conclusions.

In the first part of this chapter, we began to develop a line of thought potentially linking acquaintanceship with the victim–offender overlap for household offences. For those in the offender sample who listed a victimisation, the incident sheet therefore included the question: 'I don't want to know any names, but do you know or suspect who did this?' Those who replied to this question that they knew 'definitely' or 'probably' who had committed the offence are treated as having replied affirmatively, while those who said they had no idea, or that they didn't really know but they had a hunch, are treated as having answered negatively. The overall pattern of replies is given in Table 5.9, broken down into four broad offence groups. Not surprisingly, given the definition of the offence (see Note 8), the overwhelming majority (94 per cent) of thefts in a dwelling were committed by people known to the offender; but much more unexpectedly, the proportion of burglaries (actual or attempted) where the offender was known to the victim was

Table 5.9 Frequency with which offenders in an opportunity sample reported that they knew 'certainly' or 'probably' who had victimised them

Victimisation type	N	% where 'offender known'
Residential burglary (with entry or attempted)	49	57.1
Theft in dwelling	34	94.1
Criminal damage to household or vehicle	11	36.4
Other household offences (theft outside dwelling, TWOC, theft from vehicle)	22	0.0
All	116	55.2

also very high at 57 per cent. (This is, of course, a figure that is much higher than would be obtained from any general sample of burglary victims.) The rate for the small number of cases of damage is lower at 37 per cent, and for the other household offences (theft outside the dwelling, and vehicle thefts) there were no known victimisations by acquaintances. As with the data about reporting to the police, the type of offence was by far the strongest factor relating to whether the offender was known to the victim. On this occasion, however, the offender being on drugs was also significant – those on drugs were more likely to know the identity of 'their' offender.

One might hypothesise (see earlier discussion) that probable knowledge of the offender's identity would be negatively correlated with the likelihood of reporting the offence to the police. In fact, however, taking the sample as a whole this was not the case, and there was no significant association between these two variables; and this finding was replicated even when type of offence was controlled for. Reasons for not reporting did however vary significantly according to whether the offender's probable identity was known. In cases in which probable identity was known, significantly more victims said they did not report because the issue was a 'private matter' (a finding that would probably be replicated in a general population sample), and in a further eight cases respondents were honest enough to tell the interviewer that the non-reporting was because they were afraid of the offender.

In our earlier discussion of the work of Felson et al. (2000), we referred to three main potential motivations for acquaintance-related acquisitive offences: these were 'inside information', 'proximity and impulsiveness', and 'dispute-related offences'. All three of these motivations were sometimes mentioned by respondents in this sample as they described incidents where they had been victimised. By way of illustration, we give below one case-example of each type (in these examples, the respondent offender-victims are referred to as OV1, OV2, etc.):

(a) *Inside Information.* OV1 lived in a shared house that had four bedsits, each with a lockable door. He went out for an hour one lunchtime, locking the door of his room. When he returned, he found that the outside door of the house had been kicked in, and his bedsit door was hanging off its hinges. No other room had been entered, which suggested a planned attack based on prior information. OV1's mountain bike, knives, clothes and cash had all been stolen. OV1 strongly suspected that this offence had been committed by a friend of one of the other residents in the house, with the informant and the burglar sharing the proceeds.

(b) *Proximity and Impulsiveness.* OV2 lived in a block of flats. He was interested in computers, and used to build computers in his flat. But some drug addicts ('smackheads') lived 'across the way' (on the same floor of the block of flats) and one day they broke in and stole all of OV2's equipment, when they were short of money for drugs. Similar incidents followed, so OV2 removed all electrical equipment from his flat, except for one black-and-white television; he also placed a sofa across the outside door of the flat to prevent further break-ins. In the most recent incident, the sofa had prevented entry. OV2 said he had reported the first incident to the police, but as a result he had 'got done over' by the smackheads, so he has not reported any subsequent offences.

(c) *Dispute-related offence.* OV3 lived in a bedsit. Most nights, he took his dog for a walk at around 11.30 p.m. One night, on returning home from his walk, he saw flames through the curtains of his bedsit. By the time the fire brigade arrived, everything was burned. Evidence suggested that the fire had been started by someone throwing a lighted object through the window. OV3 believed that this offence was motivated by revenge, and was committed by a member of a family through whose window he (OV3) had previously thrown a can of lager.

For the offender sample, we attempted to code the reason for the offence, as perceived by the offender-victim, in all the 64 cases in which the respondent claimed to have known or strongly suspected the identity of the offender. It proved impossible, in most cases, to distinguish between the categories of 'inside information' and 'proximity/impulsiveness', so we combined these into a broader category of 'special opportunity'. On this basis, 43 of the 64 cases could be classified as 'special-opportunity-based' offences, with 11 as 'dispute-related' and 10 for which no motivation was ascribed by the offender-victim. The predominance of 'special-opportunity' cases over 'dispute-related' is itself interesting. It seems that this might be another way in which this sample differs from the St Louis sample (see Jacobs and Wright 2006), where revenge appears to be more prominent; and this difference might again be related to the apparently different kinds of offenders in the two studies.

When the perceived motivation of the offender was related to other variables, it was found, not surprisingly, that a 'revenge' motivation was very rarely found in thefts in a dwelling (where by definition the offender is in the dwelling with the householder's permission). Taking all offences together, where the offender-victim considered revenge to have been the motivation for the offence, the offence was more likely to be reported to the police.

An overview of two empirical studies

At this stage, it is useful to bring together the evidence collected in the recorded crime study and in the small survey of offenders. What has been established? We suggest there are three main findings:

First, it seems (from both studies, but particularly from the recorded crime study) that there is strong evidence for a victim–offender overlap at least for some household offences, even when the neighbourhood crime rate is controlled for. Given the relative absence of previous research on the victim–offender overlap for household offences, this is important in adding to the overall volume of evidence confirming the existence of such overlaps.

Secondly, there is substantial evidence from both studies that those living in offender households, and frequently offenders themselves, are – except in the case of theft in a dwelling – fairly often willing to report their victimisations to the police. This appears to be largely a new finding in the criminological literature on the victim–offender overlap. We do not suggest that it is a finding that will be valid in all social circumstances, and in this respect we have noted the contrast with the important series of studies of 'the criminal underworld' in St Louis. Nevertheless, in those contexts in which the finding holds, we consider that it has significant policy implications.

Thirdly, there is direct evidence in the offender survey, and indirect evidence from the data on clear-up rates in the recorded crime study, that household offences committed against known offenders might be disproportionately often committed by acquaintances. There is also some interesting instantiation, in the interview study, of Felson *et al.*'s (2000) suggestions about the possible mechanisms underlying acquaintance-based acquisitive crimes. Given the limitations of the data sources in the present study, all these matters clearly require further research before they are treated as established, not least because of some discrepancies between the findings of the recorded crime study and the interview study.[26] Nevertheless, they raise the possibility that acquaintanceship could be a key element in the explanation of the victim–offender overlap in household offences. If that should prove to be the case, then perhaps this factor would also help to explain the differing patterns of recorded crime data found for TWOC and for theft from vehicles in Tables 5.4, 5.5, and 5.6: perhaps TWOC has more victimisations by acquaintances in offender-based households? Intuitively, that sounds plausible, but it is of course an empirical question – and one on which at present we have no data.

Explaining the victim–offender overlap

In this section, we aim to locate our research findings within the wider explanatory literature on the victim–offender overlap. In their overview article, Lauritsen and Laub (2007) draw a distinction between explanations of the overlap that are based on 'risk heterogeneity', and those that are based on 'state (or event) dependence'. These are familiar concepts to criminologists, and especially to those interested in repeat victimisation (see Bottoms and Costello 2009 for further discussion in that context), and they are derived originally from the field of statistics. 'Risk heterogeneity', in the present context, refers to 'explanations ... that assert that individuals differ according to some generally stable characteristics that are correlated with both offending and victimisation' (Lauritsen and Laub 2007: 61); these might include, for example, individually based factors such as low self-control (see Schreck 1999), or more community-oriented variables such as living in an economically deprived, high-crime area. 'State dependence' explanations, by contrast, postulate that, on occasion, an individual's *specific life experiences will 'operate in such a way as to alter [his/her] future risk of the event'* (Lauritsen and Laub 2007: 61, emphasis added). In the present context, the most obvious possibilities for 'state dependence' explanations are *first*, that the experience of victimisation might, over a short period, lead causally to the victim deciding to offend (perhaps by way of specific retaliation, or more generalised anger); and *secondly*, that the experience of becoming an offender will in some way lead causally to the offender becoming a victim.

Let us consider these two types of explanation separately. The 'risk heterogeneity' type of explanation (see above) is concerned to identify 'characteristics that are correlated with both offending and victimisation'. If this type of explanation is correct (or partially correct), it follows that such characteristics will explain (or partially explain) the existence of identified victim–offender overlaps. Clearly, the risk heterogeneity approach has something to offer to explanation, as is suggested by the examples already given of low self-control and the influence of criminal areas. However, this type of explanatory approach, when pursued to its logical conclusion, inevitably raises an important question. That question, as the authors of a recent article on violence put it, is whether those involved in violent incidents:

... have a clear tendency to differentiate into offender or victim roles. If no evidence is available to indicate that people differ in this respect, then we cannot meaningfully distinguish between offenders and victims except as chance outcomes of an incident. (Schreck, Stewart and Osgood 2008: 880)

In their research study, these authors found 'significant and stable levels of differentiation between offenders and victims', and they found also that this differentiation was 'predictable with explanatory variables' (2008: 872). Accordingly, their analysis supports, though with enhanced statistical rigour, some previous research findings to a similar effect. This body of work, taken as a whole, therefore shows that offenders and victims are not indistinguishable, even for violent offences where such a thesis might seem to be intuitively most plausible. Thus, although the 'risk heterogeneity' approach to the explanation of the victim–offender overlap clearly has some plausibility (see above), it cannot be pushed to the point where any distinction between victims and offenders is obliterated.

What then of 'state dependence' explanations? There is now a strong group of research studies which together provide evidence *both* that victimisation frequently follows offending, apparently causally, *and* that offending frequently follows victimisation, apparently causally (see for example Sampson and Lauritsen 1990; Lauritsen, Sampson and Laub 1991; Shaffer and Ruback 2002; Stewart, Schreck and Simons 2006; Smith and Ecob 2007). The most recent study is by Smith and Ecob (2007), and is based on personal offences as measured in the Edinburgh Youth Study (see Note 4). The conclusions of these authors, after a careful analysis, are complex but very interesting:

> The effects of offending on later victimization are clearest, and these *are not explained by the ten explanatory variables included in this analysis.* Offending leads to an increase in victimization up to two years later, but the effect is then cancelled out over the longer term. The effects of victimization on offending are more equivocal, but there is evidence that over the longer term victimization leads to an increase in offending, *although this effect becomes weaker after allowing for the ten explanatory variables.* These findings lend support to the theory that there are reciprocal causal influences running between victimization and offending in the teenage years. (2007: 654, emphasis added)

It is, however, important to note these authors' observations (italicised in the quotation above) that the included 'explanatory variables' (gender, impulsivity, neighbourhood deprivation, risky spare-time activities, etc.) failed to explain the first ('offending to victimisation') result, and only partially explained the second ('victimisation to offending'). Results of a similar kind were noted by Sampson and Lauritsen (1994: 34) as long ago as the mid-1990s,[27] and this type of finding led Lauritsen and Laub (2007: 62), in their overview article, to comment that 'to date, we know much more about the factors that do *not* account for the relationship between victimisation and offending than we do about those that might be responsible' (emphasis in original).

In the present chapter, we have no data relating to a possible 'victimisation to offending' trajectory, and the recorded crime data used in the first part of the chapter, being cross-sectional, are necessarily neutral as regards any possible direction of influence. However, the small Sheffield offender survey certainly suggests (though it does not definitively establish) a likely causal influence whereby being 'an offender' has enhanced the likelihood of subsequent victimisation.

Two aspects of this tentative suggestion seem worth emphasis and development. First, the overwhelming weight of the empirical evidence previously published in support of a possible 'offending to victimisation' trajectory has been based on personal offences, especially violence. Therefore, the data in the Sheffield offender survey, while tentative, seem to open up some new territory for research exploration in the field of household offences. Secondly, there is the important issue of role of delinquent peers. On this question, Jennifer Shaffer's (2003: 2) summary, written in the context of a study of violence among adolescents, remains more generally apposite:

> Nearly every study of the victim–offender overlap argues that understanding the relationship between victimization and offending requires an understanding of peer impact. However, these assertions are largely untested. Moreover, although research consistently indicates that peers influence adolescent *offending*, there is little attention to whether peers affect adolescent *victimization* [emphasis added].

It is also the case that the research literature on this issue does not speak entirely with one voice (among the more important studies, see Sampson and Lauritsen 1990; Schreck *et al.* 2004; and Shaffer 2003). Moreover, the literature has only rarely focused on the precise mechanisms whereby the specific actions of peers might be postulated to contribute to the overlap, although a general comment frequently made is that (in the words of Shaffer and Ruback's (2002: 2) useful précis) 'offenders are more likely than non-offenders to become victims, because their lifestyles frequently bring them in contact with other offenders'. Against this background, the suggestions of Felson *et al.* (2000) as regards the possible mechanisms underpinning acquisitive crimes committed against acquaintances, and the significant support for the existence of these mechanisms in the small Sheffield offender survey, are potentially important because they offer the promise of greater precision in understanding how peer-group-related mechanisms might explain the victim–offender overlap for household crimes. This line of thought therefore again seems to raise fresh hypotheses that are worth further exploration and testing.

Implications for criminal policy

In this final section, we concentrate on the policy implications of two of our main findings, namely that identified offenders appear to be disproportionately at risk of victimisation for household offences, and that such victimisations are not infrequently reported to the police.

'It must be recognised', say Lauritsen and Laub (2007: 66), 'that there is political reticence to tackle the victim–offender issue.' It must indeed. An interesting example of this may be found in the presentation of the findings of Shaffer and Ruback (2002) based on research at Pennsylvania State University. These authors analysed data from a survey of adolescents across two separate years. In their 'Key Findings' section (p. 4), they focused on the longitudinal dimension of the study, and listed two central results, with equal emphasis. These were first, a 'victimisation to offending' result and secondly, an 'offending to victimisation' result; and, as regards both, it was indicated that in general (and congruently with earlier research – see above) these patterns held 'regardless of age, gender, race, level of physical development or drug use'. The authors' research was both funded and published by an agency of the US Federal Government (the 'Office of Juvenile Justice and Delinquency Prevention'), so not unnaturally a 'policy implications' section appeared at the end of the paper. In this section, four main policy implications are highlighted, namely:

- 'Some groups are at higher risk than others for violent victimisation';
- 'Violent victimisation is a warning signal for future violent victimisation';
- 'Violent victimisation is a warning signal for future violent offending';
- 'Many of the risk factors associated with juvenile violence suggest opportunities for intervention'.

Interestingly, the longitudinal 'offending to victimisation' result (one of the two key longitudinal results previously flagged) has totally disappeared when it comes to the headlines of the policy implications. Closer scrutiny of the publication shows that this result is also given very secondary treatment even in the detailed text of the policy section, presumably reflecting what Lauritsen and Laub (2007) describe as 'political reticence'. This is unfortunate, because the research analysis that precedes the policy section is very instructive.

An entirely different approach to policy in this field is offered by Jacobs and Wright (2006) at the conclusion of their book on (as their subtitle puts it) 'retaliation in the criminal underworld' in St Louis, Missouri. This, as we noted earlier, is an underworld in which retaliation is rife, the police are viewed with deep suspicion or even hatred, and offences committed against street criminals, although common, are very rarely reported. Thus, the official criminal justice system scarcely features in the main descriptive sections of the book. But on their final page, Jacobs and Wright (2006: 135) say this:

> If we accept the proposition that much criminal violence is the result of retaliation, then it follows that one way to tackle it is for authorities to take steps to deal with incubating disputes before they escalate, whether or not the disputants seek their help. To do otherwise risks perpetuating a subculture beyond the law, a 'violent land' ... regulated by the threat and reality of personal vengeance.

In other words, Jacobs and Wright are here postulating the possible existence, in certain parts of American cities, of a subculture that is close to the Hobbesian war of all against all (see Tuck 1991). And, they suggest – in an argument that bears marked similarities to that of Matt Matravers in Chapter 1 of this volume – that this is a state of affairs that no civilised State can contemplate with equanimity. Pursuing the argument, they further contend that an urgent priority, in the kind of social context that they describe, is the restoration of a greater degree of *legitimacy* to the police (and other players in the criminal justice system) in the eyes of street criminals. But 'respect is the bedrock on which legitimacy rests', while 'most serious street offenders despise formal authority and all it stands for'. Such contempt, say the authors, 'cannot be erased or even reduced through simple policy changes' (Jacobs and Wright 2006: 131), but a promising way forward would be to try to construct officially sponsored and highly localised forms of dispute resolution based on a mediating role offered by so-called 'old heads', that is, 'senior members of street culture whose years of experience "on the corner"' might give them 'the pull necessary to stymie conflicts before they mushroomed into full-blown confrontations' (Jacobs and Wright 2006: 133).

The offenders encountered in the Sheffield study are less alienated from the police and the criminal justice system than are Jacobs and Wright's 'street criminals'. Indeed, in one of the most interesting findings of the small Sheffield survey of offenders, the household victimisations they suffered were reported to the police only a little less often than were the victimisations of the general public (as reported in the British Crime Survey) (Table 5.8). Moreover, respondents' views about the police response when victimisations were reported were sometimes – though not always – positive; there was thus little corroboration, in a Sheffield context, for Jacobs and Wright's (2006: 4) observation that, in St Louis, offenders' 'desire for safety and justice are of little or no concern to most police officers anyway'.

In the light of these findings, it would appear that, for 'volume' offenders in a UK context, it ought to be more easily possible to develop policies along the lines of those recommended by Jacobs and Wright (2006). We do not see it as our task to formulate detailed and specific policy recommendations, but we believe it is appropriate to spell out three broad policy principles arising from the analysis in this chapter.

First, the police and the criminal justice system should take seriously known offenders' reports of their victimisations. There are two justifications for this suggestion. The first is based on grounds of principle: offenders are citizens, and have the same rights as other citizens to call upon the State to assist them in dealing with offences committed against them. The second justification is more empirical; it seems probable (although, owing to a lack of specific empirical evidence, not certain) that taking offenders' victimisations seriously will enhance the legitimacy of the criminal justice system in their eyes, and that should, on the general evidence of studies of legitimacy (see for example Tyler 2003), lead to more compliant future behaviour. This proposal might sound impossibly utopian, but in fact there are precedents of a not dissimilar kind, as Jacobs and Wright (2006: 130) have pointed out:

> Pressures from the women's movement over the past two decades have made the police more responsive to sex workers' reports of criminal victimization. The police are now more likely to treat prostitutes as genuine victims and credible complainants when they report a crime. Nothing prevents police from granting other street offenders the same opportunities for legitimate access to the law.

Secondly, the move to treat offenders' victimisations seriously should be linked to the growing trend (in many countries, including the UK) towards the adoption of neighbourhood policing strategies. To develop this point, we may note briefly some results from the evaluation of the so-called 'Local Management of Community Safety' (LMCS) in Milton Keynes (Singer 2004). In this study, it was found that there were improvements in victim satisfaction following the introduction of a 'reassurance policing' project in two socially deprived neighbourhoods. Moreover, in the view of relevant police officers, this improvement was principally attributable to closer police–community links. As one officer put it: 'this estate now has local officers and we do tend to pick up most of the victims that are being harassed on a regular basis ... we're picking up more ongoing situations than we used to pick up' (Singer 2004: 58).[28] As we have previously noted, there is strong evidence of the clustering of the residences of known offenders in certain localities (Craglia and

Costello 2005), and a well-trained local police presence in such areas, working to neighbourhood policing principles, should assist the development of policies to take offenders' victimisations seriously, as well as making it easier for offenders to report such victimisations.

Thirdly, when formulating public policy relating to victims (of the kind addressed in several other chapters of this book), it must be recognised that among the victims to whom the policy will be applied there will, in all probability, be a non-trivial number of offender-victims. It is easy to see why facing this fact will, for some political actors, be uncomfortable. But the systematic evasion of uncomfortable truths is very rarely a good policy, either in personal or in political life.

Notes

1   See for example Fagan, Piper and Cheng (1987, Appendix B), where the question 'Has anyone broken into your home?' was one of seven victimisation questions asked of a population of US inner city youths; however, in the final paper on this study, results for this crime were reported only as one of a group of four 'property offences', the others being personal thefts. Again, in their British self-reported offending survey, Graham and Bowling (1995) – and, in a replication, Farrall and Maltby (2003: 39) – used four victimisation questions; one of these was criminal damage to the household, and another a general question on theft and attempted theft, including thefts 'from . . . your home' but also including personal theft.

2   A number of authors have also found stronger evidence for the victim–offender overlap in respect of personal or violent crime than for property crime: see for example Farrall and Maltby (2003: 40–1) and Gottfredson (1984: chs 2 and 3).

3   Among recent studies of the victim–offender overlap in violent offences, see Dobrin 2001; Shaffer and Ruback 2002; and Schreck, Stewart and Osgood 2008.

4   On the victim–offender overlap in the Edinburgh Study of Youth Transitions and Crime, see Smith (2004) and Smith and Ecob (2007). Five kinds of victimisation are covered in this research; two of these are assaults (with and without a weapon), one is threatened assault, one robbery, and one theft of personal property. For the victim–offender overlap in the Home Office's longitudinal Offending, Crime and Justice Survey (OCJS), see for example Wood (2005) and Roe and Ashe (2008: ch. 4). Types of victimisation covered in these publications are assaults (with and without injury), robbery, theft from the person and 'other personal thefts' (i.e. where 'there is no direct contact between victim and offender, e.g. sports equipment from changing rooms'). The OCJS has also asked questions of its respondents about victimisations for household offences, but the Home Office has not assigned priority to the analysis or publication of these data, so they remain unpublished (information from Home Office, January 2009).

5   Perhaps the most systematic previous study of the victim–offender overlap in relation to household crime is that by Gottfredson (1984: ch. 3), using victimisation and self-report data from the first (1982) sweep of the British

Crime Survey. He considered two main types of household victimisation, namely residential burglary and criminal damage to the household. Three self-reported measures of offending were used, namely 'assault and violence', 'non-predatory minor theft' (e.g. theft of office supplies, not buying a television licence) and 'delinquencies' (including shoplifting, taking cannabis, deliberately travelling without a ticket) (1984: 35). Residential burglary victimisation was not significantly related to any of the three self-reported offending measures, but criminal damage to the household was related to all three, although only weakly so as regards 'delinquencies'. However, the validity of all these results is to a degree placed into question by the fact that, in the 1982 British Crime Survey, the level of self-reported offending admissions was for various reasons improbably low: see, on this, Mayhew and Elliott (1990).

6 One of the classic early studies of the victim–offender overlap was Simon Singer's (1981) follow-up survey of Wolfgang, Sellin and Figlio's *Delinquency in a Birth Cohort* (1972) longitudinal sample. Singer asked respondents to provide retrospectively self-reports of victimisation at three periods of their lives, and then correlated these victimisation data against official data on arrests. Some later research analysts have used official data sources to study the extent to which known offenders become homicide victims (Lattimore, Linster and MacDonald 1997; Dobrin 2001). We have not been able to discover any previous published non-homicide study that relies, as we do in the first part of this chapter, on official records for *both* victimisation *and* offending data.

7 'TWOC' is in England a commonly used abbreviation for the offence of 'taking [a vehicle] without consent'. 'TWOC' is not theft, because theft requires an intention by the offender to deprive the owner permanently of the property, whereas most offenders committing TWOC use the vehicle temporarily and then abandon it.

8 'Thefts in the home' are legally distinct from residential burglaries (although the latter of course often involve theft) because a central element of the offence of burglary is that the offender must be a trespasser. 'Thefts in the home' are therefore committed by people who are in the home with the permission of the householder – for example, friends or tradepersons fixing household defects (plumbers, etc.).

9 We wish to express warm thanks to South Yorkshire Police for their kindness and co-operation in making these data available. This chapter is published with the permission of South Yorkshire Police, but any views expressed are those of the authors and do not necessarily represent the views of South Yorkshire Police.

10 Normally, this means that an offender has been convicted or formally cautioned for a standard list offence in 1995. There are, however, a small number of instances in which the police have good reason to list the person as an 'offender' with no conviction or caution recorded (e.g. where the person has died).

11 For this purpose we used so-called 'Enumeration Districts' (EDs) from the 1991 National Census. There were 1,057 EDs in Sheffield in 1991, with an average of 209 households per ED. The number of households per quintile varied from 38,964 in Quintile 5 to 42,930 in Quintile 2 – see Table 5.1.

12 'Prevalence', in a criminological context, means the proportion of persons or households victimised for a given crime or crimes, regardless of whether they are once-only victims or repeat victims during the study period. The total

incidence of crime in a given area for a given period is given by the formula 'Prevalence × Repeat Victimisation'.

13 Many incidents of repeat victimisation occur within three months of the initial victimisation (see the bar chart in Bottoms and Costello 2009: 43). As writers on repeat victimisation have frequently pointed out, this means that measuring this phenomenon over a fixed and short period of time – such as, in the present instance, a calendar year – gives a necessarily incomplete account of the extent of RV, because of arbitrary cut-offs at each end of the period.

14 The decision to place Quintile 3 with Quintiles 1 and 2, rather than with Quintiles 4 and 5, was made on the grounds of the differing number of offender households in each quintile. Quintiles 1–3 together include 2,347 offender households, as against 3,226 in Quintiles 4 and 5 together (see Table 5.1).

15 Further supporting evidence of a victim–offender overlap for repeat victimisation in household offences may be found in a longitudinal study by the present authors for the period 1998–2006. It was found that, among a group of 641 'long-term chronically victimized households', 53 per cent were also 'offender households' (Bottoms and Costello 2009: 39, 48).

16 Moreover, Felson *et al.* (2000: 300) reported that 'school-age youths are particularly likely to be victims of acquaintance robbery' and that 'youths are much less likely than older victims to report robbery incidents' to the police, partly because many of the incidents are minor. Although the authors do not make the point, this presumably means that adults who experienced acquaintance robbery were very much more likely than other adult victims to report the crime to the police.

17 Wright and Decker's (1997) study was restricted to armed robbery. However, in a previous study of burglary (Wright and Decker 1994), the findings were very similar – a point of some importance for the present study of household offences.

18 The population interviewed in this longitudinal study consisted of 113 male offenders who, at the time of their first interview (from which the data given in the text are derived), had a mean age of 20 years and nine months and a mean number of eight conviction occasions for a standard list offence.

19 We are most grateful to the South Yorkshire Probation Service for their help in facilitating our research in this way. The notices in the waiting room did not disclose the principal subject matter for the research interview, although of course this was explained as part of the consent procedure at the beginning of the interview itself.

20 Some interviews in the early part of the study were conducted by each of the authors, but the majority were the responsibility of our research assistant, Gary Potter, to whom we wish to express our thanks.

21 The Home Office in 2001 published 'first results' relating to BCS data for the year 2000 (Kershaw *et al.* 2001). This was a transitional year for the BCS, prior to drawing a much larger annual sample based on continuous interviewing. Initial results using these new methods were published in 2002 (Simmons *et al.* 2002), in many tables alongside data for earlier years, including the year 2000. In some tables, the data for 2000 were revised in the 2002 publication, and therefore in the present chapter, wherever possible, we present BCS data from Simmons *et al.* (2002). However, the earlier report included data for 2000 on a number of topics not covered in the later report, and in such instances we rely

on Kershaw *et al.* (2001). Differences between the sources are in all cases relatively small.

22 In the source cited, Kershaw *et al.* (2001) do not give an overall figure for household offences. However, for individual offences the proportion of single victims among all victims was below 70 per cent for only one household crime (damage to households, 60 per cent), and other typical figures were 'all burglaries' (including attempts) 79 per cent, 'other household theft' 77 per cent, 'all vehicle thefts' 77 per cent.

23 A small number of respondents had been victimised so often for a given offence that they said they could not give a precise estimate. In such cases we have assigned a coding of five victimisations.

24 The British Crime Survey for 2000 records victimisation prevalence rates per vehicle-using household as follows: TWOC (full crime) 1.8 per cent; theft from vehicle (full crime) 7.2 per cent; attempted TWOC or theft from vehicle 3.3 per cent (Simmons *et al.* 2002: Table 3.03).

25 The victimisation rate for persons living in hostels was the same as for those living in households of two or more. It seems therefore to be the fact of living alone in a non-protected housing context that enhances the risk of victimisation.

26 In particular, the recorded crime study found no difference in the clear-up rates for residential burglary as between offender households and others, by contrast to TWOC and criminal damage, where offender households had higher clear-up rates (Table 5.6). However, in the offender survey, the proportion of residential burglary cases where the offender-victim said he/she could identify the offender (58 per cent) was substantially higher than the equivalent figure for other household offences (including criminal damage and TWOC: 12 per cent) (Table 5.9).

27 Sampson and Lauritsen (1994) noted evidence of causal effects in both directions, and added that the data 'strongly suggest that violent offending and violent victimisation are intimately connected and that this relationship cannot be explained away by traditional demographic and social correlates of crime' (p. 34).

28 A more rigorous research evaluation of reassurance policing strategies was later completed by the Home Office in six sites in different geographical areas (Tuffin *et al.* 2006). There were positive results on a range of outcome indicators such as crime, perceptions of antisocial behaviour and public confidence in the police, but unfortunately sample sizes were too small to determine whether or not there was a programme effect on victim satisfaction (p. 52).

References

Bottoms, A.E. and Costello, A. (2009) 'Crime prevention and the understanding of repeat victimization: a longitudinal study', in P. Knepper, J. Doak and J. Shapland (eds), *Urban Crime Prevention, Surveillance, and Restorative Justice: Effects of social technologies*. Boca Raton, FL: CRC Press, pp. 23–53.

Bottoms, A.E., Shapland, J., Costello, A., Holmes, D.J. and Muir, G. (2004) 'Towards desistance: theoretical underpinnings for an empirical study', *Howard Journal of Criminal Justice*, 43(4): 368–89.

Craglia, M. and Costello, A. (2005) 'A model of offenders in England', in F. Toppen and M. Painho (eds), *Proceedings of AGILE 2005: Eighth Conference on Geographic Information Science.* Lisbon: Universidade Nova de Lisboa, pp. 489–97.

Dobrin, A. (2001) 'The risk of offending on homicide victimization: a case control study', *Journal of Research in Crime and Delinquency,* 38(2): 154–73.

Fagan, J., Piper, E. and Cheng, Y.-T. (1987) 'Contributions of victimization to delinquency in inner cities', *Journal of Criminal Law and Criminology,* 78(3): 586–613.

Farrall, S. and Maltby, S. (2003) 'The victimisation of probationers', *Howard Journal of Criminal Justice,* 42(1): 32–54.

Felson, R.B., Baumer, E.P. and Messner, S.F. (2000) 'Acquaintance robbery', *Journal of Research in Crime and Delinquency,* 37(3): 284–305.

Garland, D. (2001) *The Culture of Control: Crime and social order in contemporary society.* Oxford: Oxford University Press.

Gottfredson, M.R. (1984) *Victims of Crime: The Dimensions of Risk.* Home Office Research Study 81. London: HMSO.

Graham, J. and Bowling, B. (1995) *Young People and Crime* Home Office Research Study 145. London: Home Office. http://www.homeoffice.gov.uk/rds/pdfs2/hors145.pdf

Hedström, P. (2005) *Dissecting the Social: On the principles of analytic sociology.* Cambridge: Cambridge University Press.

Home Office (1996) *Criminal Statistics England and Wales 1995* Cm. 3421. London: The Stationery Office.

Jacobs, B. and Wright, R. (2006) *Street Justice: Retaliation in the criminal underworld,* Cambridge Studies in Criminology. New York: Cambridge University Press.

Kershaw, C., Chivite-Matthews, N., Thomas, C. and Aust, R. (2001) *The 2001 British Crime Survey: First results, England and Wales* Home Office Statistical Bulletin 18/01. London: Home Office. http://www.homeoffice.gov.uk/rds/pdfs/hosb1801.pdf

Lattimore, P.K., Linster, R.L. and MacDonald, J.M. (1997) 'Risk of death among serious young offenders', *Journal of Research in Crime and Delinquency,* 34(2): 187–209.

Lauritsen, J.L. and Laub, J.H. (2007) 'Understanding the link between victimization and offending: new reflections on an old idea', in M. Hough and M. Maxfield (eds), *Surveying Crime in the 21st Century,* Crime Prevention Studies, Vol. 22. Monsey, NY: Criminal Justice Press and Cullompton: Willan Publishing, pp. 55–75.

Lauritsen, J.L., Sampson, R.J. and Laub, J.H. (1991) 'The link between offending and victimization among adolescents', *Criminology,* 29(2): 265–92.

Maguire, M. (2007) 'Crime data and statistics', in M. Maguire, R. Morgan and R. Reiner (eds), *The Oxford Handbook of Criminology* (4th edn). Oxford: Oxford University Press, pp. 241–301.

Matza, D. (1964) *Delinquency and Drift.* New York: John Wiley and Sons.

Mayhew, P. and Elliott, D. (1990) 'Self-reported offending, victimization, and the British Crime Survey', *Violence and Victims,* 5(2): 83–96.

National Crime Reduction Board (2008) 'Summary minutes from meeting number 2', held on 15 February 2008 in Committee Room 17, House of Commons.

Roe, S. and Ashe, J. (2008) *Young People and Crime: Findings from the 2006 Offending, Crime and Justice Survey* Home Office Statistical Bulletin 09/08. London: Home Office. http://www.homeoffice.gov.uk/rds/hosb2008.html

Sampson, R.J. and Lauritsen, J.L. (1990) 'Deviant lifestyles, proximity to crime, and the offender–victim link in personal violence', *Journal of Research in Crime and Delinquency*, 27: 110–39.

Sampson, R.J. and Lauritsen, J.L. (1994) 'Violent victimization and offending: individual-, situational- and community-level risk factors', in A.J. Reiss Jr. and J.A. Roth (eds), *Understanding and Preventing Violence*, Vol. 3: *Social Influences*. Washington, DC: National Academy Press, pp. 1–114.

Schreck, C.J. (1999) 'Criminal victimization and low self-control; an extension and test of a general theory of crime', *Justice Quarterly*, 16(3): 633–54.

Schreck, C.J., Fisher, B. and Miller, M. (2004) 'The social context of violent victimization: a study of the delinquent peer effect', *Justice Quarterly*, 21(1): 23–47.

Schreck, C.J., Stewart, E.A. and Osgood, D.W. (2008) 'A reappraisal of the overlap of violent offenders and victims', *Criminology*, 46(4): 871–906.

Shaffer, J.N. (2003) 'The victim–offender overlap: specifying the role of peer groups', unpublished Ph.D. thesis, Pennsylvania State University; also National Criminal Justice Reference Service Unpublished Document No. 205126 (2004), Report of NCJRS Award No. 2002-IJ-CX-0008.

Shaffer, J.N. and Ruback, R.B. (2002) *Violent Victimization as a Risk Factor for Violent Offending Among Juveniles*. Washington, DC: US Department of Justice, Office of Juvenile Justice and Delinquency Prevention. http://www.ncjrs.gov/html/ojjdp/jjbul2002_12_1/conten ts.html

Simmons, J. and colleagues (2002) *Crime in England and Wales 2001/2002* Home Office Statistical Bulletin 07/02. London: Home Office. http://www.homeoffice.gov.uk/rds/hosb2002.html

Singer, L. (2004) *Reassurance Policing: An evaluation of the local management of community safety*. Home Office Research Study No. 288. London: Home Office. http://www.homeoffice.gov.uk/rds/hors2004.html

Singer, S.I. (1981) 'Homogeneous victim–offender populations: a review and some research implications', *Journal of Criminal Law and Criminology*, 72: 779–88.

Smith, D.J. (2004) 'The links between victimisation and offending: the Edinburgh study of youth transitions and crime, No. 5'. Edinburgh: University of Edinburgh, Centre for Law and Society.

Smith, D.J. and Ecob, R. (2007) 'An investigation into causal links between victimization and offending in adolescents', *British Journal of Sociology*, 58(4): 633–59.

Stewart, E., Schreck, C. and Simons, R. (2006) '"I ain't gonna let no one disrespect me": Does the code of the street reduce or increase violent victimization among African American adolescents?', *Journal of Research in Crime and Delinquency*, 43: 427–58.

Tuck, R. (ed.) (1991) *Hobbes: Leviathan*. Cambridge: Cambridge University Press.

Tuffin, R., Morris, J. and Poole, A. (2006) *An Evaluation of the Impact of the National Reassurance Policing Programme*, Home Office Research Study 296. London: Home Office. http://www.homeoffice.gov.uk/rds/hors2006.html

Tyler, T. (2003) 'Procedural justice, legitimacy and the effective rule of law', in M. Tonry (ed.), *Crime and Justice: A Review of Research*, Vol. 30: 283–357.

Widom, C.S. (1997) 'Child abuse, neglect, and witnessing violence', in D.M. Stoff, J. Breiling and J.D. Maser (eds), *Handbook of Antisocial Behavior*. New York, NY: Wiley, pp. 159–70.

Wolfgang, M.E., Figlio, R. and Sellin, T. (1972) *Delinquency in a Birth Cohort.* Chicago: University of Chicago Press.

Wood, M. (2005) *The Victimisation of Young People: Findings from the Crime and Justice Survey 2003* Home Office Research Findings 246. London: Home Office. http://www.crimereduction.homeoffice.gov.uk/youth/youth62.htm

Wright, R.T. and Decker, S.H. (1994) *Burglars on the Job: Streetlife and residential break-ins.* Boston, MA: Northeastern University Press.

Wright, R.T. and Decker, S.H. (1997) *Armed Robbers in Action: Stickups and street culture.* Boston, MA: Northeastern University Press.

Chapter 6

The victim and the prosecutor

John Spencer

The victim as the prosecutor, to the victim and the prosecutor: an historical overview

In the next chapter of this book, Shapland and Hall contrast the practical position of the victim in criminal proceedings today with his or her position as it used to be by looking at the case of George Fisher, who was prosecuted in 1831 for breaking and entering the warehouse of one Abraham Isaacs and stealing a bag of almonds. As they say, in those days 'the victim had to be the prosecutor'. What exactly did the requirement to be a prosecutor mean for him? And when and how did his position change, so that he became (as they say) a 'bit part player' rather than the central actor? The story has been told before, in particular by Sir Leon Radzinowicz in his monumental *History* (Radzinowicz 1956); but it merits a brief retelling at the start of this chapter, in order to set the scene for today.

In many parts of Europe, including not only France but Scotland, public prosecutors have been around for centuries, and the prosecution of offenders has long been regarded as a function of the State. In England and Wales, however, the enforcement of the criminal law was historically seen as a matter of private enterprise. For a small minority of important cases, including murders, the prosecution was brought not only in the name of the King, but by his officers, the Attorney General and his deputy the Solicitor General, aided by the Treasury Solicitor. But for all other crimes, the prosecution was brought by private citizens: the victim, or his relatives, or such other citizens as could be persuaded to undertake the task.

This task was not one that citizens were necessarily prepared to take on willingly, even where they were the victim, and in consequence a range of incentives was provided in the hope of ensuring that the criminal law was actually enforced. These included 'carrots' in the form of rewards.

These were usually, of course, cash payments, but for a time they included the so-called 'Tyburn ticket': an official exemption from a range of burdensome civic duties, which – like commissions in the army – could be bought and sold, and hence were valuable items of property.[1] The incentives also included 'sticks' in the form of various penalties. A particular weakness with the system of private prosecutions was, it seems, the tendency of victims to desert the pleasures of the criminal courts when they were offered compensation, and it was thought necessary to create a number of official disincentives in the hope – all too often vain, it seems – that they would do their official duty to the end. One of these was the rule, invented by the judges, that 'where injuries are inflicted on an individual under circumstances which constitute a felony, that felony cannot be made the foundation of a civil action at the suit of the person injured against the person who inflicted the injuries until the latter has been prosecuted or a reasonable excuse shown for his non-prosecution'.[2] So where, as in the leading case, a woman had allegedly been drugged and raped, no action for damages against the suspected rapist lay unless and until he had been brought before the criminal courts. Another was the criminal offence of 'compounding'. At common law, fortified by a series of statutes, it was a criminal offence for anyone – including the victim – to take money in return for compounding, i.e. not prosecuting, a felony. By statute this offence was, until 1816, punishable by, among other things, the pillory. A third was a criminal offence of advertising a reward for the return of stolen goods 'with no questions asked'. All three of these incentives to ensure that private citizens did their public duty by the criminal courts continued to clutter up the law long after the creation of professional police forces, and the consequent decline of private prosecutions. The first two lasted until the abolition of felonies as a separate class of offences in 1967, and the last one is still with us, as section 23 of the Theft Act 1968.

During the first half of the nineteenth century, England and Wales gradually acquired professional policemen, but not professional prosecutors. The practical result of this was that, for most criminal offences, the police took over the job of prosecuting. To do so they were given no special powers, and used the general power of prosecution that belonged to every citizen – so giving rise to the oft-repeated assertion that, when he is enforcing the law, 'the policeman is to be treated as if he were an ordinary citizen' (Devlin 1960: 14). But private prosecutors continued to play a small but still significant role: first, in prosecutions for assault, which police forces everywhere left to the victim, and secondly in prosecutions for shoplifting, which some police forces left, as a matter of individual force policy, to the shops (Philips 1981b: §171; Lidstone *et al.* 1980: 104).[3]

All this radically changed in 1986 with the creation of the Crown Prosecution Service – usually known as 'the CPS'. This came into being when Parliament carried out the recommendations of the Philips Commission (Philips 1981a) which had proposed an expansion and codification of the powers of the police to gather evidence, balanced by the removal from the police of the power to prosecute and its transfer to a new official public prosecutor. The Philips Commission thought that, as part of the 'new deal', the unlimited right of private citizens to prosecute should be curtailed. Criminal prosecutions, they said, were appropriate only when 'the community's interests are at risk', and of this they thought the new Crown prosecutor ought to be the judge. To this end, they said that 'an attempt must be made under the auspices of the Director of Public Prosecutions to develop and promulgate throughout the police and prosecution services criteria for the exercise of the discretion to prosecute' (Philips 1981a: §8.10); a recommendation which in due course led to the official *Code for Crown Prosecutors*.[4] Private citizens who wanted their fellow citizens prosecuted, the Commission said, should have to ask the Crown prosecutor to do this, and should be permitted to 'go it alone' only if on his refusal they were given leave by the court. But Mrs Thatcher's Government, friendly towards private enterprise in criminal justice as well as in other areas of public life, thought otherwise, and this part of the Philips Commission's recommendations was not carried out. Instead, by section 6 of the Prosecution of Offences Act 1985 – the statute by which the CPS was created – the private citizen's unlimited right to bring a private prosecution was retained; though subject, as it was before, to the power of the Director of Prosecutions to take it over, and having done so, to either run it, or to kill it.

About this new system and its impact on the position of the victim there are two key points to note, both of which are important to the understanding of the rest of this chapter. The first is that, in practice, since 1986 private prosecutions have become even rarer than they were before, the prosecution of both common assaults and shoplifting[5] now being handled by the CPS. The second is that, while maintaining the theoretically unlimited right of all citizens to bring a private prosecution, the new system denied the victim, and *a fortiori* any other private citizen, any official right to participate in a public one.

Initially, the policy of excluding the private citizen from public prosecutions was taken to the extreme of erecting an official barrier between the victim and the new decision-maker, namely the CPS. At first, the rule was that the CPS was insulated from victims, and vice versa. The Home Office guide to the Prosecution of Offences Act said: 'It is not envisaged that the new service will have direct or personal contact with witnesses and it will be under no duty to make contact with victims, witnesses or others after disposal of the case' (Home Office 1985: 29). As before the CPS was created, the victim's point of contact with the criminal justice system was the police: but under the new arrangements the police were no longer the decision-makers, merely the channel of communication with the apparently faceless bureaucracy that had taken the decision-making function over from them.

This became a matter of grievance among victims and those who speak on their behalf, and, as is explained more fully later in this chapter, this 'no access' policy has now been reversed.[6] Since 2001 it has been the official policy of the CPS to enter into direct contact with victims, and a whole series of official Government documents have proclaimed, in ever more emphatic terms, that it is part of the official duty of the CPS to look after their interests. The number of official documents relating to victims has multiplied to the point at which, in February 2009, the CPS website contained no fewer than 31. One of the more recent in the series, *The Prosecutors' Pledge*, appeared in 2005. Under a photograph of Lord Goldsmith, the then Attorney General, wearing an expression of earnest concern, this sets out a list of 10 'pledges' towards victims which the CPS now undertakes to honour: including 'to take into account the impact on the victim or their family when making a charging decision', 'when practical [to] seek a victim's view or that of the family when considering the acceptability of a plea', to 'promote and encourage two-way communication between victim and prosecutor at court', and 'on conviction [to] apply for appropriate order for compensation, restitution or future protection of the victim'. But to the sceptical lawyer these documents, if high on rhetoric, look low on solid legal content. If the CPS neglects to honour any of the 'pledges' to the victim that Lord Goldsmith made on its behalf, there is usually no legal redress available to him or her. The route for the enforcement of these pledges, insofar as there is one, is political, not legal: the disgruntled victim must write a letter of complaint to the Director of Public Prosecutions (DPP), and if that produces nothing, a further letter of complaint to the local Member of Parliament, who in the last resort can refer the matter to the Parliamentary Ombudsman. As another of these documents, the Government's 'Code of Practice for the Victims of Crime' bluntly puts it: 'Where a person fails to comply with this Code, that does not, of itself, make him or her liable to any legal proceedings'(Office for Criminal Justice Reform 2005: §1.3).[7]

During 2009 the CPS was the subject of an investigation and report by the House of Commons Justice Committee (Justice Committee 2009). Among other things, it looked at the relationship between the CPS and victims, and suggested that the stream of official pronouncements mentioned in the previous paragraph might have raised expectations that cannot realistically be met. The summary that appeared at the head of the Report contained the following:

> The prosecutor's role in relation to victims also seems to be generally misunderstood. The prosecutor is not able to be an advocate for the victim in the way that the defence counsel is for the defendant, yet government proclamations that the prosecutor is the champion of

victims' rights may falsely give this impression. Much of the prosecutor's work by its nature serves the needs of victims, and we should strive for a better service to victims, but there needs to be a better understanding of what it is possible for the prosecutor to be and to do in relation to victims.

In the next section of this chapter, the legal steps available to victims to make sure the CPS takes notice of their interests will be examined. Then in the third and final section we shall examine how well the current regime of unenforceable duties towards the victim actually works in practice, and whether his or her position is really any worse than it is in countries where, unlike in England and Wales, the victim has a legally enforceable right to participate in a public prosecution.

The victim and the public prosecutor in England and Wales today: the legal position

(i) Private prosecution

The victim who is dissatisfied because the offender has not been prosecuted – or not prosecuted for what he considers to be a sufficiently serious offence – has in principle the right to start a private prosecution. In theory this right is very wide, because in principle any citizen can prosecute anyone for any criminal offence, unless it is one of those for which by statute the permission of the DPP or the Attorney General is required before a prosecution is started. In practice, however, the right to bring a private prosecution is of less use to the victim than at first appears. First, the private prosecutor has no legal right to require the police (or anyone else) to help him put the case together; thus, for example, he cannot force the police to let him see their files.[8] Secondly, the private prosecutor has to pay for the proceedings out of his own pocket, because for private prosecutions there is no legal aid. This difficulty is magnified by the fact that if the case ends up in the Crown Court the private prosecutor is in principle obliged to employ a barrister, and cannot, as he can in the magistrates' courts, 'go it alone' as a litigant in person.[9] Although the difficulty is potentially mitigated by the power of the court, if he obtains a conviction, to order his costs to be paid out of public funds, these costs will be paid only retrospectively, and when he gets them they will cover only his expenditure, and will not compensate him for his time and trouble.[10] Thirdly, if the prosecution is unsuccessful and the court concludes that the prosecutor was guilty of 'an unnecessary or improper act or omission', it may order him to pay all or part of the successful defendant's costs;[11] and in addition to this, the defendant may bring separate civil proceedings against him for malicious prosecution.[12] And fourthly, as previously mentioned, the DPP has a statutory right to intervene at any time to take a private prosecution over, and having done so, may close it down.[13]

To the long list of hazards described in the last paragraph, all of which have long existed, case law in recent years has now added a new one: the risk that, if the DPP does not intervene to stop the private prosecution, the court itself will do so because it considers it to be 'an abuse of process'.

Case law dating back to the 1960s affirms that the criminal courts have a general duty to prevent their procedure being put to improper use, one aspect of which is that they must suppress a prosecution if it amounts to 'an abuse of process'. The concept of 'abuse of process' is a nebulous one. At a high level of abstraction, it is said to exist either where the defendant in the case would not receive a fair trial, or more broadly, where his eventual trial might be a fair one, but it is not fair for him to be tried.[14] In concrete terms, the concept of abuse of process can be understood only by examining the various factual categories of case in which the courts have decided that there was an abuse of process. Of these, there are two which are particularly relevant to private prosecutions. The first is that a prosecution is an abuse of process where it has been brought for an improper purpose. The second is that it is an abuse of process when the authorities officially inform the defendant that he will not be prosecuted, and then go back upon their word.

The 'improper purpose' line of argument was successfully deployed to defeat a private prosecution in *R v. Belmarsh JJ ex pte Watts*.[15] In this case, a Mr Tivnan, who had served a term of imprisonment for drug trafficking, sought to bring a private prosecution against a customs officer for criminal libel and misconduct in public office, on the basis of her allegedly having made deliberate false statements in her official report about his smuggling activities. His purpose in bringing the proceedings, as he admitted, was to undermine his conviction; and this, said the Divisional Court, was an 'improper purpose' given that, three years earlier, he had not bothered to challenge his conviction by the obvious route of appealing against it. In ruling that Tivnan's private prosecution must for this reason be stayed as an abuse of process, Buxton LJ made some further and much wider comments (p. 200):

> ... a private prosecutor such as Mr Tivnan is still a prosecutor, and subject to the same obligations as a minister of justice as are the public prosecuting authorities. We think that if a public prosecutor had brought proceedings in anything like comparable circumstances to those in which the summonses were issued it would have been thought self-evident that they should be stayed.

Taken to its logical conclusion, this line of thought would place a severe limit on attempts to bring a private prosecution in any case in which the

CPS had made a decision not to prosecute – particularly if the decision was made on grounds of 'public interest'. It would enable the defendant who was then privately prosecuted to say, in effect, 'A private prosecutor, like the public prosecutor, can prosecute only when a prosecution is in the public interest; the CPS is the guardian of the public interest; and if the CPS has decided that it is not in the public interest to prosecute, a private prosecutor can institute a prosecution only if he can show that the decision of the CPS was flawed; if he cannot do this, the private prosecution will necessarily amount to an abuse of process.'

Yet in a series of later cases, other courts have refused to follow the logic of this argument to its end. In *R (Dacre and Another) v. Westminster Magistrates' Court*[16] the Divisional Court said that Buxton LJ's remarks in ex pte *Watts* must be 'kept firmly in context', and should not be interpreted to mean that a private prosecution was an abuse of process just because the prosecutor had brought it for 'mixed motives'. In similar vein, in *Ewing v. Davis* Mitting J, holding that a magistrate had been wrong to treat a private prosecution arising from a dispute between neighbours as an abuse of process, said that there was no 'requirement that a private prosecutor had to demonstrate that it was in the public interest that he should bring a prosecution for an offence against the provision of a public statute'.[17] And in *R (Charlson) v. Guildford Magistrates' Court* the Administrative Court expressly rejected the argument that, when the CPS has made a decision not to prosecute, any subsequent attempt to bring a private prosecution will be abusive unless there are 'special circumstances, such as apparent bad faith on the part of the Crown prosecutor'.[18] In this case, the claimant's three-year-old son had been run down by a car and killed when on a pelican crossing. After a public prosecution against the driver for careless driving had been instituted the CPS discontinued it, whereupon the claimant, deeply dissatisfied, sought to institute a private prosecution for dangerous driving. The magistrates refused to allow the prosecution to proceed on the ground that it was an abuse of process, but Silber J quashed their decision.

However, defendants who are privately prosecuted following decisions by the public authorities not to prosecute can derive more comfort from another case that approaches the issue via the other aspect of abuse of process previously mentioned: namely, that it is an abuse of process when the authorities officially inform the defendant that he will not be prosecuted, and then go back on their word. In *Jones v. Whalley*,[19] Whalley had attacked and injured Jones, and instead of prosecuting Whalley the police had issued him with a 'formal caution'[20] and let him go. Dissatisfied with this outcome, Jones then sought to institute a private prosecution against Whalley for assault occasioning actual bodily harm; but the magistrates refused to allow the case to proceed on the ground that a private prosecution following a decision by the police to end the proceedings with a caution amounted to an abuse of process. The written form used by the police when notifying Whalley of their decision to let him off with a caution contained a statement informing him that, in consequence, he would not now have to go to court: and in the light of this, the House of Lords held that the magistrates had correctly decided that the private prosecution would now amount to an abuse of process. In so holding, different Law Lords expressed different views as to whether, when the police issue formal cautions, they ought to give assurances that there will be no court proceedings, as the Greater Manchester police had done in the case in hand. In essence, of course, this case raised the same practical issue as came before Silber J just a few weeks later in R (Charlson) v. Guildford Magistrates' Court, in which the outcome was the opposite. In the Charlson case the arguments were different, as we have seen, and Silber J was not referred to Jones v. Whalley. In consequence we do not know whether the CPS in the Charlson case, like the police in Jones v. Whalley, told the defendant when informing him of their decision to drop the case that this meant that he would not now have to go to court. If it did, then in the light of Jones v. Whalley the result ought to have been different.

The outcome of these cases is, to put it bluntly, something of a muddle. The reason for this, I believe, is that judges, like those who comment on their decisions (Blakely 2007; cf. Bennion 2006a, b), are divided among themselves about the proper place (if any) for private prosecutions in a system like ours today, where criminal offences are widely defined, defences to criminal liability are narrowly construed, and the resulting over criminalisation is kept in check by a discretion to prosecute, exercised according to published principles by a public prosecutor whose decisions are subject to judicial review. The two opposing views appear clearly in the speeches of the Law Lords in Jones v. Whalley, where Lord Bingham said, '[16] The surviving right of private prosecution is of questionable value, and can be exercised in a way damaging to the public interest', whereas Lord Mance said, '[43] The right of private prosecution operates and has been explained at the highest level as a safeguard against wrong refusal or failure by public prosecuting authorities to institute proceedings ... Further ... it cannot always be assumed that, if it is wrong to bring a public prosecution, then it is also wrong to bring a private prosecution.'

(ii) Judicial review

The reason for the increasing scepticism of at least some judges towards private prosecutions as a tool for controlling the exercise of the discretion to prosecute is, of course, the fact that the courts themselves are now increasingly prepared to control its exercise themselves, in particular by means of judicial review. To what extent does judicial review enable the victim to challenge decisions by the CPS which he or she feels are made without consideration for his or her proper interests?

The possibility of victims using judicial review as an effective means of challenging CPS decisions not to prosecute was clearly demonstrated for the first time in *R v. DPP* ex pte *C*[21] in 1994. In this case an Asian woman who had come to the UK for an arranged marriage had complained to the police that, for the five months of their cohabitation, her husband had subjected her to repeated anal rape. Despite the existence of some medical evidence that corroborated part of her story the CPS declined to prosecute. In its judgement the Divisional Court asserted that, in principle, the courts could quash a CPS decision not to prosecute on any of three grounds: first, illegality, for example, a blanket policy of never prosecuting certain types of criminal offence; secondly, where the decision contradicted the policy set out in the DPP's official *Code for Crown Prosecutors*;[22] and thirdly, if it was perverse, in the sense of being 'a decision at which no reasonable prosecutor could have arrived'. Then it quashed the decision not to prosecute, because the reasons that the Crown Prosecutor had given to support it could not be intelligibly squared with the statements about 'evidential sufficiency' contained in the *Code for Crown Prosecutors*.

A similar outcome was reached a few years later in *R v. DPP* ex pte *Manning*.[23] In this case the Divisional Court quashed the DPP's decision not to prosecute any of the members of a group of prison officers who appeared to have been involved in the death of a prisoner in custody, in respect of which a coroner's jury had returned a unanimous verdict of unlawful killing. Given the gravity of the case and the verdict at the inquest, the laconic reasons the DPP had given for not prosecuting were inadequate, and in deciding that the evidence was not strong enough to justify a prosecution the CPS had 'applied a test higher than that laid down in the Code'. Building on the *Manning* case, the family of Jean Charles de Menezes, shot dead at Stockwell tube station by armed police who had mistaken him for a terrorist about to set off a bomb, sought judicial review against the decision of the CPS not to prosecute any of the police officers for murder or manslaughter; but in this case the attempt to overturn the decision failed. In justifying his decision the DPP had said that, in order to secure their conviction for murder, the Crown would have to show that the officers did not honestly believe the man they shot was a terrorist about to explode a bomb, or for manslaughter, that the mistakes the officers had made were so negligent 'that they could be considered criminal': neither of which looked likely on the evidence. This, said the Divisional Court, was a reasonable assessment, adding, 'Indeed, though it is not necessary for us to go this far, we see no reason to disagree with the decision.'[24]

But in a third and more recent case a disgruntled victim once again persuaded the courts to quash the public prosecutor's decision to drop the case. In *R (B) v. DPP*[25] the applicant (V) was attacked, and had part of his ear bitten off when a fight broke out in a cafe on Boxing Day. He identified X as the person responsible, whom the CPS then prosecuted for the serious offences of wounding with intent to cause grievous bodily harm and witness intimidation. On the morning of the trial, the barrister who had been briefed to prosecute noticed a doctor's report in the case file indicating that V had a history of mental illness, and after a hurried consultation with the CPS decided that the Crown could therefore not put him forward as a witness who was credible. And so, without consultation with V, the Crown offered no evidence, X was acquitted, and V was sent home without the court having heard his evidence. The Divisional Court quashed the decision to drop the case, describing it as 'irrational':

> [55] The reasoning process . . . for concluding that [V] could not be placed before the jury as a credible witness was irrational in the true sense of the term. It did not follow from Dr C's report that the jury could not properly be invited to regard [V] as a true witness when he described the assault which he undoubtedly suffered. The conclusion that he could not be put forward as a credible witness, despite the apparent factual credibility of his account, suggests either a misreading of Dr C's report (as though it had said that [V] was incapable of being regarded as a credible witness) or an unfounded stereotyping of [V] as someone who was not to be regarded as credible on any matter because of his history of mental problems.

As by now X had been acquitted it was too late for the CPS to reconsider its decision to drop the case. But the Divisional Court held that the failure of the CPS, a public authority, to apply the criminal law so as to provide V with proper protection against a brutal physical attack infringed his human rights under Article 3[26] of the European Convention on Human Rights, and they ordered the CPS to pay him £8,000 compensation.

And still more recently, a fourth disgruntled victim persuaded the Administrative Court to quash the decision of the CPS not to prosecute. In *R (Guest) v. DPP*[27] a man forced his way into the house of a neighbour who had sent him an offensive text message and, in the presence of the neighbour's terrified partner, gave him a beating that sent him to hospital in an ambulance, where stitches and butterfly clips were required to mend his face. For this, a Deputy Crown Prosecutor decided not to prosecute, but to let the attacker off with a 'conditional caution',[28] the condition being that he pay the victim £200. When the victim refused to accept the money and complained to the Chief Crown Prosecutor, the Chief Crown Prosecutor apologised and accepted that the decision was contrary to the DPP's official guidance on conditional cautions, but said that nothing could be done about the blunder because to reverse the decision and to start a prosecution at this stage would amount to an abuse of process. The Divisional Court quashed the decision not to prosecute, and suggested that, where the initial decision not to prosecute had been quashed, a subsequent prosecution could not be attacked as an abuse of process.

How effective is judicial review as a mechanism to enable victims to ensure that the CPS acts with the consideration for their interests promised by the Code for Crown Prosecutors, the 'Prosecutors' Pledge' and a range of other official documents?

From the perspective of the victim (or in the case of homicides, his family), in the individual case the answer is 'not wholly'. The quashing of a decision by the CPS to drop a case does not guarantee that there will be a prosecution. As in *R (B) v. DPP* it may now be too late to prosecute because the defendant has been formally acquitted. Even if it is made in time, a court order quashing a decision to drop the case does not require the public prosecutor to prosecute, only to reconsider his decision; and having done so, the CPS may reach the same decision once again – as it did, indeed, in ex pte *Manning*.[29] Much less, of course, does such an order ensure that a conviction will result, if having examined the file again the CPS does decide this time to 'run with it'.[30]

On the other hand, when viewed from the perspective of victims generally, the existence of judicial review is clearly beneficial. It stops the CPS (or certain parts of it) from pursuing prosecution policies that are clearly undesirable: for example, not prosecuting in sex cases which depend upon the word of the complainant, or for any offences in which the key witness has a history of mental illness. More generally, the fact that the decisions of public prosecutors to drop cases can be publicly examined by the courts, and that public prosecutors are aware of this, undoubtedly encourages them to approach decision-making carefully. Finally, from the broader perspective of criminal justice, judicial review of decisions to drop cases does not distort the prosecution process by pressuring prosecutors to proceed with cases which they ought to drop, because unreasonable decisions to proceed with cases are also liable to be judicially reviewed.[31]

(iii) Legal redress against decisions relating to the conduct of the case

If private prosecutions and judicial review give the victim an indirect legal means of seeing that his interests are properly considered when the decision is made as to whether a public prosecution shall be instituted, he has no legal means of ensuring that they are taken account of in the way the public prosecution is then conducted. As we saw earlier, the Government has issued official 'pledges' that victims' interests will be properly considered, and as we shall see later, various informal mechanisms have been created with the aim of seeing these are honoured. But if they are not, the law gives the victim no redress.

This point was graphically illustrated in the recent case of *R (Faithfull) v. Crown Court at Ipswich*.[32] Faithfull was an employer whose dishonest employee, Underwood, stole from him £15,579.01 – a sum which, unusually, on her conviction she was in a position to repay. But instead of asking the Crown Court to impose a *compensation order* requiring her to repay the money to Faithfull, the barrister conducting the prosecution asked the judge to impose a *confiscation order* under which the money was forfeited to the State. Under the convoluted legislation that governs confiscation orders, the court, when asked by the prosecutor to make a confiscation order against a defendant who (like the employee in this case) has profited from his crime, is legally required to make one – and so it promptly did. The judge, if he had thought of it, could have made a compensation order too, and could then have ordered the compensation to be paid out of the money extracted by the State under the confiscation order. But he did not think to do this, and the prosecutor did not remind him. In consequence, not only did the victim fail to get his stolen property back by means of a compensation order, but his chances of getting it back by any other means were much reduced.

In this situation the victim could do nothing. Against improper sentences, and matters ancillary to them such as compensation orders, appeal lies in principle to the Criminal Division of the Court of Appeal: but only at the instance of the defendant, and in certain limited circumstances (of which this was not one) the prosecutor. In the light of this, the victim tried to challenge the order by means of an application for judicial review in the Administrative Court; but in this he failed, because section 29(3) of the Supreme Court Act 1981 puts outside the reach of judicial review a range of rulings made in the Crown Court, including, in the view of the Administrative Court, the one that was made here.[33] All this was most unfortunate, but as Gibbs J explained:

> [29] . . . the real reason why it is said that this court should assume jurisdiction is that the claimant, as a victim of the offence, not being a party to the criminal proceedings, cannot bring the case before the Court of Appeal (Criminal Division). Thus he cannot himself, otherwise than by application to this court, prompt a review of that aspect of the sentence which affects him adversely, in the sense that the judge failed to make an order to the claimant's benefit, which he could and should have made.

> [30] It is clear that the interests of the victim are rightly afforded great (and growing) importance in the criminal process . . . However, the general position is that it is still the prosecution's responsibility to ensure that the interests of victims are properly catered for in the criminal process. We do not have a system in which the victims are parties to it . . .

In a final attempt to persuade the Administrative Court to grant him a remedy, the claimant said that the official blunders in this case had infringed his right to peaceful enjoyment of his possessions as guaranteed by the First Protocol to the European Convention on Human Rights; but this argument was rejected. Mr Faithfull, said the Administrative Court, could still sue the defendant for the return of the money in the civil courts: (if, it might have added, he was prepared to throw good money after bad by bringing civil proceedings against a defendant from whose pockets the State had removed the money he wanted to reclaim).

The victim and the public prosecutor in England and Wales today: is there a case for change?

In the previous section we saw three recent cases, *R (B) v. DPP* and *R (Guest) v. DPP* from 2009 and *R (Faithfull) v. Crown Court at Ipswich* from 2007, in which, despite the 'Prosecutors' Pledge' and similar pronouncements, the public prosecutor contrived to let the victim down badly. In France the victim has a legal right to become a party to a public prosecution; and as what is called *une partie* civile, or civil party, he has a right to be legally represented at the trial (Brienen and Hoegen 2000; Hodgson 2005). Arrangements that are broadly similar exist in many other parts of Continental Europe, and indeed in the wider world beyond. If this possibility had been open to the victim in this country, and the victims in these three cases had taken advantage of it, it seems unlikely that any of the prosecutions would have ended as disastrously for the victim as they did. Is there a case for the introduction of such a system here?

As one of the recommendations attached to his report into the Stephen Lawrence affair (Macpherson 1999), Sir William Macpherson said that the introduction of such a system should be considered. The Government responded to this by arranging for the Home Office to organise a private two-day conference on the subject, which took place in Macclesfield in September 1999. Among those who attended, and spoke, were two Dutch researchers who were then completing a large-scale study, later published, of the legal position of the victim in 22 different criminal justice systems in Europe (Brienen and Hoegen 2000). At this conference the idea of creating a *partie civile* system in England and Wales was not well received. According to the final report (Home Office 1999: 42):

> The broad conclusion of the conference was that neither the civil party system nor the assistant prosecutor system[34] delivered significant benefits to victims within inquisitorial systems, and were unlikely to do so in an adversarial system. It was felt that an improved system of Victim Statements, together with other measures being taken to bring victims closer to the heart of the criminal justice process, would be far more effective in England and Wales.

From that point on, the Government has indeed made efforts to improve the position of the victim in the prosecution process but, to put it crudely, it has done so by making 'pledges' to them, rather than by giving them any further legal rights. In essence, the Government's policy has been to encourage the CPS to look after their interests; and also, regrettably, to use its own supposed concern to improve the position of victims as an excuse for authoritarian 'tough on crime' measures, the true purpose and effect of which are to worsen the legal position of defendants.[35]

The Government, so far as I am aware, has never published detailed reasons for rejecting the idea of creating a *partie civile* procedure in this country. But from what was said at the Home Office conference in 1999, the official view is that, contrary to what is often stated, the victim who can make himself a *partie civile* in one of the Continental systems is not significantly better off than his counterpart in this country who cannot; and that if our system, under which the CPS is charged with looking after the interests of the victim, has deficiencies, these can be resolved by administrative fine-tuning. Although it has not been stated publicly, it also seems likely that a further – and entirely respectable – reason for resistance to the idea of a *partie civile* procedure is fear that it would add to the cost of criminal justice, while at the same time causing it to operate more slowly.

Whether this opposition to the idea of giving the victim the right to be a formal party in the proceedings is justified is a complicated question, in which at least three elements are involved: first, how good or bad, in reality, is the present system at taking account of the interests of victims? Secondly, if and insofar as it fails to look after them properly, would a *partie civile* system really help to fill the gap? And thirdly, if it would, would the advantages for victims be outweighed by other disadvantages for the criminal justice system – for example, increased cost and delay? To examine these three questions fully, much more needs to be said than can be considered here; but it is possible to outline the main issues briefly.

First, how well are the interests of victims looked after in the 'informal' system as it exists today? There can be no doubt that, since 1999, the Government and the CPS have collaborated in a genuine effort to improve procedures so that, in public prosecutions, greater notice is now taken of the interests of victims. Over the last 10 years Government has repeatedly announced that its official policy is 'to rebalance justice' so that the victim is 'at the heart of the system'.[36] In England and Wales the CPS, for good or ill, is one of the branches of the national civil service and, like the rest of it, regards itself as duty-bound to carry out the stated policies of the democratically elected government; unsurprisingly, therefore, the Government's official policy of trying to put the victim 'centre-stage' is faithfully reflected by the CPS in its public statements about the role and purpose of the service. In the *CPS Vision* published on its official website, 'championing justice and the rights of victims' is set out as the second of the six main objectives listed, ranking only behind 'strengthening the prosecution process to bring offenders to justice'.[37] The Code for Crown Prosecutors has been amended to amplify what is said about the place of victims. The current version says '... when considering the public interest, Crown Prosecutors should always take into account the consequences for the victim of whether or not to prosecute, and any views expressed by the victim or the victim's family', and adds that 'it is important that a victim is told about a decision which makes a significant difference to the case in which they are involved'.[38] As mentioned earlier, the CPS website now contains no fewer than 31 documents about victims. These include 'Care and Treatment of Victims and Witnesses', 'CPS Public Policy Statement on the Delivery of Services to Victims', 'Direct Communication with Victims', and 'Victim Focus Scheme – Guidance on Enhanced CPS Service for Bereaved Families'. As part of this new policy, the CPS, which originally left all contact with victims to the police, now follows an official policy of communicating with them directly.

What does this new policy of 'direct communication' mean in practice?[39]

When taking the initial decision on whether to prosecute, and if so for what offence, the CPS does not usually make contact with the victim: for information about the views and interests of victims it is normally dependent, as it always has been, on such information as there may be in the witness statements taken by the police. At this crucial stage, the CPS will not usually hear the victim's views at first hand unless (as occasionally happens) the victim takes the initiative and contacts the CPS. The current policy[40] is that, in cases in which the police and CPS reach an early decision that there is no evidence on which to prosecute, the news that nobody is to be prosecuted will be passed to the alleged victim by the police; when someone is charged, or when after reflection an initial charge is dropped or modified, the CPS communicates the information to the alleged victim by letter; and when the CPS decides to drop or reduce charges in cases of alleged homicide, child abuse, sexual offences, or 'racially and religiously aggravated offences and offences with a homophobic or transphobic element',[41] the Crown Prosecutor will then offer those who claim to be the victims, or their families, a meeting to explain. In addition to this, the CPS is now developing a separate scheme under which, contrary to the long-standing practice, Crown Prosecutors meet and interview key witnesses ahead of trial.[42] The purpose of these meetings is not to hear the views of victims as to what the CPS should do for them, but to enable the CPS to gain a clearer idea of how the witness would perform at an eventual trial. Inevitably, however, at these meetings the victim's views do sometimes come across.

All this falls a long way short, of course, of a system in which the CPS actually seeks out the victim's views before deciding whether a defendant shall be charged. But this does not mean that, from the victim's point of view, it is completely useless. If the Crown Prosecutor does not consult the victim in advance of charge, he knows that he will now have to explain to the victim afterwards what he has done; and this thought, like the much remoter possibility of judicial review, is likely to concentrate the prosecutor's mind. And quite apart from whether the new policy of 'direct contact' really gives victims any new degree of leverage, meetings between victims and Crown Prosecutors clearly have, for certain victims or their families, a useful cathartic effect. As to how thoroughly the 'direct contact' policy has been implemented, an audit by the CPS Inspectorate in 2007 found that compliance had been rather patchy, some CPS areas taking it more seriously than others. To this, the response from CPS headquarters was (in effect) 'We shall try harder.' And as the three unhappy cases mentioned at the beginning of this section illustrate, there are still at least a few occasions on which communication with the victim breaks down.[43] I believe a true verdict on the new arrangements is that they are an improvement, and one that is genuine and not purely cosmetic; but from the victim's point of view, they remain less than perfect. And as the House of Commons Justice Committee said in the Report quoted earlier, a public prosecutor has a range of duties and obligations, and 'is not able to be an advocate for the victim in the way that defence counsel is for the defendant'.

That being so, would the creation of a new *partie civile* procedure solve any of the remaining problems?

In my view, the answer to this is not a simple 'yes' or 'no', but depends on what in concrete terms the new procedure actually consisted of. In the countries which give the victim the possibility of a formal status in a public prosecution, there is no standard model. According to Brienen and Hoegen (2000), the Dutch researchers mentioned earlier, in some countries in which the victim has the option of making himself a civil party the practical result is that the public prosecutor leaves him to 'fight his corner' on his own: so putting him, in practice, in a worse position than he is in England and Wales, where the CPS at least tries to be helpful and informative. Similarly, *partie civile* systems do not necessarily mean that the victim is more likely to receive compensation. In France, and in many other countries, the criminal courts award the *partie civile* damages on the same scale as would be awarded by the civil courts, and hence the sums awarded are much larger that they are in England, where compensation orders are calculated according to what the defendant is actually in a position to pay. In England the courts enforce the payment of compensation orders automatically, by using the same mechanism as is used for fines; by contrast, in France the victim is left to enforce the judgement for himself. So if the English victim is awarded a much smaller sum, he is more likely in practice actually to get it.

And the same answer, 'it all depends', must be given to the third question: whether giving the victim the status of a *partie civile* in this country would produce incidental disadvantages for the criminal justice system; in particular, increased cost and delay. Once again, the devil – or the absence of one – is in the detail. A comprehensive *partie civile* system under which the prosecutor was formally required to consult the alleged victim before he took any step, and in which any alleged victim was entitled to the services of a lawyer paid for by the State, would presumably produce both these disadvantages. On the other hand, a minimalist system which merely allowed the victim, at his own cost, to be represented at the sentencing hearing in order to apply for a compensation order, should in principle produce neither. As scientists – particularly those working on research grants – are inclined to say at the conclusion of their papers, more research is clearly needed.

A final point should be made about the inherent compatibility, or otherwise, of a *partie civile* system with the adversarial tradition. Those who are suspicious of proposals to give the victim in this country some kind of formal legal status in a public prosecution are inclined to view the idea as an unsuitable import from an alien legal culture. 'It may work in France and Germany, but there they have the inquisitorial system. Here we have the adversarial system.' As a matter of legal history, the reverse is true. It was France that first borrowed the idea from England. In France, the inquisitorial tradition originally meant a powerful public prosecutor, whose legal muscle represented the power in criminal justice of an autocratic king; and the idea of giving private victims an official status was, like juries and the right to silence, an import from across the Channel, made by Revolutionaries who admired English institutions – and who were looking, in those days, at an English system in which private citizens played a central part (Schnapper 1991). As with the European Convention on Human Rights, which the popular press daily denounces as an alien imposition forced upon us from across the Channel, it seems that the ultimate origins of the *partie civile* are to be found in the common law.

Notes

1 This strange institution got its name from the fact that most of the offences to which it applied were punishable by hanging, which in London then meant a public execution at Tyburn.
2 *Smith v. Selwyn* [1914] 3 KB 98.
3 In addition to police prosecutions and prosecutions brought by private citizens, there were also a substantial number of prosecutions brought by a range of public agencies, such as the Customs and Excise, the Inland Revenue and the Health and Safety Executive: see Lidstone *et al.* (1980): ch. 3. These public agencies were allowed to retain control of their own prosecutions after the Crown Prosecution Service was created, and – perhaps surprisingly – some still

control them now. As the offences in question do not usually have direct human victims, I have not dealt with this type of public prosecution in this paper, although I have discussed it elsewhere (Spencer 2006).

4 Which the DPP is required to publish by s. 10 of the Prosecution of Offences Act 1985. The current version, which can be found online on the CPS website, dates from 2004. At the time of writing, a consultation process is in progress about a revised version.

5 Insofar as shoplifting is ever prosecuted at all; under sections 1 and 2 of the Criminal Justice and Police Act 2001 the police are now able to deal with theft of all types by issuing a 'fixed penalty', and many shoplifters are now dealt with in this way.

6 As a response, *inter alia*, to recommendations in the Glidewell Review of the CPS (Glidewell 1998) and the Macpherson Report into the Stephen Lawrence affair (Macpherson 1999).

7 The Office for Criminal Justice Reform (OCJR) is a group within the Civil Service that attempts to co-ordinate the efforts of the Home Office, the Crown Prosecution Service and the Ministry of Justice.

8 *R v. DPP* ex pte *Hallas* (1988) 87 Cr App R 340.

9 *R v. George Maxwell Developments Ltd* (1980) 72 Cr App R 83; in *R v. Southwark Crown Court*, ex pte *Tawfick* [1995] Crim LR 658, (1995) 7 Admin LR 410; [1995] Crim LR 658; [1995] COD 168; *Times*, 1 December 1994, however, the Divisional Court held that section 27(2) of the Courts and Legal Services Act 1990 now gives the Crown Court a discretion to allow a private prosecutor to appear in person, but stressed that it should be exercised only rarely.

10 *R v. Stockport JJ*, ex pte *Cooper* (1984) 148 JP 261, [1984] Crim LR 233.

11 Costs in Criminal Cases (General) Regulations 1986 (SI 1986 no. 1335) paragraph 3. See generally, Archbold (2009) §6.53 *et seq.*

12 On which see any textbook on the law of tort; for example, W.V.H. Horton Rogers (ed.) (2006), *Winfield and Jolowicz on Tort*, ch. 18.

13 His decision to do so, or not to do so, can be judicially reviewed; and so where he refused to intervene and stop a private prosecution for an offence in respect of which he had said that, in his view, the defendant had no case to answer, his decision not to intervene was quashed: *R v. DPP* ex pte *Duckenfield* [2000] 1 WLR. This case was one of the many pieces of litigation arising from the Hillsborough Disaster. Relatives of persons killed in the disaster sought to prosecute the police officers whom they believed to be responsible. The police officers responded (*inter alia*) by asking the DPP to take the prosecutions over and stop them, and when he refused, sought judicial review against his refusal. The end of the story was that one of the private prosecutions went ahead and the former Chief Constable of South Yorkshire was tried for manslaughter: proceedings that ended inconclusively when, after a six-week trial, the jury disagreed: see *The Independent*, 25 July 2000; and the judge (Hooper J) then refused to order a retrial.

14 The leading case is *R v. Horseferry Road JJ*, ex pte *Bennett* [1994] 1 AC 42, [1992] 3 WLR 90.

15 [1999] 2 Cr App R 188.

16 [2008] EWHC 1667 (Admin); [2009] 1 Cr App R 6.

17 [2007] EWHC 1730 (Admin); [2007] 1 WLR 3223.

18 [2006] EWHC 2318 (Admin), [2007] 1 WLR 3494, at [16]; explicitly disapproving of a statement to that effect in the 2005 edition of *Stone's Justices Manual*.

19 [2006] UKHL 41; [2007] 2 AC 63.

20 A 'formal caution' is an official warning given by the police as an alternative to instituting criminal proceedings. The procedure has no statutory basis, but is regulated by Circulars issued by the Home Office from time to time, of which the current one is HO 30/2005. For juveniles the equivalent procedures are 'reprimands' and 'warnings', which are regulated by the Crime and Disorder Act 1998. A related but distinct procedure is the 'conditional caution' which can now be issued by the CPS under Part 3 of the Criminal Justice Act 2003. For a brief account of all these procedures see Sprack (2008), §5.05 onwards.

21 [1995] 1 Cr App R 136.

22 See note 4 above.

23 [2000] 3 WLR 463, [2001] QB 330.

24 *R (da Silva) v. DPP* [2006] EWHC 3204, at [58].

25 [2009] EWHC 106 (Admin), [2009] 1 WLR 2072; and see Robertshaw (2009).

26 'No one shall be subjected to torture or to inhuman or degrading treatment or punishment.'

27 [2009] EWHC 594 (Admin), [2009] Cr App R 26.

28 As provided for by the Criminal Justice Act 2003, ss. 22 to 27.

29 See the statement from the CPS Press Office, *CPS Statement on Alton George Manning (deceased)*, 25 January 2002.

30 In *R v. DPP*, ex pte C the CPS did eventually prosecute, but the proceedings ended inconclusively because the jury disagreed (private communication from a source within the CPS).

31 Although in principle subject to judicial review, an unreasonable decision to prosecute is more likely in practice to be challenged by the defendant asking the trial court to stay the proceedings as an abuse of process. See Lord Bingham's comments in *Sharma v. DPP of Trinidad and Tobago* [2006] UKPC 57; [2007] 1 WLR 780.

32 [2007] EWHC 2763 (Admin), [2008] 1 WLR 1636.

33 Proceedings in the magistrates' court are in general subject to judicial review, and so the outcome might have been different if the defendant had been tried summarily instead of on indictment.

34 An account in English of the 'assistant prosecutor system' in Germany is given by Sanders and Jones (2007); and by Brienen and Hoegen (2000).

35 The most brazen example of this was the press release on 19 April 2006 in which the then Home Secretary justified his decision to cut compensation for wrongful imprisonment payable to defendants whose convictions had been overturned by saying, 'The Government is committed to putting victims' interests at the heart of the criminal justice system.'

36 'We need to rebalance the system in a way that gives the law-abiding public much greater involvement in the criminal justice services they receive. That starts with ensuring the needs of victims must be at the heart of what the criminal justice system does' (Home Office 2006: 4); and 'The Crown Prosecution Service has undergone a quiet revolution and now has the interests of the victim centre stage . . .' (Straw 2008).

37 Presumably as a side effect of the 'rebalancing' mentioned in the previous note, the 'CPS Vision' makes no mention of ensuring fairness for defendants, a key objective which used to appear in its earlier statements of this sort; for example, the CPS *Statement of Purpose and Values* (CPS 1993: 10). In the light of

that significant absence, it is a relief to see that, in a speech in January 2009, the new Director of Public Prosecutions said, 'Respect for and protection of human rights should be at the heart of a transparent, contemporary prosecution service' (Starmer 2009).

38 §5.12 and §5.13.
39 For information in the following paragraphs I am indebted to Richard Crowley, the Chief Crown Prosecutor for Cambridgeshire, who was kind enough to allow me to interview him.
40 Set out in the document entitled 'Direct Communication with Victims', published on the CPS website.
41 *Ibid.*, section 2, paragraph 6.
42 The policy and practice is set out in a document entitled *Pre-Trial Witness Interviews – Guidance for Prosecutors*, which is published on the CPS website.
43 In two of these cases the blunder seems to have arisen as the result of an off-the-cuff decision by the independent barrister whom the CPS had briefed to present the case. If more CPS prosecutions could be presented to the court by the Crown Prosecutors who had prepared them, instead of by barristers who may be less familiar with the file, it is possible that some mistakes of this sort would be avoided.

References

Bennion, Francis (2006a) '*Jones v Whalley*: constitutional errors by the Appellate Committee', 170 *Justice of the Peace*, 847–50. http://www.francisbennion.com/2006/039.htm

Bennion, F. (2006b) 'The prosecution circus continued', 170 *Justice of the Peace*, 944–8. www.francisbennion.com/pdfs/fb/.../2006-043-prosecution-circus.pdf

Blakeley, R. (2007) 'To the fullest extent of the law? *Jones v Whalley* and the right to private prosecution', *Cambridge Law Journal*, 66(1): 11–13.

Brienen M.E.I. and Hoegen, E.H. (2000) *Victims of Crime in 22 European Criminal Justice Systems: The implementation of Recommendation (85) 11 of the Council of Europe on the Position of the Victim in the Framework of Criminal Law and Procedure.* Nijmegen: Wolf Legal Productions.

Carr, A.P., Turner, A.J. and Starmer, K. (2005) *Stone's Justices' Manual 2005.* London: Lexis/Nexis UK.

Crown Prosecution Service (1993) *Statement of Purpose and Values.* London: Crown Prosecution Service Publicity Office.

Crown Prosecution Service (2002) *CPS Statement on Alton George Manning (deceased).*

Crown Prosecution Service (2004) *Code for Crown Prosecutors.* http://www.cps.gov.uk/Publications/docs/code2004english.pdf

Crown Prosecution Service (2005) *The Prosecutors' Pledge.* London: Crown Prosecution Service Corporate Communication Team. http://www.cps.gov.uk/publications/prosecution/

Crown Prosecution Service (undated) *The CPS Vision.* http://www.cps.gov.uk/about/aims.html

Crown Prosecution Service (undated) *Direct Communication with Victims.* http://www.cps.gov.uk/legal/d_to_g/direct_communication_with_victims_/

Crown Prosecution Service (undated) *Pre-Trial Witness Interviews – Guidance for prosecutors*. http://www.cps.gov.uk/legal/p_to_r/pre_-trial_witness_inter views/

Devlin, Patrick (1960) *The Criminal Prosecution in England*. London, Oxford University Press.

Glidewell, Sir Ian (1998) *The Review of the Crown Prosecution Service: A report*, Cm. 3960. London: The Stationery Office.

HM Crown Prosecution Service Inspectorate (2007) *Direct Communication with Victims: An audit of CPS performance in relation to keeping victims informed*. http:// hmcpsi.gov.uk/index.php?id=47&docID=289

Hodgson, J. (2005) *French Criminal Justice: A comparative account of the investigation and prosecution of crime in France*. Oxford: Hart Publishing.

Home Office (1985) *The Prosecution of Offences Act 1985: A guide*. (An internal document, described in the Introduction as '. . . the product of discussions between the Home Office, The Director of Public Prosecutions' Department and the Association of Chief Police Officers'.)

Home Office (1999) Home Office Special Conferences Unit, Criminal Justice Conferences, *The Role of Victims in the Criminal Justice Process*, 13–15 September 1999, Shrigley Hall Hotel, Macclesfield, Conference Report. (Circulated to participants, but not otherwise published.)

Home Office (2006) *Rebalancing the Criminal Justice System in Favour of the Law-abiding Majority: Cutting crime, reducing reoffending and protecting the public*. London: Home Office. http://www.homeoffice.gov.uk/documents/CJS-re view.pdf/

House of Commons Justice Committee (2009) *The Crown Prosecution Service: Gatekeeper of the Criminal Justice System*, Ninth Report of Session 2008–9, HC 186. http://www.publications.parliament.uk/pa/cm200809/cmselect/cmjust/186/186.pdf

Lidstone, K.W., Hogg, R. and Sutcliffe, F., in collaboration with Bottoms, A.E. and Walker, M.A. (1980) *Prosecutions by Private Individuals and Non-Police Agencies*, Research Study, Royal Commission on Criminal Procedure, No. 10. London, HM Stationery Office.

Macpherson, Sir William (1999) *The Stephen Lawrence Inquiry: Report of an Inquiry by Sir William Macpherson of Cluny*. Cm. 4262-I. London: The Stationery Office. http://www.archive.official-documents.co.uk/document/cm42/4262/4262.htm

Office for Criminal Justice Reform (2005) *Code of Practice for the Victims of Crime*. http://www.cps.gov.uk/legal/v_to_z/victims_code_operational_guidance/

Philips, Sir Cyril (1981a) *Report of the Royal Commission on Criminal Procedure*. Chairman, Sir Cyril Philips), Cmnd. 8092. London: The Stationery Office.

Philips, Sir Cyril (1981b) *Royal Commission on Criminal Procedure* (Chairman Sir Cyril Philips), *The Investigation and Prosecution of Criminal Offences in England and Wales: the Law and the Procedure*, Cmnd. 8092-1. London: The Stationery Office.

Radzinowicz, L. (1956) *A History of English Criminal Law and its Administration from 1750, Vol. 2, The Enforcement of the Law*. London: Stevens and Sons.

Richardson, P.J. (ed.) (2009) *Archbold: Criminal Pleading, Evidence and Practice*. London: Sweet & Maxwell.

Robertshaw, P.E. (2009) 'R (FB) v DPP [2009] EWHC 106: the Prosecutor and the Bookmaker', *Archbold News*, 2: 4–5

Rogers, W.V.H. Horton (ed.) (2006) *Winfield and Jolowicz on Tort* (17th edn). London: Sweet & Maxwell, ch. 18.

Sanders, A. and Jones, I. (2007) 'The victim in court', in S. Walklate (ed.), *Handbook of Victims and Victimology*. London: Willian Publishing, pp. 282–308.

Schnapper, B. (1991) 'L'action pénale, le ministère public et les associations. Naissance et contestation d'un quasi-monopole (XIXe–XXe siècles)', in B. Schnapper, *Voies Nouvelles en Histoire du Droit. La justice, la famille, la répression pénale (XIXe–XXe siècles)*. Paris: Presses Universitaires de France, pp. 375–91.

Spencer, J.R. (2006) 'Droit pénal des affaires en Europe: Angleterre', in Geneviève Giudicelli-Délage (ed.) *Droit pénal des affaires en Europe (Allemagne, Angleterre, Espagne, France, Italie)*. Paris: Presses Universitaires de France.

Sprack, J. (2008) *A Practical Approach to Criminal Procedure* (12th edn). Oxford: Oxford University Press.

Starmer, K. (2009) 'A prosecution service for the 21st century'. Public address given at the London Metropolitan University on 9 January 2009. http://www.cps.gov.uk/news/articles/prosecuting_service_for_the_21st_century/

Straw, J. (2008) 'Working for everyone: building community confidence in the criminal justice system.' Public lecture to the Royal Society of Arts, London, 26 March 2008. http://www.justice.gov.uk/news/sp260308a.htm

Chapter 7

Victims at court: necessary accessories or principal players at centre stage?

Joanna Shapland and Matthew Hall

Problematising the role of the victim

The essence of a modern, common law, adversarial criminal justice system, such as that of England and Wales, is primarily that it is a contest between the State and the offender. The State plays two roles with different tasks and rules, that of prosecuting and that of acting as judge. Pared down to these basics, there is no part for anyone else, except perhaps as onlooker, in the tradition of open justice. Yet these three actors – judge, prosecutor and offender – cannot actually create criminal justice by themselves. Such a minimalist cast would rapidly turn into a pantomime of 'yes, he did it', 'no, I didn't'. For a trial, they need the whole panoply of witnesses and evidence, which necessarily opens up to inspection the offence itself, those involved with it as victims or witnesses, and the pre-trial processes of detection, investigation and interviewing the offender. For sentencing, they need information and action from another cast – pre-sentence report writers, the correctional services, the victim in relation to the effects and financial consequences of the offence, and potentially more witnesses.

The key tension we shall explore in this chapter is that between the minimalist cast and the additional participants, concentrating on the victim. The minimalist cast is dependent on the others, yet, as we shall see, it is loath to give them billing, wishing to write the script and, in relation to lay participants, reluctant to facilitate their communication. The victim appears as a bit player in cast lists for both trials and sentencing. As a result, we would argue that there has been an unfortunate tendency to conflate the victim's role in the two parts of the process. Instead, there is a need to clarify each role separately, looking at whether the victim should be seen in each merely as a necessary accessory to the main characters or whether, in order to create a justice system which is and can be seen to be fair towards all parties, the victim should be encouraged to venture further towards centre stage. We shall therefore look at each phase separately but first, to clarify the essence of each key role in State criminal justice (offender, prosecutor, judge), we shall look back to how they were fulfilled when the victim was one of those key players – the prosecutor. That will illustrate how the prosecutor could then provide the key evidence needed and it will start to indicate the tensions which appeared when the roles of prosecutor and victim were separated.

Where do we need the victim in criminal justice?

The fascinating Old Bailey online project, a record of all criminal proceedings at the Old Bailey from 1674 to 1913, provides the record of the indictment, evidence, verdict and sentence for all cases in that period (Emsley, Shoemaker and Hitchcock 2005). For 12 May 1831, the indictment of the case of George Fisher, in a very typical case, states: 'George Fisher was indicted for feloniously breaking and entering the warehouse of Abraham Isaacs, on the 7th of May, and stealing 6 pecks of almonds, value 20s., and 1 bag, value 1s., his property' (at http://www.oldbaileyon-line.org/browse.jsp?id = t18310512-60-defend480&div = t18310512-60#highlight).

There are of course cultural and historical differences to the Old Bailey today. Compared to a modern indictment or a charge sheet, the legal offence has changed, as have the legal units of measurement (both shillings and pecks), but the overall form remains unchanged[1] and indeed an indictment from the 1600s would be very similar. The basics are that the offender is indicted – accused – of committing a burglary against a named individual victim who owned the property. The point we are making is that indictments are necessarily personal, not just in relation to the offender, but for the victim as well. The 'eternal triangle' of offender, victim and State is still current.

Why do we still need an individual named 'victim' to be so centrally involved in the charge or indictment, the basis of criminal law and criminal justice? We think it is largely because of the way in which harm is experienced and perceived in relation to crimes. The primary harm centre is the victim and offender. However, an offence creates harm and disorder outwards in ripples from this centre. That is why the State is involved at all – because the harm and potential damage has reached beyond the offender and the victim potentially to touch others in the local area, to cause disquiet there and eventually in the general public (as the headlines in the media constantly remind us) and, if nothing is done about it, potentially to threaten the perceived efficacy of the State. The ripples spread outwards:

victim→friends and relations of victim→local neighbourhood
→town/court area→State

The news about the offence, we know, can spread in this way, with the key source of information for people about crime in the area coming from friends and relations who have experienced crime (Skogan 1994). When a local shop is burgled, it has a far greater effect on the neighbourhood's crime consciousness and 'crime talk'[2] than does burglary of a local house because of the larger number of people who hear about the offence and the number who use the shop and who start feeling that it is directly relevant to their lives (Shapland and Vagg 1988). One feature about our current criminal justice system which we want to examine in this chapter is whether it has only recently begun to remember about that ripple effect.

At the time of the 1831 indictment, the victim had to be the prosecutor. This was clearly shown in the evidence of Thomas Bicknell, who was at the station-house when the victim, Mr Isaacs, arrived after the arrest of the offender. Thomas Bicknell states, from the Old Bailey records: 'I was at the station-house. The prisoner was brought in there, and when the prosecutor came he said, "Is that Mr Isaacs? pray do not be too hard with me."' Indeed, the verdict and report of sentencing says, 'Guilty. Aged 21. Recommended to Mercy by the Prosecutor. Confined Three Months.' That was a very lenient sentence for those times. So in 1831, the victim was not only prosecutor, and witness (as in this trial), but also important to sentencing.

Today, we have victim-absent charging and victim-absent prosecution. It is the State authorities of police and prosecution who charge and review charges in England and Wales. It is no longer necessary for the victim to press charges, or indicate they would wish a prosecution. This is particularly relevant in domestic violence cases, in which the offender may intimidate the victim into withdrawing their complaint. In fact, as the JUSTICE Society Committee noted, before the move to victim-absent charging, it was very strange that victims of, for example, street violence generally tended not to be asked whether they wished to press charges, particularly if there were serious injuries, but victims of domestic violence were almost routinely so asked (JUSTICE 1998). Practice today has moved to the point that the victim's 'consent' is no longer required for the public interest test of the Code of Practice of Crown Prosecutors (Crown Prosecution Service 2004, 2006).[3] Though this is clearly beneficial in the sense that prosecutions can be taken if the victim is being intimidated, there are tensions with ideas of empowering victims or of putting victims at the centre of criminal justice. They have come into sharp focus in relation to domestic violence (JUSTICE 1998; Crown Prosecution Service 2006), but can occur with many other offence scenarios.

So, in England and Wales there is victim-absent charging and prosecution. However, we have not yet moved to victim-absent evidence.[4] Mr Isaacs would be likely to recognise both the court layout and much of the court's procedure if he were giving evidence today.[5] At this point in modern procedure, however, there is a significant difference. The victim is certainly no longer the prosecutor. But neither would he or she be termed a victim – the victim has become reincarnated as a witness of the prosecution. In a legal sense, as well as in practice, the victim's evidence is no longer 'owned' by the victim and, as we shall see, is no longer given in the victim's own words and style of speech. Whether the victim is called as a witness, what the victim is asked about, and in what manner, is a matter for the prosecutor (moderated by the judge).[6] In terms of the eternal triangle, power to shape the case has very definitely passed from the victim to the State.

What do victims think about all this? There is a remarkable absence of empirical research on victims at court in recent years in England and Wales: remarkable because of the focus on victims in political discourse on crime and disorder (see, for example, Garland 2001) and in legislation.[7] It seems as though the rhetoric and the legislation have not been accompanied by seeking victims' views as to what they think or would prefer, or consideration of how they would recommend things should change. For victims' views of the whole process we have to rely on some quite old studies (such as Shapland et al. 1985).

The recent information we do have about victims is derived from three main sources: the British Crime Survey (BCS), the Witness Survey, and the International Crime Victims Survey (ICVS). One problem is that these three sets of data cannot be easily amalgamated into one complete picture. The BCS is a survey of a large sample of the general population in England and Wales (Dodd et al. 2004; Allen et al. 2005), the ICVS a similar survey with samples taken from different countries (van Kesteren et al. 2000). Both are useful in terms of their large sample sizes and breadth of questioning, but we know, both from the surveys themselves and from comparison with police statistics, that very few of these victims will have had any contact with the court or given evidence as witnesses (Dodd et al, 2004). The Witness Survey is what it says, a survey of witnesses, recruited via court records (Angle et al. 2003; Moore and Blakeborough 2008). Though the survey could have chosen to focus on victims as victims and phrased questions in this way, in fact it reflects the recasting of victims into the role of witness. In other words, the survey is concerned with witnesses, some of whom will be victims, rather than victims who are witnesses.

As such, not only is it difficult to reconcile the three sets of data we have on victims, it is also the case that none of these sources is specifically concerned with victims within court processes.[8] In terms of the trial process, the Witness Survey sees victims in only one role at court – as witnesses. We, however, would distinguish at least three such roles: victims as members of the public, victims as witnesses, and victims *as* victims. We turn now to look at these three roles played by victims.

The trial phase

Victims at court as members of the public

With the obvious exception of police officers victimised in the course of their duty, most victims who visit a court are lay members of the public and generally have little prior experience of a court or the courtroom setting. Yet these are public courts, with open proceedings,[9] designed to show openly to members of the public that justice is being done. This open nature of justice was specifically organised originally to reassure the first few ripples of concern emanating from the offence: those of the victim, of the victim's family and friends, and of the local neighbourhood. Court-houses were considered a local resource where people could take their problems and have them resolved (Judicature 1997).

In recent times, however, we would argue that the public's view of courts has become very different and, in the process, courts have lost their 'local' character. To most members of the public, the court has now become an alien environment into which one rarely ventures, and then only at the express invitation (or compulsion) of the State. In other words, victims, like other members of the public, have become 'strangers' in the courthouse and, indeed, within the court process. The notion that victims as members of the public are strangers in the courthouse is well illustrated by Rock's (1993) portrayal of the working practices in the Crown Court as comprising a distinctive 'social world'. He described four 'circles', three of which were to some degree 'insiders': the judiciary, who knew what was going on and controlled the environment within the courtroom; the resident court staff and professionals who formed a close-knit, relatively permanent group ('the team'); and the lawyers and other professionals who visited occasionally. The outermost circle was the lay people: victims, witnesses, defendants, jurors, the public:

> The public tended characteristically to enter the courthouse as strangers and would then proceed to wait dejectedly on the benches or in the canteen, at a remove from insiders, smoking, talking to companions perhaps, or in morose seclusion. After all, in the main, it was their problems that were about to be exposed or reanimated painfully and in public. In a sense they represented the emotional and disorderly in crime and public life that the very orderliness of the Court was designed to balance. (p. 195)

As Rock shows, the public (including victims) were seen as unreliable, ephemeral and potentially embarrassing. They were kept apart from the really important people in the court setting spatially, both outside and inside the courtroom. The architecture of the modern courthouse does not put the public at its centre. Unlike the judiciary, court staff, lawyers, probation staff etc., they tend to be kept locked out of central space and controlled rigorously outside the courtroom. As Carlen (1976) demonstrated earlier in the magistrates' court, they are also on the fringes of the courtroom (except when, as witnesses, they are on the witness stand).

Thus, victims attending court are effectively entering a different world; one which is at the very least confusing and stressful, but can also be frightening and intimidating (Dodd *et al.* 2004). With increased attention being focused by academics and policy-makers on the difficulties encountered by lay court users, recent years have witnessed a number of developments aimed at improving this situation; effectively to make the court's 'social world' more receptive to and approachable by members of the public, including victims. Thus, in recent years the Government has emphasised the provision of information to the public about the criminal justice system. For example, the Code of Practice for Victims of Crime (Criminal Justice System 2005a; Home Office 2003) makes it clear that all victims should receive a copy of the 'Victims of Crime' leaflet from the police. Similarly, all victims are free to access the 'online walkthrough' of a criminal court via cjsonline.[10] Courthouses themselves are now mostly equipped with public information desks, as well as a collection of informational leaflets and signposts, including courtroom plans.

However, this need for signposts flags up the other recent trend, towards centralisation and amalgamation of court centres. Magistrates' courts are no longer local resources at the neighbourhood level. They exist at the town or city level (and are increasingly, in rural areas, available only in major population centres). Professionals no longer travel out to local areas to conduct cases which are more serious. Instead, the lay people affected are required to travel in to the professionals. It is highly unlikely that the general public from the local neighbourhood will be able to attend. The ripple of concern of the local neighbourhood can be assuaged, today, only by the media. However, media reporting of criminal cases in England and Wales is not notorious for its assuaging, calming effect or for reporting cases to show that justice has been done. Instead, as Hough and Roberts (1998) have shown, it focuses on cases in which it is considered justice has not been done. Moreover, there is no adequate and specific information service to victims – or witnesses. Some 20 years after early research showed that victims' key need was for information on the case (Maguire 1982; Shapland *et al.* 1985), and despite constant findings from the British Crime Survey that victims feel inadequately informed and this relates strongly to dissatisfaction,[11] there is still no nationally implemented, consistent service to inform victims of the progress of a case. This is a matter of priorities and of resources, not of ignorance.

An important recent innovation, however, is the expansion of the Witness Service to the majority of magistrates' courts and Crown Court centres. The Witness Service is a branch of the victim assistance charity, Victim Support, which provides volunteers to help witnesses attending court. By supplying witnesses with information on the court process and keeping them updated as to the progress of the case, the Service acts as an intermediary between the social world of the court and that of the public. There is a question, however, as to what extent such support reaches victims who are not attending court as witnesses. In the South Yorkshire region, Victim Support's own statistics suggest that very few 'non-witness' victims are being supported by the Witness Service (Victim Support South Yorkshire 2004).[12] Prosecution witnesses have also recently been given some space to themselves in court buildings, in witness waiting rooms (though these seem still not to be universal: Shapland and Bell 1998; Criminal Justice System 2005a). Victims, however, are still in their incarnation as prosecution witnesses.[13]

As such, victims attending trials as observing members of the public might well lack the essential umbilical cord connecting them with the internal world of the court. To give a practical example, such victims will be reliant on the good will of the court staff (usually the ushers) to tell them when to enter the public gallery, when a case will start, how long any delays will take and why such delays have occurred. In short, victims attending court simply to observe a case which concerns them may currently be given no greater consideration than that afforded to any member of the public attending court on the same day (which is not much).[14] The 2005 Code of Practice does not require *any* services to be afforded to victims by the Witness Service unless the victim is attending as a witness. At court, one corner of the eternal triangle seems to have disappeared, in terms of being related to a real, live person. The evidence being given at court may be about the victim (and indeed the victim may be present in bodily form, watching), but this seems to be a conceptually ethereal victim.[15]

If the victim does in fact come to court, then proceedings are certainly not organised around their availability and for their convenience. After all, many criminal trials in the Crown Court take several days, and magistrates' court trials usually involve sacrificing at least one day. Furthermore, trials are of *indeterminate* length and, particularly in the magistrates' courts, can extend into the evening at the discretion of the bench. In addition, most courts employ a listing system whereby all business to be heard in a specific court is scheduled to begin at 10 or 10.30 a.m., which can be confusing for lay observers, as can the frequent delays and, indeed, the frequent adjournments of cases to a future date. It may therefore come as no surprise that victims do not seem disposed to attend court very often just to watch a case.

What attributes would a victim-centred court possess? An expectation that victims might decide to attend (in their role as victims)? A recognition they are not only witnesses and should not be shooed out of the door if they have finished giving evidence (or do not give evidence)? A specific welcome for them? A specific role for the Witness Service in relation to victims, not just victims as witnesses? A named waiting space? A central place in the courtroom (as defendants have)? A welcome by the judge? Our reaction as to the extent to which these would be seen as heresies is an indication of the extent to which victims are not now central (and how far things have moved since 1831).

Victims as witnesses

Victims attending court as a witness face many of the difficulties enumerated above. In addition to these are the specific stresses of acting as a witness. Rock's (1993) conclusion further reveals that witnesses in general have been kept very much at the margins of the court's social community, receiving little help or comfort. This is due mainly to the fact that criminal justice professionals (who of course held the answers to the witnesses' many questions) were afraid of being professionally compromised by talking to them: 'their [witnesses'] marginality is built into the physical fabric and temporal structure of the courthouse itself. They are confused and confusing, often distressed, a threat to the insiders who will not and cannot comfort them.' (Rock 1993: 283)

We have already established that the victim at court is reincarnated as a witness. The extra challenges which come with actually giving evidence in court have been well documented elsewhere (Shapland et al. 1985; Jackson et al. 1991; Rock 1993; Ellison 2001), but a brief reprise of the key issues will prove useful in the present context.

First, a courtroom is an unfamiliar environment for most people and can be frightening and intimidating. One also needs to bear in mind that the timescale of the effects of offences on victims is such that, although the effects of many property offences will have receded before the typical time a trial takes place, longitudinal studies show this is not true for many victims of violence, robbery or sexual assault, where psychological effects can last for months or years (Shapland et al. 1985; Norris and Kaniasty 1994; Denkers and Winkel 1998; Shapland and Hall 2007). The effects a crime has on its victims, along with their duration, are also likely to be affected by the level and type of support individual victims receive (Andrews et al. 2003).

These aspects can make it physically difficult for witnesses to give clear and forceful evidence, especially if they are wary of the defendants or their supporters in the public gallery (Hamlyn et al. 2004). Even in more conventional settings, many people simply have an aversion to speaking in public, particularly in front of people they don't know. The result is that witnesses' voices will tend to squeak or mutter – only for the witness constantly to be told to speak up. Confusingly, though, in several courts the audio equipment which looks like a microphone is there only for recording, not for amplification. Speaking close to this does not help (Hall 2009). Despite the centrality of the orality principle for evidence, a number of courtrooms have extremely bad acoustics, which neither help witnesses nor allow victims as members of the public to hear what is going on (Criminal Justice Review Team 2000; Hall 2009). We do not understand why there is neither adequate amplification in all courts, nor water and clean beakers readily available for all witnesses, nor comfortable chairs in the witness box, and all are asked to sit – all of which would be expected in any other public forum. It doesn't help nervousness, or in generating the best evidence.

Recently, recognising the strains of the witness box, a considerable number of testimonial aids have been introduced into criminal trials to help vulnerable or intimidated witnesses give their best evidence. Originally introduced for child witnesses, the Youth Justice and Criminal Evidence Act 1999 expanded the 'special provisions' to all vulnerable witnesses and they now include giving evidence via a television link; pre-recorded examination in chief and cross-examination; screening witnesses off from the defendants; clearing the public gallery of the court; the removal of lawyers' wigs and gowns in the Crown Court; and giving evidence through intermediaries. The evaluation of these measures clearly shows they have been found to be very beneficial to these witnesses (Hamlyn *et al.* 2004), though their use in practice still requires much further improvement (Burton *et al.* 2006). They depend, however, on the identification of vulnerable witnesses at the pre-trial stage. Burton *et al.* (2006) estimate that there is a considerable gap here, with 24 per cent of witnesses being considered by them to be potentially vulnerable or intimidated, compared to 9 per cent actually identified by agencies in their sample and the 7–10 per cent envisaged by the report preceding the Act (Home Office 1998).

Secondly, when actually giving evidence during criminal trials, witnesses are asked to relay information in a very unnatural, unfamiliar way. The evidence itself is elicited from witnesses in a manner quite unlike any normal conversation, or even public speaking; with witnesses usually being told to present their answers towards the bench or jury while simultaneously receiving the questions from a lawyer standing in another direction (Jackson *et al.* 1991; Hall 2009). In addition, the fact that notes of a witness's evidence must be taken by hand by more than one person in the room means that witnesses are required to present the information at an unnatural speed and volume, persistently being interrupted in their flow and asked to slow down or speed up or speak more loudly (Rock

1993; Hall 2009). Frustratingly, victims will often be asked to elaborate on what they consider to be very small details while passing over what are, to them, more important ones.

Thirdly, particularly during cross-examination, the questions being asked may be embarrassing and accusatory, as well as confusing, coercive and insulting. For example, the evidential requirement that if the defence will present a different story, relevant prosecution witnesses should be challenged on all contradictory points, tends to involve their being accused of lying, implicitly and explicitly (or its euphemism, 'being mistaken'). Yet witnesses are normally not briefed that this will occur: they see it as an attack on their character (Shapland *et al.* 1985). For victims as witnesses, these constraints are likely to be even more problematic. They are telling the story of the offence against them to the official and public forum still seen as the supreme forum of the criminal justice system: the court and the judge. But they are not allowed to say it in their own way, in their own words, emphasising what they see as the most important elements.[16]

The Old Bailey material from the 1660s to the 1830s is the court records, which cannot be considered as a verbatim transcript. Nonetheless, the way in which victims' evidence is presented suggests strongly that witnesses then were at least initially allowed to tell their story, with there then being clarificatory questions and cross-examination. Mr Isaacs said:

> I am a fruit-merchant, and live at No. 11, North-street, Spitalfields market. The prisoner had been employed on my premises, but was discharged about a month or six weeks since; he had to attend a horse in my yard. On the 7th of May I received information and went to the station; I saw the bag of almonds – I knew the bag; it is marked R. – it is a particular mark that we buy; I missed almonds of this description – I had such in my warehouse the night before; I went to the prisoner – as soon as he saw me he said, 'Mr Isaacs, I hope you will have mercy – I took the tiles off the warehouse, and took the bag and the almonds;' my warehouse is in the parish of Christchurch, Spitalfields.

This is not the rigorously chronological story elicited by prosecution lawyers, but the way someone would normally tell things. Other trials in the series similarly clearly separate the initial story from later cross-examination.

Ellison (2001) places some of the blame for the problems faced by witnesses (specifically vulnerable and intimidated witnesses) on the system's continued reliance on the orality principle (evidence should typically be presented out loud).[17] She also notes that the special measures introduced to assist vulnerable and intimidated witnesses are restricted in the sense that they are still fundamentally based on this same orality principle and the traditional rules of evidence. That said, Government guidelines to police officers on the conduct of pre-recorded examination in chief interviews with child witnesses (to be recorded on video and played in the court) suggest these should include a 'free narrative' phase (Home Office 2001a). The free narrative phase is a portion of the interview in which children are allowed to say what they wish about the incident without being interrupted. This represents a notable break with traditional techniques of eliciting evidence from young victims and other witnesses. Note, however, that the advantages of this free narrative stage are gained through a victim's status as a vulnerable, intimidated and young *witness*. A witness's role *as a victim* does not itself afford her any extra benefit. One key question is whether witnesses should all be allowed the same 'privileges' currently granted to vulnerable witnesses. Alternatively, should victims, given they are victims and harmed by the offence, normally be treated as vulnerable witnesses?

Fourthly, in many cases witnesses are also asked to cope with some very unfamiliar concepts and uses of language. Hearsay can be highlighted as a particularly good example of an issue causing confusion for many victims and witnesses in general. The rules related to hearsay evidence are an entirely legal construction which dictate what information a court can hear from a witness and what must be excluded. The confusion this causes for the witness lies in the distinction between 'legally knowing' a fact and 'knowing' a fact in the ordinary sense of the word. For example, if a trusted relative tells us about an incident they witnessed outside our presence, the natural use of language would leave us with no reservations about telling people that we too 'know' about that incident. In a courtroom, however, we would be prevented from giving details of this incident on the basis that, legally speaking, we don't know about it because we were not actually present.

Confusion over hearsay can only be increased by the marked lack of any information given to witnesses about the hearsay rules before attending to give evidence (Home Office 2003). This is despite the fact that these rules represent such an important aspect of the process they are about to undergo. The frustration of witnesses stems not only from the experience of being confusingly informed that they don't 'know' about something which in their eyes they do, but also from an impression that lawyers and criminal justice workers believe the friend or relative who originally provided the information is lying (Hall 2009).

Overall, then, it can be appreciated that victims who attend court as witnesses are not there, from the system's perspective, to 'tell a story' in the natural way that people tend to express information as a narrative (Gergen and Gergen 1988), but are instead there to give evidence. This is a far more unnatural and challenging process for victims of crime. Indeed, research confirms that a skilled advocate will largely dictate the answers received to questions posed to witnesses during evidence (Luchjenbroers

1997; Doak 2005). While the introduction of a so-called 'free narrative' phase within the video-recorded interviews of young children hints at the first signs of a break with traditional evidential conventions (including hearsay), attending court to give evidence as a witness remains a difficult and unsettling experience for many victims of crime.

Victims as victims in the trial phase

So far we have discussed victims in the guise of members of the public and of witnesses/potential witnesses: their normal incarnation at court during the trial phase. Additionally, however, victims face particular limitations as victims. It should be remembered that, in England and Wales, despite all the recent moves to put victims more 'at the heart' of criminal justice, victims still have no actual standing in the criminal procedure. That is to say, they lack party status and, along with it, the capacity to gain information and directly affect proceedings. The practical implication of this is that victims in England and Wales do not have their own lawyers to represent their interests. Hence, the victim is unable to *converse* with the system or to put across their own story.

The Criminal Justice System consultation paper (2005c) suggested the introduction of victims' advocates in murder and manslaughter cases, who might be qualified lawyers or lay people. This was piloted from April 2006 (Sweeting *et al.* 2008). Though the major part of the scheme was in relation to sentencing, where advocates were able to describe the impact of the offence on the victim's family (see below), they were also there to communicate between the family and the system at pre-trial and trial phases. However, 'it is not proposed that a victim's advocate would participate in the trial as a party to it, for example he or she would not examine or cross-examine witnesses, or make submissions or speeches which addressed the issue of guilt or innocence' (2005c: 14). Sweeting *et al.* (2008) discovered that the families found the pre-trial contact very helpful, particularly that provided by the Crown Prosecution System, and it has now been announced that this service will be rolled out for homicide cases throughout England and Wales. However, we need to note that, though such advocates do help the family of victims in this very important but tiny minority of cases, such a reform, at the trial stage, essentially provides a translation service, rather than making the trial itself comprehensible to lay people. It is also an expensive translation service, which is highly unlikely to be extended to other victims on reasons of cost alone.

Going hand-in-hand with the victim's lack of party status, the criminal procedure adopted in English courts has no component specifically dedicated to victims in their role *as* victims. At no stage in the substantive trial procedure is the victim considered *as a victim*. The resulting situation is that victims effectively have little chance to express all the information they might wish during the trial procedure. The contradiction apparent here is that while the impact of crime on victims is fluid and dynamic, the process of giving evidence calls for the elicitation of very rigid, set information. Moreover, this is normally information acquired at one time point – and this also affects the ability of the victims to tell their story, including whether they are able to give their best evidence, having had the opportunity to reflect on what happened. Because oral evidence necessarily means that a witness is giving evidence at a different time to the offence, normally much later, we have to think which of three time points best encompasses the principle of orality. Is evidence ideally intended to be the victim's story and recollection during the offence, or when the victim first makes a statement to the police, or at the point of trial? At the first point, the victim is highly likely to be in some shock and certainly adversely affected by the offence. Police procedure is now to delay taking statements until victims have recovered from the initial shock. Clear recollections of events – and lists of property taken or injuries sustained – are far better sought after some hours, or the next morning. However, for victims of violent crime, we know that the process of starting to recover from the offence is not just a matter of some hours, but a much longer process. It is then, we think, unclear as to when 'best' evidence should be obtained.

Like all witnesses, victims of crime are in practice asked questions based largely on what they have said in their witness statements to the police (the second time point). Broadly speaking, it is the prosecutor's role during examination in chief to draw out the same information from the victim 'live' in court to provide the main plank of the Crown's case. The defence, on the other hand, must test this evidence during cross-examination and one of the main ways this is done is by pointing out inconsistencies between what a victim has said in her statement and what she has said on the day in court. In this way the defence can undermine the credibility of the evidence. Naturally, this can be quite disconcerting for the victim in question. It of course means that victims giving evidence are dissuaded from reporting on any developments in their understanding of the events in question since making the original statement. In other words, the way in which the principle of orality has been operationalised does not take into account modern understandings of how victims are affected by serious offences, how witnesses remember, nor how witnesses can be best persuaded to recount what they remember as having happened. Are we really trying to help victims give their best evidence, feel that they have done so, and so assuage the ripples of concern by showing that justice is being done?

Before leaving the issue of victims in the court procedure, and by way of summing up this section of our paper, it is important to emphasise again the court's status as a public forum. The audience to this forum is varied; from the professional criminal justice actors, to lay participants, to uninvolved parties watching from the public gallery. Overall, one of the key limitations placed on victims as members of the public, witnesses and as victims is that while their affairs are being made public through this forum, this is not able to be done at any point through the victim's own normal means of communication. Instead, the victim's grievance is expressed through a legalistic, intimidating and alien procedure. Indeed, if one wishes to speak in terms of making victims' affairs 'public' in the wider sense, then this is usually achieved only through the news media, in a few unusual cases, and affected by news values which are often very different to those of victims.

The victim's role between conviction and sentence

If the victim at court prior to conviction has been reincarnated as a witness or possible witness, the role of the victim between conviction and sentence is now extremely fuzzy and unclear. This, we would argue, is precisely the problem now affecting sentencers and victims. The previous incarnation as a prosecution witness, to be used as the prosecution shall determine, is insufficient, because the effect of the offence on victims is a significant element in sentencing, as we shall show – and the prosecution has only a very limited role between conviction and sentence in England and Wales. The victim now has to emerge from the prosecutor's shadow. Moreover, judges are encouraged, in pronouncing sentence, to acknowledge the effect of the offence on the victim and indeed the victim's presence in court. So, the victim needs to change identity at conviction, but that new incarnation is not yet formalised, nor has it been directly addressed in sentencing policy.

The confusion over the victim's role at this point is also leading to concern by victims' groups and some public disquiet. This is hardly surprising. Very simplistically, the pre-trial and trial processes can be seen by the ripples of the family and friends of the victim, the local neighbourhood, and the city-wide general public in terms of *whether* justice is prepared to intervene after an offence is committed. But sentencing shows *how seriously* justice regards that particular offence. If the victim is ignored or no account appears to be taken of the effects of the offence, then these groups are likely to see the criminal justice system as not attending to the effects on themselves either. It is not a recipe for calming ripples.[18]

There are three aspects relating to sentencing and victims with which we need to deal. The first is whether sentencers actually have information on the effects on the victim. The second is the extent to which sentencing does take account of those effects. The third is how victims are treated in court between conviction and sentence. In the first two sections, we shall look at the empirical evidence (including case law) on what is happening.

In the final section, we shall consider whether these changing identities of the victim do matter – the 'should' question.

Do sentencers have information on the effects of the offence on the victim?

The first question must be whether judges actually have information about the effects of the offence on the victim which can, where appropriate, be used in sentencing. If there is no information, it cannot be taken into account.

If there has been a not guilty plea and therefore a trial, the assumption has been in practice that it is unnecessary to have further information or evidence about effects: the victim has already given evidence and will have addressed the effects of the crime. However, we saw above that this is unlikely to have occurred, in terms of having full information on effects. Proving the elements of the offence normally requires only minimal information on effects. Typically, this is a list of property and its value for property offences, or medical evidence on immediate injuries for offences of violence. The victim's story may not be sought at all on this: psychological effects never touched upon, the effects of losing property irrelevant. As we saw above, lawyers can tightly control the information provided by witnesses in answer to their questions, and much is restricted to the time point of the witness statement to the police. Hence even the short-term effects of crime on victims may not be addressed in evidence during the trial.

Secondly, and using the evidence from longitudinal studies, the problems faced by victims in expressing in evidence the affects and effects of crime are compounded by the fact that the impact of crime on victims is not a static phenomenon, but one that develops and changes over time (Shapland and Hall 2007). In most cases, witness statements made to the police shortly after the offence have been the main means of accessing information on effects. Where there was a guilty plea or the victim was not called as a witness – which together account for the vast majority of cases – of course there is no direct verbal evidence by the victim on the effects of the offence.[19] So, using the previous standard criminal procedure of the State, information on the effects on victims is unlikely to reach the sentencer.

Recognising this, one means by which victims are now able to communicate more detailed information to the court on the developing effects of crime is through victim personal statements, following a pilot in the late 1990s (Hoyle et al. 1998). These are statements, in England and Wales, written by the victim under police supervision, or told to the police, to give victims of crime an opportunity to comment on how a crime has affected them 'physically; emotionally; psychologically; financially or in any other way' (Home Office 2001b: 2).

Victim personal statements were rolled out as a national initiative in October 2001 but their implementation has now been acknowledged as very patchy (Graham *et al.* 2004; Office for Criminal Justice Reform 2005; Criminal Justice System 2005c: 11). The recent national Witness and Victim Experience Survey found that only just over one third of victims interviewed recalled being given the opportunity to make a victim personal statement, while 53 per cent said they had definitely not been told about this (Moore and Blakeborough 2008). The authors say: 'There is some evidence that standards highlighted in the Victim and Witness Delivery Plan are not being met. Most noteworthy is the severe lack of availability of the Victim Personal Statement. With more than half of victims not recalling having been offered the opportunity to make such a statement, there is a need for the CJS [Criminal Justice System] agencies to revisit the use and promotion of this intervention' (p. v). There seems to have been little pressure on practitioners to undertake the task and, as far as we are aware, achieving consistent availability of victim personal statements to sentencers (or indeed their being offered to victims) has not figured in performance targets for relevant criminal justice practitioners.

Nor do we think the judiciary have been pointing out where they have not occurred. As one of us has argued elsewhere, implementation of new initiatives in criminal justice in England and Wales is strongly affected by whether there are consequences if the initiative is not undertaken by individual practitioners or statutory agencies (Shapland *et al.* 2004). The most potent adverse consequence for a criminal justice practitioner if a report relevant to sentence is not produced is if the judiciary are likely to comment on its non-availability. We know of no such judicial policy in relation to victim personal statements.

There is an additional factor in relation to victim personal statements which we think reflects strongly on the lack of agreed role for the victim in relation to sentencing. The pilot study conducted by Hoyle *et al.* (1998) reported confusion among criminal justice practitioners as to what use should be made of personal statements. A subsequent investigation from Morgan and Sanders (1999) concluded that 'victim statements' were seen primarily as an aid to sentencing by criminal justice professionals but that *in practice* they still had little or no impact on most sentencing decisions. This is similar to the findings in South Australia by Erez and Rogers (1999).

A Practice Direction issued by the then Lord Chancellor's Department in 2001 soon after the national roll-out of the scheme suggested that a rather restrictive use and interpretation of victim personal statements was to be adopted by the court. Putting it simplistically, descriptions of effects were fine; victims' opinions were not:

> The opinions of the victim or the victim's close relatives as to what the sentence should be are therefore not relevant, unlike the consequences of the offence on them. Victims should be advised of this. If despite the advice, opinions as to sentence are included in a statement, the court should pay no attention to them.[20]

This is of course contrary to what Mr Isaacs was doing in 1831, when he requested the court to have mercy – which is the victim expressing a view on sentence.

Sanders and Jones (2007) would prefer expert testimony on effects, rather than a direct statement by victims, because victims 'not only vary unpredictably in their reactions to victimisation, but . . . are liable to over or understate these reactions in statements of the VIS kind' (p. 297). We disagree. The effects of victimisation are different for different victims – but they are still the effects on those victims. It is rather patronising or paternalistic to state that (adult) victims are unable to express the effect that being a victim has had on them. What effect this should then have on sentence is another matter, which we consider below.

Even in their current format and use, however, a key to the disadvantage of the scheme from the victims' perspective is that the use and interpretation of these statements are in the hands of the prosecutor presenting the case. Unlike the equivalent schemes in several US states (Erez 2000), the English and Welsh version of victim personal statements does not currently allow the victims themselves to read the statement orally in court, except in the pilot for homicide cases (JUSTICE 1998). Thus the victim must rely on the prosecutor presenting the statement to the court, referring to it in a speech or eliciting information contained within it during the victim's examination in chief.

It is of course the prosecutor's duty to ensure that relevant information is provided to the court. The Court of Appeal stressed as long ago as 1992 in *Hobstaff* (1992) (14 Cr App R (S) 605), the leading case dealing with the evidence of psychological harm in child sex abuse, that the sentencer must have evidence on which to proceed. They said the evidence 'must be available in a proper form whether as an expert's report, witness statement or otherwise'.

In 1995, the Court of Appeal considered the status of a statement from the victim as to the psychological effects of the offence. In *Doe*,[21] Sedley J, giving the judgement of the Court, said:

> The valuable practice of putting before the sentencing court what is sometimes called a 'victim impact statement' which was followed in this case, served to illustrate the profound and enduring impact of the rape on the life and well-being of a young victim on the threshold of adult life.

In *Attorney General's Reference No. 2 of 1995 (R v. S)*,[22] a further witness statement had been taken from the victim of indecent assault by her father setting out the effects on her. The Lord Chief Justice, Lord Taylor, sitting in the Court of Appeal, said of this:

> We consider it wholly appropriate that a judge should receive factual information as to the impact of the offending on a victim. The judge

is well equipped to know whether the statement put before him contained evidence of fact relevant to sentencing or whether an attempt had been made to try to hot up the case against the offender. However that may be, we consider that the gravity of the offence is aggravated by the impact on this particular victim.

Cases hence suggest strongly that the sentencer should have relevant information at the point of sentence. The Government now agrees: 'Everyone agrees that when it comes to sentencing the judge should take into account the effect of the crime on the [victim]' (Criminal Justice System 2005c: 13). The difficulty is in getting it there.

There have been some attempts to try to increase the use of victim personal statements. They include the promotion of personal statements in the Toolkit issued to Local Criminal Justice Boards (Office for Criminal Justice Reform 2005). However, this Board route has been tried before, with conspicuous lack of success. It will require a major culture change in criminal justice agencies and among the judiciary to ensure implementation this time.

The direct route – victims preparing a statement which is read in court, by a lawyer, a lay person or by victims themselves – has recently been piloted for relatives of victims in homicide cases, as is described by Paul Rock in Chapter 8 in this volume. The pilot was in five Crown Court centres between April 2006 and April 2008. Its official evaluation showed that the possibility of making a family impact statement (as the statements were called in the pilot) was welcomed by many families of homicide victims, primarily because it created a sense of active involvement in the legal proceedings (Sweeting et al. 2008). If, however, the opportunity to make the statement was denied, or the statement was edited, or the statement seemed to make no impact on the judge, then there was distress. In those circumstances, relatives were, we would argue, feeling shunned again by criminal justice.

The possibility of being shunned, of expectations denied, has been a key argument in the controversy over victim statements in the UK. Hoyle et al. (1998), in their pilot, later rephrased more strongly in their Criminal Law Review article (Sanders et al. 2001), suggest that victim experiences with statements led to disappointment – victims did not know whether they had been used in sentencing; they were not often decisive in affecting sentencers – and that as a result victim statements should not be a part of the process between conviction and sentencing. The title of their article, 'Victim impact statements: don't work, can't work' conveys their message. Chalmers et al. (2007), however, who evaluated the Scottish pilot, have cast doubt on Sanders et al.'s interpretation of their figures re England and Wales – and obtained rather different Scottish results. Chalmers et al. point out that though positive views from victims in England and Wales as to whether making a statement had been the right decision apparently dropped from 77 per cent to 57 per cent by the end of the case, this is still a majority of victims believing it was the right decision – not a statement of major disappointment.[23] In Scotland, the vast majority of the victims interviewed at the end of the case (86 per cent) still thought their decision to make a statement was 'definitely' or 'probably' the right one.

Whether victims are disappointed depends very much, we would argue, on why they decide to make such a statement in the first place – and on whether anyone bothers to let victims know what happened at sentence.[24] Influencing sentencers is one reason for making a statement, but simply to express the effect of the offence (therapeutic or cathartic effects) is another. Chalmers *et al.* (2007) found that in Scotland only relatively few victims overall decided to make a statement, but that this was strongly related to the seriousness of the offence: a majority of victims made statements for very serious offences. The most common reason was expressive (34 per cent), with 23 per cent wishing to influence sentencers. Many found the process of making the statement helpful or therapeutic, even if for some it was also upsetting.[25]

Chalmers *et al.* make the important point that victim statements *per se* should seldom be expected to have major effects on sentence, because the information contained in them should have reached sentencers by other means (e.g. from the prosecution) or be the majority effects from that kind of offence, already, hopefully, known to sentencers. In other words, it should usually be a confirmatory back-up and so not be expected to have a radical effect on sentencing by itself. That does not of course deny its expressive effect for victims.

Does information about the effects of the offence matter to current sentencing?

We have seen that information about effects may not always reach the sentencer. But does this matter? Does current sentencing practice need any information about the victim? We would argue that, even without considering the 'should' questions (should victims be relevant to sentencing? should they have any active role?), current case law requires that sentencers obtain and consider information pertaining to victims. There are several aspects to consider here.

First, as the JUSTICE (1998) report argues, aspects of the offence relating to the victim can have a major influence on how serious an offence is judged to be, and so on sentence, particularly given that seriousness is relevant both to a just deserts philosophy of sentencing and to risk and public protection arguments. The consequences of the offence on the victim may, in some cases, make a fundamental difference to the offence that is charged, for example the difference between causing grievous bodily harm with intent and the offence of assault occasioning actual bodily harm. In other cases, the consequences for the victim may be relevant to prove an element of the offence. Thus, if a defendant is charged with arson intending or being reckless as to endangering life, the fact that a victim's life was, in fact, endangered will be admissible in any trial. Indeed, it is the centrality of the consequences of the offence to the victim which makes the victim often a principal prosecution witness in any trial.

Secondly, in a wide range of offences, courts now routinely receive and act on evidence of the consequences for the victim. As well as the more obvious property loss, damage or physical harm, this has increasingly included a recognition of psychological effects ('jewellery of sentimental value') and reflects research findings of the harm done by different offences ('the sense of shock and uncleanliness produced by burglaries where clothing has been scattered and defiled': *Smith and Woollard*[26]).[27] The courts also increasingly reflect understanding of the potential for longer-term harm for different kinds of victims (robbery or burglary of elderly people). Sentencing therefore needs to include consideration of the seriousness of the offence in producing short- or long-term psychological harm to victims.

A particular area in which there has been recognition of the potential for grave long-term effects, and the need for the courts to act on evidence of it, is in relation to sexual offences against both adults and children. So, for example, in *Billam*,[28] it is said that an offence of rape should be treated as aggravated in circumstances in which 'the effect upon the victim whether physical or mental is of special seriousness' and in *Attorney General's Reference No. 1 of 1989* an aggravating feature of incest would be where the 'girl has suffered physical or psychological harm'.[29]

An obvious factor here is the vulnerability of the victim. This may arise through age, with both the young and the old being seen as vulnerable,[30] or in relation to mental handicap (as in *Mason*).[31] Another group of particularly vulnerable victims is those who are exposed to violence because of the work they do, such as bus drivers and conductors, taxi drivers, publicans, police officers etc. Thus, sentence is intended to depend on the vulnerability of the victim and on the extent to which the offence causes that victim physical or psychological harm. It is easy to justify this approach in those cases in which the consequences fall within the 'normal' range for that kind of offence, so an offender may be said to have been reckless as to whether his offence would have such consequences even though he did not know that it would. For example, a burglar can reasonably be expected to know that many people place great sentimental value on objects that have small intrinsic worth because, for instance, they belonged to a deceased loved one, or to know that some householders are devastated by a burglary. Similarly with some sexual offences, the range of catastrophic effects is well known. More difficult to justify logically is the taking account of effects that are wholly unforeseeable. In these cases, the courts have tended to act only on those consequences where the public would instinctively, and reasonably, feel that they should.

There is one particularly difficult issue in the case law which also needs to be addressed in discussing the victim and sentencing. It involves the relationship between the victim and offender and, particularly, whether the offender feels remorse; whether the offender apologises to the victim or takes part in restorative practices; and whether the victim then forgives the offender. We think this underlines the current fuzziness in relation to the role of the victim. Essentially, remorse shown by the offender towards the victim, particularly if backed up by evidence that the remorse is genuine (having done reparative work for the victim, offering/paying compensation, etc.) has long been a mitigating factor for sentence. The Court of Appeal has even held, in a burglary case, *R v. Collins*,[32] that an offender being prepared to attend a restorative justice conference could be considered a mitigating factor in sentence. The reason is that just going through the preparation and agreeing to meet the victim (whether or not the restorative justice conference actually took place) was difficult and stressful for the offender.

But these principles are very offender-centred: they concentrate upon the offender's remorse or effort. They seem to ignore the victim and the victim's part in being prepared to meet the offender or accept the apology. One of us has argued elsewhere that apologies in restorative justice, situated within criminal justice, should be seen as intrinsically triadic, with the apology from the offender being to both the victim and the State, but, as Bottoms (2003) has pointed out, the response from the victim to the apology is also integral to it (Shapland *et al.* 2006). Referring back to the eternal triangle, one could develop this argument to say that, in criminal justice or restorative justice, the State also needs to respond, both through reintegrative measures towards the offender for having offered the apology *and* by acknowledging any response from the victim.[33] We are not here centrally concerned with restorative justice, but the courts in criminal justice do not seem to have addressed coherently the need to recognise the response of the victim where that has occurred. This is very different from the embedded acknowledgement in the 1830s, where the victim's recommendation for mercy clearly carried great weight (Emsley, Shoemaker and Hitchcock 2005).

The Court of Appeal in *Nunn*[34] in 1996 set out the current main principles of the courts in relation to victims who forgive. They said it is

> an elementary principle that the damaging and distressing effects of a crime on the victim represent an important factor in the sentencing decision, and those consequences may include the anguish and emotional suffering of the victim, or in the cause of a death, his or her surviving close family. The opinions of the victim or the surviving family member about the appropriate level of sentence do not provide any sound basis for assessing a sentence. If the victim feels utterly merciful towards the criminal, as some do, the crime has still been committed and must be punished as it deserves. If the victim is obsessed with vengeance, as sometimes happens, the punishment

cannot be made longer than would otherwise be appropriate. Otherwise cases with identical features would be dealt with in widely different ways leading to improper and unfair disparity. If carried to its logical conclusion, the process would end up by imposing unfair pressures on the victim or survivors of a crime resulting in death to play a part in the sentencing process which many would find painful and distasteful. This is very far from the court being kept properly informed of the anguish and suffering inflicted on the victim.

A very interesting article by Edwards (2002) has taken further this discussion of the Court of Appeal's view on forgiveness or anger. He cites the case of *Perks*, in which the husband of a robbery victim had addressed a document to the CPS talking about his anger towards the offender.[35] In *Perks*, the Court of Appeal reiterated:

> The opinion of the victim and the victim's close relatives on the appropriate level of sentence should not be taken into account. The court must pass what it judges to be the appropriate sentence having regard to the circumstances of the offence and of the offender subject to two exceptions: (i) where the sentence passed on the offender is aggravating the victim's distress, the sentence must be moderated to some degree. (ii) where the victim's forgiveness or unwillingness to press charges provide [sic] evidence that his or her psychological or mental suffering must be very much less than would normally be the case.[36]

A subsequent case, *Robinson (Sean)* has reiterated that a sentence which aggravates the victim's distress should be moderated to some degree.[37]

So, currently, it seems that whether the victim does forgive is irrelevant to sentence. The victim's views can usually safely be ignored. But if there is evidence that there have been effects on the victim, whether because of the sentence passed, or simply because of that forgiveness, then forgiveness is relevant. Similarly, in *Roche*,[38] Edwards again brings out the Court of Appeal's view that 'whereas the court can never ignore the public interest element of offences of this kind and can never become an instrument of vengeance, nonetheless it can in appropriate circumstances, and to some degree, become an instrument of compassion'. Even more confusingly, in an offence of criminal damage, the sentence was reduced for various reasons including that the court had 'taken insufficient account of the statements made by the victims as to [the appellant's] good character and mild mannered nature'.[39] This surely is an opinion from the victim. Edwards argues that this is confusing: why is forgiveness relevant, but vengeance is not? He also argues that taking into account forgiveness is allowing too much of chance factors to be brought into the sentencing of the offender on a strict retributive view of sentencing (although it is relevant to a restorative viewpoint).

Walker (1999) similarly deplores the lack of clarity by the Court of Appeal on the role of forgiveness and in relation to victims generally. He asks whether it is proper for a criminal court to go further than is justified by a plea in mitigation and act mercifully, and argues that the Court has used the concept of mercy[40] loosely: 'It tends to resort to what it calls "mercy" when it has a vague compassion for the offender but cannot articulate a precise justification for reducing the severity of the sentence.' Walker, in a similar argument to Edwards, seems primarily to be very wary of introducing forgiveness by victims because it would introduce a 'chance' element (the individual victim involved, whether that victim forgives) into what he considers should be a logical, rational process between the State and the offender.

We would certainly agree with both Edwards and Walker that we need much more clarity from the Court of Appeal on the question of victims' reactions to offenders. However, we do not think the sentencer, representing the State, can ignore the fact that both offender and victim have been involved during the course of the offence and that there may have been interaction between them since then – particularly if that would be seen as important by the local community (as in our ripples model). It is illogical to acknowledge certain types of interaction (expressed remorse, previous reparation/payment of compensation) and try to ignore others (forgiveness). Interestingly, Murphy (1988: 179–80) argues that, because punishment is the State's right, but not its duty,

> A judge or head of state may show mercy *if* (and this is a very big 'if') it can be shown that such an official is acting not merely on his own sentiments, but as a vehicle for expressing the sentiments of all those who have been victimised by the criminal and who, given those sentiments, wish to waive the right that each has that the criminal be punished.

This is clearly, as Walker notes, close to ideas in Islamic jurisprudence, but it can also be taken as indicating the claim of both the victim and the local community (indirectly victimised, on our ripples argument) to comment on and even be invoked in sentencing by the State.

We think that the necessary clarification in sentencing needs additionally to take into account two elements. The first is the strong historical tradition in England and Wales of the relevance of mercy from victims (as in the case of Mr Isaacs, described at the beginning of this chapter). Perhaps it is because of the intrinsic tensions between retribution and mercy and the dominance of retribution in current sentencing philosophy[41] that there is such difficulty in considering mercy and forgiveness. The second factor is that it seems to us to be really rather insulting to take into account victim-related factors, such as effects, and even victim decisions on forgiveness in as far as they affect victims' health, but to ignore the victim as a person – i.e. to ignore what the victim is actually expressing as their views or what they say they feel. It is as though the current conceptualisation of the victim at sentence is that of a bag of effects, but not as a whole person capable of acting as a person in their own right. It is a very disempowering view.

How does victim input relate to the job of the sentencer?

Our final question is how the role of victims relates to the job of the sentencer. Answering this means starting to set out how victims might be reincarnated post-conviction, as they step out of the pre-conviction shadow of the prosecution into the spotlight of the homily and the media. It is a very difficult discussion, partly because previous discourse has been so dominated by one procedural suggestion (the victim impact statement/ victim personal statement), partly because there has been little systematic consideration of how the task of sentencing and philosophies of sentencing require either participation by the victim or, at minimum, information about the victim. Sentencing has been seen as a matter between State and offender, with the State needing to keep one eye on public views, but being able largely to ignore victims.

We would argue, however, that many of the purposes of sentencing for adult offenders require participation by victims or information about victims.[42] In this we are saying not only that the effects on victims should be considered at sentencing, or that current sentencing practice is that such information should be obtained and considered, but that victim input is *necessary* for proper sentencing. Sentencing without victim input is impoverished sentencing.

Sentencing according to the seriousness of the offence, an underlying principle for proportionate punishment and for deterrence, requires adequate information on seriousness, including, as we saw above, information about the effects on the victim. Even in relation to the protection of the public, victim participation is important. One key element for the State in relation to public protection is protection of the victim from revictimisation.[43] For the future protection of the victim, the role of the victim needs to include information to the sentencer on potential risks to the victim. The information may be relevant to curfews, to electronic tagging and other means of physical separation, to licence conditions and so forth. In asking for such information (currently done at several stages of criminal justice: re bail, special measures for vulnerable and intimidated witnesses, sentence, pre-release), the criminal justice practitioner is not just asking for information, but also for victims' *views*. The risks are then weighed up by sentencers or other practitioners.

Reparative measures clearly also require information about losses and injuries to the victim. The importance of reparation being ordered as part of the sentence has strongly been supported by the general public and by victims themselves (Shapland *et al*. 1985; Roberts and Stalans 2004). The extent of the damage done to the victim has to be appreciated, so that the amount of financial compensation, for example, is seen as appropriate to the seriousness of the offence, and not an insult (Shapland *et al*. 1985; Cozijn 1984).

In order to reduce crime by rehabilitation, it is important for the sentencer to be precise about the offence and its circumstances, not just about the circumstances of the offender taken in isolation. It is quite strange how modern ideas of rehabilitation have seen change in offending behaviour as a matter for the offender seen in isolation, abstracted from his or her family, community – and victim. Considering the reform and rehabilitation of offenders implies considering how offenders might be helped to desist. Desistance is increasingly being seen as a process in which cognitive changes in attitudes towards offending are intertwined with the formation of affective bonds with significant others and opportunities for legitimate activity (or, more popularly phrased, the good woman and the job) (Farrall and Calverley 2006; McNeill and Whyte 2007; Bottoms *et al*. 2004). Getting to that point could also involve appreciating the effects on victims and being able to apologise to victims – which is the theory behind restorative justice and much victim impact work. One of us has argued elsewhere that restorative justice events may be important staging posts on the path to desistance, at which offenders' desires to change are encouraged by both victims and their own family (Robinson and Shapland 2008). In other words, we are suggesting that the role of the victim needs to go beyond being seen as an empty bundle of effects, to becoming a person who may interact with the offender, may hear apologies, and may respond to those apologies – all of which needs to be acknowledged by the State at sentence.

Accurate and recent information about victims is therefore crucial for reparation and punishment. Interaction with the victim may be helpful for encouraging desistance and creating opportunities for rehabilitation. The discussion on victims and sentencing has tended to be based on what victims themselves may need. We are arguing that victims are also intrinsic to the job of sentencing itself. It is perhaps not surprising that the Sentencing Advisory Panel has recently, in its research reports, made significant attempts to find out the views of victims, particularly where the offence is known to have major effects.[44]

Using victims to help sentencing, but ignoring their own needs, is, however, a dangerous trap to fall into, because it may call into question for the public the perceived legitimacy of sentencing. It is strange that questions of legitimacy have often not been raised in discussions of sentencing philosophy and practice. It may be because the State in England and Wales has tended over the last century or so to feel itself secure against major public disquiet about justice.[45] However, public disquiet over the performance of justice practitioners at home, as well as more violent manifestations of disquiet in other European countries, have led to States reaching out more obviously to their publics (Shapland 2008), as well as to measures of public confidence becoming targets for the justice system to attain in England and Wales.[46]

Recent surveys in this country and internationally have shown that what undermines public confidence in the criminal justice system generally is:

- a perceived lack of accountability and legitimacy of the courts, which are felt to be too insulated from the public;

- biased treatment of some defendants, especially minorities;

- poor treatment of victims and their exclusion from the criminal process; and

- the media reporting of crime, especially its concentration on violent crime and its focus on the failures of the system (Hough and Roberts 2004).

Again, we see the role of the victim becoming important.

The legitimacy of criminal justice and the role of the victim

Our original premise about the ripple effects of crime showed disquiet and harm spreading outwards:

victim→friends and relations of victim→local neighbourhood →town/court area→State

The evidence on confidence in criminal justice and the courts indicates that the views of the public, whether broadly from the town or court area, or more narrowly from the local neighbourhood, are intimately tied up with what happens to the victim – or, rather, the system's failings in respect of the victim.

We have seen that the victim's role as an important actor pre-trial becomes reincarnated, for the trial process, as that of a prosecution witness. For many victims it may be no more than the role of a spectator member of the public. There will be few mentions of the victim and very few references or elements relating to the victim as victim. Although the trial process is the part of criminal justice where the minimalist cast of actors (judge, prosecutor, offender) is most dominant, even here we do not see why the victim is completely unacknowledged as victim (in terms of consideration, place in court, etc.). After all, the indictment itself (both in 1831 and now) singles out the victim from other witnesses. Though the victim at trial may be a minor player, he or she should surely be a respected player. With the current rules of evidence, witnesses – apart from vulnerable witnesses – are unable to tell their story in a normal way. We think some of these restrictions and the extent of direction by lawyers may not be necessary, and the lack of explanation of the more insulting rules and lack of consideration and audibility quite unnecessary. None of it produces confidence that the court has understood the burdens and constraints on witnesses, let alone victims.

After conviction, the role of the victim has not, we consider, been properly addressed. The victim can no longer masquerade as just a prosecution witness. Indeed, both current sentencing practice and the principles of sentencing demand that information be obtained from the victim. However, it seems to have been convenient to continue to hide the victim under the cloak of a witness. The means of obtaining the necessary information have not been routinised, nor comment made when they fail and the information is not there.

More fundamentally and more controversially, we consider the victim between conviction and sentence can no longer be just a provider of information – a bag or bundle of separate effects on which evidence is given, which can be 'taken into account' in the sentencing of the offender and the meting out of a relevant quantum of punishment. Our reasoning stems from the purposes of sentencing, as well as from common decency and for public confidence. Many purposes require not just 'information on effects' but ascertaining views from the victim. For example, insisting on reparation against the consent of the victim would be an insult and a travesty, but asking for that consent is asking for a view on the potential sentence. Similarly, protection against future harm requires views on that harm and on what might prevent it. Rehabilitation and desistance may be facilitated by communication between the victim and the offender, but that will necessarily be about what will happen in the future – which in the context of sentencing is a view on sentence. In other words, we think the distinction in the 2001 Practice Direction[47] between information and views is no longer tenable.

However, we are not arguing for the introduction of an American-style victim impact statement as a panacea, though this kind of oral statement has been found to be helpful for some relatives of homicide victims. We are completely against the compulsory or 'normal' expectation of such an oral statement being made. That would strongly suggest to the victim that the system expects the victim to form an opinion on sentence and to take the risk of expressing it publicly (whether it be hanging and flogging, or forgiveness and leniency). Judges are employed to take the responsibility and the 'brickbats' in expressing public views on sentencing. We should not offload that responsibility on victims.

Instead, we suggest that the victim, at conviction, be allowed to emerge from the witness cloak and to be treated as a person: a person whose hurt is acknowledged, who has useful information, who may have helpful views and who may sometimes even, if they wish, be able to assist in what might help the offender and society. That is, after all, already the premise of referral panels for young offenders and of the pilots in restorative justice with adult offenders. It is not suggesting that the victim should determine sentence: it is suggesting that the victim should be a respected and acknowledged person during the sentencing phase. A court and criminal justice system with these views about the role of the victim would seek to explore which avenues of communication would be most helpful to the victim. Possibilities might be that the victim himself or herself complete a written victim personal statement which is given to the sentencer;[48] or that the victim might attend a restorative justice event, the results of which would be passed on to the sentencer; or that the prosecutor read out a statement; or that a victim advocate speak on behalf of the victim; or that the victim speak. The setting might be the normal court setting or a panel or conference setting with the offender, or whatever. The victim would be invited to be present.

Traditionally, the minimalist cast has objected to these proposals. Rock, in his history of the formation of victim policy in the 1990s says: 'Time after time, action mooted by the Home Office and 10 Downing Street met with stout opposition from those in the judiciary and the Lord Chancellor's Department who guarded defendant rights, the maintenance of professionally controlled and emotionally unencumbered trials, and the doctrine that crime is at heart an offence against Society, State, or Sovereign' (2004: 567). One argument is that the judge might be biased after communication with the victim. We have always found such arguments very disrespectful to the abilities of the judiciary. We do not see why judges could not be trusted to give victims' views the weight they should bear, just as they do for defendants' pleas in mitigation. How can one really say that a judge who could well have heard evidence from a victim is then likely to be 'biased' by a victim's views on sentence? Judges are trained, in court and chairing public inquiries, to give due weight to relevant elements and to disregard others.

But will this not disadvantage the offender if 'their' victim were to hold really vengeful or intimidatory views? This is a serious point, but not one fatal to the new potential role for the victim to be treated as a person. The key comes in what is seen to be a 'relevant' element for sentence and in the boundaries set on the application of each principle. Those depend upon the particular principle or principles of sentencing adopted. If we consider compensation, for example, the upper boundary for property loss is the value of the property lost; the boundary for injury the likely award of a civil court (or that of the Criminal Injuries Compensation Authority). Deterrence has the legal boundary of the maximum statutory sentence for the offence, but in practice much lower boundaries set by previous guidance to the courts of first instance. In other words, there are elements of proportionality (to loss, to seriousness) related to all the sentencing principles. We do not see why such elements could not also apply to victim input.

The recent proposals for victim advocates in the very serious cases of murder and manslaughter begin to give some identity to the victim in the sentencing phase. They seem to have proved very helpful to victims in terms of advice and support (as, essentially, a legal version of the Witness Service) and we would not wish to take away such opportunities, particularly for these offences. However, they are essentially substituting the victim with another (normally legally trained) person. They are allowing lawyers to interact only with lawyers, and so taking the courts further away from ordinary people and the ripples of disquiet. Instead, for the vast bulk of offences, we would argue that, for confidence and for legitimacy, the courts need to turn again to acknowledge the victim as a real person and to communicate with that person; and, by means of that communication, show they care about the disquiet caused by offending.

Notes

1 For a modern form of an indictment, see Rock (1993: 63).
2 Loader *et al.* (1998) first formulated the evocative phrase 'crime talk' to describe the everyday discourse in homes, shops and pubs about the crime and disorder occurring in the local neighbourhood.
3 The Code states: 'The Crown Prosecution Service does not act for victims or the families of victims in the same way as solicitors act for their clients. Crown Prosecutors act on behalf of the public and not just in the interests of any particular individual. However, when considering the public interest, Crown Prosecutors should always take into account the consequences for the victim of whether or not to prosecute, and any views expressed by the victim or the victim's family' (para 5.12, p. 12). Their guidance booklet on domestic violence states: 'Sometimes victims will ask the police not to proceed any further with the case and say that they no longer wish to give evidence. This does *not* mean that the case will automatically be stopped. As a general rule we will prosecute cases where there is sufficient evidence and it is in the public interest to do so' (Crown Prosecution Service 2006: para 5.5).
4 Victim-distant evidence has been introduced for vulnerable witnesses and, in different ways, for witnesses from other countries, via live video links, but this has merely shown up how essential victim evidence is.
5 Though of course the Old Bailey itself, like other Crown Court centres, has been considerably modernised to incorporate security features.
6 This point is well addressed and buttressed jurisprudentially in Doak (2005).
7 For example, the Domestic Violence, Crime and Victims Act 2004.
8 From 2005, the Witness Survey turned into the Witness and Victim Experience Survey (WAVES) to monitor, among other things, the satisfaction of witnesses and victims with their experience at court. However, though it separates the

views of victims from those of non-victim witnesses, its priority is not to concentrate on victims *as* victims.

9 The youth court and, very occasionally, proceedings in adult courts in which the safety of the participants is an issue, are exceptions to the general rule of proceedings being open to the general public.

10 Although, given what we know about the economic means of the typical victim, it is questionable whether a large proportion of them are able to make use of this resource (Kershaw *et al.* 2000; Dodd *et al.* 2004).

11 The British Crime Survey results show that 58 per cent of victims felt that they were not kept informed about the progress of the case, despite this being one of the four key targets for the police in relation to the performance of the criminal justice system on confidence in criminal justice, one of the two main Home Office performance targets (Allen *et al.* 2005).

12 There are, revealingly, no recent statistics or research available on the number of victims attending court in different capacities.

13 We should also note the proposed Victim Care Units, which may be useful in providing support to victims at court – though they may concentrate more upon needs assessment close to the time of the crime and pre-court support (Criminal Justice System 2005b). It is not clear how the Victim Care Units are relating to the Witness Service.

14 The Code of Practice for Victims (Criminal Justice System 2005a) says victims should have a place in the courtroom, a suggestion made at least as far back as 1985 (Shapland *et al.* 1985), but it is not clear how victims who do not give evidence can be identified and welcomed.

15 Even more confusingly, the victim is often called the 'complainant' at court, a concept stemming from the historical role of the victim being needed as the initial prosecutor (i.e. lay a complaint before the court). The term then became used to designate the person who reported the offence to the police and was designated as the complainant on police forms. This is of course not necessarily the victim. The term 'complainant' hence is now not only conceptually ethereal (in the sense the person is not often actually present) but also very fuzzy. Its continued use suggests a reluctance to dignify the victim with that appellation until the offender is convicted.

16 We are not arguing at this point for the inclusion of material which might be 'unfair' to the defendant or potentially misleading, just because it is important to the victim. We are merely pointing out that a non-vulnerable victim, as a witness 'owned' and controlled by the prosecution, does not normally have the opportunity at any stage to tell the story of the offence in their own words, despite the orality principle.

17 Sanders and Jones (2007) make similar points in their very interesting comparison of adversarial and inquisitorial systems.

18 This is clearly recognised by the Lord Chancellor in the 2005 consultation paper: 'We want victims to be heard where they should be heard: properly, inside the court – where it's important, where it really matters, where it should be. Part of the process of the court – not outside the process of the court' (Criminal Justice System 2005c: 3).

19 It is possible for the judge to call evidence between conviction and sentence on any relevant matter, which would include the effects of the offence on the victim in many cases. Equally, if the defence contradict a significant element in

the statement of the victim to the police (for example, which property was taken or the extent of injuries), evidence can be heard and the matter resolved in a so-called *Newton* hearing after conviction. However, the calling of victims to give evidence after trial is in practice extremely rare (Shapland 1981; Hall 2009).

20 Practice Direction [2001] 4 All ER 640.

21 (1995) 16 Cr App R (S) 718.

22 [1995] Crim LR 835.

23 They also found that it was not at all clear in Sanders *et al.*'s research how many victims received 'end' interviews at the end of the case, in order to make such a comparison, because not all cases had finished by the time of the 'end' interviews.

24 There is a rather long, sorry history of victims not being given information about what has happened to offenders, whether at sentence, or in relation to undertaking rehabilitational programmes (Moore and Blakeborough 2008; Shapland *et al.* 2007). Certainly, most victims in the Hoyle *et al.* (1998) pilot of victim statements in England and Wales did not know what had happened to their statements.

25 In Scotland, victims were sent a statement pack and made statements themselves. In England and Wales, statements are taken by police officers. We would argue that the direct communicative method operating in Scotland may be more helpful (and less costly), though involving police officers does demonstrate that the criminal justice system is attending to victims (but also, when the service is not offered, that it is not).

26 *R v. Smith and Woollard* (1978) 67 Cr App R 211: 'The Court knows that when there is a burglary in a house great distress is caused. Not only is there the loss of property but there is induced a feeling of insecurity. This court knows that where the householders are women they sometimes worry a great deal about what has happened to them. It has been said that when a house is burgled it never seems the same again.'

27 *R. v. Dixon (Ross Linsey)* [2003] EWCA Crim 235, for example, includes the evidence provided by an impact statement that the victim had suffered a loss of confidence after being assaulted during a burglary.

28 *R v. Billam* (1986) 8 Cr App R (S) 489. See also *R. v. Bamforth (Jason)* [1999] 1 Cr App R (S) 123, a rape case, in which the victim had become frightened and depressed and had not completed her first year at university.

29 *AG's Reference No. 1 of 1989* (1989) 11 Cr App R (S) 409.

30 For example, in *Attorney General's Reference No. 43 of 1994* (16 Cr App R (s) 815) or in *Boswell* (1982) 4 Cr App R (S) 317 – re the very young; or in *Attorney General's References Nos 32 + 33 of 1995* (1996) Cr App R (S) 346; *or Attorney General's Reference No. 104 of 2002 sub nom R v. B* (2003) Cr App R (S) 116 – re violent offences against the elderly.

31 [1995] 16 Cr App R (S) 860.

32 *R v. Collins (David Guy)*, Court of Appeal (Criminal Division), 18 March 2003, [2003] EWCA Crim 1687, *The Times* 14 April 2003.

33 The victim cannot necessarily, of course, be expected to respond by accepting an apology or forgiving the offender. Indeed, one of us has argued elsewhere that, for serious offences, an apology is not sufficient to mark the harm caused by the offence. Symbolic reparation (an apology) may need to be accompanied

by concrete evidence of action to show remorse, apology and willingness to transform one's life (willingness to undertake rehabilitative measures) (Shapland *et al.* 2006).

34 [1996] Crim LR 210.

35 [2000] Crim LR 606.

36 At 607. The importance of forgiveness by the victim was a factor in reducing a sentence for unlawful wounding: *R. v. Barnes (Ashley)* [2001] EWCA Crim 1038 and in a case of grievous bodily harm on a wife: 'reduced to four years owing to her forgiveness as expressed in a statement which had not been before the sentencing judge': *R v. Higgins (Michael Anthony)* [2001] EWCA Crim 929.

37 [2003] 2 Cr App R (S) 86. The deceased's mother was used to visiting the cemetery with the appellant, who had driven the power boat which had killed her son, a friend of his.

38 [1999] 2 Cr App R (S) 105.

39 *R. v. Burke (Michael)* [2002] EWCA Crim 2213.

40 Walker (1999) would prefer to see mercy being kept firmly out of the sentencing process and used solely by the executive post-sentence. On purely retributive grounds, he makes a good case for this.

41 Under the Criminal Justice Act 1991 retribution was the dominant sentencing philosophy. It continues to be a major element under the Criminal Justice Act 2003.

42 The purposes of sentencing for adult offenders as set out in the Criminal Justice Act 2003, s. 142, are: the punishment of offenders; the reduction of crime (including its reduction by deterrence); the reform and rehabilitation of offenders; the protection of the public; and the making of reparation by offenders to persons affected by their offences.

43 An area touched upon by the European Court of Human Rights in its commentary on *Osman v. United Kingdom* (2000) 29 EHRR 245.

44 The Sentencing Advisory Panel has undertaken research which has deliberately sought the views of victims, for example, in its report on the sentencing of offences involving death by dangerous driving (where relatives of the victim were interviewed: Hough *et al.* 2008) and in its report on factors which might influence the sentencing of rape (where individual interviews were carried out with victims/survivors of rape: Clarke *et al.* 2002).

45 This complacency has not been shared by other parts of the UK, such as Northern Ireland.

46 The Public Service Agreement target 2 for the Ministry of Justice, which is also shared by the Home Office and the Attorney General's Office, is: 'to improve public confidence in the [criminal justice system], including increasing that of ethnic minorities and increasing year-on-year the satisfaction of victims and witnesses, while respecting the rights of defendants' (Ministry of Justice 2008).

47 Practice Direction [2001] 4 All ER 640.

48 Pre-sentence restorative justice conferencing or mediation was found to be helpful by a large number of victims who attended such sessions, particularly for serious offences (Shapland *et al.* 2007). The outcome agreement from the event and, in some instances, reports from the facilitator of the event were given to sentencers.

References

Allen, J., El Komy, M., Lovbakke, J. and Roy, H. (2005) *Policing and the Criminal Justice System – Public Confidence and Perceptions: Findings from the 2003/4 British Crime Survey*. Home Office Online Report 31/05. London: Home Office. http://www.homeoffice.gov.uk/rds/pdfs05/rdsolr3105.pdf

Andrews, B., Brewin, C. and Rose, S. (2003) 'Gender, social support and PTSD in victims of violent crime', *Journal of Traumatic Stress*, 16(4): 421–7.

Angle, H., Malam, S. and Carey, C. (2003) *Key Findings from the Witness Satisfaction Survey 2002*. Home Office Research Findings 189. London: Home Office. http://www.homeoffice.gov.uk/rds/pdfs2/r189.pdf

Bottoms, A.E. (2003) 'Some sociological reflections on restorative justice', in A. von Hirsch, J. Roberts, A.E. Bottoms, K. Roach and M. Schiff (eds), *Restorative Justice and Criminal Justice: Competing or Reconcilable Paradigms?* Oxford: Hart Publishing, pp. 79–113.

Bottoms, A.E., Shapland, J., Costello, A., Holmes, D. and Muir, G. (2004) 'Towards desistance: theoretical underpinnings for an empirical study', *Howard Journal*, 43(4): 368–89.

Burton, M., Evans, R. and Sanders, A. (2006) *Are Special Measures for Vulnerable and Intimidated Witnesses Working? Evidence from the criminal justice agencies*. Home Office Online Report 01/06. London: Home Office. http://www.homeoffice.gov.uk/rds/pdfs06/rdsolr0106.pdf

Carlen, P. (1976) *Magistrates' Justice*. London: Martin Robertson.

Chalmers, J., Duff, P. and Leverick, F. (2007) 'Victim impact statements: can work, do work (for those who bother to make them)', *Criminal Law Review*: 360–79.

Clarke, A., Moran-Ellis, J. and Sleney, J. (2002) *Attitudes to Date Rape and Relationship Rape: A qualitative study*. Sentencing Advisory Panel Research Report 2. London: Sentencing Advisory Panel. http://www.sentencing-guidelines.gov.uk/docs/research.pdf

Cozijn, C. (1984) *Schadefonds Geweldsmisdrijven*. The Hague: Ministry of Justice.

Criminal Justice Review Team (2000) *Review of Criminal Justice in Northern Ireland*. Belfast: The Stationery Office. http://www.nio.gov.uk/review_of_the_criminal_justice_system_in_northern_ireland.pdf

Criminal Justice System (2005a) *The Code of Practice for Victims of Crime*. London: Criminal Justice System. http://www.homeoffice.gov.uk/documents/victims-code-of-practice

Criminal Justice System (2005b) *Rebuilding Lives, Supporting Victims of Crime*, Cm 6705. London: The Stationery Office. http://www.official-documents.gov.uk/document/cm67/6705/6705.pdf

Criminal Justice System (2005c) *Hearing the Relatives of Murder and Manslaughter Victims*. Consultation paper, September 2005. London: Criminal Justice System. http://www.restorativejustice.org.uk/.../pdf/murder_mansl.Consultation.pdf

Crown Prosecution Service (2004) *The Code for Crown Prosecutors*. London: Crown Prosecution Service. http://www.cps.gov.uk/publications/docs/code2004english.pdf

Crown Prosecution Service (2006) *CPS Policy for Prosecuting Cases of Domestic Violence*. London: Crown Prosecution Service. http://www.cps.gov.uk/publications/docs/DomesticViolencePolicy.pdf

Denkers, A. and Winkel, F. (1998) 'Crime victims' well being and fear in a prospective and longitudinal study', *International Review of Victimology*, 5: 141–62.

Doak, J. (2005) 'Victims' rights in criminal trials: prospects for participation', *Journal of Law and Society* 32(2): 294–316.

Dodd, T., Nicholas, S., Povey, D. and Walker, A. (2004) *Crime in England and Wales 2003/2004*. Home Office Statistical Bulletin 10/04. London: Home Office. http://www.homeoffice.gov.uk/rds/pdfs04/hosb1004.pdf

Edwards, I. (2002) 'The place of victims' preferences in the sentencing of "their" offenders', *Criminal Law Review*: 689–702.

Ellison, L. (2001) *The Adversarial Process and the Vulnerable Witness*. Oxford: Oxford University Press.

Emsley, C., Shoemaker, R. and Hitchcock, T. (2005) *The Old Bailey Proceedings Online Project*. http://www.oldbaileyonline.org

Erez, E. (2000) 'Integrating a victim perspective in criminal justice through victim impact statements', in A. Crawford and J. Goodey (eds), *Integrating a Victim Perspective Within Criminal Justice: International debates*. Aldershot: Ashgate Dartmouth, pp. 165–84.

Erez, E. and Rogers, L. (1999) 'The effects of victim impact statements on criminal justice outcomes and processes: the perspectives of legal professionals', *British Journal of Criminology*, 39: 216–39.

Farrall, S. and Calverley, A. (2006) *Understanding Desistance from Crime: Emerging theoretical developments in resettlement and rehabilitation*. Milton Keynes: Open University Press.

Garland, D. (2001) *The Culture of Control: Crime and social order in contemporary society*. Oxford: Oxford University Press.

Gergen, K. and Gergen, M. (1988) 'Narrative and the self as relationship', *Advances in Experimental Social Psychology*, 21: 17–55.

Graham, J., Woodfield, K., Tibble, M. and Kitchen, S. (2004) *Testaments of Harm: a qualitative evaluation of the Victim Personal Statements scheme*. London: National Centre. http://www.natcen.ac.uk/natcen/pages/publications/AcrC2101.pdf

Hall, M. (2009) *Victims of Crime: Policy and practice in criminal justice*. Cullompton: Willan Publishing.

Hamlyn, B., Phelps, A., Turtle, J. and Sattar, G. (2004) *Are Special Measures Working? Evidence from surveys of vulnerable and intimidated witnesses*. Home Office Research Study 283. London: Home Office. http://www.homeoffice.gov.uk/rds/pdfs04/hors283.pdf

Home Office (1998) *Speaking Up for Justice: Report of the Interdepartmental Working Group on the treatment of vulnerable or intimidated witnesses in the criminal justice system*. London: Home Office. http://www.homeoffice.gov.uk/documents/sufj.pdf

Home Office (2001a) *Achieving Best Evidence in Criminal Proceedings: Guidance for vulnerable or intimidated witnesses, including children*. London: Home Office. http://www.homeoffice.gov.uk/documents/ach-best-evidence/

Home Office (2001b) *The Victim Personal Statement Scheme: guidance note for practitioners or those operating the scheme*. London: Home Office.

Home Office (2003) *Victims of Crime – the help and advice that's available*. London: Home Office. http://www.cjsonline.gov.uk/downloads/application/pdf/victimsofcrime.pdf

Hough, M. and Roberts, J. (1998) *Attitudes to Punishment: findings from the British Crime Survey*. Home Office Research Report 179. London: Home Office. www.homeoffice.gov.uk/rds/pdfs/hors179.pdf

Hough, M. and Roberts, J. (2004) *Confidence in Justice: an international review*. Home Office Research Findings 243. London: Home Office. www.homeoffice.gov.uk/rds/pdfs04/r243.pdf

Hough, M., Roberts, J., Jacobson, J., Bredee, A. and Moon, N. (2008) *Attitudes to the Sentencing of Offences Involving Death by Driving*. Sentencing Advisory Panel Research Report 5. London: Sentencing Advisory Panel. http://www.sentencing-guidelines.gov.uk/research/index.html

Hoyle, C., Cape, E., Morgan, R. and Sanders, A. (1998) *Evaluation of the 'One Stop Shop' and Victim Statement Pilot Projects*. London: Home Office. http://www.homeoffice.gov.uk/rds/pdfs/occ-one.pdf

Jackson, J., Kilpatrick, R. and Harvey, C. (1991) *Called to Court: A public review of criminal justice in Northern Ireland*. Belfast: SLS Legal Publications.

Judicature (1997) Special issue on *Courts and the Community*, March–April, 80: 5. American Judicature Society.

JUSTICE (1998) *Victims in Criminal Justice, Report of the Justice Society Committee on the Role of Victims in Criminal Justice*. London: Justice.

Kershaw, C., Budd, T., Kinshott, G., Mattinson, J., Mayhew, P. and Myhill, A. (2000) *The 2000 British Crime Survey*. Home Office Statistical Bulletin 18/00. London: Home Office. http://www.crimereduction.homeoffice.gov.uk/statistics/statistics12.htm

van Kesteren, J., Mayhew, P. and Nieuwbeerta, P. (2000) *Criminal Victimisation in Seventeen Industrialised Countries: key findings from the 2000 International Crime Victims Survey*. The Hague: Ministry of Justice Research and Documentation Centre. http://www.minjust.nl:8080/b_organ/wodc/publications/08-icvs-h2.pdf

Loader, I., Girling, E. and Sparks, R. (1998) 'Narratives of decline: youth, dis/order and community in an English "Middletown"', *British Journal of Criminology*, 38(3): 388–403.

Luchjenbroers, J. (1997) '"In your own words . . .": questions and answers in a Supreme Court trial', *Journal of Pragmatics* 27: 477–503.

McNeill, F. and Whyte, B. (2007) *Reducing Reoffending: Social work and community justice in Scotland*. Cullompton: Willan Publishing.

Maguire, M. (in collaboration with T. Bennett) (1982) *Burglary in a Dwelling: The offence, the offender, and the victim*. Cambridge Studies in Criminology, 49. London: Heinemann.

Ministry of Justice (2008) 'Performance in 2007/08', *Ministry of Justice Departmental Report 2007/08*, Chapter 2. London: Ministry of Justice. http://www.justice.gov.uk/publications/annual-report-2008.htm

Moore, L. and Blakeborough, L. (2008) *Early findings from WAVES: Information and service provision*. Ministry of Justice Research Series 11/08. London: Ministry of Justice. http://www.cjsonline.gov.uk/downloads/application/pdf/WAVES.pdf

Morgan, R. and Sanders, A. (1999) *The Use of Victim Statements*. London: Home Office.

Murphy, J. (1988) 'Mercy and legal justice', in J. Murphy and J. Hampton (eds), *Forgiveness and Mercy*. Cambridge: Cambridge University Press, pp. 162–87.

Norris, F. and Kaniasty, K. (1994) 'Psychological distress following criminal victimization in the general population: cross-sectional, longitudinal and prospective analyses', *Journal of Consulting and Clinical Psychology*, 62(1): 111–23.

Office for Criminal Justice Reform (2005) *Local Criminal Justice Board Victim and Witness Delivery Toolkit 4: Taking Victims' Views into Account (Victim Personal Statements)*. London: Office for Criminal Justice Reform. http://frontline.cjson line.gov.uk/search/index.php?searchterm=Toolkit+4

Roberts, J. and Stalans, L. (2004) 'Restorative sentencing: exploring the views of the public', *Social Justice Research*, 17(3): 315–34.

Robinson, G. and Shapland, J. (2008) 'Reducing recidivism: a task for restorative justice?', *British Journal of Criminology*, 48(3): 337–58.

Rock, P. (1993) *The Social World of an English Crown Court: Witnesses and professionals in the Crown Court Centre at Wood Green*. Oxford: Clarendon Press.

Rock, P. (2004) *Constructing Victims' Rights: The Home Office, New Labour and victims*. Oxford: Clarendon Press.

Sanders, A., Hoyle, C., Morgan, R. and Cape, E. (2001) 'Victim impact statements: don't work, can't work', *Criminal Law Review* (June): 447–58.

Sanders, A. and Jones, I. (2007) 'The victim in court', in S. Walklate (ed.), *Handbook of Victims and Victimology*. Cullompton: Willan Publishing, pp. 282–308.

Shapland, J. (1981) *Between Conviction and Sentence: The process of mitigation*. London: Routledge.

Shapland, J. (ed.) (2008) *Justice, Community and Civil Society: A contested terrain*. Cullompton: Willan Publishing.

Shapland, J., Atkinson, A., Colledge, E., Dignan, J., Howes, M., Johnstone, J., Pennant, R., Robinson, G. and Sorsby, A. (2004) *Implementing Restorative Justice Schemes (Crime Reduction Programme): A report on the first year*. Home Office Online Report 32/04. London: Home Office. www.homeoffice.gov.uk/rds/pdfs04/rdsolr3204.pdf

Shapland, J., Atkinson, A., Atkinson, H., Colledge, E., Dignan, J., Howes, M., Johnstone, J., Robinson, G. and Sorsby, A. (2006) 'Situating restorative justice within criminal justice', *Theoretical Criminology*, 10(4): 505–32.

Shapland, J., Atkinson, A., Atkinson, H., Chapman, B., Dignan, J., Howes, M., Johnstone, J., Robinson, G. and Sorsby, A. (2007) *Restorative Justice: The views of victims and offenders*. Ministry of Justice Research Series 3/07. London: Ministry of Justice. http://www.justice.gov.uk/docs/Restorative-Justice.pdf

Shapland, J. and Bell, E. (1998) 'Victims at the Magistrates' Court and Crown Court', *Criminal Law Review*: 537–46.

Shapland, J. and Hall, M. (2007) 'What do we know about the effects of crime on victims?', *International Review of Victimology*, 14(2), *Special Issue on Crime, Fear of Crime and Well-being: Towards measuring the intangible costs*: 175–218.

Shapland, J. and Vagg, J. (1988) *Policing by the Public*. London: Routledge & Kegan Paul.

Shapland, J., Willmore, J. and Duff, P. (1985) *Victims and the Criminal Justice System*. Aldershot: Gower.

Skogan, W. (1994) *Contacts between Police and Public: Findings from the 1992 British Crime Survey*. Home Office Research Study 134. London: HM Stationery Office. http://www.homeoffice.gov.uk/rds/hors1994.html

Sweeting, A., Owen, R., Turley, C., Rock, P., Garcia-Sanche, M., Wilson, L. and Khan, U. (2008) *Evaluation of the Victims' Advocate Scheme Pilots*. Ministry of

Justice Research Series 17/08. London: Ministry of Justice. http://www.justice.gov.uk/publications/docs/research-victims-advocates.pdf

Victim Support South Yorkshire (2004) *Annual Report 2004*. Wath-upon-Dearne, Rotherham: Victim Support.

Walker, N. (1999) *Aggravation, Mitigation and Mercy in English Criminal Justice*. London: Blackstone.

Chapter 8

'Hearing victims of crime': the delivery of impact statements as ritual behaviour in four London trials for murder and manslaughter

*Paul Rock**

Introduction

Victim impact statements have been introduced in a number of criminal justice systems, including those of Canada, New Zealand and Australia and, most particularly, of the United States, where they were launched first in the 1970s.[1] They are characteristically delivered after conviction but before sentence, and their possible use in shaping the sentencing decision tends to be ill-defined.[2] In some parts of the United States,[3] the statement is quite explicitly intended to have an effect (see Flatman and Bagaric 2001; O'Hear 2006), even – and contentiously[4] – in capital cases (see Myers and Greene 2004), where there is some evidence that it does indeed affect severity (see Luginbuhl and Burkhead 1995).

In England and Wales, what were originally called Victim Impact Statements and later Family Impact Statements[5] were introduced experimentally in trials for murder and manslaughter in five Crown Court centres in April 2006. They emerged in the wake of a somewhat terse election manifesto commitment of 2005[6] and a subsequent consultation paper, *Hearing the Relatives of Murder and Manslaughter Victims* (http://www.dca.gov.uk/consult/manslaughter/manslaughter.pdf), in September 2005, and they reflected the growing importance of activist or campaigning secondary victims, 'co-victims' or survivors, those who might be called victims *für sich*, members of self-conscious and organised groups, who had long worked for greater rights and had grown to prominence with the establishment of a Victims' Advisory Panel inside government by the Domestic Violence, Crime and Victims Act 2004, Chapter 28.

The Panel had seemed at first to have been of little importance, the subject of almost no discussion in Home Office preparatory papers and meetings.[7] But it did succeed in installing a hitherto excluded group into the very heart of policy-making, and it gave alienated and distressed relatives of victims the presence and recognition that they had long demanded. Public advertisements called for 'victim[s] of crime or [those who] have a good understanding of the needs of victims of crime ... to share their experiences and to generate ideas and practical proposals for improving services to victims and witnesses'. Those who came forward were people who defined themselves *as* victims of crime, and it was inevitable that they were self-selected, activist victims.

Campaigning and self-help organisations were heavily represented on the Panel (after all, where else could such victims be recruited?). They stemmed from groups such as SAMM (Support After Murder and Manslaughter), NEVA (The North of England Victims Association, 'a service provider to the families of homicide'), The Zito Trust (whose 'primary focus [is] on supporting and advising victims of mentally disordered offenders'), Victims' Voice (a federation of groups which 'raises issues that arise when people are bereaved by sudden and traumatic death'[8]) and other survivors' groups. Six of the initial 12 members were themselves homicide survivors, one a victim of a stalker, one a victim of an aggravated burglary, one a victim of sexual assault, and another a victim of rape. The Panel's website announced that 'For too long the needs of victims of crime have not been considered paramount and they have not always been treated appropriately. We are working to put that right. Critical to this is the need to listen to victims of crime and take account of their thoughts on how we can improve services at every stage of the system.'

Meetings of the Victims' Advisory Panel were chaired by a Minister, at first chiefly Baroness Scotland, then of the Home Office, the Department of State then responsible for policies for victims and for criminal legislation; and they were attended from time to time by other Ministers such as Fiona McTaggart, also of the Home Office;[9] Harriet Harman, then Solicitor General, responsible for legal advice to Government and for prosecutions; and the then Lord Chancellor, Lord Falconer, responsible at a remove for the judiciary and courts. Politicians were to be confronted at first hand with the anger and distress of the victims of major crime (although the victims claimed it took time before they were heard. One said: 'We didn't have in the beginning, a great deal of influence. I felt we were used. But we fought hard and they did say it was a powerful group. So ... we were given the opportunity to push and then we eventually said, "Well, we want to set the agenda because the government was setting it."'). A member of SAMM was eventually able to report that she had managed, 'with the other lay members, to raise the awareness of Ministers and Officials of the need for better services for victims and the gross inequalities in the law and legal rights, favouring the offender'.[10]

At the very outset of the Panel's deliberations, the then Lord Chancellor reflected that 'They are a vocal – and for us – challenging group that ask pointed questions on our commitment to deliver and meet the needs of people like them. We see the panel as a key part of our drive to ensure a victim-centred approach to Criminal Justice.'[11] The matters that the Panel discussed became, by extension, largely of consequence to activist victims, touching on the obtaining of trial transcripts (although no more than 3 per cent of crimes in England and Wales go to trial, and even fewer to courts of record where such transcripts are prepared, a mere 4 per cent of total proceedings in 2005); a review of the Coroners' Service (responsible for inquests); and on one occasion, and significantly, support in the management of post-traumatic stress disorder, the condition associated particularly with serious crime and sudden bereavement.

There was also to be a growing number of ancillary meetings between Ministers and individual or small groups of bereaved victims who were starting to become the acknowledged representatives of victims at large. A Government minister told me that 'I would say that over, since 2002, I have met the . . . whole range of victims and I've also met lawyers and judges over a long period of time and discussed these issues. I've met victims at court, victims through SAMM . . .' And very much the same issues kept coming to the fore: 'they have very little good to say about the trial . . .', said the then Parliamentary Private Secretary first to Lord Irvine, the Lord Chancellor, and subsequently to his successor, Lord Falconer (Clark 2004: 24). Ministers listened: Harriet Harman was reported to have said that:

'During my four years as solicitor general . . . I was very struck by the sense among the bereaved relatives that they were completely excluded from the system. It seemed to me an incredible paradox that the people for whom that case matters most in the world are silent in court.' (in 'Making the right connections', *New Statesman*, 1 August 2005)

There are disputed claims about the paternity of the proposal to award victims and survivors legal representation and a voice in the courtroom. Victims' Voice asserted that it was responsible for the idea ('We got the impact statement from America in the first place,' said a member, remembering the role played by the Manwaring Victims Trust[12] and how Diana Lamplugh of the Lamplugh Trust had visited the United States and returned with the idea of impact statements). But officials and politicians insisted that the proposal had not been initially broached at the Victims' Advisory Panel, and that there had been divisions on the Panel when it *was* presented.

Whatever its origins may have been, what was mooted and then adopted was undoubtedly a direct or indirect consequence of the new intimacy that had arisen between politicians and activist victims. The imagery, composition and politics of significant victims had changed radically in the political mind (see Rock 2006), and they had changed in some measure because the victims newly facing Ministers were the survivors of heinous crimes whose arguments were personal, hot, urgent and unfettered. One Government minister told me:

> I've met victims a whole variety of ways. The Victims' Advisory Panel. I've seen Support Against Murder and Manslaughter, both in their northern capacity and in their southern capacity ...[13] I saw a group of knife-crime victims of which there were six people, two of whom had basically children who had been murdered. They are ... expressing a completely different view ...

That different view was designed to accommodate the appalling events that have befallen the families of those who have been killed. Those bereaved by homicide are often distressed, isolated, emotional and angry. They may try to restore order to their moral universe by turning to a strong, elemental set of binary oppositions which pitches the murderer against the victim; evil against innocence; a life still lived against a life lost for ever. How the killer is treated can become, by extension, a measure of the value placed on the victim, and there may be point-by-point comparisons made to establish how well and fairly institutions, including institutions of the criminal justice system, behave: a Ministry of Justice should be matched by a Ministry for Victims; the loss of a victim's life by life imprisonment; the defendant's right to testify by the victim's family's right to testify; mitigation speeches by victim impact statements; and legal advice and aid to defendants by advice and aid to victims or survivors (see Rock 1998). Legal representation at trial had strong appeal. 'Many victims' families', wrote Sandra Sullivan of Victims' Voice, 'are shocked by the lack of balance in the system: the defendant has a social worker, legal aid, rehab schemes, resettlement officers etc. Families have only the Family Liaison Officer,[14] and often the amount of contact depends on how busy the officer is at that time' (no date: 1). Just as defendants were afforded legal advice, legal representation and a right to speak, so should the victim's family.

The Department for Constitutional Affairs' consultation paper on oral impact statements (and two other new measures) elicited a battery of responses, many respondents being nervous of the prospect that the emotional tone of trials for murder and manslaughter would rise to inappropriate levels; that judges would be subjected to improper pressure; and that families would have expectations unduly raised about their ability to influence sentence. And the Government's formal response was to argue 'that the best way to deal with worries about the proposals is to try them out in practice. The Government therefore intends to pilot victims' advocates in five Crown Court centres from April 2006' (*Hearing the Relatives of Murder and Manslaughter Victims*, 2005: no page number; and see the statement made by Lord Falconer to the House of Lords on 27 February 2006).

This essay is based upon my own unpublished contribution to the evaluation of those pilots, a contribution that consisted of case studies based on intensive fieldwork in the Central Criminal Court at the Old Bailey in London, a contribution which complemented and fed into other work conducted by BMRB, the British Market Research Bureau, a market research organisation which surveyed families and practitioners across all five courts,[15] and by Matrix, a consultancy firm, which examined the financial costs and benefits of the new proposals. To the best of my knowledge, what follows reports the first analytic incision made into what might be called the black box of procedures centred on victim impact statements. It cannot pretend to provide much of a foundation for generalisation, although there is no reason to suppose that the cases were at all unusual, but its lack of breadth may be offset by the thickness of its description of the hitherto unexplored workings of social processes that are normally treated by evaluation studies as little more than a mass of inputs and outputs.

The cases studied

Four cases that opened at the Central Criminal Court in 2007 were studied, three in their entirety. Two were conducted throughout at the Old Bailey, and two were transferred to other Crown Court centres in London. Proceedings were observed in their entirety and, apart from the defendants, all the principals were interviewed, sometimes more than once. In the description that follows, the most pertinent features of the cases are reported intact, but minor details have been altered to preserve confidentiality and anonymity.

None of the victims was from a minority ethnic group. All were male, one in his twenties, two in their thirties, and one in his forties. One of the four could be described as middle class, although, in many particulars, the class background of the family had little perceptible bearing on how they reacted to the facts of the death, or to the prosecution, verdict and penalty.

The first case, in which a man killed his business partner, marked the quarrelsome climax of a lengthy bout of drinking and drug-taking and it led to a charge of murder, a conviction for manslaughter, and a sentence of a minimum term of eight years' imprisonment. The second was that of a young man who had been drinking in several establishments and was eventually killed by a doorman at a public house after having been ejected in ambiguous circumstances, and, in that case, the defendant was acquitted, much to the distress of the victim's family. The third case arose in an altercation between members of two loosely connected families while they were drinking in a public place, and that resulted in a conviction for 'single punch manslaughter' and an 18-month sentence, again to the family's acute distress. The last was that of a man who was killed by a rough-sleeping alcoholic while himself sleeping in an open space after a bout of drinking, and the defendant was convicted of murder and sentenced to a minimum term of 13 years' imprisonment.

Three of the victims themselves had been convicted of violent offences in the past,[16] one being on bail and awaiting trial for an offence of violence at the time of his death; giving rise to problems of presenting a creditable moral and social identity in the Family Impact Statement and, in one instance, to appreciable incredulity evinced by the defence about the laudatory manner in which the victim and his family were portrayed in the statement (counsel protested to me at the end of proceedings that the victim and his partner had 'been separated and in her evidence, she said that the cause of the separation was his increasingly erratic behaviour and potentially violent behaviour due to his predilection for cocaine'. She declared her intention to appeal against sentence, an intention which was apparently acted upon). However, and following the pattern in evidence elsewhere in the pilot sites, none of the impact statements was subject to cross-examination because the defence held that no good purpose would be served by their being tested (one barrister remarked that 'it is traditionally regarded as counterproductive for the defence counsel to rubbish the deceased for obvious reasons ... if you start kicking the deceased for six, you are likely to lose the favour of the court'; and another said, 'I didn't think that cross-examining would assist my cause at all in mitigation and might simply inflame the family. I could see nothing to gain from it.').

Rather than give detailed *vignettes* of each case, a few cross-cutting conclusions will be drawn. Those conclusions cannot be described as readily generalisable, but they do present a new and detailed account of the social dynamics entailed in making victim impact statements. In pursuing my central argument, analysis will be simplified in the interests of economy and clarity.

Distress as an underlying condition

The families and partners of the victims of murder and manslaughter undergo a series of deeply disturbing experiences as they move towards the pre-trial and trial procedures touched on by the new Victims' Advocate Scheme. They will have learned the appalling and unexpected news that a killing or critical injury has taken place (a Family Liaison Officer said of one family: 'as most families are . . . they are deeply, deeply upset. At the end of the day, their son went out for a drink, he had a few drinks, he was undoubtedly . . . drunk to an extent, but he's been punched and he's died and they are completely and utterly horrified by it.'). Questions of complicity, blame, family involvement and victim-precipita- tion necessarily arose to trouble the families (see Lamb 1996; Wolfgang 1957). Families may well reproach themselves for having failed to protect the victim, prevent the crime or reduce the risk of its occurring. Police and press inquiries can make unwelcome disclosures about the family's and victim's lifestyle and history; disclosures which are difficult to reconcile with the idealised memory of the dead that mourners seek to construct and retain. The bereaved may well have been objects of police suspicion themselves, and that can be a source of anguish at a time when they may believe they deserve immediate and unqualified support and sympathy. Witnesses and potential witnesses may be intimidated. Post-mortem examinations may be repeated and inquests delayed, resulting in the family's having to wait before a funeral can take place. Coroners may limit or delay the family's access to the body of their relative for forensic or other reasons, and the result can be frustration and a sense that there has been no satisfactory leave-taking. The partner of one victim recalled, for instance, how 'I could not view the body, like, to view the body weeks and weeks after . . .! I had to view it afterwards. It was horrible, weeks afterwards . . . and I mean the head was already starting to . . . deteriorate and everything.'

Families may ingenuously or disingenuously be taken aback by the ferocity of questioning in the adversarial system, and by fresh disclosures or allegations made at trial about the death, the victim and his family ('The trial will be distressing for you because the defence will put [the victim] in a different light', one family was warned at a pre-trial conference).

In short, the family may approach and then attend the courts in an acute and perhaps increasingly angry, confused and bitter frame of mind, unable always to make calm judgements about what is happening to and about them. Theirs can be a state of general resentment which seeks targets and fuels grievances, a state that can be so aggravated by a succession of problems – including revelations that the jury may not agree on a verdict or may acquit; actual acquittals; attempts to control their conduct and demeanour in and around the courtroom; the release of defendants on bail and consequent chance meetings with them or their supporters in the public spaces in and about the courthouse; what they regarded as inappropriately short sentences; reductions in charge or conviction from murder to manslaughter; the defendant engaging in what was seen to be inappropriate behaviour; real or imagined slights from defence counsel; and revelations about the circumstances of the death – that it is not remarkable that the bundle of new pilot measures (usually reduced in practice to the delivery of a Family Impact Statement alone) could not always have a decisive influence on their satisfaction with the courts and criminal justice system.

This must be borne in mind because it shaped and permeated almost all their responses, and any checks, slights and obstacles would rankle in proportion. What must also be borne in mind is that they had no manner of gauging how very much more indifferent and alienating had been the treatment meted out to their predecessors in the past; how great the improvements in service have actually been; and how much effort has been expended in introducing them (a barrister commented of the experience of one family: 'They probably don't appreciate it because they haven't been in this situation before – that they were given really gold-plated treatment.').

The preparation of Family Impact Statements

The police Family Liaison Officers who assisted the four families in the preparation of Family Impact Statements asserted that they had had little or no formal training or preparation for the task, that theirs was an unavoidably improvised and *ad hoc* method of proceeding ('it was so rushed out that everyone hit the street running'), and that they tended *faut de mieux* to model the drafting process on the older and more familiar techniques involved in preparing witness statements and Victim Personal Statements, an earlier (and still extant) form of impact statement that had not been delivered orally. After what could be the first faltering attempts, however, they had learned to become quite emphatic about what the statement should and should not include. References to sentencing should be omitted but:

> Basically, this is your opportunity to say how this has affected you, how the murder or manslaughter has affected your family. And it's the only occasion really because if we take any other statement from them, it's generally just a historical thing or to detail the person that's died. So we wouldn't go into their own feelings almost other than perhaps a very short sentence at the end saying this has you know, totally destroyed my life. Some sort of catch-all statement which really isn't sufficient. So until this came in, they didn't have the opportunity to say how they felt.

Drafting was a negotiated process, akin to the writing of a witness statement. Family Liaison Officers would ascertain verbally from the family what it was that they wished to say, or urge the family to sketch a rough copy or keep notes, perhaps in the form of a diary, that could serve as a skeleton statement. They would then compose their own summary version, written as if by the family member; read it back to the family; and accept (where permissible and according to their understanding of the process) amendments of style, words or substance. I observed one such procedure at length – the drafting of a late, supplementary statement – and noted how it was punctuated by very precise questioning about wording, because words in an impact statement at a trial for homicide carry an unusually heavy load. Family Impact Statements convey deeply felt, personal sentiments, offered at a critical point in the family's fortunes, and Family Liaison Officers believed they had little right to tamper with what the bereaved wished to say. One Family Liaison Officer remarked: 'I think we should allow the family to say what they want to say, as long as it's evidentially correct . . . I've found it better for them to write it in their own words and it actually expresses what they feel.'[17]

The procedure I witnessed was conducted painstakingly. At one point, for instance, the partner of the victim was asked, 'Would you call him a binge drinker or an alcoholic? I don't want to put words in your mouth', and she replied, 'A serious drink problem, I'd say. He'd only go to London for the drink and to see his so-called friends.' She was again invited to consider whether the victim had been 'sleeping rough' – an activity which conjures up images of dereliction and social exclusion – and she insisted that 'X certainly was *not* homeless': 'When he was with me, he had a home and a family . . . He certainly did not sleep rough but when he went binge drinking he'd sleep anywhere. It could be a bench, a train or a park.' She said to me afterwards:

> When [the prosecutor] opened that first [opening] statement, I thought 'Yeah, he was homeless. I met him homeless but well he was in rehab at the time.' But you know, I was a bit shocked, 'cause that's wrong. But then the defence, the other guys did say . . . he was in his sleeping bag and I thought, 'I wonder if they're depicting the right picture of X there? He wasn't actually homeless you know, he did have a bed to sleep in.' . . . I said that they should read that [portion of the amended statement] out . . . Right from the beginning I wanted to tell them he did have a home and he had someone that cared for him. He had family.

The final, written version of the supplementary statement, delivered by counsel in court, then contained the agreed sections, taken virtually *verbatim* from the conversations held at the preparatory stage:

> X did sleep rough but this was only when he went binge drinking in [Z City] every two to three months. He would get so drunk that he would just sleep anywhere, it could be a bench, a train or a park . . .

When not binge drinking X was with me for long periods at a time where he did not drink, would work and would lead what you would call a 'normal life'.

Those passages, and others like them, were at the heart of what family members wished to convey, they constituted the prime message and purpose of the statements, and I shall enlarge on their significance below.

Despite the gingerly manner in which editing took place, there *were* excisions, omissions or rewordings imposed by the Family Liaison Officer, and, very occasionally, by prosecution counsel, and it was prosecution counsel who would then later police their delivery in open court. There could, for instance, be no critical reference to the judge, jury, trial or defendant (in later, amended versions of the statement), none to sentence, and none to forbidden words such as 'murder' or 'murderer' where charges or convictions had been reduced to manslaughter. Although family members mostly deferred, and without much resistance, to the authority of the police and lawyers, such efforts at editorial control could induce considerable vexation and dissatisfaction with the scheme itself.

The purposes of Family Impact Statements

Documents and papers accompanying the new scheme make it clear what the Family Impact Statement was supposed *not* to achieve. Advice tendered by the CPS, for instance, stated that it should be 'focused on the impact of the events on the family and, if appropriate, its members'; but it should 'not contain any evidential material which should properly be put before the court in another form', and should 'not refer to any matters or issues that would render the statement inadmissible, or can be construed as falling outside the purpose of the FIS scheme, for example, statements on matters of public policy, or statements of a political nature.'[18] A leaflet given to the families themselves recited that 'These statements give the families of murder and manslaughter victims a voice in the criminal justice system. Making a statement enables you to tell the court about how the murder or manslaughter has affected your family.' It was not made entirely evident in those documents what concrete object was actually to be achieved by telling the court about those effects, although it may be presumed that one important purpose was catharsis, and a member of Victims' Voice did indeed tell me that 'That's the only way we have to get rid of anything we feel. I mean that's very, very elementary.' The statement was to be about 'who we've lost, who the world's lost'. It would restore balance and give the dead a presence:

... the victim would be a person and the value of his life. And that is the most important thing because he's not there and can't answer

209

anything, we're the representative. I'm his representative in that courtroom and I've been voiceless and I've been nobody.

Those and allied themes seemed to infuse the Family Impact Statements prepared in the case studies, but at the time I met them, the families had not yet formulated their intentions clearly, and it was difficult at that stage to establish through questioning precisely what they thought their intentions to be. Most replies and comments suggested that the Family Impact Statement was written and delivered because that was what the families had been told was expected of them – chiefly by the Family Liaison Officer – and they dutifully did what they were told to do as responsible and compliant participants in courtroom procedure. But families also cited a number of other aspirations which fluctuated over time, the most obvious being a public description of the impact of the crime on the family because that is again what they had been told to provide by officials whom they trusted.

Although they could be sympathetic to the scheme and not averse to its continuation (all the Family Liaison Officers being especially convinced of its value), practitioners sometimes also professed to be bemused about what it might accomplish and they were split in deciding whether its new, oral form was necessarily the best way of proceeding ('I think everyone's a little puzzled as to what the purpose is and my own view of it is really a gimmick and that . . . it's not quite clear what the purpose is. Because it certainly doesn't have an impact on sentence,' said one counsel). What they *did* recognise was its potential for catharsis, and catharsis was not necessarily treated as an unwelcome or unreasonable objective. Indeed, more than one lawyer and judge could imagine or was able to recall an experience of having been a victim, and their ability to do so led to the fostering of fellow-feeling with the families. One judge remarked of a statement, for instance: 'I hope that it made her feel better 'cause I think it's a cathartic experience. And I think it may be helpful for you as an academic to know that I personally have been the victim of a knife-point burglary. I wasn't in fact injured but I do know what fear is.' She had been affected by what she had heard, but she was also confident that her sentencing decision had not been compromised. She had in any event already been fully briefed by the bundle of trial papers. And, in all this, she was at one with her other fellow judges interviewed in the case studies and with judges in other jurisdictions who had had long experience of listening to Victim Impact Statements. She continued:

It's a difference in style because you've got the words of the victim which are very potent and actually can be quite emotional. And they do have an effect on, in my case, judicial emotion but emotion isn't something which you deal with in sentence. You look at seriousness and culpability, background of the defendant and how bad was his behaviour and the context of a whole raft of comparable cases that I had very helpfully from the Judicial Studies Board, a document with a hundred sentences on manslaughter of this type with a vast area of different fact situations.

Family Impact Statements and the adversarial system

The judge's observation is important because it introduces explicitly and implicitly several pivotal features of the Family Impact Statement. Her recollection was that she had listened to the statement but had followed the sentencing guidelines. Yet the protagonists in the trial over which she had presided emphatically did not all agree with her or among themselves on its impact, utility and fairness. The statement had been delivered at a crucial stage in a highly contested, adversarial system in which perspectives, if only for professional purposes, are locked into structured opposition, and that divergence of views ran across all the four trials. The statement served as a Rorschach blot, the prosecution and the judge believing that the sentence was 'about right' (the judge said, 'I passed what I thought was correct, reflecting the facts of the case and paying some attention, but unquantifiable in terms of years, as to the effect on those closest to the deceased'); the defence that it was far too severe ('the sentence was inordinately high ... [the Family Impact Statement] had compromised the sentencing procedure and the judge, unfortunately, did not take into account sufficiently or at all, that the deceased was a very bad man'); and the victim's partner that it was excessively lenient ('So he's basically going to serve four years and one month [after parole] and that's it. And that's what [his] life's worth. Now I told my son that he's got eight years. He was mortified that he got eight years. When am I going to tell him that he's only serving four years for his dad's life? Disgusting!').

Partly because of its apparently strategic location between the stages of conviction and sentence, two of the four families remained persuaded or still hoped privately that the Family Impact Statement would influence sentencing, although in both cases they had been told that it would not and could not do so in any transparent way. The inherent ambiguity of the procedure thus remained. What they *were* told was that anything they said about the impact of the crime might be taken unto account by the judge but that they could not talk about penalties. None the less, in both cases, they were incandescent at the length of sentence imposed, the way in which it apparently weighed the victim's life and what they consequently regarded as the utter futility of the statement they had delivered.

The Family Impact Statements did not conform to a strict model, there was no such model on offer, but they did tend to possess traits in common. All listed the many areas of life and the many people affected by the death, and in so doing, they adhered precisely to the stated aims of the scheme. In the words of one family member, the defendant, as the prime target, should be made to know that:

> He's taken the immediate family, grandchildren that he'll never see, their children, I mean he probably wouldn't have been alive by then but what about the community that he's grown up in and the people that have loved him over the years ... they [must] understand the damage, that he hasn't just caused by one killing, but the damage and the effects that we've got to carry for the rest of our lives, he needs to know the exact importancy of what he has done.

The sentiments in the statements had been rehearsed and discussed before – in at least two of the cases in interviews with the mass media (see Chermak 1995: 1) – and there had been prolonged honing over time. In the versions eventually agreed between the family and with the Family Liaison Officers, there was a description of the appalling shock and grief that the death had caused; the irreparable damage and loss that had been incurred; how difficult it was to explain to others – and especially young children – what had happened; the illness and strains it had engendered; and the multitude of dependants, often separately named, who had been left behind. The scale of the loss, it was said, could be measured by the many relationships, present and future, that had been blighted (see Bakan 1966; Bauer and McAdams 2000: 277); and the promise that had been lost through the death of one who was often still relatively young (the obituaries editor of *The Times* newspaper reflected in interview that in such cases 'you're having to write more ... about promise and potential than would be the case in a lot of the pieces we have where clearly potential's been more than fulfilled or not fulfilled'). There were accounts of the victim's humanity, loving nature, wit and kindness; the irreplaceable position which he had occupied in their lives; and the irreparable way in which the continuity and coherence of the victim's and family's life had been fractured (see Crossley 2000; McAdams 1996: 297).

In short, the Family Impact Statement was an effort to construct a favourable public representation of the victim and his family. Its medium could be a form of disjointed story-telling consisting of pointed anecdotes (Fleckenstein 1996: 914; Peacock and Holland 1993; Thompson 1995: 210). Its audience was variously intended to be the defendant, the judge (who sometimes – but not always – acknowledged what was said at the point of sentencing), the jury and the wider world, who were invited to understand the family's extraordinary loss, desolation and isolation.

Key among those who were intended to hear what was said was the defendant, and members of the families were anxious that he be made to understand what he had done. They would stare closely at him, sometimes for long periods at a time, trying to fathom whether he was registering any sign of remorse ('I would ... so love to actually speak to him myself ... I would like to say to him, if he or even one of his family ... had sent one card of an apology, I would have felt that much better,' said the mother of one victim). It was evident that they sought not only catharsis but signs of repentance.

Excerpts from Family Impact Statements illustrate how they played on those themes of loss, grief and devastation across the ranks of the family:

As a Mother and Grandmother I have seen many things go before me, but never in a million years would I have ever thought I would loose a beloved son so dear to me and my family. The very nature in which my son was taken has destroyed my faith in human nature. If it were not for the fact I am the sole head of our family and my responsibility to all my children and grandchildren I feel my life would serve no purpose to carry on. However it is my duty to hold my family together united we stand to try our very best to go forward with a reason to live as best we can ... X has six children four girls and two boys, three of them adults with families of their own and the three youngest just little ones and what the future holds for them remains to be seen ... Grandfather to Y I wish he had been given the chance to hold his new grandchild and enjoy his little granddaughter Z. (Case 1)

X made me very happy, he was an extraordinary man. The day I was told that [he] had been killed I was in total shock. I felt totally alone, I actually got the news from his niece, [Y]. I was in total denial at first until the police came to visit me and more or less confirmed that it was X that had died. It was then that it began to sink in that this could be true. From that time on I was in a dream state, just totally numb. I found myself talking to X but also knowing that I would never see him again. I felt he was too young to die, we had so much left to do ... I think it has affected my daughter, Z, she often says that she misses him and she knows that it hurts me to be left alone again. I miss having someone to talk to and be there to help share the load. I miss the security of him being around, I felt secure with him around. X [has] left a massive hole, the home is quiet and there just seems to be a big void. I just can't get around the fact I will never see him again. (Case 2)

In 1996 I gave birth to X's son Z. X became a great dad to both Z and Y and would always be there for them both ... X told me he wasn't happy with his life at the time and we talked seriously about him changing his ways ... and moving to Spain with the kids for a fresh start. Those plans that we had have now been shattered completely and I have been left devastated that someone I loved has been taken away from me. I am now left with only dreams of what may have been for the kids and me. (Case 3)

Imagine that you were awoken early in the morning by a telephone call to tell you that the person had been brutally injured by a 'bouncer' ... Imagine being collected in a police car and driven at high speed through the early morning streets to a hospital where your beloved is lying on a life-support machine. Imagine being told by a doctor with an ashen face that your beloved has been so badly injured that they have a 'very small chance of survival'. Imagine sitting by your beloved and holding their hand, kissing them and saying anything you can think of to let them know that you love them dearly and pleading that by some miracle they won't die. Imagine sitting there for nearly two days – what would go through your mind? Imagine after all that time being told that the position is 'hopeless' and asked permission for the life-support machine to be turned off ... Not one life but many were destroyed by this man, Y. Those who remain behind, X's parents, Z and A, his brother B, his grandparents, his aunts and uncles, his cousins, his friends and colleagues and everyone who loved him have all been irreparably damaged and our lives will never be the same again. Ours will truly be a life sentence. I don't know if this has helped you understand our feelings and how this terrible crime has changed our lives forever. We loved X from his first breath, and we will love, mourn and miss him until we are also dead. (Case 4)

The delivery of Family Impact Statements as ritual behaviour

There was another strand, perhaps even more important, threading itself through the preparation and presentation of Family Impact Statements. I have remarked that after the death, in the period running up to the trial, and at trial itself, the victim and his family would often be seen to have been traduced. They could be traduced in the press and at trial. They were certainly vulnerable to humiliation (and a sensitivity to slight and disrespect is ever with the ranks of the poor and the marginal from whom many victims are recruited (see Sennett 2003; Young 2007: 54)). The victims had all been drinking alcohol, sometimes in great quantities, at the time of the killing. In all the cases, there was the possibility introduced at trial that they had been provocative, such an allegation being a stock part of defence instructions in trials for crimes of violence. There is, further, always a larger strain towards blaming the victim for what happened, because in a just, well-ordered world terrible things should not happen to the innocent (Lerner 1980). And, predictably enough, three of the victims had had criminal records, two of them extensive, and all including offences of violence. The outcome could be the very public shaming, amounting at an extreme to vilification, both of the victim and, directly or indirectly, his relatives. The partner of one victim protested:

X come out being the big monster, a gun-wielding drugs baron from oh, it was. And he started off, X was five foot nine and a half. I don't know, by the end of it, he was five foot eleven. They read out a part of the *Godfather* which I thought, and our one didn't even moan about that, read out a part of the *Godfather* about respect and everything. He tripled in size, they said you know, when he got angry, he tripled in size. I mean what's all that?

Families wondered in all four cases why they and others had not been allowed to undo that damage by testifying as character witnesses for the victim, rebutting, in the one case, the assertion that their son ever used words like 'wanker' and 'jobsworth' ('he wouldn't have known what they meant'); in another that their son had been a drunk who had engaged in wanton, public sexual behaviour; in a third that the victim was a homeless alcoholic, and in the fourth that he was a villain. The partner of the victim in the last case, the woman whom I quoted as deploring his portrayal as a monster, said, 'None of us could put our side. I mean we had X's best mate Y up there. He couldn't say anything. You know, it's like we have not put our side. Where is this big monster you know? I just never heard of, I've never, the things that they said about X. [It] really was absolutely appalling!' They wondered why vital context and history had been omitted in the prosecution's stark presentation of the 'facts of the case', leaving behind only a meagre and distorting image of the victim, stripped of the relationships and biography which gave him social and moral identity, an image at odds with their own attempt to construct a tolerable 'inner representation' of the dead (see Silverman and Klass 1996), and they would have liked to have been able to brief counsel about those omissions and distortions ('They didn't want to speak to me or have anything to do with me and if they'd let me work with them, they'd have found out about the person they were prosecuting for,' said a mother). A member of one family protested that his son had been 'a piece of evidence essentially and they didn't really need us to be there'; another that the victim was 'not just a name or a piece of paper but a real person whose death affected everybody'; a third that 'he's not so black and white and cold and just on paper'; and a fourth that 'He was real. He was somebody's son. Somebody's father. Somebody's grandfather.'

In sum, they believed that vital information had been lost: the victim had been maligned, reified and belittled; they as his family had also been maligned; their identity as a family had been suborned (Howarth 2007: 169); the relations between the victim and his family had been thrown into question, and, at a critical turning-point in a formal, perhaps definitive and very public casting of the character of the dead, in a transitional period, they wished to do remedial work and assert openly the continuing strength of the family and the grievous loss of the victim. One mother said in two successive draft statements:

My life and feelings will never change my darling son is gone and my heart is in two. Just as everyone else is so upset Iv tried to stay strong for all my Familie ... I do believe X had great faith in me that I would not let him down even upon his death, that I his mother would do my very best to ensure continuity while I still have breath in my lungs.

The families and memorialisation

One of the prime roles all families can assume is the preservation and transmission of collective memory. Theirs is an obligation to construct and police proper ways of remembering and memorialising the dead and, in the case of traumatic death, where confusion abounds, to do so in a robust fashion (Finch and Mason 2000: 17, 165; Marris 1974: 10; Rock 1998). The Family Impact Statement may then be treated as an important device to put right the harmful imagery which had been laid before the public. It was, above all, a tool formally to redeem the family, and to restore respect and *normalise* the dead, to make him again appear through biographical construction (Howarth 2007: 212) as a rounded, admirable figure, free of, or despite, the taint that had been levelled against him (a mother said that she wanted the court to know 'basically that he was a good boy, he was a good son and he was a good boy ... It is important that his name should be cleared'), and do so before an audience of professionals who, in the very nature of a trial for homicide, could never have known the deceased. So it was that the statements further said:

> *X was a larger than life character* who since his death has now left in our lives a massive gap, which in my opinion will never be filled by anyone else ... When Y [my daughter] was one and a half years old X came into my life. He wasn't the biological father of Y but in the sixteen years that he has known Y she saw X as her real dad as she had little or no contact over those years with her real father. She called him dad and X called her his daughter. X was always loving, kind, generous and considerate and she loved him dearly. (Case 1) [Emphasis added]

> *X was certainly not homeless.* In the time he was with me he had a home and a family ... When not binge drinking X was with me for long periods at a time where he did not drink, would work and would lead what you would call a *'normal life'*. (Case 2) [Emphasis added]

> *Nobody is perfect we all have fault to some degree* but my son would never wish to take or spoil a life in the form in which he met his own death ... [He] took a keen interest in all his children, supporting their goals and achievements. [He] enjoyed school plays, concerts and celebra-

tions with great pride, a very proud father. He may not have been a millionaire but what he did leave for all his children is LOVE. (Case 3) [Emphasis added]

Such a mobilisation of a public response to death marks a status passage, one of the significant transitions or crises in the life cycle which require 'institutions and organizations to manage, direct, and control them' (Glaser and Strauss 1971: 15), and manage and direct them, frequently, through ritual practice (see Hughes 1958: 13; Van Gennep 1960), the dedicated formal procedure that is set apart from the mundane world to accomplish important symbolic work (Bocock 1974: 39). Families would regularly appear in court in force, bearing visible witness in their numbers and unity to the strength of their grief and the nature of their loss, not unlike a Greek chorus (see Finch 2007): 'A lot of people it'll stick in their mind 'cause they will realise how this family . . . what this family really means when there's a family. We are a close-knit family. We do love one another,' said one mother. And, said a partner of another victim, 'it is to show them or him [the defendant] as well, that there was someone out there for him you know, who did care for him [the victim]'.

The presentation of a Family Impact Statement itself was a dramatic event in a criminal justice system marked by its dramas (Christie 1986; Garland 2006: 420), delivered nervously and expectantly in full court, before a bewigged judge and counsel, the defendant and his supporters, the victim's family's supporters, and, from time to time, the jury. It was delivered from the witness box, sometimes on oath, by a family member, selected on the basis of his or her rank importance, or by an advocate in counsels' row, both of whom might stand as if to mark the gravity of the occasion. It was delivered by the appointed guardian of the family's memory in the pregnant space between two of the most solemn and emotionally fraught episodes in a trial for murder or manslaughter, conviction and sentence. It revealed the naked emotions of the mourner and laid them before his or her audience. It was a peroration that had much of the appearance of a ritual of lamentation (Zehr 1990: 208) or a funeral oration.

In essence, then, the reading of a Family Impact Statement conformed in every important respect to *The Oxford English Dictionary*'s definition of a ritual as 'A formal procedure or act in a . . . solemn observance . . . A custom or practice of a formal kind'. It was part of a newly instituted mourning ceremony that 'dramatise[d] death, at once expressing grief and guiding it towards consoling gestures. [It] enable[d] the bereaved, for a while, to give the dead person as central a place in their lives as they had before: the rituals honour the dead, secure their memory . . .' (Marris 1974: 84).

As a ritual, relying on the manipulation of context, actor and perform-ance as much as on content; intended to lend a peculiar ceremoniousness to what was said (Moore and Myerhoff 1977: 4); uttered often in a special, studied language, it was devised to convey sentiments and aspire to effects – chiefly of shared understanding or empathy (see Bandes 1996; Habermas 1984) – that were greater and more expressive than the plain wording of more banal and utilitarian speech. That was in large measure what made it a *ritual*. A barrister who read out a statement in one of the cases observed, said of another occasion on which he had spoken:

> I remember thinking at the time this is taking an awful long time. This statement was, I don't know eight, nine pages long and I was very aware, not that I've not read out long statements in past, but I felt the delivery had to be different. I felt in order to give it meaning, you had to read it in a way which was quite different to the way you might read an ordinary factual statement. And I remember remarking to one of my colleagues here that I found it extraordinarily difficult and frankly, we shouldn't really be asked to do these things. . . . I mean I'm not flat anyway but you can afford flatness in a factual statement. But it's far more difficult because you've got the person who's written the statement or been party to it, listening to somebody else reading it. And their expectation, if it's to have any impact at all, is that you should read it in a way that they would want you to . . . [It's] entirely a departure and that's why it's so alien for the system in which we move.

In this manner an impact statement went beyond conventional courtroom speech alone, and that is perhaps why the families and practitioners were sometimes at a loss fully to explain what purposes the new statements were to serve.

The problematics of ritual performance

Ritual is staged and, like all staged performances, it may be difficult to execute effectively. New and unfamiliar rituals are especially fragile because they lack the authority of tradition. Randall Collins of the University of Pennsylvania told me that there has been little or no scholarly writing on failed or frail rituals, but he has listed some of the prerequisites of *effective* ritual, and they include the sharing of a 'momentarily shared reality, which thereby generates solidarity' (2004: 7); 'a high degree of intersubjectivity, together with a high degree of emotional entrainment . . . result[ing] in feelings of membership' (42); the existence of 'boundaries to outsiders so that participants have a sense of who is taking part and who is excluded' (48); 'participants share a common mood . . . an emotional contagion among the persons present' (107); and 'the individual feels that they have the community's support

. . .' (127). When those elements are not present, the outcome can be 'a low level of collective effervescence, the lack of momentary buzz . . . little or no feeling of group solidarity; no sense of one's identity as affirmed or changed; no respect for the group's symbols; no heightened emotional energy . . .' (52) There is, in other words, an absence of collaborative work, of mutually choreographed engrossment, in which 'the people present become entrained in each other's emotions and bodily rhythms, and caught up in a common focus of attention' (Collins 2008: 19).

Collectively, those prerequisites point to the obstacles lying before the wholly successful delivery of Family Impact Statements: the courtroom contains no well-defined congregation of like-thinking, like-feeling, supportive and sympathetic insiders in an adversarial trial for murder or manslaughter. To the contrary. Judges, counsel and court staff practise a studied disinterest when the statement is made (as they do when listening to opening and closing statements – the other segments of the trial which are equally partisan and non-evidential). They convey civil inattention, signalling that they recognise the solemnity of the event but that they cannot be a proper part of its congregation, and that it would be inappropriate for them to register a response to what they see and hear. They are in that sense on the margins, not full members but observers, largely immune to 'emotional contagion' and discomfited when that immunity breaks down,[19] distant from whatever shared reality there may be in the making, not wholly complicit in the ends of the exercise. The defendant and his supporters (if any), on the other hand, are manifestly remote, inscrutable, passive or hostile, and almost certainly not participants in any common mood, although, again, there may be different readings of their reactions across the adversarial structure of the trial. In the often sparsely attended courtroom, it is only the victim's partner or family who may be moved without reservation, who sense that their identity has been confirmed, and they are in a small minority in a room wracked by division.

There is a second obstacle. Courtrooms are already deeply embedded in long-standing ritual processes, but they are processes designed to achieve ends quite different in kind from that of the Family Impact Statement. Counsel and judges talk of their practice as *clinical*: it is intended to be controlled, calm and calming; rational and purposeful; well-mannered and dignified; forensic and professional; conspicuously distant from emotion and emotional display. The rituals of the Family Impact Statement and of routine courtroom procedure do not sit well together (see Arrigo and Williams 2003: 604, 614), and that misalignment may explain some of the discomfort with which a number of lawyers greeted the new procedure. Families and lawyers may in this sense be talking past one another, neither quite understanding – or wishing fully to understand – the speech and objectives of the other: the one working on the moral sentiments to inculcate a new, shared and heightened emotional sensibility ('barbaric' was one otherwise sympathetic prosecutor's observation), the other intended to produce clear, unruffled decisions about guilt and punishment (see Cogley 1968: 72; Eliade 1959: 186). A clergyman, trained for the criminal bar before becoming ordained, who had officiated at a number of funerals (whose orations are akin to the making of Family Impact Statements) and who had studied ritual practices as a theology student, reflected:

> I suppose the thing that . . . makes a ritual successful is a common sense of purpose and awareness of involvement in that ritual and what it's about . . . [But here] you've got various people involved in . . . several different rituals, they happen to be overlapping at the same time. The victims and the families are involved, engaged in one particular ritual which is being witnessed by others, but the lawyers and the court are involved in another. And the two possibly jar . . . basically two rituals [are] happening at the same time, . . . they're overlapping. And they both have their own way of operating and they're not, they're not using the same language, they're [not] operating on the same level . . . so it'd be a bit like throwing part of the wedding service in the middle of a funeral service. The legal world works on . . . rules, protocols, interpretation, the specific use of language, distinctions, definitions, and people know how to play this . . . this sort of swordplay of language in order to fight and defend a case. But then you have some emotionality coming in . . . there isn't emotionality in the argument for the law. The law *is* and it's just an argument as [to] whether it is or is not. There isn't space for the emotion in that.

That there were divergent rituals with different purposes and different emotional pitches was clear. One judge commented of the cathartic role of a Family Impact Statement delivered orally, 'I don't see how that can really help anybody and I don't see how that adds to the dignity of the proceedings or anything really.' His colleague in another case reflected:

> If you've got . . . the relatives of the deceased coming into court every day . . . I think it is an emotional thing for them, a highly emotional thing. And I just think that then, to inject into it just another emotional facet, to no good purpose as far as the court is concerned, although I can understand there may be an advantage to the relatives, I just think the overall situation leads to problems . . .

And, most pointedly, a prosecutor said:

> Unless it has some effect in sentencing, I query why we do it at all unless it is for the cathartic experience or simply the idea of getting

families more involved in the whole process. Now the question [is]: why are we doing that and should we be doing that or should we be keeping the court process very separate, very clinical? ... I think we've probably gone, we're going a little too far in bringing them into the court process because I think the court process should be absolutely clinical so you don't run the risk of the emotion coming in.

There were, he said, dangers in the families' oral presentation of a Family Impact Statement, the dangers of them going 'off script, the emotional side of it and danger of it becoming a rather unnecessary dramatic, staged event'. It was not that such emotional work could not be managed and contained – judges were perfectly confident of their ability to control their courtroom – but that it was quite tangential to the proper business and sentimental order of the court.

The families' difficulties will be compounded when ritual is terminated in mid-flow, as happened in the case where the mother and daughter were severally stopped by counsel from speaking because they had gone 'off script'. Said one, pointing to the text where the word 'murder' had been introduced after a conviction of manslaughter, 'Right from the first we've been shut down! We haven't been allowed to read out our statement! We were only allowed to read from there to there! [The Family Liaison Officer] says "If you can't say what you feel what's the point?" Whether they like it or not, the court, it is a murder charge.' After the pronouncement of the sentence of 18 months' imprisonment for 'single punch manslaughter', she swept out shouting, 'I don't know how you sleep. You fucking pigs! Bastards! Wankers!' The prosecutor who had intervened subsequently reflected:

> What happened in this case was a very good example of why it shouldn't be allowed for family members to read it out, because both of them began reading out additional statements. And I didn't want to prevent them doing that, but this scheme must be strictly adhered to, otherwise it does descend into a free for all. And Mrs X had written out reams of additions and criticising the trial judge and criticising the defendant which is not what the statement's for.

It was the view of defence counsel that the prosecution had intervened quite correctly: 'It was inappropriate material. It was a criticism of the jury, of their verdict, of the judge's conduct of the trial. Now that's not the purpose it seems to me of a victim impact statement at all.' And the judge himself concluded that 'If it had been read out and it had been ... frightfully critical of ... counsel or me or the police or the CPS, I don't see that would have done anything to help ... But what happened I would have thought made no difference at all.' Overall, he asserted, 'Of course, one takes it into account and it's very moving and heartrending stuff it has been today, I'm sure you would agree. [But it] doesn't make any difference to the sentence.'

Difficulties will be compounded further where there is prior editing of the Family Impact Statement; where, as in a second case, the ritual was still-born and the family could not speak at all because there was an acquittal ('The big thing is what was the verdict and everything else is unimportant, isn't that right?' said a father in just such an eventuality); and where, as in the first and third cases, the sentences awarded were taken to be so disproportionately lenient that the Family Impact Statement must have made no effective or worthwhile impression. In the first of those two last instances, the sister of the victim commented in an email:

> There after [we] get a kick in the face with how this judge has made us to feel the guilty and accused. this by far is in fact injustice, and i no untill we have this for the sake of my brother and his children we can never get on and walk forward in life . . . the impact statements are ment for the victim family the judge had time for us yet passed A comment how he agreed of the jurys verdict. what about how its left us as a family what about all the pain and suffering we have felt how about what we had to say ???.

And, in the second, the victim's partner said:

> I was speaking for [my daughter] as well, yeah, 'cause she helped me with the statement as well. But just to, you know, just to stand there and say, look, you're all listening to [the defendant]. That wasn't the X [I knew]. That was [the defendant's] lies. . . . [But I failed] . . . All it done was brought me pain, heartache and that was that.

But the ritual *did* appear to have been satisfactory for a number of the principals in the fourth case, and that was where events manifestly conspired to bring about success. The victim's partner had wanted well in advance to talk about him:

> I said, oh yeah, I'd be very interested because of . . . what I could understand in the courts, they didn't really mention anything of the victim's family and . . . it was all very dry . . . [The statement] gives a picture, I think, of what's going on, what's happened, the murder's happened, this is who he was. This is how I understood it. Some sort of background . . . to give it a sort of a bit of life . . . I'd written down who he was, who he was to me and my daughter and how it affected us . . . [to] personalise it a little bit . . . which I think it's so much better than this, there's a body that's dead and this is who he was and that's that, and that's just a name.

She did not overreach herself or have great expectations. She did not idealise the deceased (he 'was a pisshead and he would ... have tantrums ... [He] talked crap most of the time. But I just wanted them to know ... he was so full of life. He really was a big loud person who wanted the party to never end'). She did not unduly strain credulity or the possibility of some accord between different audiences (although the defence were not to be drawn in). The judge was to comment on her statement, 'It wasn't judgemental either. It was just saying really affectionate things about him but identifying his, not fault, that's the wrong word, his defects and his shortcomings.' She was succinct ('I'd written a precise but quite short statement, not to be so long-winded about it'). She wanted to restore character and vitality to a victim who could no longer be viewed or heard ('I just thought everyone should get a chance to do this, get this out, put on paper who this person was to them, and how much they're really going to miss him, you know? Just to make it a bit more human ... so people could get a face and think there's a life there'). She wanted to make public what had hitherto been private ('I did want everybody to hear it, including the defendant there ... I wanted the jury, the judge and everybody connected really to hear who X was, 'cause at the moment, it's just ... the body').

She alluded neither to the sentence nor to the defendant. Indeed, she was relatively sympathetic to the defendant, and hoped that his alcoholism might be treated in prison (but 'I got the impression he wasn't with it anyway ... It would be nice if I could have got that message across to him. I would have liked to have done that, yes ... But the point is, I don't think the man's really with it'). She nevertheless believed that the defendant was penitent ('I think ... he's really remorseful'), a view also taken by the judge (who said that the affair had been a tragedy for victim and defendant alike), and by counsel and the solicitor, who talked of suicide attempts in remand.

There *was* a conviction for murder and a relatively substantial sentence, signifying a recognition of the magnitude of the loss. Because the statement was issued immediately after conviction, the jury was present and attentive ('the jury heard and the judge. I know it didn't matter so much, [but] I wanted the jury to know ...') The defendant had no supporters visibly in attendance. The statement was read out in a measured way by counsel while the partner sobbed, oblivious to how others in the courtroom were responding and whether or not there was a 'momentarily shared reality': 'I was bawling my eyes out. I meant to look up and see is anyone taking any notice of this statement?' It was a ritual that she claimed to have found very satisfying indeed:

> I think I covered everything in it and I'm glad it was read out. Didn't hear anything about him throughout the trial really and the way that the defendant, you know, was saying he's a wanker. He didn't

deserve to die. Didn't say very much about him at all. I'm so glad, yeah, it was read out ... You have to know the background to the person, you know. I just think, instead of everything's so black and white, it throws a bit of light on the whole thing you know? Makes it more human ..., *Archbold* [a standard law book in use in the Crown Court] and books and all that kind of legal talk ... it's that bit that you need. I think the jury and the judge listen to that bit, the personal bit. It's very important ... I think this is a really good scheme. I think it's really important to have the victim's family put things down on paper if they feel they want to. I really do think that's a very good scheme ... as I say, I can't stop saying it, this is a brilliant idea.

The judge in the case was equally persuaded of its success:

I thought today that was handled particularly well, if I may say so. It was read in fact, unemotionally. It was a prosecutor who was not shoving emotion down my throat ... He knows exactly what he's doing. No. I thought the whole thing – she was upset, I could see that – but I thought she retained composure in full measure and dignity from beginning to end ... I've found that it's been an opportunity for people to demonstrate how measured and dignified they are in their sadness ... You'll think this very unadventurous, [but there should be] more of the same. More of the same. I think it really is something which should be factored into the whole picture.

And it may have had a modest impact on sentence:

It painted a picture, didn't it, of someone who could be modestly bizarre in drink but not overtly so ... so yes, it did influence me in the sense that this woman's seen him in drink on many occasions and her perception clearly was that he wasn't a sort of unmitigated aggressive individual.

Yet even where events coalesced so well together for some principals, the adversarial system and divergent rituals continued to play their parts. Prosecution counsel had not been markedly impressed by what had happened:

I think if you did a straw poll of most of us who prosecute these cases day in and day out, most of us when it came in said it was a complete waste of time. Because the problem is, yes, it's cathartic up to a point ... I mean it provides some form of closure. But as long as victims understand that there is really nothing in it for them other than that, that they have no expectation that the sentence will be increased.

And defence counsel had been equally unimpressed:

> I don't see what role the witness or victim impact statement actually has ... I personally ... don't see the need for these statements other than to give ease to the person perhaps who's doing it ... I think we've imported [it] without actually being clear in our own minds as to why we want this actually as part of our system ... I wouldn't have them at all, to be honest. Because I just do not see the purpose in the criminal justice system ... I don't see what purpose it has if it's not going to be used for sentencing purposes. I don't see what the role is in a criminal system.

The outcome of the initiative

Even before the pilot project was complete and the report of its evaluation had been published, Charles Falconer and Harriet Harman, its original patrons, had moved on, and the initiative was superseded by another, better favoured by lawyers and judges, launched by Lord Goldsmith, the then Attorney General, in June 2007, and 'rolled out' nationally by his successor, Baroness Scotland, four months later. What was to be called the Victims Focus Scheme restricted the delivery of impact statements (called once more victim personal statements) in homicide trials[20] to written statements passed to the judge or, where it was to be oral, the safer vehicle of counsel who could be trusted not to behave too expressively or go 'off script'. Endemic ambiguities about the possible impact on sentence remained,[21] but the perils of improperly enacted and damaging rituals were curtailed, and there was a retreat from allowing secondary victims to penetrate significantly into the fabric of the trial.

Conclusions

Evaluations of victim impact statements across the world have reported that they generally contribute only a little to victims' satisfaction and have a negligible effect on sentencing (see Erez, Roeger and Morgan 1994; Erez and Tontodonato 1992; Leverick, Chalmers and Duff 2007; and Roberts 2002), although there has been too little examination in the past of their expressive role (Roberts and Erez 2004).

What has been reported here is no more than a first sighting of the fledgling stage of a new initiative which was soon aborted. But these case studies do similarly indicate that the statements, in three of the four trials, appeared to have had only a modest effect on the families' satisfaction and very little effect on sentencing, and they did meet with a measure of structured resistance from professionals.

Statements were earnestly desired as a means of restoring respect to victims and their families, but they could not always accomplish their object because there was too much competing anguish, too deeply entrenched an adversarial system, and too many problems, at least at the outset, with staging a novel form of ritual performance. In confronting those impediments, their introduction illuminates some important properties of the grief that attends violent death, on the one hand, and of culture and process in the Crown Court of England and Wales, on the other.

It was in this sense that they acted as a scouting expedition which mapped and then reinforced the place of the victim in the moral topography of the courtroom. If the first, somewhat murky, marker that came into view proved to be a refusal to grant the bereaved any greater power to make or perceptibly sway judicial decisions, the second was radically to tamp down displays of expressive behaviour. The roles of victims and their survivors in England and Wales are, at least for the foreseeable future, hedged about by tight proscriptions on their ability to participate as parties, decide outcomes or induce emotional contagion.

Acknowledgements

*I am grateful to the Ministry of Justice for inviting me to undertake this work, funding it and allowing me to publish this paper. Any views expressed are mine alone. I am also most grateful to Susan Lee and her colleagues in the Ministry of the Attorney General of Ontario, and to Judges Cole and Vaillancourt of Toronto; to Judges Lerner, Temin and Greenspan, and to Ed McCann, Assistant District Attorney and his colleagues, in Philadelphia; to Joyce Lorinstein for transcribing the interviews conducted for this paper; and to Ian Brunskill, Randall Collins, Frances Heidensohn, Janet Finch, Tim Newburn, Julian Roberts, Laurie Robinson, Lawrence Sherman and Heather Strang for their help and advice.

Notes

1 The first Victim Impact Statement was reported to have been introduced in Fresno County, California, in 1976 (see Alexander and Lord 1994).
2 Julian Roberts stated, for instance, that in Canada, where victim impact statements are similarly expressly intended not to address questions of sentence, 'The [Criminal] *Code* provides no guidance with respect to the critical question of the way in which a court should use the information contained in the victim impact statement. How should a sentencing court incorporate the victim impact information into the complex determination of sanction? The

statutory statement of purpose and principle is of little use to judges in this respect because it does not relate those principles to the question of victim impact. The matter is left to judicial discretion to resolve . . .' (undated: 4). Canadian victims themselves would concur about that ambiguity. Interviews with focus groups composed of Canadians who had delivered Victim Impact Statements disclosed, for example, that 'The first perceived goal was that the statements should allow victims to have a say in the sentencing process by presenting to the court how the crime has affected their lives . . . They believe that to some degree, the statements reduce the perceived anonymity of the victim in the trial process . . . the second perceived aim [was given by] most victims [as indicating] that they expected that their statements would have an effect on the sentence actually imposed in the cases. At the same time, they stated that they recognized that judges must take into account a number of factors in reaching their decisions on sentencing' (Meredith and Paquette 2001: 6).

3   At the Federal level, for instance, the Victim and Witness Protection Act 1982 stated that a pre-sentence report could include not only 'information concerning any harm, including financial, social, psychological and physical harm done to or loss suffered by the victim of the offense' but also 'any other information that may aid the court in sentencing . . .'; and the later, and more radical, 2004 Crime Victims' Rights Act and ensuing case of *Kenna* (*Kenna v. District Court* 435 F.3d 1011 (9th Cir. 2006) confirmed that a victim had a right to be heard and make representations about plea, sentence, bail and parole, and that those representations could and should touch on sentencing (although it appears that federal prosecutors are sometimes reluctant to allow victims and their families to make a *mitigating* plea at the point of sentence). In Pennsylvania, on the other hand, the position was identical to that of the Victim Personal Statement (VPS) and Family Impact Statement (FIS) in England and Wales. The Victim Impact Unit of the Philadelphia District Attorney's office, for example, formally instructed those about to give victim impact statements that a number of topics could be addressed in a statement, but not one of those topics touched on sentencing. At the same time, 'co-victims' were told that 'Your Victim Impact Statement will be used by the judge, in addition to information obtained by other sources related to the defendant (past criminal history and mental status examinations) to determine whether an appropriate sentence for the crime is committed.' In death penalty cases, the 'co-victim' would be informed that 'The Judge will review your statement and may edit sentences from it that he/she may think are too "inflammatory" for the jury to hear. **Your statement will be restricted to information about the character of the victim and effects that the crime has had on you and your family. You will be instructed to read your statement without crying.** You must maintain your composure, or the Judge may stop you from speaking.' (Emphasis in the original)

4   Bandes argues flatly that 'victim impact statements are stories that should not be told, at least not in the context of capital sentencing, because they block the jury's ability to hear the defendant's story. Moreover, they evoke emotions that do not belong in that context . . . the emotions they evoke – hatred, bigotry, and unreflective empathy – demean the dignity of both victim and defendant' (1996: 392–3, 394).

5 The term is also in use in Australia and parts of the United States. It signifies that the victim himself or herself is unable to testify and that the impact of the crime has now shifted to his or her family.

6 The manifesto itself stated that the Government would 'Expand [. . .] specialist courts to deal with domestic violence and specialist advocates to support the victims of such crime and of other serious crimes like murder and rape'.

7 The history of that Act is traced in my *Constructing Victims' Rights* (2004).

8 All descriptions are taken from the organisations' websites.

9 Who told a SAMM Annual General Meeting in October 2005: 'We've made big strides in giving victims a voice through the VAP. We're trying to put the victim's voice into the judicial system. So long as victims aren't part of the criminal conversation we are not going to have an emotionally intelligent system. You've been there, you've been through it, you know it. We need to use your voice to make a difference. We are determined to listen to the voice of the victim.'

10 *Report and Financial Statements*, SAMM, 31 March 2005: 3.

11 Lord Falconer of Thoroton, Secretary of State for Constitutional Affairs and Lord Chancellor: *Audit Commission Conference on Victims and Witnesses*, Video Conference, 3 December 2003.

12 '. . . started by Mark Manwaring, whose father and sister were brutally murdered all for the sake of a red Escort car. He had a terrible experience as a victim, and so he set up the Trust to help others who are touched by murder.' (www.tparents.org/UNews/unws9411/PEACE.htm)

13 There were important regional splits in SAMM reflecting differences in style and culture.

14 A detective, specialising in serious crime inquiries and a member of the investigating team, who is assigned on secondment to act as a bridge between the family and the investigating officers.

15 BMRB's own findings, not expressed in numerical form, were wholly consistent with those presented here.

16 In that they followed a common pattern. Commenting on research conducted in the USA (where the murder rate is admittedly much higher than in the UK), Smith and Ecob remark that 'People who had ever been arrested were . . . more likely to become homicide victims than those never arrested . . .' (2007: 635).

17 He later recalled of a particular case, 'And all she said, "I really want to say, how do I want to start this statement? I'd like to fucking kill the bastard who's killed my son. That's what I want to say", and we actually did, you know, we wrote that in because in her words, that was what she wanted to say. And . . . she actually appreciated that she was allowed to say that because she said, "That's really, you know, if anybody asked me what I want, you know."'

18 And that reflected apprehensions that the statement would be used for purposes of campaigning by activists.

19 An email from one of the pilot courts reported that 'In one murder case leading Counsel for the Pros read out the statement. In this particular case the Judge in the case commented later. He said that the content of the statements had caused much distress to an already distressed Jury who had returned guilty verdicts to murder and had clearly found it difficult. During the statement being read 5 of the 12 Jury members were reduced to tears. The Judge was

minded to rise but then thought it better to continue as that would make the situation worse.'

20 The scheme was also extended to deaths in custody and in road traffic accidents.

21 Under paras. 23–25 of the guidance accompanying the new scheme (http://www.cps.gov.uk/victims_witnesses/focus_scheme.html), it was stated that 'In the direction provided by Judge LJ, the Family Impact Statement cannot affect the sentence that the Judge may pass and the family will not be able to comment on what they think the sentence should be. However, the Family Impact Statement may help to provide a fuller understanding of the nature and impact of the crime when passing sentence. Prosecutors are advised to adopt a conservative view when advising the family – namely that the VPS is very unlikely to affect the sentence. While this may be unwelcome news to the family it will prevent expectations being unduly raised. Some families may be sceptical about the value of making a VPS at all if it has little or no effect on sentence . . .'

References

Alexander, E. and Lord, J. (1994) *A Victim's Right to Speak: A nation's responsibility to listen*. Washington, DC: US Department of Justice, Office for Victims of Crime.

Arrigo, B. and Williams, C. (2003) 'Victim vices, victim voices, and impact statements: on the place of emotion and the role of restorative justice in capital sentencing', *Crime and Delinquency*, 49(4): 603–26.

Bakan, D. (1966) *The Duality of Human Existence: An essay on psychology and religion*. Chicago: Rand McNally.

Bandes, S. (1996) 'Empathy, narrative, and victim impact statements', *The University of Chicago Law Review*, 63(2): 361–412.

Bauer, J. and McAdams, D. (2000) 'Competence, relatedness, and autonomy in life stories', *Psychological Inquiry*, 11(4): 276–9.

Bocock, R. (1974) *Ritual in Industrial Society: A sociological analysis of ritualism in modern England*. London: George Allen & Unwin.

Chermak, S. (1995), *Victims in the News: Crime and the American news media*. Boulder, CO: Westview Press.

Christie, N. (1986) 'Crime control as drama', *Journal of Law and Society*, 13(1): 1–8.

Clark, P. (2004) 'Redressing the balance: The Criminal Justice Bill 2002', in E. Cape (ed.), *Reconcilable Rights? Analysing the tension between victims and defendants*. London: Legal Action Group, pp. 19–26.

Cogley, J. (1968) *Religion in a Secular Age: The search for final meaning*. London: Pall Mall Press.

Collins, R. (2004) *Interaction Ritual Chains*. Princeton, NJ: Princeton University Press.

Collins, R. (2008) *Violence: A micro-sociological theory*. Princeton, NJ: Princeton University Press.

Crossley, M. (2000) 'Narrative psychology, trauma and the study of self/identity', *Theory and Psychology*, 10(4): 527–46.

Eliade, M. (1959) (trans. W.R. Trask), *The Sacred and the Profane: The nature of religion*. New York: Harcourt, Brace and World.

Erez, E., Roeger, L. and Morgan, F. (1994) 'Victim impact statements in South Australia: an evaluation', South Australia Office of Crime Statistics Research Report No. 6. Adelaide: South Australian Attorney General's Department.

Erez, E. and Tontodonato, P. (1992), 'Victim participation in sentencing and satisfaction with justice', *Justice Quarterly*, 9(3): 393–417.

Finch, J. (2007) 'Displaying families', *Sociology*, 41(1): 65–81.

Finch, J. and Mason J. (2000) *Passing On: Kinship and inheritance in England*. London: Routledge.

Flatman, G. and Bagaric, M. (2001) 'The victim and the prosecutor: the relevance of victims in prosecution decision making', *Deakin Law Review*, 6(2): 238–58.

Fleckenstein, K. (1996) 'Images, words, and narrative epistemology', *College English*, 58(8): 914–33.

Garland, D. (2006) 'Concepts of culture in the sociology of punishment', *Theoretical Criminology*, 10(4): 419–47.

Glaser, B. and Strauss, A. (1971) *Status Passage*. London: Routledge and Kegan Paul.

Habermas, J. (1984) (trans. T. McCarthy) *The Theory of Communicative Action, Vol. 1, Reason and the rationalization of society*. Boston, MA: Beacon Press.

Howarth, G. (2007) *Death and Dying: A sociologial introduction*. Cambridge: Polity.

Hughes, E. (1958) *Men and Their Work*. Glencoe, IL: Free Press.

Lamb, S. (1996) *The Trouble with Blaming*. Cambridge, MA: Harvard University Press.

Lerner, M. (1980) *The Belief in a Just World: A fundamental delusion*. New York: Plenum Press.

Leverick, F., Chalmers, J. and Duff, P. (2007) *An Evaluation of the Pilot Victim Statement Schemes in Scotland*, Research Findings No. 92/2007. Edinburgh: Scottish Executive Social Research. http://www.scotland.gov.uk/Publications/2007/03/27152708/0

Luginbuhl, J. and Burkhead, M. (1995) 'Victim impact evidence in a capital trial: encouraging votes for death', *American Journal of Criminal Justice*, 20(1): 1–16.

Marris, P. (1974) *Loss and Change*. London: Routledge and Kegan Paul.

McAdams, D. (1996) 'Personality, modernity, and the storied self: a contemporary framework for studying persons', *Psychological Inquiry*, 7(4): 295–321.

Meredith, C. and Paquette, C. (2001) *Summary Report on Victim Impact Statement Focus Groups*, Victims of Crime Research Series. Ottawa: Department of Justice. http://www.justice.gc.ca/eng/pi/rs/rep-rap/2000/rr00_vic21/inde x.html

Moore, S. and Myerhoff, B. (eds) (1977) *Secular Ritual*. Assen/Amsterdam: Van Gorcum.

Myers, B. and Greene, E. (2004) 'The prejudicial nature of victim impact statements: implications for capital sentencing policy', *Psychology, Public Policy, and Law*, 10(4): 492–515.

O'Hear, M. (2006) 'Punishment, democracy, and victims', *Federal Sentencing Reporter*, 19(1): 1–4.

Peacock, J. and Holland, D. (1993) 'The narrated self: life stories in process', *Ethos*, 21(4): 367–83.

Roberts, J. (undated) 'Victim impact statements and the sentencing process: recent developments and research findings', mimeo.

Roberts, J. (2002) *The Use of Victim Impact Statements in Sentencing: A Review of International Research Findings*, Report for the Policy Centre for Victim Issues. Ottawa: Department of Justice.

Roberts, J.V. and Erez, E. (2004) 'Communication in sentencing: exploring the expressive and the impact model of victim impact statements', *International Review of Victimology*, 10(3): 223–44.

Rock, P. (1998) *After Homicide: Practical and political responses to bereavement*. Clarendon Studies in Criminology. Oxford: Clarendon Press.

Rock, P. (2004) *Constructing Victims' Rights: The Home Office, New Labour and victims*. Oxford: Oxford University Press.

Rock, P. (2006) 'The politics of victimhood', *Safer Society: The Journal of Crime Reduction and Community Safety*, 29: 11–13.

Sennett, R. (2003) *Respect: The formation of character in a world of inequality*. London: Allen Lane.

Silverman, P. and Klass, D. (1996) 'Introduction: what's the problem?', in D. Klass, P. Silverman and S. Nickman (eds), *Continuing Bonds: New understandings of grief*. Washington, DC: Taylor and Francis, pp. 3–30.

Smith, D. and Ecob, R. (2007) 'An investigation into causal links between victimization and offending in adolescents', *The British Journal of Sociology*, 58(4): 633–59.

Thompson. J. (1995) *The Media and Modernity: A social theory of the media*. Cambridge: Polity.

Wolfgang, M. (1957) 'Victim precipitated criminal homicide', *Journal of Criminal Law, Criminology and Police Science*, 48: 1–11.

Van Gennep, A. (1960) *The Rites of Passage*. Chicago, IL: University of Chicago Press.

Young, J. (2007) *The Vertigo of Late Modernity*. London: Sage.

Zehr, H. (1990) *Changing Lenses: A New Focus for Crime and Justice*. Scottsdale, PA: Herald Press.

Chapter 9

Communication at sentencing: the expressive function of Victim Impact Statements

Julian V. Roberts and Edna Erez

The role of the victim in the sentencing process continues to generate controversy among scholars and practitioners across many common law jurisdictions. The debate has focused on the propriety of allowing victims to have input into the sentencing process in an adversarial legal system, as well as the specific ways in which this input should be structured. In particular, legal professionals (e.g. Office of Victims of Crime 1998: 99) and some sentencing scholars (e.g. Ashworth 2000) have argued that victim input may undermine the foundation of adversarial legal systems, adversely affect court schedules and outcomes, and erode the due process rights of defendants (Erez 1994).

Victim participation of some kind is now a requirement of legal proceedings throughout the criminal process. Victims' rights have been created by several national and international organisations: the United Nations (Declaration of Basic Principles of Justice for Victims of Crime and Abuse of Power [1985]), the Council of Europe Recommendations for Victims of Crime (R [85] 11) and more recently, the Council Framework Decision of the European Union [2001/220/HA]). The latter is a binding decision that obliges signatory States to ensure that victims play a significant role in the criminal legal system (Article 2) and to ensure that victims are heard during proceedings (Article 3).

In the adversarial legal systems of some countries (such as the US), victims acquired the right to provide input into sentencing and parole as early as the 1980s, when most jurisdictions introduced the Victim Impact Statement (hereafter VIS). In Canada, impact statements at sentencing received statutory recognition with Criminal Code amendments in 1989.

Other common law jurisdictions such as New Zealand and several Australian States also introduced impact statements during the 1980s. There is now general recognition that 'victim participation of some kind is here to stay' (Sanders *et al*. 2001: 448), although objections remain. Opposition to the use of victim impact statements at sentencing is based primarily on divergent views about the purpose, function and consequences of using such statements in sentencing: whether VISs exist to have an impact on sentencing patterns, or to serve an expressive function.

Purpose of this chapter

In this chapter we first discuss the conceptions of victim impact statements that have emerged over the last two decades. Then, by situating the debate on victim input in its historical context, we describe how the expressive or communicative conception of victim input – originally envisioned by the reform movement as its principal justification – was replaced by a model that stressed the impact of victim input on the sentence imposed. We argue that the instrumental focus is misplaced; it fails to reflect the true purpose of a VIS at sentencing, namely its expressive and communicative aims (see also Young 1993; Erez 1999). Furthermore, the instrumental model ignores the possible therapeutic or restorative benefits associated with communication involving other participants at sentencing. The chapter argues that much of the lingering opposition to victim input rights has been animated by the instrumental model, which we argue is theoretically misconceived, empirically unsupported, and at odds with major sentencing aims. Having reintroduced an alternative, communicative model, we discuss its potential for victims and offenders, and summarise findings from relevant research in a number of common law jurisdictions. We conclude with a call to reassess current theory and practice regarding victim integration in sentencing, and offer some practical recommendations regarding the optimal way to facilitate victim input.

Competing perspectives on Victim Impact Statements

Two alternative models of VISs have emerged since victims were given the right to submit an impact statement at sentencing. The first model stresses the effect that these statements should have on the sentence imposed; we term this the *instrumental* model. In contrast, VISs can be conceived as vehicles of *communication* or expression. According to this alternative model the statements provide victims with a means of communicating with other actors in the sentencing process. These two conceptions also relate (although they do not map directly on to) another analytic dichotomy: *punitive* versus *restorative*. The instrumental perspective on the VIS exemplifies what Kent Roach has described as the 'punitive model' of victims' rights (see Roach 1999a: 700–6).

This perspective regards the conservative 'law and order' ideology as underlying the movement to provide victims with input rights and the purpose of VISs is to increase the severity of sentencing (Henderson 1985; Erez 1994; Roach 1999b: 292). Some critics of victim input have asserted that the intention of victims' rights is to foment hostility towards offenders or to highlight the leniency of the sentencing system (e.g. Henderson 1985; Elias 1993) and that crime victims are often used as 'pawns' in the politics of law and order (Fattah 1997). Opponents of victim participatory rights have also argued that victims are vindictive, and, by and large, motivated by a desire to maximise sentence severity (see review in Erez 1994). Some critics contend that the movement to provide victim participatory rights seems to go hand in hand with an increase in sentence severity or that participatory rights were established to benefit the prosecution (Mosteller 1998).

In contrast, the 'non-punitive model' or restorative model of victim rights promotes the interests of the victim from a restorative justice perspective[1] (Roach 1999a: 706–12). This approach accords priority to the communicative and expressive functions of a VIS at sentencing. Here the purpose of the statement is to provide information about the effect of the crime, and to communicate with the principal players in the proceeding – but not to demand a specific penalty, or to enhance severity. In contemporary debates concerning the integration of victim input into criminal proceedings, however, the two models of justice are often perceived as distinct and mutually exclusive, and victim communication is considered appropriate for restorative justice but not for retributive justice.

Victim voice and the politics of Victim Impact Statements

The public discussion regarding victim input into sentencing was originally prompted by concern over the absence of victim input into criminal justice proceedings and the 'secondary victimisation' inflicted on victims by the criminal justice process. A movement to ameliorate the plight of victims and to integrate victims in the criminal justice process subsequently emerged. This movement sought measures that would empower victims and provide them with a voice at sentencing and parole. In most common law jurisdictions, the VIS[2] has become the principal vehicle for facilitating victim input. The VIS was supposed to address victims' 'perceived justice needs' (Sebba 1996), as well as to promote their psychological welfare. It was expected to provide victims with a public forum in which to communicate a message to the court about the harm they had sustained, an opportunity to be recognised as the injured party, and a measure of achieving psychological catharsis (see Erez 1994).[3]

The use of victim impact statements has been criticised on conceptual as well as practical grounds (e.g. Henderson 1985; Sanders 2002). Some of the opposition to victim input is based upon its potentially adverse effects on sentencing outcomes, court proceedings and defendants' due process rights (see Erez 1994 for a review). There has also been opposition to allowing victims to deliver their impact statement in person – exercising their allocution right – as this may be particularly moving for the judge, and may further enhance any aggravating effect on sentencing patterns.[4] Practical objections have also been raised regarding the effect that victim input and allocution rights may have on an overburdened judicial system in terms of time to process cases.[5]

As the campaign to provide victims with a voice has faced significant opposition, particularly from some members of the legal profession (e.g. Henderson 1985), the justification for the proposed reform was redirected to highlight the potential of VISs to assist judges in imposing sentences commensurate with the harm inflicted on the victim.[6] Although the VIS was created to provide victims with a voice at sentencing, the rationale for it has been rapidly transformed to accommodate a conservative legal profession that has been reluctant to integrate victims in adversarial criminal justice systems (Erez 2004). Representing the VIS as a tool that helps judges in imposing a 'just' sentence was a strategy to bring victims into the process. Hence, the discourse of victim input more often underscores the value of VIS for participants in the process *other* than victims, or for the sentencing system as a whole (Erez 2004).

The list of justifications for the use of impact statements thus included benefits for criminal justice participants and processes. For the offender, the VIS may provide rehabilitative benefits when offenders are sensitised to the full extent of the harm that they have inflicted on the victim. From the criminal justice system's perspective, the VIS provides the court with an opportunity to recognise the wrong committed against an individual victim, promoting the idea that although crimes are committed against the State, it is individual victims who sustain the loss, damage or injury. For the prosecution, and ultimately for the court, the VIS can provide information about the impact of the crime on the victim, and on victims' needs with respect to reparative sanctions (for discussion of the purposes of VIS and their benefits for criminal justice see Erez 1994; Kelly and Erez 1997: Roberts 2003).

The potential for communication has been overlooked by scholars and legal practitioners. In most jurisdictions (e.g. the US, Australia and Canada), the impact statement is represented as a source of information for the judge about the harm suffered by the victim as a result of the crime. For example, a leading Canadian case (*R v. Gabriel*) identifies four principal purposes of the VIS at sentencing, none of which invokes communication between the parties giving rise to the criminal proceeding in the first place: the victim and the offender. This emphasis on the significance of victim input for sentencing decisions precipitated the impact perspective of the VIS and diverted attention from the benefits involved in victims communicating their experiences in court – even though this provided the impetus behind the movement to provide victims with a voice at sentencing.

Whether the avowed aims of the VIS are phrased in terms of benefits to the victim, to other participants in the process, or the sentencing system as a whole, promoting victim welfare emerges, directly or indirectly, as a major aim behind the reform (see Erez and Rogers 1999). Beyond the symbolic recognition of victims in the criminal justice process, the expressive function of the VIS can help promote the welfare of crime victims. The VIS is situated at a critical point in the criminal process, namely the ultimate disposition of the crime. It may thus precipitate beneficial reactions and serve various therapeutic ends[7] (Wiebe 1996; Herman 2003). The VIS presentation may also prompt offenders to respond to victim statements, thereby helping to dispel stereotypes about offenders.

The exchange of perspectives or information in the sentencing hearing may contribute to dispelling stereotypes about both victims and offenders. It is well known that the public (including victims) subscribe to stereo-types of offenders who are seen as a small, well-defined group that is different from the rest of society. Offenders are often perceived as multiple recidivists who do not share the characteristics of law-abiding citizens (see Stalans and Diamond (1990) and Roberts and Hough (2005) for a review of research on public attitudes towards offenders). The prevalence of these stereotypes explains in part the punitive attitudes displayed by the public when asked to sentence in the absence of specific information about the case. Research reveals that people become more sympathetic towards offending, and assign less severe sanctions, when they have more information about a case (see for example Roberts 2002). Victims may also be more understanding as a result of hearing the offender's story, particularly if preceded or accompanied by the expression of remorse.

The expressive and communicative potential of VISs merits further exploration. We argue that the victim *expresses*[8] his or her perspective or feelings about the effect of the crime, and this expression *communicates* messages to several parties. In addition to communicating information about the effects of the crime to the judge, the VIS constitutes an important form of communication between the victim and the offender, as well as the judge and the offender. Further, the expressive function more accurately reflects the original purpose of the VIS, and offers benefits that cannot be achieved if these statements are used exclusively to influence the sentence imposed. The VIS as originally conceived may in fact introduce a restorative element to adversarial proceedings, without undermining important and, in some jurisdictions, codified principles of sentencing, such as equity and proportionality.[9] Encouraging these additional forms of communication will not transform the sentencing hearing into a tripartite proceeding; nor will it undermine the central assumption of the adversarial system – that a crime is committed against the State and not a private party.

Placing impact information before the court

The manner in which victim impact information is placed before the court may affect the 'victim voice': it may either enhance or diminish the communicative potential of the VIS for victims as well as for other participants in the sentencing process, particularly the offender.

Most jurisdictions employ VIS forms that are completed by the victim. In other jurisdictions, criminal justice professionals prepare the statement, after having solicited the information from the victim. Both methods have advantages and disadvantages in terms of providing victims with a voice. Self-administered VIS forms are less costly, and reflect the true voice of the victim. However, an often-raised drawback of this approach is that some victims may insert opinions into their statements that are irrelevant to sentencing. If justice officials prepare the statement, it is less likely to include new material that is not part of the record or inadmissible statements – such as inflammatory or prejudicial comments about the offender. On the other hand, impact statements prepared by justice officials may neither accurately reflect the feelings of the victim, nor incorporate the exact wording employed by the victim to describe the impact upon his or her life. Because justice officials (particularly if overburdened with other responsibilities) may present victim harm in generic terms or rush through the 'extra' work (e.g. Erez and Rogers 1999), statements prepared by professionals may understate the impact of the crime and might not reflect the true voice of victims.

The way in which the content of the VIS is conveyed to the court also varies across jurisdictions. Some countries (e.g. most US jurisdictions and Canada) require a VIS to be submitted to the court directly, either in a written form or by means of an oral statement (if there is a right of allocution) or both. Others rely on prosecutors to convey the content of the impact statement to the court. Each method has its strengths and weaknesses. From a 'victim voice' viewpoint, one of the major disadvantages of having prosecutors convey the impact information to the court is that there is likelihood of editing, withholding or 'losing' information (e.g. Rogers, Laster and Inglis 1994), particularly if the interests of the prosecutor are not aligned with those of the victim (Erez 1999). The tendency of legal professionals to 'sanitise' impact information, or to represent the harm in 'clinical' terms (particularly when they think the statement is exaggerated), has been documented in past research (Erez and Rogers 1999; Rogers *et al.* 1994).

The VIS forms commonly used in various countries convey two principal messages about the purpose of a VIS at sentencing. First, the purpose of the VIS is to communicate with the judge and/or the criminal justice system. For example, the instructions given to victims in England and Wales who are contemplating completion of a Victim Personal Statement indicate that the statement gives the victim 'the chance to tell us [i.e. the criminal justice system] about how the crime has affected you' (Home Office 2002: 2). Second, the contents of the VIS should be restricted to information relevant to the impact of the crime in terms of the kind of harm suffered, its extent and lasting effects on the victim.

VIS forms often explicitly direct the victim's attention away from communicating with the offender. The VIS guide given to victims in the State of Washington directs victims to 'Remember at all times that you are talking or writing to the judge about how the crime has affected you.'[10] In other jurisdictions (such as some Australian States) the forms note that the defence has the right to see the statement (or receive a copy). This language may suggest to victims that there is no communicative purpose involving the offender, a curious message, since it implies that the person who committed the crime has no interest in hearing about the impact on the victim. Language of this kind diminishes the communicative function of the VIS to anyone other than the sentencing judge. Thus victims have been encouraged to regard a VIS exclusively in terms of a unidirectional communication with the court.

The emphasis on the VIS solely as a tool for judges also conveys a mixed message to victims about the likely effect of their statement on the sentencing outcome. Although victims in some jurisdictions are told that the VIS will not affect the sentence imposed, they are simultaneously encouraged to write anything they believe is important to the judge in determining sanction. This potentially confusing message may be the reason some victims expect their VIS to influence the sentencing outcome and are therefore disappointed when they believe the statement had no effect on the nature or severity of sentence (e.g. Erez and Tontodonato 1992). Instructing victims that the statement is as much addressed to the offender as it is to the court may prevent such an outcome.[11]

An illustration of the hegemony of the instrumental over communicative models can be found in a Canadian case, in which a victim's request to make an oral presentation of the VIS was denied by the court.[12] In Canada, section 722 of the *Criminal Code* permits victims to make an oral presentation of their statement. In this case, the offender had been convicted of first-degree murder, an offence carrying a mandatory sentence of life imprisonment with no possibility of parole until the offender has served at least 25 years in prison. Because there is no judicial discretion with respect to the sentence that may be imposed for this crime, the court declined to hear the victim's statement. From the court's perspective, there was no point in hearing about victim impact, since nothing the victim might say could affect the nature of sentence imposed – the judge ascribed no purpose to the statement except to influence the sentence imposed. This narrow perspective on the function of a VIS at sentencing deprived the victim's family of communicating a sense of their loss to the court and to the offender. Preventing the victims from speaking can only have exacerbated their suffering and sense of alienation from the sentencing process. We would argue that the need to hear from the victims is important in such cases, given the seriousness of the crime, regardless of the existence of a mandatory sentence (see also discussion in Rock, Chapter 8, this volume).

Theories of sentencing and the Victim Impact Statement

The communicative element of the VIS is important for theoretical as well as practical reasons. Communication lies at the heart of many contemporary theories of sentencing. The retributive theories that have become so pervasive across Western jurisdictions are essentially communicative theories of sentencing. The just deserts perspective espoused by von Hirsch (1993), for example, is concerned with communicating a message to the offender by means of the severity of the sentence imposed. According to the just deserts model, a sentence conveys a message of disapprobation to the offender, and the severity of the sentence represents the means by which the measure of legal censure is expressed. But the communication is not a single message conveyed from a legal authority to an offender. The message of legal censure treats the offender as a person capable of moral decisions, and creates the opportunity (even if in practice declined) for the offender to respond, by acknowledging the harm caused and accepting responsibility for the offence.

The sentence also carries a communication for the victim of the crime. The imposition of a sanction represents official recognition that this individual has been wronged (see Sebba 1996: ch. 7, for further discussion of the implications of desert-based sentencing theories for crime victims). By permitting a victim to submit a VIS, the sentencing process opens up another avenue of communication: between the victim and the offender. Victim impact is also relevant to other retributive theories. Duff argues that criminal punishment should be understood (and is justified) as 'a communicative, penitential process that aims to persuade offenders to recognize and repent the wrongs they have done, to reform themselves, and so to reconcile themselves with those they have wronged' (2001: 175). Recognition of wrongfulness and repentance is a more likely outcome of a sentencing hearing in which the impact of the crime is described directly by the victim, rather than through the words of a proxy, such as a prosecutor (Herman 2003; Petrucci 2002). No relationship exists between the prosecution and the offender. However, one has been created between the offender and the victim as a result of the offence. Moreover, for many crimes of violence a social relationship between the two parties will have pre-dated the commission of the crime.

Forms of reciprocal communication

In contrast to the conventional view of VISs as offering victims a means of communicating exclusively with the sentencing judge, we argue that the VIS can promote *reciprocal* communication: between the victim and the judge, as well as between the victim and the offender. The first form of communication is familiar to all; the second, however, is equally important and should be considered in scholarly debates and policy formulation.

Communication between the court and the crime victim

The VIS provides a way for the victim to communicate with the court. However, the VIS also creates an opportunity for the court to communicate State recognition of the harm that victims have suffered. This is not simply a message of sympathy towards an injured party, but recognition that these individuals have been *wronged* (see von Hirsch 1993). Moreover, if the victim is present in court, the sentencing judge has the opportunity to speak directly to the victim of the crime, and to provide State recognition of harm he or she has suffered. Members of the judiciary appear aware of their power to recognise victims as the injured person, and that referring to the VIS or citing victims' own words may further enhance victims' sense of being recognised.[13] Judges appreciate the therapeutic value that such recognition has for victims and often make use of it in court. A survey of judges in Canada found that two-thirds of the respondents availed themselves of the opportunity to address the victim if he or she was present at the sentencing hearing (Roberts and Edgar 2006). Even if the victim was not present, judges stated that they often incorporated reference to the VIS in their reasons for sentence.

Likewise, judges in Australia stated that, whenever possible, they referred to the VIS in their sentencing remarks. They were cognisant of the positive impact that quoting victims' words has on victim satisfaction with justice and that using the victim's own words in sentencing signifies court recognition and hence validation of the harm sustained by victims (Erez and Rogers 1999). Victim advocates also confirm the satisfaction that victims express when their input is quoted by the judge in sentencing remarks (Erez 1999). Research with crime victims in Canada has also demonstrated that victims appreciate being recognised in this manner. This research has found that acknowledgement by the judge of the contents of the statements was greatly appreciated by crime victims (Meredith and Paquette 2001).[14]

Communication between victims and offenders

In a traditional sentencing hearing, victims and offenders have few opportunities to communicate with one another. Communication is practically impossible because they are seated in separate areas of the courtroom. The opportunity arises only if one of the two parties gives evidence, delivers a VIS, or addresses the court prior to the imposition of sentence. For those cases in which the court attempts to achieve 'restoration' between the victim and offender (by imposing a sentence with restorative goals), an opportunity to advance restoration or reconciliation is thereby lost.

Encouraging communication in open court between the victim and the offender is a way of achieving some of the benefits of victim–offender reconciliation programmes that have existed for decades. At the heart of these programmes lies the idea that victims can communicate their feelings directly to offenders, who can then have an opportunity to accept responsibility and express remorse directly to the victim. Such exchanges are of mutual benefit to the two parties.[15] However, many victims are reluctant to become involved in such meetings, in part because they do not wish to abandon the formal and protective setting of the courtroom for a setting in which they may feel vulnerable or subjected to pressure. The communication of victim impact information in open court permits hesitant victims to express their feelings without the necessity of a private meeting with the offender.

The limited opportunity for communicative interaction between the victim and the offender underlines the importance of allowing the victim to present the impact information directly to the court by means of a VIS and/or an oral presentation of the statement. The victim is ideally situated to sensitise the offender to the consequences of the crime. Only some offenders are going to be moved by VISs, and research has shown that some offenders have little or no capacity for empathy (e.g. Herman 2003). However, hearing victims describe their suffering and harm may make a difference to the future behaviour of certain offenders. Encouraging this kind of communication should not transform the sentencing hearing into a tripartite proceeding, nor would it undermine the central assumption of the adversarial system, namely that a crime is committed against the State and not a private party (Talbert 1988).

One of the leading judgements that relates to the use of victim impact information in Canada makes an important point when it notes that: 'the words of the victim of a crime might well serve to educate the offender as to the effects of his or her criminal behaviour' (R v. Redhead). The relationship between the prosecutor and the offender is inherently antagonistic in nature, particularly if the conviction arises as a result of a trial rather than a guilty plea. If the prosecutor delivers the VIS, the offender may well be less willing to listen, accept the accuracy of the statement or appreciate its significance. The offender may regard the victim impact information simply as a continuation of evidence adduced at trial, or additional information used by the prosecutor while attempting to secure a harsher disposition. The prosecutor is a legal professional discharging his or her professional duty to represent the State. For defendants, this role may dilute the unique character of the VIS and strip the statement of its human qualities, and hence its impact.

On the other hand, the victim is dissociated from the prosecution – except as a witness – and carries no legal authority to secure conviction or establish the level of punishment. The victim is a 'civilian' in a highly professionalised legal environment. Like offenders, victims are generally unfamiliar with judicial proceedings and usually lack the necessary training to understand specialised terminology or follow legal manoeuvres. In this regard, offenders and victims may have more in common with each other than with the legal professionals who represent their interests or litigate their case. Research has confirmed that many victims share the same social characteristics as their offenders (e.g. Fattah 1992; Bottoms and Costello, Chapter 5, this volume), adding to the likelihood that direct appeal by the victim to the offender may be better understood, thereby enhancing the effectiveness of the communication.

Empirical evidence relating to victims' wishes to communicate

Although past research has not focused specifically on the communicative elements of the VIS, several studies have revealed that victims have an interest in communicating with more participants than simply the sentencing judge. Why do victims elect to submit a VIS? What do they hope to achieve by completing the statement, and in some cases delivering it orally at a sentencing hearing? A number of studies have asked victims questions such as these. This research also helps to resolve the question of whether VISs fall into the punitive or non-punitive categories proposed by Roach (1999a).

The results suggest that no single objective is uppermost in victims' minds. As with punishment in general (see Orth 2002) multiple goals for participating at sentencing exist. VISs serve different purposes for different people and, for some, meet several objectives. Differences in the specific questions posed to victims render it difficult to make comparisons across studies. In addition, since victims' opinions on this issue are generally solicited *after* they have been given information about the programme in their jurisdiction, their views may in part reflect the 'official' objectives described in materials provided to them or what they have been told by victim services personnel. Nevertheless, victims' responses across studies do reveal some consistent trends.

First, there appears to be more support for the expressive rather than the utilitarian function. Thus Leverick, Chalmers, and Duff (2007: Table

6.14) found that the most frequently cited reason for making a statement was expressive rather than instrumental. Indeed, this study of victims in Scotland provides strong support for the expressive function of victim input, as fully half the participants who had submitted a statement acknowledged that they did not know whether, or to what degree, the court had considered their statement, yet they were still intending to submit a statement in the future in the event of further victimisation.

A survey of victims in South Australia found that communicating with the offender was the most frequent reason offered by victims for completing a VIS (Justice Strategy Unit 2000: Table 11). Similarly, more than half (60 per cent) of the victims interviewed by Hoyle *et al.* (1998: 26) cited expressive reasons for submitting a statement. Erez, Roeger and Morgan found that only five per cent of their victims sought to influence the sentence imposed on the offender – suggesting expressive and communicative motives were more important (1994: 49). Results from Canadian research reveal that victims were divided between wishing to communicate a message to the offender, wanting to perform a 'civic duty' and to ensure that 'justice was done' (Giliberti 1990: 14). Miller reports that all the participants in her qualitative study of sexual assault victims 'explained that they had been primarily motivated in the expressive purpose of the VIS, namely the use of the victim VIS *to communicate to offenders and to judges'* (2008: 33; emphasis added). Similarly, the most frequently cited reasons for submitting a statement among victims in another national study in Canada were to help the court understand the effect of the crime *and* to make the offender understand the effect of the crime. One of these two reasons was cited by more than 90 per cent of the sample (Prairie Research Associates 2005: Table 28).

Research in Ohio (Erez and Tontodonato 1992), Australia (Erez *et al.* 1994) and Canada (Giliberti 1990; Meredith and Paquette 2001) has found that many victims cited communicating with the offender a sense of the harm inflicted as a reason for submitting impact statements. The comments of two victims cited by Hoyle *et al.* (1998: 26) illustrate victims' interest in communicating with more parties than just the sentencing judge. One said that 'I wanted to show the defendant that what they did does affect someone's life'; the other hoped that the statement would be read aloud 'so that all his friends and family . . . would know what I had suffered'. Similar findings emerged from qualitative research in Canada (see Young and Roberts 2001).

Encouraging communication between offenders and victims

Offenders typically say little during a sentencing hearing, and there are several reasons for their reticence in this respect. In some instances, they may have been advised by their counsel to remain silent. Offenders may be apprehensive about speaking in a public forum, or they may feel shamed by the experience. Many offenders decline to speak even if given the opportunity by the court before sentence is pronounced.[16] In most criminal courts, the imposition of sentence follows immediately after sentencing submissions, and the offender may well feel intimidated by the formality of the proceedings. Offenders also may feel that their 'opportunity to speak' is more an invitation to express remorse or to disavow any further offending; courts have neither the time nor the interest at this point to entertain explanations or exculpatory statements from the offender.

However, the offender may have other messages to communicate, including making a statement of apology (Petrucci 2002), and these messages need to be heard if the sentencing process is to live up to its claim to constitute a 'hearing' of all interested participants. Indeed, it is vital for the moral standing of the sentencing court to listen to the offender if the message of censure is to be received. Sentencing from a desert-based perspective involves treating offenders as moral agents, capable of making moral decisions; as such these agents need to be heard at the time at which legal punishment is imposed.

There may well be grounds for mitigation, or partial exculpation, that the offender wishes to communicate to the court, and possibly to the victim if he or she is present. Many offenders can cite background factors – such as social deprivation – that may have precipitated or contributed to the incident giving rise to the conviction. Circumstances such as these may lessen the offender's level of culpability. Traditionally, defence counsel places this information before the court; nevertheless, there may be reasons for encouraging the offender to speak for him or herself at this point.

Crime victims are seldom in attendance at the sentencing hearing. One explanation is that there is little incentive for them to be present. Having completed a VIS, the victim assumes the role of passive onlooker, listening to a legal professional summarise their experience in a way that may strip the account of its significance or uniqueness.[17] The prosecutor may well focus on the elements of the VIS likely to attract the attention of the judge, or to secure a harsher disposition. The victim, however, may wish to place the emphasis elsewhere. Ironically, the only opportunity, in some jurisdictions, for the victim to address the court directly will arise if he or she is cross-examined by a defence counsel on the contents of the VIS. But cross-examination is unlikely to provide the forum for communication with the judge or the offender. Indeed, although it happens rarely (Erez et al. 1994; Roberts and Edgar 2006),[18] cross-examination is a difficult experience for crime victims, and often exacerbates their distress.

Some victims may decline the opportunity to communicate the impact of the crime to the court, preferring to delegate this task to the prosecutor. Other victims may use the opportunity to criticise or censure the offender. This is outside the remit of all victim impact schemes, and represents an encroachment on the court's jurisdiction. Under the adversarial system, only the court holds the authority and occupies the disinterested position to express legal censure and impose appropriate punishment. If the victim pursues this route, either in a written VIS, or oral delivery of the impact information, the court has the discretion to intervene or prevent the communication. Similarly, if the offender uses the occasion to impugn the victim in some way, or undermine the legitimacy of the court, the court should react. The decorum of the sentencing hearing needs to be protected in order that *legitimate communications* may thrive. In most cases, the court authority is sufficient to prevent inappropriate exchanges.

There is an important restorative element to these reciprocal communications. Restoration of victim and offender, or the restoration of the offender to the community against whom he has offended, cannot be imposed, but only facilitated by the court. Encouraging the communication of victim impact information therefore establishes one of the preconditions of restorative justice: awareness of the consequences of the crime to the victim. Direct communication by the victim about the harm he or she sustained may also encourage an apology from the defendant. Research indicates that victims can be empowered by their ability to confer or withhold forgiveness, and that aggressive feelings on the part of the victim are likely to be attenuated following genuine requests for forgiveness (Petrucci 2002.)

Communicating a broader message to the community

Finally, Szmania and Gracyalny (2006) draw attention to attempts at communication that reach beyond the courtroom. These researchers found that crime victims in their study also expressed views to the larger community. This suggests that there may well be a communicative function which includes a much wider constituency than simply the individuals present in court at the time of sentencing. A high-profile case in Canada provides another illustration of this broader form of communication. The parents of a young woman who had been shot on the streets of Toronto presented an impact statement in which they appeared to wish to sensitise the community to the fact that the 'people of Toronto have been forever changed by the Boxing Day shootings'. It is noteworthy that whatever their private feelings regarding the sentence that should be imposed, the public communication contained no recommendation to the court.[19]

Victim Impact Panels

Additional insight into the benefits that may accrue from permitting victims to express themselves can be gained from an examination of the experience to date with Victim Impact Panels (VIPs). Such panels are generally constituted as a court sanction in certain jurisdictions for perpetrators of domestic violence or for drunk drivers. Victim volunteers are brought together in a small group, to encounter a larger group of offenders (excluding the specific offender in their case). The victims (or family members of victims who were killed) describe the effect that the perpetrator's criminal conduct has had upon their lives. It therefore represents a court sanction designed simultaneously to benefit the victim and educate the offender. An experimental study of VIPs involving wife batterers reported a high level of victim satisfaction following the panel experience (Fulkerson 2001). The panel's aim was to provide a non-confrontational setting for victims as 'a means to express their feelings' and 'to provide the offenders with an understanding of some of the consequences of their behavior' (Fulkerson 2001: 358).

Although VIPs are not the same as the submission of a VIS at sentencing – the two differ in terms of the forum of presenting the crime impact, and in relation to the possibility of influencing court outcomes – the results of the study are relevant to the issue of communication between victims and offenders. The overwhelming majority (85 per cent) of participants stated that they would recommend the use of VIPs as part of the disposition in domestic violence cases. Most (73 per cent) of the participants also thought that the VIP had been a positive experience (Fulkerson 2001: 365). This high level of victim satisfaction was reported despite the fact that the experience served no instrumental function with respect to the sentence imposed. These findings underline the importance of the communicative versus the impact function of victim reactions.

Improving victim satisfaction with impact statements

We conclude this section by addressing the question of victim satisfaction. A number of studies have attempted to determine whether victims are more satisfied if they submit a statement, and the results are generally positive. A recent review of all such research projects concluded that victims appear to benefit from the experience (Roberts 2009). The earliest studies found little 'lift' in victim satisfaction for individuals who submitted a statement. However, recent studies have shown more positive outcomes. For example, the Scottish study reported by Leverick, Chalmers and Duff (2007: 42) found that the vast majority of victims who submitted a VIS had concluded that it was the right decision. Perhaps a more telling outcome variable is whether victims who deliver a statement would do so if they were victimised again. Leverick *et al.* (2007) note that two-thirds of victims in Scotland who had submitted a VIS reported that they 'definitely would' submit a statement again in the event of further victimisation – clearly a positive outcome. Moreover, among victims who had *not* submitted a statement, over half (57 per cent) stated that they would submit a statement if they were victimised again, compared to only one third who predicted that they would not submit in the future (Leverick *et al.* 2007: Table 6.28). An earlier study in England and Wales found that fully three-quarters of the participating victims said that they would submit another statement if they were victimised again (Hoyle *et al.* 1998: 33). Similar findings emerge in other jurisdictions (see Roberts 2009 for a review).

The principal cause of dissatisfaction is misunderstanding about the purpose of VISs. If victims expect their statements to have an appreciable impact on the sentence imposed, or their expressed desires for particular dispositions to be followed, disappointment and resentment will surely ensue. This suggests that reorienting VIS regimes towards a more expressive model may well enhance victim satisfaction, or at least minimise the likelihood that victims will leave the court disappointed because their unrealistic expectations have not been met.

Objections to permitting the communication of victim impact

Some of the objections to allowing victims to express their views at sentencing, or to provide the right for VIS in the first place, are based on the erroneous assumption that the primary purpose of such statements is to influence the sentence (e.g. Sanders *et al.* 2001) or an unsubstantiated fear that such statements may lead to more severe sentencing (Hills and Thomson 1999; Fattah 1997). There are no obvious objections in this regard to encouraging victim–offender communication at sentencing. Such communication is unlikely to undermine the principles of sentencing or to affect the quantum of the sentence imposed. However, there are some practical objections, and it is to these that we now turn.

First, encouraging the victim to communicate impact information to the court and to the offender may well consume additional court time. This is particularly true if the victim wishes to deliver the VIS orally. A judge can read a written victim's statement in seconds; allowing the victim to deliver the same information orally will take longer. However, it is important to remember that, in many jurisdictions, victims have exercised these rights without imposing an undue burden on court schedules. The solution adopted in some jurisdictions is to devote more resources and more court time to the most serious personal injury offences (if the victim has indicated an interest in submitting a VIS). The experience in many US jurisdictions, some of which involved high-profile offenders or televised crimes, has demonstrated that allowing victims to present their VIS does not cause delays, nor is it associated with taking undue amount of court time (see also Erez and Rogers (1999) for the Australian experience).

A second possible objection is that VISs may influence judges to impose harsher sentences. As previously indicated, this outcome has not been supported by research in various jurisdictions. Judges are trained to ignore testimony that has no probative value, and they are not easily moved by the affective demeanour of victims.[20] On some, albeit rare occasions, offenders direct abuse at the prosecutor, the court, or even victims, yet there is no supporting evidence that such emotional outbursts provoke the presiding judge to impose a more punitive sentence. Judges are surely capable of distinguishing legally relevant from irrelevant information, whether contained in VISs or in offenders' communications.

Conclusions

The right to participate in the process of justice, including the right to attend criminal proceedings and to be heard at various points in the criminal justice process, is important for crime victims (Office of Victims of Crime 1998). Most victims are interested in participating in the justice process and report wanting to tell, in their own words, their stories about how the crime has affected them (Kilpatrick, Beatty and Howley 1998). Court procedures rarely provide such an opportunity; rather, the court requires them to respond to a series of questions, without being able to construct a coherent and meaningful narrative (Herman 2003). VISs represent a means of providing victims with a voice at sentencing.

In this chapter we have focused on the communicative value of the VIS in order to highlight the role of the statement as reciprocal communication and the compatibility of this function of the VIS with current sentencing theories. We have also furnished examples of court-sanctioned procedures in which reciprocal communication of crime impact has been shown to have positive effects on victims and offenders. We have challenged the conclusion that the communication of crime impact by victims is bound to be associated with victims' dissatisfaction, showing the benefits inherent in being heard and listened to, regardless of the outcome. While there is a persistent belief that VISs and the right of allocution 'can only lead to harsher sentences, longer terms of imprisonment and delayed release of prisoners' (Fattah 1997: 268), research has not demonstrated that victim input at sentencing consistently or inevitably results in harsher sentencing (see Roberts 2009, for a review of relevant research). The preceding discussion carries practical implications for the way in which victim impact information should be used in the sentencing process. First, information provided to victims by victim service personnel or prosecutors about the purpose of the VIS should emphasise the expressive and communicative aspects of the VIS. If victims are encouraged to view the statement as an exercise in communication for the court and for the offender, they are less likely to be disenchanted than if they are encouraged to see the statement as a way of influencing the sentencing decision. Second, victims of serious personal injury offences who intend to submit a VIS should be permitted to deliver the statement orally at the time of sentencing. Oral presentation of the VIS may delay sentencing and create a need for adjournment, as on many occasions the victim may not be ready to appear to make the statement. This should not create an undue hardship unless the offender is in custody, in which case the court will consider whether the interests of justice are best served by adjourning the sentencing until the victim is able to deliver the statement in court. Third, the most important actor in the process – the sentencing judge – should take steps to ensure that communication is possible, wherever this seems appropriate. Thus the offender should be encouraged to read the statement, and to respond prior to the imposition of sentence.[21]

Research findings about the benefits for victims and offenders of reciprocal communication such as those discussed in this chapter high-light the value of communication and of providing victims with the opportunity to exercise their allocution right. Concerns that victims will become dissatisfied as a result of presenting the VIS can be addressed by ensuring that victims are informed about the purpose of the statement and its role in criminal proceedings (e.g. by prosecutors or those who reorient victims in the direction of communicating with the offender in addition to the court).[22] Judges can also validate victim input by citing or referring to the content of the VIS in their sentencing remarks. Moving away from an approach which emphasises the instrumental function and towards the expressive function will redirect the concept and practice of the VIS and bring it back to its original course – providing victims with a voice in the sentencing process.

Notes

1   This model has been offered as a complement, or in some cases replacement, to the traditional criminal justice model (e.g. Braithwaite 1999). The similarity between restorative justice and therapeutic jurisprudence in terms of its emphasis on empathy for human survivors of legal conflicts has been noted (Braithwaite 2002). Both traditions incorporate a commitment to legal proceedings that are restorative and are therefore relevant to discussions regarding the VIS as an expressive and communicative tool in court.

2   In this chapter we discuss only the VIS, which is a written or oral statement made by the victim prior to sentencing, describing the impact of the crime on his or her life. The victim allocution right refers to making an oral statement in court prior to sentencing. We do not include in our discussion the victim statement of opinion (VSO), which allows victims to provide their opinion about an appropriate sentence (the VSO is practised in only a small number of jurisdictions and is generally not considered as a widely accepted part of the victim rights package). We see clear dangers for the sentencing process if victims are encouraged or allowed to suggest specific sentences, except in very exceptional circumstances (see discussion in Roberts 2003). In many of the discussions about the VIS, however, authors use VIS and VSO interchangeably, and occasionally critics challenge one by referring to the effects of the other.

3   We do not deal here with the use of victim impact evidence in capital trials. It is clear that the role of impact statements raises a very different set of issues,

not least of which is the nature of the decision-maker, namely a jury charged with deciding whether to impose the death penalty rather than life imprisonment.

4 It should be noted that research in various jurisdictions has demonstrated that filing VISs does not generally lead to aggregate increases in sentence severity (see review in Roberts 2009). Probation officers in California reported that the contents of allocution statements were not always as expected and that they had heard victims' pleas for leniency that resulted in a more lenient sentence (Villmoare and Neto 1987: 55). Research on mock jurors suggests that the use of VISs in capital cases is associated with mock jurors' imposition of death sentences (e.g. Myers and Arbuthnot 1999), although later research indicated that mock jurors were influenced by the degree of harm presented in the VIS (a legally relevant consideration), but not by the demeanour, or emotionality level, of the victim (Myers et al. 2002). In any case, these findings pertain to mock jurors in capital cases and are not necessarily applicable to judges trying cases in court.

5 Research on this issue has also shown that allowing victim input did not result in substantially longer trials or sentencing hearings, nor in delays or special burdens on court resources (e.g. Erez and Rogers 1999; Kelly and Erez 1997).

6 The time was ripe for arguing that victims can help the court by providing input about the harm they sustained: the 1970s were characterised by disenchantment with, on the one hand, the rehabilitative model of punishment (which was associated with sentence disparity), and with the rise of the 'just deserts' model, which calls for punishment based on harm and culpability. Thus, the idea that victims, who suffered the brunt of the harm, can provide information to the court about the harm they suffered seemed logical and acceptable to the legal profession (for details see Erez and Sebba 1999).

7 The emerging field of therapeutic jurisprudence focuses on the therapeutic benefits and antitherapeutic consequences associated with engaging with legal proceedings. It examines how the law or justice interventions, remedies and procedures can be applied in such a way as to support, or at least not harm, the psychological well-being of those they affect (e.g. Wexler 2000). Victim rights (including providing input) are of interest in this regard (e.g. Wiebe 1996; Herman 2003; see also Erez, Kilchling and Wemmers forthcoming).

8 R.A. Duff (2001) makes an important distinction between 'expression' and 'communication', with the latter connoting an attempt to engage another party, a motive absent from mere expression. In our view, the VIS involves both expressive and communicative functions, although we will use the terms interchangeably throughout this chapter.

9 These principles were codified in Canada in 1996 and New Zealand in 2002.

10 Available at www.gcvwu.com/victimimpactstatements.htm.

11 Much of the criticism against the VIS is that it presumably leads victims to expect that their input will affect the sentence and increase sentence severity. Representing the VIS as a means to address the defendant may have beneficial effects in this regard.

12 Unreported case; see Globe and Mail, 20 June 2002, page A3.

13 The report by the Office of Victims of Crime (1998: 108) recognises that 'It is significant for victims' healing that the judge acknowledge at the time of sentencing that victims have been injured [and] solicit specific information from victims on the crime's impact on their lives . . .'

14 There may well be an incidental benefit associated with judicial recognition of the harm caused to the victim. This may attenuate victims' criticism of the judge, and of the sentencing process in those cases in which a sentence is imposed the severity of which falls short of the victim's expectations.

15 A pertinent example from the international scene about public presentation and acknowledgement of personal suffering that may bring both individual and national healing is the Truth and Reconciliation Commissions (see Andrews 2003).

16 In several jurisdictions the duty of the court to permit the offender to speak to sentence has been codified. For example, s. 726 of the Canadian Criminal Code states that 'Before determining the sentence to be imposed, the court shall ask whether the offender, if present, has anything to say.'

17 An experienced prosecutor may have read hundreds of VISs, and this may well diminish the impact on him or her, the way he or she presents the statement to the court and, subsequently, the significance of the statement for the court (e.g., Erez and Rogers 1999).

18 Research suggests that the reason for the rarity of cross-examination of victims on their VIS is that defence counsel do not wish to antagonise the court or risk increasing sympathy for the victim, and thereby attract a more severe penalty.

19 See *Globe and Mail*, 8 April 2009; available at www.theglobeandmail.com/servlet/story

20 As previously stated, research on mock jurors has demonstrated that their decisions were not influenced by the affective demeanour of victims (Myers *et al.* 2002). It is even less likely that such demeanour would influence judges.

21 Recently, Hoyle (forthcoming) has suggested that the VIS be read in open court after sentence has been imposed. This proposal certainly strips the statement of any power to influence the sentence imposed, and is therefore consistent with the non-instrumental perspective we have advocated here. However, we feel that this sequencing will also denude the VIS of much of its significance. The offender may well be less inclined to listen to the victim's views if the business of the court has been concluded. Most importantly, however, presenting the statement after sentencing assumes that VISs have no informational value for the purposes of sentencing. Research with legal professionals, and in particular judges, has clearly demonstrated that VISs contain legally relevant information for a sentencing court (see Roberts 2009 for a review).

22 Victims should also be given information on the range of prevailing sentences for various crimes and on the factors that judges consider in determining a punishment. Such explanations (possibly in the form of a brochure) will help victims better understand the outcome in their case, thus preventing disappointment (Erez 1999).

References

Andrews, M. (2000) 'Victims' Rights, Defendants' rights and Criminal Procedure', in A. Crawford and J. Goodey (eds), *Integrating a Victim Perspective in Criminal Justice: International Debates*. Aldershot: Dartmouth.

Andrews, M. (2003) 'Grand National Narratives and the Project of Truth Commissions: a comparative analysis', *Media, Culture & Society*, 25: 45–65.

Ashworth, A. (2000) 'Victims' rights, defendants' rights and criminal procedure', in A. Crawford and J. Goodey (eds), *Integrating a Victim Perspective within Criminal Justice*. Aldershot: Ashgate.

Braithwaite, J. (1999) 'Restorative Justice: Assessing optimistic and pessimistic accounts', in M. Tonry (ed.), *Crime and Justice: A Review of Research*. Chicago: University of Chicago Press.

Braithwaite, J. (2002) 'Restorative Justice and Therapeutic Jurisprudence', *Criminal Law Bulletin*, 38(2): 244–62.

Duff, R.A. (2001) *Punishment, Communication, and Community*. New York: Oxford University Press.

Elias, R. (1993) *Victims Still*. Newberry Park, CA: Sage.

Erez, E. (1994) 'Victim Participation in Sentencing: And the Debate Goes On . . .', *International Review of Victimology*, 3: 17–32.

Erez, E. (1999) 'Who's Afraid of the Big Bad Victim: Victim Impact Statements as Victim Empowerment and Enhancement of Justice', *Criminal Law Review*, July: 545–56.

Erez, E. (2004) 'Victim Voice, Impact Statements and Sentencing: Integrating Restorative Justice and Therapeutic Jurisprudence Principles in Adversarial Proceedings', *Criminal Law Bulletin*, Sept.–Oct.: 483–500.

Erez, E., Kilchling, M. and Wemmers, J. (forthcoming) *Victim Participation in Justice: Therapeutic Jurisprudence Perspectives*. Oxford: Hart Publications.

Erez, E., Roeger, L. and Morgan, F. (1994) *Victim Impact Statements in South Australia: An Evaluation*. Adelaide: South Australian Attorney-General's Department.

Erez, E. and Rogers L. (1999) 'Victim Impact Statements and Sentencing Outcomes and Processes: The Perspectives of Legal Professionals', *British Journal of Criminology*, 39: 216–39.

Erez, E. and Sebba, L. (1999) 'From Individualization of the Offender to Individualization of the Victim', in W. Laufer and F. Adler (eds), *Advances in Criminological Theory*. New Brunswick, NJ: Transaction.

Erez. E. and Tontodonato, P. (1992) 'Victim Participation in Justice and Satisfaction with Justice', *Justice Quarterly*, 9: 393–427.

Fattah, E. (1992) *Understanding Criminal Victimization*. Cliffside, NJ: Prentice-Hall.

Fattah, E. (1997) 'Towards a Victim Policy Aimed at Healing, Not Suffering', in R.C. Davis, L.J. Lurigio and W. Skogan (eds), *Victims of Crime*. Thousand Oaks, CA: Sage.

Fulkerson, A. (2001) 'The use of victim impact panels in domestic violence cases: A restorative justice approach', *Contemporary Justice Review*, 4: 355–68.

Giliberti, C. (1990) *Victim Impact Statements in Canada. Volume 7*. Ottawa: Research and Development Directorate, Department of Justice Canada.

Henderson J. (1985) 'The Wrongs of Victim Rights', *Stanford Law Review*, 37: 937–1021.

Herman, J.L. (2003) 'The Mental Health of Crime Victims: Impact of Legal Intervention', *Journal of Traumatic Stress*, 16: 159–66.

Hills, A.M and Thomson, D.M. (1999) 'Should victim impact influence sentences? Understanding the community's justice reasoning', *Behavioral Sciences & the Law*, 17: 661–71.

Home Office (2002) *Making a Victim Personal Statement*. London: Home Office.

Hoyle, C. (forthcoming) 'Empowerment through Emotion: The Use and Abuse of Victim Impact Evidence', in E. Erez. M. Kilchling and J. Wemmers, *Victim*

Participation in Justice: Therapeutic Jurisprudence Perspectives. Oxford: Hart Publications.

Hoyle, C., Cape, E., Morgan, R. and Sanders, A. (1998) *Evaluation of the 'One Stop Shop' and Victim Statement Pilot Projects.* London: Home Office, Research Development and Statistics Directorate.

Justice Strategy Unit (2000) *Victims of Crime Review. Report 2. Survey of Crime Victims.* Available at: http://www.voc.sa.gov.au

Kelly, D. and Erez, E. (1997) 'Victim Participation in the Criminal Justice System', in R.C. Davis, L.J. Lurigio and W. Skogan (eds), *Victims of Crime.* Thousand Oaks, CA: Sage.

Kilpatrick, D.G., Beatty, D. and Howley, S.S. (1998) *The Rights of Crime Victims – Does Legal Protection Make a Difference?* National Institute of Justice. Research in Brief. US Department of Justice, Office of Justice Programs. Washington, DC: US Government Printing Office.

Leverick, F., Chalmers, J. and Duff, P. (2007) *An Evaluation of the Pilot Victim Statement Schemes in Scotland.* Available at: www.scotland.gov.uk/publications.

Meredith, C. and Paquette, C. (2001) *Summary Report on Victim Impact Statement Focus Groups.* Ottawa: Policy Centre for Victim Issues, Department of Justice Canada.

Miller, K. (2008) *Empowering Victims: the Use of the Victim Impact Statement in the case of sexual assault in Nova Scotia: the perspective of victims and victim services staff.* Toronto: Centre of Criminology, University of Toronto.

Mosteller, R.P. (1998) 'Victims' Rights and the Constitution: moving from guaranteeing participatory rights to benefiting the prosecution', *St Mary Law Journal,* 29: 1053–65.

Myers B. and Arbuthnot, J. (1999) 'The Effects of Victim Impact Evidence on the Verdicts and Sentencing Judgments of Mock Jurors', *Journal of Offender Rehabilitation,* 29(3/4): 95–112.

Myers, B., Lynn S.J. and Arbuthnot, J. (2002) 'Victim Impact Testimony and Juror Judgments: the effects of harm information and witness demeanor', *Journal of Applied Social Psychology,* 32: 2393–412.

Office of Victims of Crime (1998) *New Directions from the Field: victims' rights and services for the 21st Century.* Washington, DC: U.S. Department of Justice.

Orth, U. (2002) Secondary Victimization of Crime Victims by Criminal Proceedings. *Social Justice Research,* 15: 313–26.

Petrucci, C.J. (2002) 'Apology in Criminal Justice Setting: evidence for including apology as an additional component in the legal system', *Behavioral Sciences and the Law,* 20: 337–62.

Prairie Research Associates (2005) *Multisite Survey of Victims of Crime and Criminal Justice Professionals across Canada.* Ottawa: Department of Justice Canada, Policy Centre for Victim Issues.

R v. Gabriel (1999) 26 *Criminal Reports* (5th) 364 (Ont. Sup. Ct.).

R v. Redhead [2001] BCJ No. 1810 (Prov. Ct.).

Roach, K. (1999a) 'Four Models of the Criminal Process', *The Journal of Criminal Law & Criminology,* 89: 671–716.

Roach, K. (1999b) *Due Process and Victims' Rights. The new law and politics of criminal justice.* Toronto: University of Toronto Press.

Roberts, J.V. (2002) 'Determining Parole Eligibility Dates for Life Prisoners in Canada', *Punishment & Society,* 4: 103–14.

Roberts, J.V. (2003) 'Victim Impact Statements and the Sentencing Process: recent developments and research findings', *Criminal Law Quarterly*, 47: 365–96.

Roberts, J.V. (2009) 'Listening to Crime Victims: evaluating victim input into sentencing and parole', in M. Tonry (ed.), *Crime and Justice. A Review of Research.* Volume 38. Chicago: University of Chicago Press.

Roberts, J.V. and Edgar, A. (2006) *Victim Impact Statements at Sentencing: judicial experiences and perceptions.* Ottawa: Policy Centre for Victim Issues, Department of Justice Canada.

Roberts, J.V. and Hough, M. (2005) *Understanding Public Attitudes to Criminal Justice.* Maidenhead: Open University Press.

Rogers, D., Laster, K. and Inglis, N. (1994) 'Victims of Efficiency: tracking victim impact information through the system in Victoria, Australia', *International Review of Victimology*, 3: 95–110.

Sanders, A. (2002) 'Victim Participation in an Exclusionary Criminal Justice System', in C. Hoyle and R. Young (eds), *New Visions of Crime Victims.* Oxford: Hart Publishing.

Sanders, A., Hoyle, C., Morgan, R. and Cape, E. (2001) 'Victim Impact Statements: don't work, can't work', *Criminal Law Review*, 447–58.

Sebba, L. (1996) *Third Parties: Victims and the Criminal Justice System.* Columbus, OH: Ohio State University Press.

Stalans, L.S. and Diamond, S. (1990) 'Formation and Change in Lay Evaluations of Criminal Sentencing: misperception and discontent', *Law and Human Behavior*, 14: 199–214.

Szmania, S. and Gracyalny, M. (2006) 'Addressing the Court, the Offender, and the Community: a communication analysis of victim impact statements in a non-capital sentencing hearing', *International Review of Criminology*, 13: 231–49.

Talbert, P.A. (1988) 'The Relevance of Victim Impact Statements to Criminal Sentencing Decisions', *UCLA Law Review*, 36: 199–232.

US Department of Justice (1998) *New Directions from the Field: victims' rights and services for the 21st century.* Washington, DC: US Department of Justice.

US Department of Justice (2002) 'Victim Input Into Plea Agreements', *Legal Series Bulletin Number 7.* Washington, DC: NCJ 189188.

Villmoare E. and Neto, V.V. (1987) *Victim Appearances at Sentencing Hearings Under the California Bill of Rights.* Washington, DC: US Department of Justice, Institute of Justice.

von Hirsch, A. (1993) *Censure and Sanctions.* Oxford: Clarendon Press.

Wexler, D.B. (2000) 'Practicing Therapeutic Jurisprudence: psycholegal soft spots and strategies', in D.P. Stolle, D.B. Wexler and B.J. Winick (eds), *Practicing Therapeutic Jurisprudence: law as a helping profession.* Durham, NC: North Carolina Academic Press.

Wiebe, R.P. (1996) 'The Mental Health Implications of Crime Victims' Rights', in D.B. Wexler and B.J. Winick (eds), *Law in a Therapeutic Key: developments in therapeutic jurisprudence.* Durham, NC: North Carolina Academic Press.

Young, A. (1993) 'Two Scales of Justice: a reply', *Criminal Law Quarterly*, 35: 355–75.

Young, A. and Roberts, J.V. (2001) *Research on the role of the victim in the criminal process.* Ottawa: Department of Justice Canada.

Chapter 10

Victim input at parole: probative or prejudicial?

Nicola Padfield and Julian V. Roberts

Should crime victims have a right to participate in the decision to release an offender from prison? If victims are given a role in the decision to grant or deny parole, what should be the nature of their input? Can victims make a contribution to more effective parole decision-making? Is victim participation in the release process a natural extension of victim input at other stages of the criminal process? These are some of the difficult questions addressed in this chapter. In light of the ambiguity which surrounds the role of the victim at the sentencing stage of the criminal process, it is hardly surprising that uncertainties exist when it comes to the decision to release an offender from prison.

Early release decisions and victims: general issues

The purposes of sentencing are various and contradictory and so too are the objectives underlying early (conditional) release from prison. One obvious goal of the parole system is to promote the rehabilitation of prisoners – an objective which is usually best achieved by facilitating their reintegration into the community through graduated release with supervision. On the other hand, protection of society – the primary purpose of the correctional system – may necessitate the continued detention of the offender. These twin objectives may well be in conflict. The decision regarding the precise date of the prisoner's release from custody is often hidden from public view, and is little discussed.

Almost all common law jurisdictions allow crime victims to have some input into the sentencing process. In the common law world this is usually accomplished by means of a Victim Impact Statement (VIS)[1] completed by the victim and submitted to the court as evidence at the sentencing hearing. Some US jurisdictions go further than simply allowing evidence of the impact of the crime and permit victims to express an opinion regarding the sentence that should be imposed. Victim input at sentencing may be justified in part by reference to the retributive principle of proportionality; in order to impose a sentence the severity of which is proportional to the seriousness of the crime, courts must hear evidence on the matter. This may emerge from testimony at trial, but far more frequently the source is a submission by the prosecution at sentencing. Victims' rights advocates argue that the victim is best placed to provide impact evidence, and that it should not be placed before the court filtered through the words of a legal professional.

As well as a retributive, 'desert-based' justification, the victim's role can have another important justification: that offenders should make reparation to people affected by their offences. In many civil law systems, the victim has (at least in theory) even greater participatory rights: in Sweden, France and Belgium, for example, where the victim can make him or herself a *partie civile*, the sums awarded by way of compensation to the victim far exceed those normally ordered in common law countries, where compensation orders are usually fixed according to the offender's ability to pay. Finally, claims are made that allowing the victim to submit a VIS, and possibly to deliver the statement orally, carries important benefits for crime victims, without disturbing the fundamental principles of sentencing under an adversarial model of justice (see Erez 1999).

The practice of allowing victim input into sentencing has stimulated a lively debate in many countries (e.g. Sanders *et al.* 2001; Erez 1999; see Roberts 2009 for a review of research), but, as we shall see, there has been less discussion (and little research) regarding decisions to release from (or recall) prisoners to prison. In this chapter we discuss the role of the victim in post-sentence decision-making. Our focus is on parole, but it is vital to recognise that this term has different meanings in different countries. The composition of parole boards varies considerably, as do the procedures followed. For example, considerable variation exists regarding the point in the custodial term at which prisoners become eligible for parole. In addition, there are release programmes besides parole that permit prisoners to serve part of their sentences of custody in the community. Regardless of the nature of the release procedure, the same concerns about the appropriate role for victims apply.

To illustrate our concerns about the role of the victim we examine current arrangements in two common law jurisdictions – England and Wales, and Canada. Where appropriate, we place developments in these jurisdictions in a broader international context. Many States across the US have abolished parole and employ 'flat-time' (no parole) sentences of custody where a prisoner serves every day of the sentence in custody. In England and Wales, parole board decision-making is now restricted to those serving indeterminate sentences and those recalled to prison. In contrast, the parole system in Canada continues to play an important role in the administration of a sentence of imprisonment, as most prisoners become eligible for parole after having served one third of the sentence in prison.

Having described the context of decision-making, we return to two key questions, relating to victim notification and victim input:

1. To what extent should victims be apprised of developments in the progress of the offender, now a prisoner, through the correctional process?

2. Should victims be allowed input into the decisions taken by a conditional release authority such as the Parole Board of England and Wales, or the National Parole Board in Canada?

We attempt to clarify whether increased victim participation at parole represents a belated recognition of legitimate victim interests in the criminal process, or simply another example of populist and potentially punitive justice. Much of the rhetoric of 'victims' rights' is aimed at promoting public (and victims') confidence in the conditional release system, but it should be only one element of the argument. It is our submission that public confidence in release procedures can best be achieved by improving the decision-making process, the supervision of parolees in the community, and by ensuring openness and transparency in decision-making. As Lord Auld's (2001) *Review* noted with respect to sentencing, public confidence should be a *consequence* and not a goal of an open and fair system of legal punishment. But first, we should say something about 'victims' themselves.

Victims' interests and victims' rights in the criminal process

For many victims, the imposition of sentence represents the end of their contact with the criminal justice system.[2] However, some (but by no means all) victims express a desire to be kept apprised of their offender's progress through the prison and probation system. The same individual victim may have evolving attitudes to his or her offender: the dangers of generalisations have been well catalogued elsewhere (see Chapter 3 by Reeves and Dunn in this volume). Unsurprisingly, the interests of many victims focus upon the issue of compensation; a few may also seek to influence the decision whether or not to release the prisoner on parole. Compared to sentencing, victim involvement at release hearings is a relatively recent development in the two jurisdictions discussed in this chapter, and accordingly there is less research on which to draw. In addition, it is likely that victim participation in the parole system[3] will always involve a smaller percentage of crime victims than the proportion submitting an impact statement at sentencing. Many victims may simply want no reminder of a painful event which they are trying to put behind them, or they may have lost contact, deliberately or otherwise, with the criminal justice system.

In many common law countries, there has been increasing formal interest in recognising the interests of victims throughout the criminal process. In England and Wales, for example, there has been a Code of Practice for Victims since 2005 (issued under s. 32 of the Domestic Violence, Crime and Victims Act 2004). But this is merely a Code of Practice, and hence aspirational: failure to comply with the Code does not, of itself, make a person liable in legal proceedings. Canada adopted a Statement of Basic Principles of Justice for Crime Victims in 2003,[4] although these principles are also merely aspirational in nature. Commissioners for victims have also been created at the provincial and federal levels in Canada to promote victims' interests in the criminal justice system. In Scotland, the Victim Notification Scheme (VNS) is a statutory scheme, which came into force on 1 November 2004. The scheme originally provided victims of offenders who had been sentenced to four years or more with the right to receive information about the offender's progression within the prison system and eventual release. In May 2008 the scheme was extended to include offenders who have been sentenced to 18 months or more.[5] Victims can apply to join the scheme regardless of when the crime was committed and they may make representations both to the parole board and to the Scottish prison service, which makes the decision to release offenders on home detention curfew.[6] In many other European countries, the decision to release a prisoner is heavily influenced by whether the offender has started to make payments to the victim as *partie civile*.

Prisoners in most countries seldom serve the entire period of a sentence of custody specified by the sentencing judge. There are complex rules which give powers to both judicial and administrative bodies to release the offender prior to the expiry of the custodial warrant. Indeed, many jurisdictions allow indeterminate sentences, where the sentencing court simply lays down a minimum term to be served before release may be considered. Interestingly, while both Canada and England and Wales allow indeterminate sentences for those deemed dangerous, many fewer prisoners have been detained under the relevant legislation in the former than the latter. In 2007, 1,700 offenders were sentenced in England and Wales to the indeterminate sentence of 'Imprisonment for Public Protection'. In contrast, across Canada, only 403 people were designated as dangerous offenders over the period 1978–2006, an average of 15 per year (Manson et al. 2008: 679).[7] In both jurisdictions, a parole board considers questions of release for such prisoners. In England, the parole board no longer has a role in releasing offenders sentenced to fixed terms of imprisonment, while in Canada parole remains the means to attain early release for the majority of prisoners. In comparing developments in Canada with the complex system of conditional and early release in England and Wales (which relies heavily on administrative discretion, with the parole board focusing on decisions to release only the most serious violent and sexual offenders and those who have been recalled to prison), it becomes clear that 'parole' can mean different things in different contexts.

Victim input into parole in other jurisdictions

Although victim impact schemes at sentencing have attracted most attention from scholars, victims in the United States have long had the right to provide input into parole decisions. The first jurisdictions to allow victim input into the parole process were in the US. Statutory reforms in the State of New York in the early 1980s created an obligation on parole boards to consider any written statement submitted by the victim when determining the prisoner's suitability for release on parole. A recent survey of releasing authorities noted that input from victims is now allowed almost everywhere in the US, with in-person input permissible in 87 per cent of jurisdictions (Kinnevy and Caplan 2008: Table 14). Today, victim-related provisions at parole are almost as common as at sentencing. Victim input usually takes the form of allowing victims to submit an impact statement, and to attend parole hearings, or to express their views in a separate meeting with parole board members.

Victims' rights at parole are developing in many other countries. In New Zealand, for example, the Victims' Rights Act 2002 gives both registered and unregistered victims the right to provide input and to receive information about the parole board's decisions. Registered victims are then notified when a hearing is due to take place. The victim can make a written submission to the board about the offender's case, and may apply to the board to attend a hearing and make an oral submission. Victims can apply for financial assistance to attend a hearing, and are supported by Victim Support workers.[8] According to the parole board's latest annual report, 126 victims made oral submissions and 435 made written submissions in 2007–08. Most other common law jurisdictions such as England and Wales, Scotland, Canada, New Zealand and Australia have followed the US example of introducing at least some victim involvement in the parole process.

Expressive v. instrumental objectives of victim input

What is it that the victim is invited to express at a parole hearing? Let us return to the sentencing stage of the criminal process. Although some US jurisdictions permit victims to make sentencing recommendations, victims in most common law jurisdictions are prohibited from expressing an opinion regarding the specific sentence which they believe should be

259

imposed (see Tobolowsky 1999; Roberts 2009 for reviews). The victim input regimes which permit impact evidence but not sentence recommendation make a clear distinction between the two, although in practice some victims make suggestions regarding sentence even when explicitly directed otherwise. This 'bright line' between describing the impact of the crime and recommending a specific disposition becomes blurred at the stage of parole. Victims may be asked to describe the impact that the offence has had (and continues to have) upon their lives – in this sense they are updating any impact statement that may have been submitted at sentencing. But they may also be provided with the opportunity to recommend specific conditions which may be imposed upon the prisoner if granted parole, and more worryingly, to express an opinion about the parole decision itself.

In some jurisdictions, victims are asked to describe not whether they support or oppose parole, but rather the impact that releasing the offender will have upon them. Thus in the Australian State of Tasmania, the directions to victims note the following three issues on which they are encouraged to make submissions: (i) how the crime has affected and continues to affect them; (ii) 'how they *would feel about the prisoner being released* from prison'; and (iii) the kinds of conditions they would like to see included in the parole order (Tasmania Department of Justice 2008, emphasis added).

Critics of victim impact statements at sentencing have argued, rightly in our opinion, that victim input has the potential to undermine principles of sentencing such as fairness. However, they only do so to the extent that the impact statement is deposed to secure some instrumental purpose – to elicit a harsher sentence. Erez (1999, 2004) and others (e.g. Szmania and Gracyalny 2006; Roberts and Erez 2004) have argued that this perspective constitutes a misreading of the original purpose of the victim impact statement. They assert that the purpose of victim impact statements is *Expressive* rather than *Instrumental*, and that allowing the victim to express a message to the court (and the offender) is a very different matter from allowing them to influence the sentence imposed. A review of the empirical literature suggests that victims cite a number of reasons for submitting an impact statement at sentencing and appear as interested in the expressive as the instrumental function (see Roberts 2009).[9]

How does the Expressive–Instrumental distinction relate to release from prison? At the stage of parole, the penal environment has changed. Expressive motives are far less likely to play a role. Victims have had the opportunity to express themselves to the court and the offender. Victim input is much more likely to be instrumental in nature – thereby increasing the threat to fairness identified by critics of victim input at sentencing. It is hard to conceive of many victims wishing to attend a parole hearing primarily for the purpose of communicating with the offender, although as noted this is far from uncommon at a sentencing hearing (Leverick *et al.* 2007). Similarly, although it occurs in only a small minority of cases, victims sometimes attend sentencing to appeal for a more lenient sentence (such as a non-custodial sanction); it seems unlikely that victims will attend a parole hearing to argue for the release of the prisoner.

Profile of victims and offenders at parole

The profile of victims participating in parole processes is very different from those who submit an impact statement at sentencing. Victims at sentencing represent a wide range of victimisations and motivations for participation in the criminal process. The research on crime victims has demonstrated the diversity of reasons for participating by submitting a statement or attending a hearing. This diversity is reflected in the range of outcomes at a sentencing hearing: the offender may be sentenced to custody or one of a number of non-custodial options. Parole hearings involve a more homogeneous group of victims and offenders – generally, those involved in serious crimes of violence for which the latter have been sentenced to lengthy terms of imprisonment. For example, in Canada the National Parole Board reviews applications from prisoners serving terms of two years or more. It is important to recognise that this means that parole is a possibility for those with sentences which represent only the longest custodial terms in that country.[10] Parole boards deal with prisoners serving time for the most serious offences – those sentenced to prison and often for lengthy terms of imprisonment. Victims expressing a desire to participate at parole will likely be those suffering longer-term trauma. They may be less inclined to see any merit in expressive gestures, effective resettlement or restorative justice and are likely to be focused on the single instrumental goal of impeding the prisoner's release from custody. The kaleidoscope of victim interests and inputs at sentencing has become, at parole, a microscope focused clearly on the single question of whether to grant or deny release from prison.

Effect of victim input upon parole outcomes: research in the United States

Opponents of victim input argue that allowing victims to express their views will prove prejudicial to the parole applicant. The extent to which victim participation at parole threatens a prisoner's chances of release is an empirical question. Unfortunately – in light of the prevalence of victim participation in conditional release decisions around the world – only three empirical studies have tested the effect of victim input on parole hearing outcomes. The findings of these studies demonstrate that victim input does have an impact on parole outcomes. Morgan and Smith (2005) conducted a careful analysis of parole files in Alabama and found that victim participation was a significant predictor of parole decision-making: when the victim submitted impact evidence the prisoner was less likely to be granted parole. This finding existed independently of the influence of other factors related to the parole decision, and is consistent with the two other studies from the United States that have evaluated the impact of victim input at parole (Parsonage *et al.* 1992; Smith *et al.* 1997). Such findings raise questions about the fairness of the parole decision-making process when victims are allowed to intervene. It is important to remember that these studies have been undertaken in the US where the criminal justice climate as well as the nature of parole boards is very different from that in Canada or England. At the very least, however, these studies demonstrate the potential for victim input to change the outcome of a parole hearing, to the detriment of the applicant. Unfortunately, no studies have to date been conducted of the impact of victim input into parole decision-making in Canada, England and Wales or other common law jurisdictions.

There are several reasons why one would expect victims to have more impact on parole decisions than on the decisions of sentencing courts, in the US context at least. First, as noted, victims appearing at parole hearings are likely to have suffered serious harm. Their impact statements may well therefore be particularly moving and influential. Second, the decision-makers at the stage of sentencing are legally qualified judges, with a legal training which helps to ensure that material with prejudicial value is set aside.[11] We will later suggest that parole boards should in fact be seen as courts, led by judges, and governed by due process conventions. If the role of the victim is to increase, so must the authority of a parole board as a quasi-judicial 'court'. Third, many parole boards recruit members from the ranks of victims' advocates, in order to give the process of parole more legitimacy in the eyes of the public or victims' groups. Such members may feel it is part of their mandate to take victims' impact statements into account when deciding upon whether to grant or deny parole (see Roberts 2009 for further discussion). We argue that, alongside such members, it is important that there should be judicial members to ensure legal authority and independence.[12]

Victim input into parole in Canada

Victim impact statements (VIS) for use at sentencing were introduced in Canada in 1988. The VIS provisions of the Criminal Code were amended in 1999 when victims acquired the right to present their statements orally at the sentencing hearing, if the statement has been filed in accordance with an official victim statement scheme. Victim impact statements have been the subject of more research in this jurisdiction than any other outside the United States (e.g. Giliberti 1990; Roberts 2003; Roberts and Edgar 2006; Prairie Research Associates 2005). Victim input at parole, however, is a more recent phenomenon in this jurisdiction.

The parole system in Canada plays an important role in the administration of a sentence of imprisonment: most prisoners become eligible for day parole after having served one-sixth of the sentence, and full parole at the one-third point.[13] If parole affects the sentence as served to such an extent, informing the victims that the offender has received, say, a sentence of nine years' imprisonment gives them little idea how long will be spent in custody. The offender could be living in the community after 18 months (on day parole), or may have to serve every day of nine years before leaving prison at the expiry of the court's warrant.[14] Prisoners who are denied parole, or who decline to apply for parole, are entitled to release at the two-thirds point in the sentence under the programme known as Statutory Release. This statutory entitlement contrasts with the discretionary nature of release on parole.

Parole for federal offenders (those serving sentences of two years or longer) is regulated by the Corrections and Conditional Release Act (CCRA) 1992, as amended.[15] According to s. 102 of the CCRA the criteria for release on parole are: (a) the risk of reoffending and (b) whether the release of the offender will facilitate his or her reintegration into society. Crime victims who have registered with the Correctional Services of Canada enjoy a statutory right to be notified of a prisoner's parole application. They also have the right to submit a statement to the National Parole Board regarding the impending decision to deny or grant parole of the offender in their case, and to attend the prisoner's parole hearing. The contents of the victim's statement will be disclosed to the offender – a legal requirement that is absent in many US jurisdictions.

In Canada, the National Parole Board (NPB) asserts that: 'Victims play a key role in the NPB risk assessment through their statements.'[16] This assertion assumes that victims have information about the offender's risk of reoffending (or likelihood of benefiting from parole) that is not available to the parole board from other sources. More specifically, guidelines for victims state that: 'You may want to speak about:

1. the continuing impact of the crime since sentencing. This could include information about the physical, emotional, medical and financial impact of this crime on yourself, your children and family members, or others who are close to you;

2. concerns you may have for the safety of yourself, your family, or the community with regard to the offender should he or she be released, explaining why you believe there may be a risk.'

The NPB website describes relevant information from the victim as including 'the nature and extent of harm suffered by the victim'; 'the offender's understanding of the impact of the offence' and 'conditions necessary to manage the risk which might be presented by the offender'.

Finally, the Board notes that 'Information about the harm victims have suffered is important in cases where the NPB must decide whether to detain an offender in custody.'

In our view, these directions to victims highlight the principal weakness of arguments in favour of victim input – its lack of relevance. However much we may deplore the protracted suffering of the victim, how, exactly, does this suffering shed light on the decision to detain or release guided by the statutory criteria identified above? It is hard to see how the crime victim will have unique information unavailable from another source that will be relevant to these issues. Unless the offender has communicated or attempted to communicate with the victim, the two parties will have had no contact with each other since the crime. Moreover, if the offender is now applying for parole from a federal penitentiary, the offence will have occurred years before, since, as previously noted, these offenders will have served several years in prison before becoming parole-eligible.

Victim participation statistics in Canada

A number of studies have explored the issue of participation rates in victim impact schemes at sentencing. The general conclusion is that only a minority of crime victims choose to submit an impact statement at sentencing (see Hall 1991; Tobolowsky 1999; Roberts 2009). Participation *rates* are unavailable with respect to victims and parole in Canada. However, recent statistics do reveal considerable victim interest in receiving notification about correctional developments relating to 'their' offender, and the absolute number of victims seeking to participate in parole hearings is clearly rising.

In order to receive notification of developments regarding the offender in their case victims must first register with the Correctional Service of Canada (CSC). The number of registrations therefore constitutes a measure of victim participation. The number of victims who registered rose fourfold during the period 1994 to 2008 – from 1,200 to 5,182. In 2005–06, approximately 5,000 victims registered to receive notification about the offender's progress through the correctional system and almost all (97 per cent) of these individuals were successfully contacted by the CSC (Brozowski 2007: 7). In 2002–03, 14,270 contacts were made with crime victims with respect to conditional release hearings. Requests for information grew at an even higher rate, rising 20 per cent over the previous year (Roberts 2008). The volume of contacts is likely to increase further within the next few years as victims become more aware of their rights.

Most recently (2008) the federal government announced additional funding to the Victims' Fund. Since a principal barrier to victim participation in parole hearings in a country the size of Canada is the cost of travel, it is worth noting that there has been a significant increase in the number of victims benefiting from the NPB travel fund, which started in November 2005: from 126 victims in the first year to 432 the following year, and in 2007–08, 485 people took advantage of the fund. In addition, financial support now covers a wider range of victim services. The consequence of this enhanced funding is clear: more victims have appeared at parole hearings to deliver their VIS orally. Brozowski (2007) notes that within the first five years (1 July 2001–31 March 2006) of the policy of allowing victims to make oral presentations at National Parole Board hearings, 700 such victim presentations were made (2007: 8) and with the increased funding now for a support person to attend, these numbers are expected to continue to increase still further. The statistics on victim participation make it clear that if victims are offered the opportunity to learn about developments in their offender's progress through the prison system, many will register to receive this information. A much smaller percentage will request to appear, or to submit an impact statement to the parole board reviewing an application for release. The bare statistics, however, cannot help us analyse the impact of victim input at parole on the correctional system.

Victim input into parole in England and Wales

Victim participation in oral hearings before the Parole Board has been slower to develop in England and Wales. In July 2006 a scheme was announced to enable victim representation at Parole Board hearings and the first delivery of a victim personal statement took place in November 2007. The rarity and importance of this event to the Parole Board is underlined by the fact that it is described in great detail over four pages of the Parole Board's Annual Report 2007/08 (pp. 30–3), which quotes at length the observations of various participants: the panel chair (a judge), the panel administrator, the 'public protection advocate' and the victim, the mother of the 15-year-old murder victim. The hearing concerned the prisoner's application to move to an open prison (from which he might be allowed home visits to his own mother, who attended the whole hearing). He (and others) had been convicted some 10 years earlier of the murder, in particularly horrendous circumstances, of another teenager.

At the beginning of the hearing, the victim's mother delivered her pre-prepared victim personal statement, which outlined the impact of the offence and of her son's death on her and her family. She then had to withdraw from the hearing, accompanied by the victim liaison officer, and was escorted from the prison.[17] She was not allowed to attend the whole hearing, unlike the prisoner's mother, because of objections from the prisoner's legal representative. It is not obvious what impact the mother's evidence had on the panel. They had, in any case, a written statement from her. The panel chair comments that: 'the panel understood and appreciated the passion and anger expressed by the mother of the victim and, while what she said did not contain any new information about risk, she was able to give us important information that helped us to set appropriate licence conditions for the prisoner' (at page 32). This statement valuably underlines our concern: given that the mother gave no new information on risk, was it really so valuable for the panel to learn more of the mother's 'passion and anger'? How exactly did this material enhance the parole process?

It bears repetition that the role and function of the Parole Board of England and Wales is very different from that in Canada, and indeed has changed enormously since it was created in 1967. Originally its work focused on the decisions to release determinate sentence prisoners, and until the Criminal Justice and Immigration Act 2008, the Parole Board still decided on the early release of all those sentenced to four years' imprisonment, or more (for offences committed before 4 April 2005). Today, unlike Canada, no determinate sentence prisoner has his or her release decision taken by the Parole Board. The main focus of Parole Board work now is the release of lifers and all those serving *in*determinate sentences, all of whom have the right to an oral hearing regarding their application (see Padfield 2006, 2009). The other principal focus of Parole Board work involves dealing with the increasing population of prisoners recalled to prison (Padfield and Maruna 2006).[18]

This change in caseload of the Parole Board reflects a complex variety of factors, the most obvious of which are greater flexibility in administrative early-release rules (particularly the introduction of Home Detention Curfew – see below), greater caution and risk-aversion among probation officers and their supervisors, and closer surveillance of offenders on licence. In 2007–08, the Board considered 31,172 cases, up 22 per cent in just one year. The dramatic increase in the numbers of prisoners recalled to prison has had an important impact on the workload of the Parole Board (leading to the increase in the use of single-member panels, for example), but also on both the prison population and on the nature of the second, supposedly 'non-custodial' part, of a prison sentence more generally.

It is also important to be aware of the other programmes by which prisoners may obtain early release from prison in this jurisdiction, which we now briefly discuss.

Other early-release processes in England and Wales[19]

(i) Home Detention Curfew

In England and Wales, the most significant early-release mechanism, at least in terms of prisoner numbers, is not parole but the Home Detention Curfew (HDC), first introduced in 1998.[20] Some 13,666 offenders were released from prison on HDC in 2006, and 11,428 in 2007. In 2006, 25 per cent of those male prisoners who were eligible were granted HDC, and 35 per cent of eligible women. The percentages in 2007 were 20 per cent and 30 per cent.[21] These prisoners are fixed-term prisoners who are eligible for automatic release at the halfway point of the sentence but who may apply for HDC of up to 135 days before this point. The policy is to be found in Prison Service Order (PSO) 6700. The role of the victim with respect to HDC is unclear (although in Scotland, the victim does have a right to make representations to the Prison Service). The decision to release is taken by the Governor. (In private prisons the decision is taken by the management team of the private company but 'signed off' by the Controller, a State-appointed official; see Dodgson and Mortimer 2000.) A key factor will be the report of the probation service, but resource implications mean that frequently this report will do little more than verify the proposed release address. Perhaps it is not surprising that the responsibilities of probation services specified in the Code of Practice for Victims of Crime in relation to the release of offenders focus on victims of offenders sentenced to 12 months or more for a sexual or violent offence, including mentally disordered offenders, in certain circumstances. There is certainly a need for much more analysis of the decision-making process in relation to HDC. Early research suggested wide variations between different prisons (Dodgson and Mortimer 2000), but whether victims' views are being taken into account is unclear.[22]

At first glance, considering victims' interests with respect to the decision to grant HDC might seem a stretch. After all, unlike Canada, the terms of additional supervised release in the community are brief – restricted to 135 days, and why would a victim bother to oppose release for this duration? This may explain why there has been little call on behalf of victims, and no Government initiatives to encourage victim input in this domain. In Canada, as noted, a positive parole application may mean that the offender spends years in the community under supervision rather than in prison. However, HDC does have an important impact on custodial sentence lengths. Some offenders now spend a very short proportion of their custodial sentence in prison; it is not unusual for a prisoner sentenced to nine or ten months' imprisonment to be released on HDC after four weeks. For example, any prisoner sentenced to 10 months is automatically released on licence at the halfway point of five months. But HDC means he may be released up to 135 days (4.5 months) earlier still, as long he serves a minimum four weeks.[23]

(ii) End of Custody Licence release

Release under ECL (End of Custody Licence) is another important release process which was introduced in 2007 more for pragmatic (overcrowded prisons) than rehabilitative reasons. Many short-term prisoners are now released under this scheme: during May 2008[24] there were 2,532 releases on ECL (2,262 men (89 per cent) and 270 women (11 per cent). At the end of May, it was estimated that approximately 1,300 offenders were under licence as part of the ECL scheme. As far as we know, there has been no research, and no discussion of victim concerns with respect to this new form of early release. This might suggest that victims' views are more important to policy-makers and politicians where the decisions being taken concern more 'risky' or 'dangerous' offenders?[25]

(iii) Deportation of foreign nationals in prison

Finally, there is the removal of foreign prisoners, a subject which has been the subject of much political controversy (resulting in the resignation of the Home Secretary Charles Clarke in 2006).[26] There is no evidence that victims' concerns are taken into consideration when the decision is taken whether or not to deport foreign criminals at the end of their sentence.[27] It is worth questioning why this is so. Again, it may be simply because it is not politically expedient to do so, but we would argue that it is also because here it is recognised that the victim has no role to play in this decision. Prisoners may also be sent back to their home country during their sentence under the Early Removal Scheme. Under the provisions of the Repatriation of Prisoners Act 1984, which brought into effect the 1983 Council of Europe *Convention on the Transfer of Sentenced Prisoners*, the consent of both the sentencing country and the country to which the prisoner is to be transferred, as well as of the prisoner himself, is required before a transfer may take place. The prisoner must have at least six months left to serve. But, again, there is no evidence available as to whether the view of the victim is considered.

To encourage more foreign prisoners to leave the country, a new Early Removal Scheme was introduced in July 2004.[28] It applies to all foreign prisoners sentenced to more than three months, subject to exceptions. Since 7 April 2008,[29] prisoners may be deported or removed earlier in their sentence, up to 270 days before the half-time point. There are now proposals from within the EU that prisoners should be transferred home, whether or not they consent to the transfer.[30] There are doubtless going to be many controversies surrounding the implementation of this EU Framework Decision: given that all EU countries currently have very different release rules, it is difficult to see how these transfers can work fairly. A French prisoner serving eight years in Britain will return to a very different release system to that facing the equivalent in a British prison. The ambition of the Framework Decision is avowedly rehabilitative. Perhaps it is because the focus has been on the rehabilitation of offenders that the role of the victim has not focused highly in the debates surrounding this issue. (And doubtless from the UK perspective, there is the added attraction that the UK will be net exporters of prisoners under the scheme, thus reducing the prison population.) As far as we are concerned, this is appropriate. The victim should be informed of an offender's departure from this jurisdiction but should have no role in delaying (or expediting) repatriation.

Victims and the Parole Board of England and Wales

To return to the role of the Parole Board in England and Wales, the Home Office's Code of Practice for Victims of Crime[31] states that the Board has the following obligations:

> The Parole Board must consider any representations that victims have offered to the Probation Service on the conditions to be included in the release licences of prisoners serving sentences subject to consideration by the Parole Board and reflect these considerations in the parole decisions. Conditions relating to the victim should be disclosed to the victim through the Probation Service, and where a licence condition has not been included, the Parole Board should provide an explanation for the non-inclusion.

> The Parole Board must consider any information regarding the victim that relates directly to the current risk presented by a prisoner in deciding whether or not to grant or recommend release and reflect this in the parole decision (at paras 12.1–12.2).

As McCarthy (2007) points out, in most cases where the victim's view has an impact on the Parole Board, it involves conditions relating to the prisoner's parole or life licence. The Board frequently imposes a condition to prevent the licensee attempting to contact or approach a victim; as well, geographic restrictions may be imposed to prevent contact between offenders and their victims. Usually these contact or mobility restrictions are uncontroversial; however, when the victim lives in an area where the prisoner has family of his own, or intends to work, then the proportionality test that is evoked by Article 8 of the Convention must be applied.[32] We would suggest that as long as the Board is well aware of the need to make such conditions proportionate, it is certainly appropriate to take the views of the victim into account. In this sense the victim plays an instrumental as well as a purely expressive role in the process. The case of *R (Craven) v. Secretary of State for the Home Department and the Parole Board*[33] provides an example of the conflicting interests that must be weighed by a releasing authority.

In this case a life sentence prisoner sought a declaration that a condition preventing him from entering the area of Newcastle/Tyneside without the approval of his supervising officer was unlawful. The Parole Board had recommended this licence condition based on interviews with the victim's family, who had made it clear that they wanted to be protected from any accidental contact with the offender. However, the offender's parents and close friends also lived in Newcastle, and he had to enter the city for the purposes of his employment. In order to resolve the conflicting rights of the victim's family and Mr Craven's rights under Article 8, very specific areas of Newcastle had been identified and defined by particular streets. There was no suggestion that the family of the victim were at risk of physical harm from Mr Craven, and he was entitled to have his Article 8 rights taken into account. But the Administrative Court refused to grant the declaration that the prisoner requested. As Stanley Burton J said:

> I consider that the imposition of an exclusion zone on the movements of a convicted murderer, in order to minimize the risk of accidental contact between him and the family of his victim, should be considered as capable of being necessary in a democratic society. A democratic society should be sensitive to the emotional harm caused to victims of crime, particularly of the most serious of crimes, to their anxieties and concerns, and to the risks of emotional or psychological harm in the event of an encounter between a convicted murderer and the family of his victim [at para 31].

> ... the concerns of the victim of the murder committed by Mr Craven were matters that the Parole Board and the Home Secretary were entitled, indeed bound, to take into account when deciding what conditions were to be included in the licence for Mr Craven's release [at para 34].

> I do not say that the revised zone is a perfect compromise of the interests of Mr Craven and his family and those of the family of his victim. Perfection is always difficult to achieve, and can be the enemy of the good. There remain risks of chance encounters in places outside the revised exclusion zone. However, in my judgment the revised terms of the licence and the revised exclusion zone reasonably accommodate the competing interests involved, and do so in a manner that, in relation to Mr Craven's Convention rights, meets the requirements of proportionality. They are lawful and valid [at para 40].

This is an important decision, but it does not resolve all the difficulties which may arise in such cases. Stone (2002) identifies a number of such difficulties. He suggests that a parole hearing may in fact aggravate rather than ameliorate victim concerns (for example by drawing attention to the victims' whereabouts); he points out that the decision doesn't help decide the difficult issue of how much information a victim should be given; that it fails to consider the enforceability of licence conditions; nor does it consider the legality of confinement conditions (the opposite of exclusion licence conditions). These concerns show the importance of further reflection before the English system slips into giving too great a role for victims in decisions to release. They suggest, too, the need for much more hard evidence (i.e. empirical research) into the effect of victim involvement: the impact that this involvement may have on victims, as well as on the decision to grant or deny release of the prisoner.

Influences on release decisions

Role of the probation service

Victim input may well be transmitted through indirect influences on the Parole Board. It is easy to exaggerate the role of the Parole Board in these decisions. The role of the probation service, for example, at the Parole Board is crucial. As Padfield and Liebling (2000) have shown, in the case of life sentence prisoners, if the home probation officer does not support release, the prisoner is very unlikely to be released. Even if the Parole Board makes the final decision on release for some serious prisoners, their discretion is severely constrained by the decisions taken earlier by the probation service, as well as by the prison authorities, in helping the prisoner progress through the prison system.[34] The Home Office's Code of Practice for Victims of Crime states:

> 10.2 The Probation Service has the obligations set out below in relation to:
> ... 10.3 The Probation Service must take all reasonable steps to establish whether a victim wishes to make representations about what licence conditions or supervision requirements (where it is a young offender) the offender should be subject to on their release from prison and/or conditions of discharge from hospital and to forward these to those responsible for making decisions about the prisoner's or patient's release.
> 10.4 The Probation Service must forward any requests for non-disclosure to those responsible for making decisions about the prisoner's or patient's release.
> 10.5 The Probation Service must pass on any information to the victim about whether the prisoner or patient will be subject to any conditions or requirements in the event of release or discharge and must provide the victim with details of any which relate to contact with the victim or their family and the date on which any restriction order, limitation direction or restriction direction is to cease to have effect.
> 10.6 The Probation Service shall also provide the victim with any other information which it considers appropriate in all the circumstances of the case. Generally, victims will be given information at key

stages in an offender's sentence, for example, a move to a lower category prison or a temporary release from prison on licence.

One may query whether it is the role of the probation service to deal with victims in this way, although it is consistent with probation practice in Canada where officers often respond to requests for information from crime victims. The role and function of the probation officer has changed greatly over the past century and particularly over the last decade. The emphasis is less on assisting and befriending offenders, and more on managing in the community people perceived to represent a risk to public safety.[35]

Role of prison authorities

The Parole Board is unlikely to recommend the release of a lifer or dangerous prisoner unless they have progressed through the prison system to an open prison. They will also be expected to have completed relevant courses, which are seen to help reduce the risk of reoffending. In this way, the prison authorities as well as the probation service can be seen to hold the keys to release. Yet no one (we are glad to say) seems to be arguing that victims should be represented when decisions are taken on re-categorisation or on transfers between prisons. And, as we have seen, most early-release decisions in England and Wales are no longer made by the Parole Board. The decision to release on HDC or ELC has been transferred to the prison authorities who now decide on the licence conditions, and indeed have the duty to consider changing licence conditions when something appears to be going wrong.

The Code of Practice for Victims of Crime specifies that:

11.3 . . . Governors and Controllers of Contracted Prisons must ensure that all approved conditions are inserted into release licences and that all associated administrative procedures are meeting victims' needs. In addition, prisons must ensure that this information is passed to the Probation Service so that the Probation Service can notify the victim.
11.4 Prisons must ensure that information about victims and their families, or their views and concerns about a prisoner's temporary or permanent release, is stored securely. As a general principle information provided by the victim which is pertinent to decisions about the conditions of a prisoner's release will be made available to that prisoner unless the victim requests that it is not disclosed and the Governor considers that to do so would put the victim or their family at risk of harm or would compromise any duty of confidentiality owed to the victim. Victims who wish their views not to be disclosed to the prisoner can make representations to the Governor/Controller through their Victim Liaison Officer.

Again, this is an area which has not been researched: while there is a considerable (and growing) literature on the work and role of the Parole Board (e.g. Padfield 2006, 2007, 2009) the more covert but equally important decisions taken in prison and by the probation service have remained largely unresearched. We see also a distinct contrast with early release in Canada, where parole boards continue to have a greater role in the decision to release prisoners.

The time has come for us to return to our core ambition: to identify some key principles which should apply to victims and their interests when it comes to the question of conditional release from prison.

Victim interests at parole: a principled approach

Dissemination of information to crime victims

In both our jurisdictions – but particularly Canada – the role of the victim at parole remains unclear. The nature of victim input requires careful elucidation, and in this last section of the chapter we offer some specific suggestions in this regard. Clearly, victims should be informed of some – but by no means all – developments in the criminal justice career of the prisoner in their case. It is reasonable, for example, that they should want to know when the offender is applying for parole, as they may have risk-related information that they wish to share with the board. Equally, even if they do not have any such information, and have no intention of providing an impact statement or attending the hearing, victims should be informed if the prisoner is granted parole and released to the community. If victims have a right to be informed of the sentence imposed on the offender, they should also be told what this sentence means in practice. Judges have an obligation to explain the reasons for their sentencing decisions and indeed the implications of the sentence with respect to time served. But, as we have seen in the jurisdictions which we have surveyed, release from prison is actually very flexible, both in the hands of the prison authorities and of the parole board.

In Canada, as a result of the parole arrangements, a lengthy term of imprisonment may mean very different durations of incarceration, depending upon the timing and outcome of any parole applications. In England and Wales, the prison and probation authorities also have wide powers over the release of prisoners. Information at the time of sentencing is not going to be enough. Victims should also be informed of any conditions which clearly relate to their interests. For example, if one of the conditions of parole is that the parolee stay out of the victim's neighbourhood or away from their workplace, the victim should be informed of this requirement. If the parole board or prison authority decides against such a condition, the victim should also be informed.

However, there seems little justification for providing the victim with the details of a range of issues such as the prisoner's activities in prison, his disciplinary record, the courses he has completed and the security level to which he has been assigned. Nor does the victim have a reasonable claim to information relating to the other conditions imposed if parole is granted, or the parole officer's response to any allegations of breach of these conditions. Yet some jurisdictions do disseminate exactly this kind of information to victims who have registered their interest in the case.[36] Providing this kind of information represents an intrusion into the privacy interests of the prisoner, and does nothing to promote the objectives of the prison and parole systems. Acceding to the victim's demands to have a wide range of information, or, worse, allowing victims to express an opinion about whether or when to grant parole represents a corruption of the correctional enterprise, as well as a threat to principles of fundamental justice.

Victim input into parole decision-making

Although the rights of crime victims have expanded throughout the criminal process, the arguments for allowing victims a voice are clearly stronger at some stages than others. Victims' interests are more infringed or affected at some stages of the criminal process, and the level of victim interest is not uniform from beginning to end of the justice system. In consequence, the relevance of victim input into decision-making is likely to vary. At sentencing, courts in England and Wales (as well as Canada) attempt to impose sentences proportional to the harm inflicted and the offender's level of culpability. Proportionality has been codified as the 'fundamental' principle of sentencing in Canada, thereby reflecting its status above other principles such as restraint regarding the use of imprisonment or equity.[37] Imposing a proportional sentence requires a court to determine the relative seriousness of the offence and the offender's level of culpability. The victim's input at sentencing is invaluable; the victim is best placed to describe the harm inflicted.

But once we move into the domain of conditional release from prison, matters are rather different. The parole board is not considering the seriousness of the offence or the offender's level of culpability for the crime – unless these considerations shed some light on the likelihood and gravity of future offending. We have pointed out that the aim of most parole boards is increasingly to assess the risk that the prisoner may pose to the public if released into the community. There is sometimes confusion about the true purpose of conditional release. Is it primarily aimed at rehabilitation, at reintegrating the offender into the community? Or is it about protecting the public from 'risky' offenders? In determining the offender's risk level, parole authorities will consider many factors, including the age of the offender, any substance abuse issues, the extent to which he has benefited from institutional programmes and his disciplinary record while incarcerated. When evaluating the question of whether his reintegration into the community will be promoted by release the board will consider another set of factors – whether the prisoner has a supportive family; his or her prospects of employment, the offender's attitude towards the offence[38] and so forth. Few victims will have up-to-date, reliable information relevant to these decisions that is unavailable to the parole board from other sources.

Legitimate versus unwelcome victim input

What kind of input from the victim is relevant to the decision to grant or refuse parole? Some examples spring to mind. First, as noted earlier, any conduct on the part of the prisoner – communications with the victim or other parties – which suggests that once granted release the offender will pose a threat. Second, any particular concerns that the victim may have about unplanned encounters with the offender. It may not be unreasonable for the victim to ask the parole board to ensure that the prisoner is released to a location where he is unlikely to encounter the victim of the crime.[39] Third, if the victim has information about the prisoner's previous compliance record with programmes or conditions designed to address or reduce risk of reoffending, *and this material is unavailable to the releasing authority* and it can be checked, it should be placed before the board. A victim of domestic violence, for example, may know that the offender repeatedly failed to attend anger management or substance abuse programmes in the past. In England and Wales, where the parole board is increasingly making decisions about recalled prisoners, the victim may have information relevant to these decisions. Indeed, one of the criticisms of the current process is that it is not well equipped to hear evidence.

What kind of information should be *excluded* from an impact statement at parole? Here we would identify any opinion regarding the release of the prisoner, and any views about the impact that the release of the prisoner may have on the victim or the victim's family. Both opinions are permitted in certain jurisdictions. In some US jurisdictions, victims are asked to pronounce on the question of whether the offender should be released, and in others victims are asked to specify how they would feel if the prisoner were granted parole. Taking either of these considerations into account would appear to undermine fairness and the principles of effective corrections. As well, allowing victim input in this way is likely to foster disappointment. Some crime victims will feel angry or disappointed at a prison system that releases an offender after having served 'only' half the sentence inside. But this is no different from the resentment that some victims feel when a court imposes a three-year sentence where one of double this length was possible. These reactions should not be allowed to influence the decision to grant conditional release. It is understandable that the release of the prisoner on parole may cause considerable dismay to the victim – particularly if this release occurs as early as one third of the way into the sentence. However, it is unclear how the ongoing suffering of the crime victim informs the parole board about the future dangerousness of the offender. Appreciating the seriousness of the crime, and understanding the offender's attitude to the consequences of his actions are clearly important – to a sentencing court. The link to determining the likelihood of future offending is very obscure. In addition to their opinions regarding release, and as with victim impact statements at sentencing, victims submitting a statement at parole should avoid *ad hominem* attacks on the prisoner, allegations of unprosecuted misconduct and other such material.

How can the scheme ensure that only legally relevant material be placed before the releasing authority? Once again victim input schemes at sentencing offer a guide. These schemes have had variable degrees of success in shaping victim input so that it is relevant to the determination of sentence. In some jurisdictions the instructions provided to victims are sufficiently vague as to allow the interpretation that sentence recommendations are permitted, and the result is that opinions about the sentence are inserted in the statement and have to be excised by the prosecutor, or ignored by the court. With respect to parole, in the event that this kind of material does appear in the victim's impact statement it should be excised before being read or heard by parole board members. As noted, this is the practice at sentencing.

There are two reasons for this editorial intrusion. First, the material may be highly prejudicial to the liberty interests of the prisoner and have no probative value. The victim's views are likely to be focused on the gravity of a past crime, not on the risk of future offending. Second, the exercise of discretion at parole is taken within the context of a debate between the State and the offender (now a prisoner). In most jurisdictions at the moment, the process is not really adversarial: the parole board plays a more active role in the questioning of witnesses than in traditional adversarial processes. But we would encourage a more formal approach to the receipt of evidence. In the case of life sentence prisoners, for example, applying to a parole board when they have served their minimum term, the onus should certainly be on the State to justify the need for continued detention. The role of the victim of the original crime is unlikely to be useful in proving risk. A third party, even the victim, should not be in a position to intrude into proceedings inappropriately.

Due process considerations

Regardless of the nature of the submissions made to the board by the victim, it is important that this material be disclosed to the parole applicant and subject to the same level of scrutiny as a victim impact statement at sentencing. There may be disclosure issues to be considered (disclosure may generate a risk to the victim, for example), but no information should be provided to the board which is not also known to the prisoner.[40] In addition, victims should depose their statements formally, perhaps in the form of a sworn affidavit. Crime victims in Canada normally testify under oath at a sentencing hearing and their evidence is subject to cross-examination. It might be appropriate to allow cross-examination of victim impact statements at parole hearings, but rules should be transparently clear.

We have touched on another area of legitimate concern for victims – that of reparation, or compensation. It may well be that the systems with which we are most familiar do not currently go far enough in considering the victims' right to financial compensation for the effects of their crimes. As we have mentioned, some jurisdictions put much higher weight on this factor not only when sentencing, but also when making decisions to release. Financial compensation for victims is of course vitally important: even if the State should ensure full compensation, it may well be that the offender should always, too, have to make a contribution, however small. The usual 'rule'[41] in England that prisoners sent to prison should not normally have to pay the victim compensation should be reconsidered. We would argue that there is much to be said also for encouraging reparation in other, non-financial, ways, as well. 'Restorative justice' is a term currently used to mean many things in many different contexts.[42] Within the prison system, it can be used to give prisoners the opportunity to make amends and to apologise, and can give victims a sense that they have not been excluded by the criminal justice process (see Newell and Edgar 2001, and Johnstone and Van Ness 2006). Restorative justice advocates often argue that it should be used to steer offenders away from punitive and segregating sanctions, and worry that its use in prison can be contradictory and even dangerous. But restorative initiatives can help develop rehabilitation and give relief to victims. Both these areas (financial compensation for victims, and 'restorative' processes in prison) should be examined in more detail.

Importance of providing clear directions to victims

A frequent criticism of victim impact schemes at sentencing is that they encourage victims to expect that their views at sentencing will affect the sentence imposed. Many US jurisdictions allow victims to make specific sentence recommendations, but even if this is prohibited, many victims may feel that submitting an impact statement is a way of influencing a court. When a court fails to follow the wishes of the victim, disenchantment with the sentencing process will be the result. Victims submitting an impact statement at parole should therefore be given very clear directions about the purpose of parole and of their input including the nature of information that a releasing authority will find relevant and useful. Victims have a real interest in personal protection, and this may well be a factor to be considered in assessing the risk of reoffending by dangerous offenders.

One of the weaknesses of victim input regimes at sentencing is that victims are sometimes told to avoid sentence recommendations, but do not receive an explanation of why they, the crime victim, cannot express an opinion on this issue. After all, other participants at the sentencing hearing including counsel for the defendant, the prosecutor and the probation officer (through the pre-sentence report (PSR) have the freedom (indeed the obligation) to do so. This restriction troubles many victims who see it as highly counter-intuitive, and who fail to understand the logic of the adversarial model of justice. This lack of clarity may be even more troublesome in the context of conditional release. Victims need clear explanations as well as directions. They need to understand that their role in the process cannot include offering an opinion on release any more than it can include offering a view on the initial decision to imprison.

Conclusions

We have noted in this chapter the growing awareness of the rights and needs of victims and have questioned the proper role for the crime victim in decisions taken to release the offender from prison. We counsel caution regarding victim input into releasing decisions. A court imposes sentence, and the views of the victim may be helpful in assessing the seriousness of the offence. But the decision to release (on parole or on any other release scheme) is taken for reasons which often have little to do with offence seriousness. It is obviously unfair to allow a victim's statement opposing parole to influence whether the board grants release – if the decision to release is based upon risk of reoffending and likelihood of rehabilitation. In addition, although we do not have the space to discuss it further, victim input may well interfere with sound correctional practices in terms of releasing decisions (see Roberts 2009 for further discussion). It is vital that victim input does not become so important as to overwhelm the primary considerations of a releasing authority, namely promoting offender rehabilitation and protecting society.

Uncertainties about the role of the victim have to be seen in the context of widespread uncertainties surrounding parole and release processes more generally: do prisoners enjoy a right to early release from prison? In all countries whose legal systems we know, offenders are unlikely to serve the entire sentence imposed by the sentencing court. The rules which govern release vary from jurisdiction to jurisdiction, and within jurisdictions, and are complex and subject to frequent change. Victims and offenders deserve better. While this chapter has explored the role of the victim in parole release processes, we would also urge a greater focus on release decisions more generally.[43] The role of the victim at sentencing has been considered much more fully in the literature than has their role in release processes – not least because sentencing has been discussed rather more than has release from prison. We have noted in this chapter very different release processes across different jurisdictions, and within one jurisdiction (England and Wales), much change in a short period of time. The decision to release is as important as the decision to imprison, and should be taken by accountable judicial bodies, acting according to rules that are clear to all participants.

Notes

1 England and Wales this is usually called a victim personal statement.
2 Indeed, since many victims are not called to give evidence as a result of the offender entering a guilty plea, their involvement may end much earlier, after reporting the crime to the police. Victims who follow developments in the case and who actually attend the sentencing hearing thus represent only a small proportion of the total population of victims.
3 Victims of the most serious crimes are more likely to participate in the parole process. Canadian statistics from 2007–2008 reveal that three offences involving fatalities (murder; manslaughter; impaired driving causing death) alone accounted for two-thirds of all victims who made an oral presentation at a National Parole Board hearing (National Parole Board 2008).
4 Available at: http://www.justice.gc.ca/eng/pi/pcvi-cpcv/pub/03/princ.html
5 For information on Scotland see information for victims on: www.sps.gov.uk/default.aspx?documentid = 0CDC3491-67C9-4207-AB61-538279CA6FF7
6 See also Northern Ireland Prison Service's Prisoner Release Victim Information Scheme.
7 The reason for the difference is that the Dangerous Offender provisions in Canada are more restrictive, and accordingly are invoked only very infrequently.
8 See the publicity material available at www.paroleboard.govt.nz/information-for-victims/information-for-victims.html
9 This conclusion is based upon a review of victim surveys where respondents are asked to state why they submitted an impact statement at sentencing. To a degree responses will reflect the information that victims are given about the VIS scheme in their particular jurisdiction.
10 In Canada the National Parole Board has jurisdiction over offenders sentenced to terms of custody of two years or longer; this mandate encompasses approximately 5 per cent of all admissions to custody.
11 England and Wales is the exception here; most sentencing decisions are taken by lay magistrates. In some jurisdictions juries have a role in sentencing: see, for example, the decision of the US Supreme Court on 10 November 2008 upholding the decision of the Supreme Court of California, dismissing the challenges of two death row prisoners, Kelly and Zamudio to the playing of

videotapes of the victims' lives to jurors before they decided the killers should die (*Kelly v. California; Zamudio v. California* Nos. 07–11073 and 07–11425).

12 On 15 September 2008, the Supreme Court of Victoria ruled in *Kotzmann v. Adult Parole Board of Victoria* [2008] VSC 356, that the appointment of a Supreme Court judge to chair the Parole Board would enhance public confidence in the integrity of the Board: see www.austlii.edu.au/au/cases/vic/VSC/2008/356.html.

13 In addition, some prisoners are eligible for Accelerated Parole Review (APR), a programme which will expedite their parole application and subsequent release from prison.

14 Institutional authorities have the power to detain a prisoner until warrant expiry, although the onus is upon the institution to demonstrate that the prisoner would constitute a threat to society if released at the two-thirds point of the sentence (on statutory release).

15 Three provinces have their own parole boards to regulate the release of prisoners serving terms of custody of less than two years' duration (Ontario Parole and Earned Release Board 2008). Provincial parole boards have the same mandate to consider risk and rehabilitation (e.g. Ontario Parole and Earned Release Board 2008).

16 All quotations from National Parole Board are drawn from the 'Information for Victims' page of the NPB website, accessed 6 January 2009 at: www.npb-cnlc.gc.ca/victims/factsheet-eng.shtml.

17 A detailed account of this by various participants is available in the Annual Report of the Parole Board for England and Wales 2007/08 (Parole Board 2007, available at www.official-documents.gov.uk/document/hc0809/hc07/0775/0775.asp).

18 In 2006–07, 1,210 parolees were recalled, an increase of 22 per cent from 2005–06 where it stood at 990. In 2006–07, 28 per cent of those on licence were recalled. During the year 2006–07 a total of 11,230 determinate sentence offenders were recalled to custody. This is an increase of 29 per cent on the total number of offenders recalled during the year 2005–06 (8,680). In 2006 164 offenders on life licence were recalled to prison compared with 111 in 2005 (Offender Management Caseload Statistics 2006, published December 2007, paragraphs 10.10–10.11). See also Padfield and Maruna (2006).

19 For more details see Padfield (2009).

20 Though we should perhaps look too at Release on Temporary Licence (ROTL): 400,240 ROTL temporary licences were issued in 2006. For further information about HDC, see Dodgson and Mortimer (2000) and Dodgson *et al.* (2001).

21 See Offender Management Caseload Statistics 2007, Table 9.3, page 150.

22 Prison Service Order (PSO) 6700 which governs decision-making in HDC is unclear on the role of the victim and the important subject of disclosure (see paras 7.4–7.6)

23 The current statutory provision is to be found in s. 24 of the Criminal Justice and Immigration Act 2008.

24 Ministry of Justice: statistical bulletin: End of Custody Licence releases and recalls: 1–31 May 2008, available at www.justice.gov.uk/docs/stats-ecl-0508.pdf. As in previous months, the large majority were serving sentences of under 12 months (2,071 or 82 per cent), and a majority were serving sentences of less than or equal to six months (1,770 or 70 per cent). The remaining 461 (18 per cent) were serving longer sentences.

25 Tonry (2004: 22) identifies 'an inverse relation between the government's reliance on evidence and the political salience of a subject' (p. 22). Here one might argue that where the Government's main concern is reducing the prison population, victim concerns are ignored, but where more difficult, 'riskier' decisions have to be taken, the voice of the victims is considered to be important.

26 Clarke issued a statement acknowledging that over 1,000 foreign national offenders had yet to be deported from the country following the completion of their sentences and this led to the political furore which prompted his resignation.

27 Again, complex law: this is still governed by the Immigration Act 1971, s. 46 of the Criminal Justice Act 1991 (as amended) and the Nationality, Asylum and Immigration Act 2002, though the UK Borders Act 2007 has now in s. 32 introduced 'automatic deportation' for foreign criminals (with a plethora of exceptions to be found in s. 33).

28 See PSO 6000, Chapter 9; Prison Service Instruction (PSI) 27/2004.

29 See para 7 of PSI 19/2008.

30 See, in particular, Council Framework Decision 2008/909/JHA of 27 November 2008 on the application of the principle of mutual recognition to judgements in criminal matters imposing custodial sentences or measures involving deprivation of liberty for the purpose of their enforcement in the European Union (OJ 2008 L 327/27). See also Council Framework Decision 2008/947/JHA of 27 November 2008 on the application of the principle of mutual recognition to judgements and probation decisions with a view to the supervision of probation measures and alternative sanctions (OJ 2008 L337/102). The discussion in the 39th Report of the European Scrutiny Committee of the House of Commons, Session 2005–06 (House of Commons 2006) gives useful background.

31 Available at: www.homeoffice.gov.uk/documents/victims-code-of-practice?view=Binary

32 Article 8 provides that:

 1. Everyone has the right to respect for his private and family life, his home and his correspondence.

 2. There shall be no interference by a public authority with the exercise of this right except such as is in accordance with the law and is necessary in a democratic society in the interests of national security, public safety or the economic well-being of the country, for the prevention of disorder or crime, for the protection of health or morals, or for the protection of the rights and freedoms of others.

 Proportionality in this context means simply that any restrictions on the right to private and family life must be 'necessary': and of course, both victim and prisoner have Article 8 rights. See the case of *Craven* discussed below.

33 [2001] EWHC Admin 850, QBD

34 By categorisation decisions, temporary release, courses etc.

35 There is a vast literature on the history of probation services: see, for example, Gelsthorpe and Morgan (2007).

36 For example, in New Zealand, crime victims can request to receive a list of any correctional programmes that the prisoner may have attended since admission to custody, the prisoner's security classification at any given time, as well as

any convictions that he may have acquired since beginning the sentence (New Zealand Parole Board 2007: 6).

37 *Criminal Code* of Canada, Section 718.1.

38 This issue has long been important to releasing authorities. A prisoner who denies the offence, or who expresses little regret for the crime is unlikely to be granted parole. It is however controversial as research suggests little relationship between remorse and the likelihood of reoffending. Moreover, wrongfully convicted individuals who unsurprisingly affirm their innocence pay a heavy price for contesting the conviction.

39 While on parole the offender is still serving a sentence of imprisonment. If the individual was living in a correctional facility no contact with the victim would be possible and this restriction should carry over to any portion of the sentence served in the community.

40 This is an area of law which has caused great controversy in England: see the decision of the House of Lords in *R (Roberts) v. Parole Board* [2005] 2 AC 738 and now again *R (Roberts) v. Parole Board* [2008] EWHC 2714 (Admin).

41 See for example *Jorge* (1999) 2 Cr App R (S) 1, where the Court of Appeal quashed a compensation order, holding that the passing of a sentence of imprisonment was relevant to the defendant's means when assessing a compensation order in at least three ways: (1) it would deprive him of his earning power while in prison; (2) it might make it difficult for him to find work when he came out; and (3) it would often mean that by the time he came out he would be in financial difficulty. A compensation order might well be appropriate despite an immediate prison sentence if the defendant had assets from which to pay, especially the proceeds of crime, or if he was reasonably assured of income when he came out from which it was reasonable to expect him to pay. Otherwise a compensation order was not appropriate and in some cases might operate as an incentive to further crime on release.

42 We are not here discussing restorative justice as an alternative to prosecution, on which see Sherman and Strang (2007).

43 See the House of Commons Justice Committee's Report 'Towards Effective Sentencing', July 2008 (HC 184-1) for a useful report pulling together 'front door' and 'back door' sentencing issues.

References

Auld, R.E. (2001) *Review of the Criminal Courts of England and Wales*. London: The Stationery Office.

Brozowski, J. (2007) Victim Services in Canada, 2005/2006. *Juristat*, 27(7).

Dodgson, K., Goodwin, P., Howard, P., Llewellyn-Thomas, S., Mortimer, E., Russell, N. and Weiner, M. (2001) *Electronic monitoring of released prisoners: an evaluation of the Home Detention Curfew Scheme*. Home Office Research Study 222. London: Home Office, Development and Statistics Directorate.

Dodgson, K. and Mortimer, E. (2000) *Home detention curfew – the first year of operation*. Research Findings No. 100. London: Home Office Research, Development and Statistics Directorate.

Erez, E. (1999) 'Who's afraid of the big bad victim? Victim impact statements as victim empowerment and enhancement of justice', *The Criminal Law Review*, July: . 545–56.

Erez, E. (2004) 'Victim Voice, Impact Statements and Sentencing: Integrating Restorative Justice and Therapeutic Jurisprudence Principles in Adversarial Proceedings', *Criminal Law Bulletin*, Sept.–Oct.: 483–500.

Gelsthorpe, L. and Morgan, R. (eds) (2007) *Handbook of Probation*. Cullompton: Willan Publishing.

Giliberti, C. (1990) *Victim Impact Statements in Canada. Volume 7. A Summary of the Findings*. Ottawa: Department of Justice Canada.

Hall, D. (1991) 'Victims' voices in criminal court: the need for restraint', *American Criminal Law Review*, 28: 233–66.

House of Commons (2006) *European Scrutiny Committee 39th Report*, Session 2005–6 London: Stationery Office.

House of Commons (2008) Justice Committee 'Towards Effective Sentencing' (HC 184-1). London: The Stationery Office.

Johnstone, G. and Van Ness, D. (2006) (eds) *Handbook of Restorative Justice*. Cullompton: Willan Publishing.

Kinnevy, S. and Caplan, J. (2008) *Findings from the APAI International Survey of Releasing Authorities*. Philadelphia: Centre for Research on Youth and Policy.

Leverick, F., Chalmers, J. and Duff, P. (2007) *An Evaluation of the Pilot Victim Statement Schemes in Scotland*. Edinburgh: Scottish Executive Social Research. Available at: www.scotland.gov.uk/publications

Manson, A., Healy, P., Trotter, G., Roberts, J. and Ives, D. (2008) *Sentencing and Penal Policy in Canada* (2nd edn). Toronto: Emond Montgomery.

McCarthy, T. (2007) 'Dealing with Indeterminacy: life sentences and IPP – the View from Within', in N. Padfield (ed.), *Who to Release? Parole, Fairness and Criminal Justice*. Cullompton: Willan Publishing.

Ministry of Justice (2008) Offender Management Caseload Statistics 2007.

Morgan, K. and Smith, B. (2005) 'Victims, punishment, and parole: the effect of victim participation on parole hearings', *Criminology & Public Policy*, 4: 333–60.

National Parole Board (2008) *Victims speaking at NPB hearings, 2007–2008*. Data supplied to, and available from, the authors.

Newell, T. and Edgar, K. (2001) *Restorative Justice in Prisons: A guide to making it happen*. Winchester: Waterside Press.

New Zealand Parole Board Annual Report 2007 (available at www.parole-board.govt.nz/decisions-statistics-and-publications/publications/annual_reports.html

Ontario Parole and Earned Release Board (2008) *Release Information*. Available at: www.operb.gov.on.ca/english/victim/victim.html

Padfield, N. (2006) 'The Parole Board in Transition', *Criminal Law Review*, 3–22.

Padfield, N. (ed.) (2007) *Who to release? Parole, fairness and criminal justice*. Cullompton: Willan Publishing.

Padfield, N. (2009) 'Parole and early release: the Criminal Justice and Immigration Act 2008 changes in context', *Criminal Law Review*, 166–87.

Padfield, N. and Liebling, A., with Arnold, H. (2000) *An Exploration of Decision-Making at Discretionary Lifer Panels*. Home Office Research Study No. 213. London: Home Office.

Padfield, N. and Maruna, S. (2006) 'The Revolving Door at the Prison Gate: Exploring the dramatic increase in recalls to prison', *Criminology and Criminal Justice*, 6: 329–52.

Parole Board for England and Wales (2007) *Annual Report and Accounts 2006–7*. London: The Stationery Office. http://www.official-documents.gov.uk/document/hc0607/hc10/1022/1022.asp

Parole Board for England and Wales (2008) *Annual Report and Accounts 2007/08*. London: The Stationery Office. http://www.official-documents.gov.uk/document/hc0809/hc07/0775/0775.asp

Parsonage, W., Bernat, F. and Helfgott, J. (1992) 'Victim Impact Testimony and Pennsylvania's Parole Decision-Making Process: A Pilot Study', *Criminal Justice Policy Review*, 6: 187–206.

Prairie Research Associates (2005) *Multi-Site Survey of Victims of Crime and Criminal Justice Professionals across Canada*. Summary of Probation Officer, Corrections, and Parole Board Respondents. Ottawa: Department of Justice, Policy Centre for Victim Issues.

Roberts, J.V. (2003) 'Victim Impact Statements and the sentencing process: Enhancing communication in the courtroom', *Criminal Law Quarterly*, 47: 365–96.

Roberts, J.V. (2008) 'Victim impact statements: Lessons learned and future priorities', *Victims of Crime Research Digest*, 1: 3–16.

Roberts, J.V. (2009, in press) 'Listening to Crime Victims: Evaluating Victim Input into Sentencing and Parole', in M. Tonry (ed.), *Crime and Justice*. Volume 38. Chicago: University of Chicago Press.

Roberts, J.V. and Edgar, A. (2006) *Judicial Attitudes to Victim Impact Statements. Findings from a Survey in Three Jurisdictions*. Ottawa: Policy Centre for Victim Issues, Department of Justice Canada.

Roberts, J.V. and Erez, E. (2004) 'Communication in Sentencing: Exploring the Expressive and the Impact Model of Victim Impact Statements', *International Review of Victimology*, 10: 223–44.

Sanders, A., Hoyle, C., Morgan, R. and Cape, E. (2001) 'Victim impact statements: don't work, can't work', *Criminal Law Review*, June: 447–58.

Sherman, L and Strang, H. *Restorative Justice: the Evidence* (2007, the Smith Institute) available at www.esmeefairbairn.org.uk/docs/RJ_full_report.pdf

Smith, B., Watkins, E. and Morgan, K. (1997) 'The Effect of Victim Participation on Parole Decisions: Results from a Southeastern State', *Criminal Justice Policy Review*, 8: 57–74.

Stone, N. (2002) Title, *Journal of Social Welfare and Family Law*, 24: 454–61.

Szmania S.J. and Gracyalny, M. (2006) 'Addressing the court, the offender, and the community: A communication analysis of victim impact statements in a non-capital sentencing hearing', *International Review of Victimology*, 13: 231–49.

Tasmania Department of Justice (2008) *Having your say*. Available at: www.tas.gov.au/victims/victimsregister/parole/having_your_say

Tobolowsky, P.M. (1999) 'Victim Participation in the Criminal Justice Process: Fifteen Years After the President's Task Force on Victims of Crime', *Journal of Criminal and Civil Confinement*, 25: 21–92.

Tonry, M. (2004) *Punishment and Politics: Evidence and emulation in the making of English crime control policy*. Cullompton: Willan Publishing.

Index